Frommer's®

Honolulu, Waikiki & Oahu

11th Edition

by Jeanette Foster

WILEY

Wiley Publishing, Inc.

ABOUT THE AUTHOR

A resident of the Big Island, **Jeanette Foster** has skied the slopes of Mauna Kea—during a Fourth of July ski meet, no less—and gone scuba diving with manta rays off the Kona Coast. A prolific writer widely published in travel, sports, and adventure magazines, she's also the editor of *Zagat's Survey to Hawaii's Top Restaurants*. In addition to writing this guide, Jeanette is the author of *Frommer's Hawaii Day by Day, Frommer's Hawaii, Frommer's Maui, Frommer's Hawaii from $80 a Day, Frommer's Kauai, Frommer's Hawaii with Kids,* and *Frommer's Portable Big Island*.

WILEY PUBLISHING, INC.

111 River St.
Hoboken, NJ 07030-5774

ISBN 978-0-470-49764-7

Editor: Jamie Ehrlich

Production Editor: Eric T. Schroeder

Cartographer: Roberta Stockwell

Photo Editor: Richard Fox

Production by Wiley Indianapolis Composition Services

Front cover photo: Rental surfboards at Waikiki Beach on Oahu. ©Chad Ehlers/ Alamy Images
Back cover photo: The King Kamehameha Statue draped with lei on June 11th, the day that honors him in downtown Honolulu. ©Ann Cecil/Photo Resource Hawaii/Alamy Images

For information on our other products and services or to obtain technical support, please contact our Customer Care Department within the U.S. at 877/762-2974, outside the U.S. at 317/572-3993 or fax 317/572-4002.

Wiley also publishes its books in a variety of electronic formats. Some content that appears in print may not be available in electronic formats.

Manufactured in the United States of America

5 4 3 2 1

CONTENTS

3 SUGGESTED HONOLULU, WAIKIKI & OAHU ITINERARIES   63

4 WHERE TO STAY   82

5 WHERE TO DINE   120

6 FUN IN THE SURF & SUN   153

LIST OF MAPS

ACKNOWLEDGMENT

Much love and many heartfelt thanks to Priscilla Life for her excellent research on this book.

HOW TO CONTACT US

In researching this book, we discovered many wonderful places—hotels, restaurants, shops, and more. We're sure you'll find others. Please tell us about them, so we can share the information with your fellow travelers in upcoming editions. If you were disappointed with a recommendation, we'd love to know that, too. Please write to:

Frommer's Honolulu, Waikiki & Oahu, 11th Edition
Wiley Publishing, Inc. • 111 River St. • Hoboken, NJ 07030-5774

AN ADDITIONAL NOTE

Please be advised that travel information is subject to change at any time—and this is especially true of prices. We therefore suggest that you write or call ahead for confirmation when making your travel plans. The authors, editors, and publisher cannot be held responsible for the experiences of readers while traveling. Your safety is important to us, however, so we encourage you to stay alert and be aware of your surroundings. Keep a close eye on cameras, purses, and wallets, all favorite targets of thieves and pickpockets.

FROMMER'S STAR RATINGS, ICONS & ABBREVIATIONS

Every hotel, restaurant, and attraction listing in this guide has been ranked for quality, value, service, amenities, and special features using a **star-rating system.** In country, state, and regional guides, we also rate towns and regions to help you narrow down your choices and budget your time accordingly. Hotels and restaurants are rated on a scale of zero (recommended) to three stars (exceptional). Attractions, shopping, nightlife, towns, and regions are rated according to the following scale: zero stars (recommended), one star (highly recommended), two stars (very highly recommended), and three stars (must-see).

In addition to the star-rating system, we also use **seven feature icons** that point you to the great deals, in-the-know advice, and unique experiences that separate travelers from tourists. Throughout the book, look for:

Finds	Special finds—those places only insiders know about
Fun Facts	Fun facts—details that make travelers more informed and their trips more fun
Kids	Best bets for kids, and advice for the whole family
Moments	Special moments—those experiences that memories are made of
Overrated	Places or experiences not worth your time or money
Tips	Insider tips—great ways to save time and money
Value	Great values—where to get the best deals

The following **abbreviations** are used for credit cards:

AE	American Express	**DISC**	Discover	**V**	Visa
DC	Diners Club	**MC**	MasterCard		

TRAVEL RESOURCES AT FROMMERS.COM

Frommer's travel resources don't end with this guide. **Frommers.com** has travel information on more than 4,000 destinations. We update features regularly, giving you access to the most current trip-planning information and the best airfare, lodging, and car-rental bargains. You can also listen to podcasts, connect with other Frommers.com members through our active-reader forums, share your travel photos, read blogs from guidebook editors and fellow travelers, and much more.

The Best of Oahu

Everyone ventures to Oahu seeking a different experience. Some talk about wanting to find the "real" Hawaii, some are looking for heart-pounding adventure, some yearn for the relaxing and healing powers of the islands, and others are drawn by Hawaii's aloha spirit, in which kindness and friendliness prevail.

This book is designed to help you have the vacation of your dreams. For those too excited to page through from beginning to end, this chapter highlights the very best of what Honolulu and Oahu have to offer.

1 THE BEST OAHU EXPERIENCES

To have the absolute best experiences on Oahu, be prepared for a different culture, language, cuisine, and way of doing things. Slow down—you're on an island that operates on its own schedule. To really experience Oahu, we recommend the following:

- **Get Out on the Water:** You'll take home memories of an emerald island rising out of the cobalt sea with white wispy clouds set against an azure sky, or the Waikiki shoreline colored by the setting sun. There are many different boats to choose from, ranging from tiny kayaks to 100-foot sightseeing vessels, even state-of-the-art boats guaranteed to prevent seasickness. See chapter 6 for details on all kinds of cruises and watersports.

- **Plunge Under the Water:** Don mask, fins, and snorkel and dive into the magical world beneath the surface, where clouds of colorful tropical fish flit by, craggy old turtles lumber along, and tiny marine creatures hover over exotic corals. Can't swim? Take one of the many submarines or semi-submersibles. If you come to Hawaii and ignore the underwater world, you're missing half of what makes up this paradise. See chapter 6.

- **Meet Local Folks:** If you go to Hawaii and see only people like the ones back home, you might as well stay home. Extend yourself, leave the resorts and tourist quarters, go out and learn about Hawaii and its people. Just smile and say "Howzit?" which means "How's it going?"—and you'll usually make a new friend. Oahu is remarkably cosmopolitan; every ethnic group in the world seems to be here. It's fascinating to discover the varieties of food, culture, language, and customs.

- **Drive to the North Shore:** Just an hour's drive from Honolulu, the North Shore is another world: a pastoral, rural setting with magnificent beaches and a slower way of life. During the winter months, stop and watch the professionals surf the monster waves. See chapter 7.

- **Watch the Hula:** This is Hawaii, so you have to experience the hula. A hula performance is a popular way for visitors to get a taste of traditional Hawaiian culture. For a more genuine Hawaiian hula experience, catch the hula *halau* performed Monday through Friday at 1pm at the **Bishop Museum.** See chapter 7.

- **Experience a Turning Point in America's History:** The United States could no longer turn its back on World War II after December 7, 1941, the day that Japanese warplanes bombed Pearl Harbor. Standing on the deck of the USS *Arizona* Memorial, which straddles the eternal tomb for the 1,177 sailors and Marines trapped below deck when the battleship sank in 9 minutes, is a moment you'll never forget. See chapter 7.

2 THE BEST BEACHES

See chapter 6 for complete details on all these beaches and their facilities.

- **Waikiki Beach:** This famous stretch of sand is the spot that originally put Hawaii on the tourist map. No beach anywhere is so widely known or so universally sought as this narrow, 1½-mile-long crescent of soft sand at the foot of a string of high-rise hotels. Home to the world's longest-running beach party, Waikiki attracts nearly five million visitors a year from every corner of the planet. In high season, it's packed towel-to-towel, but there's no denying the beauty of Waikiki.

- **Lanikai Beach:** Hidden and off the beaten tourist path, this beach on the windward side has a mile of powder-soft sand and water that's safe for swimming. It's the perfect isolated spot for a morning of swimming and relaxation. With the prevailing trade winds, it's also excellent for sailing and windsurfing. Sun-worshipers should arrive in the morning, as the shadow of the Koolau Mountains blocks the sun's rays in the afternoon.

- **Kailua Beach:** Imagine a 30-acre public park with a broad, grassy area with picnic tables, a public boat ramp, restrooms, a pavilion, a volleyball court, and food stands. Add a wide, sandy beach, great for diving, swimming, sailing, snorkeling, and board- and windsurfing, and you've got Kailua Beach, which is tops on the windward side of the island. On weekends, local families consider it *the* place to go. Weekdays, you practically have it all to yourself.

- **Kahana Bay Beach Park:** With salt-and-pepper sand, a crescent-shaped beach protected by ironwoods and *kamani* trees and, as a backdrop, a lush junglelike valley interrupted only by jagged cliffs, you'd swear this beach was in Tahiti or Bora Bora. Kahana offers great swimming (even safe for children), good fishing, and perfect conditions for kayaking. Combine that with picnic areas, camping, and hiking trails, and you have one of the best beaches on the island.

- **Malaekahana Beach:** If you'd like to venture back to old Hawaii, before jet planes brought millions of people to Oahu and there were few footprints on the sand, then go north to the romantic wooded beach park at Malaekahana. This is a place to sit in quiet solitude or to beachcomb along the shore. There's good swimming most of the time, and good snorkeling when it's calm, but no lifeguard. Surprisingly, very few visitors come to Malaekahana—one of the best beaches on Oahu, it's a true find.

- **Sunset Beach:** Surfers around the world know this site, famous for its spectacular winter surf—the waves can be huge, thundering peaks reaching 15 to 20 feet. In the summer months, Sunset calms down and becomes a safe swimming beach. It's a great place to people-watch year-round, as you'll spot everybody from wannabe *Baywatch* babes to King Kong surfers.

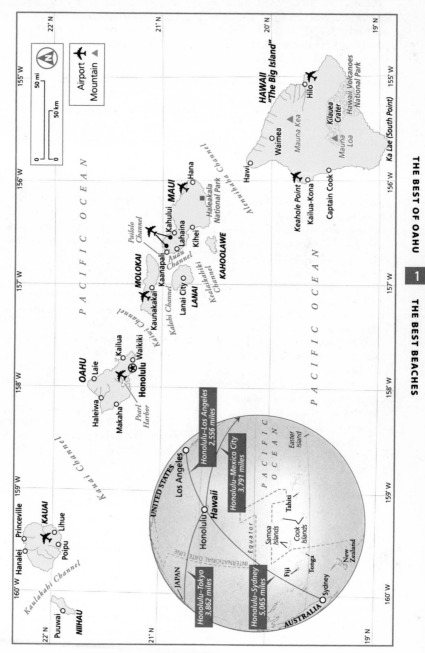

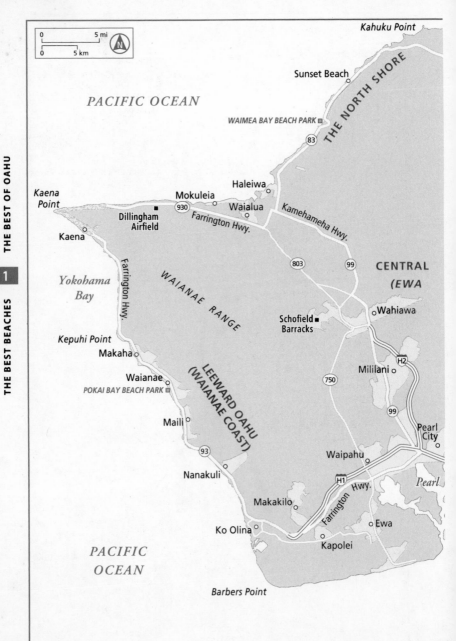

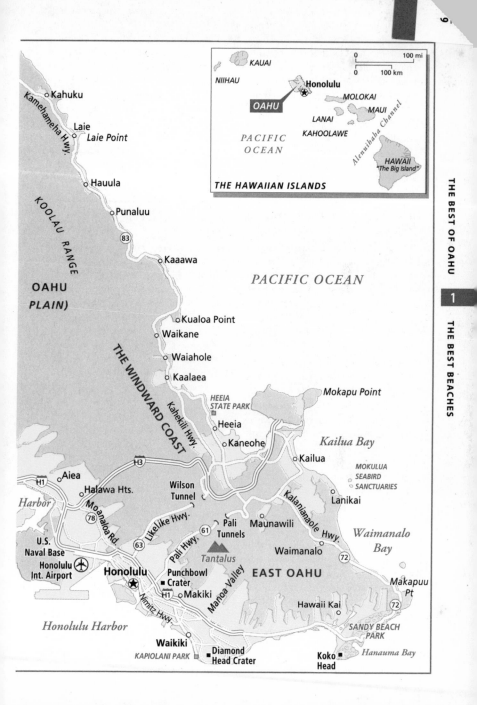

Kahuku

Kamehameha Hwy.

Laie
Laie Point

Hauula

Punaluu

83

Kaaawa

KOOLAU RANGE

OAHU
PLAIN)

THE WINDWARD COAST

Kahekili Hwy.

Kualoa Point

Waikane

Waiahole

Kaalaea

HEEIA
STATE PARK

Heeia

Kaneohe

Mokapu Point

PACIFIC OCEAN

Kailua Bay

Kailua

MOKULUA
SEABIRD
SANCTUARIES

H3

H1

Aiea

Halawa Hts.

Harbor

Moanalua Rd.

78

63

Likelike Hwy.

Wilson
Tunnel

Pali
Tunnels

61

Pali Hwy.

Maunawili

Lanikai

Kalanianaole Hwy.

Waimanalo

72

Waimanalo
Bay

U.S.
Naval Base

Honolulu
Int. Airport

Honolulu

Punchbowl
Crater

Makiki

Tantalus

Manoa Valley

EAST OAHU

Hawaii Kai

Makapuu
Pt

72

H1

Nimitz Hwy.

Honolulu Harbor

Waikiki

KAPIOLANI PARK

Diamond
Head Crater

Koko
Head

SANDY BEACH
PARK

Hanauma Bay

KAUAI

NIIHAU

OAHU

Honolulu

MOLOKAI

MAUI

LANAI

KAHOOLAWE

PACIFIC
OCEAN

Alenuihaha Channel

HAWAII
"The Big Island"

THE HAWAIIAN ISLANDS

0   100 mi
0   100 km

- **Waimea Bay:** Here is one of Oahu's most dramatic beaches. During much of the winter—October to April—huge waves come pounding in, creating strong rip currents. Even expert surfers think twice when confronted with 30-foot waves that crash on the shore with the force of a runaway locomotive. It's hard to believe that during the summer this same bay is glassy and calm—a great place for swimming, snorkeling, and diving. Oh, and by the way, despite what the Beach Boys croon in "Surfin' USA" (Why-a-*mee*-ah), it's pronounced Why-*may*-ah.

- **Pokai Bay:** If you dream of a powdered-sugar sand beach, a place you can swim, snorkel, and probably be the only one on the beach (on weekdays), try this off-the-beaten-path shoreline. Surrounded by a reef, the waters inside are calm enough for children and offer excellent snorkeling. Come with aloha spirit and a respect for local customs—the residents here don't see too many visitors.

3 THE BEST SNORKELING & DIVING SITES

A different Hawaii greets anyone with a mask, snorkel, and fins. Under the sea, you'll find schools of brilliant tropical fish, slow-moving green sea turtles, darting game fish, slack-jawed moray eels, and prehistoric-looking coral. It's a kaleidoscope of color and wonder. For more on exploring Oahu's underwater world, see chapter 6.

- **Hanauma Bay:** It can get very crowded, but—for clear, warm, calm waters, an abundance of fish that are so friendly they'll swim right up to your face mask, a beautiful setting, and easy access—there's no place like Hanauma Bay. Just wade in waist deep and look down to see more than 50 species of reef and inshore fish common to Hawaiian waters. Snorkelers hug the safe, shallow inner bay—it's really like swimming in an outdoor aquarium. Serious, experienced divers shoot "the slot," a passage through the reef, to gain access to Witch's Brew, a turbulent cove, and other outer-reef experiences.

- **Wreck of the *Mahi*:** Oahu is a wonderful place to scuba dive, especially for those interested in wreck diving. One of the more famous wrecks in Hawaii is the *Mahi*, a 185-foot former minesweeper, which is easily accessible just south of Waianae. Abundant marine life makes it a great place to shoot photos—schools of lemon butterflyfish and *ta'ape* are so comfortable with divers and photographers that they practically pose. Eagle rays, green sea turtles, manta rays, and white-tipped sharks occasionally cruise by, and eels peek out from the wreck.

- **Kahuna Canyon:** One of the most magical summer dive spots is Kahuna Canyon. Walls rise from the ocean floor to create the illusion of an underwater Grand Canyon. Inside the canyon, crab, octopi, slipper, and spiny lobsters abound (be aware that taking them in the summer is illegal), and giant trevally, parrotfish, and unicorn tangs congregate. Outside, you're likely to see the occasional shark in the distance.

- **Shark's Cove:** Braver snorkelers might want to head to Shark's Cove, on the North Shore just off Kamehameha Highway, between Haleiwa and Pupukea. Sounds risky, we know, but we've never seen or heard of any sharks in this cove; and in summer, this big, lava-edged pool is one of Oahu's best snorkeling spots. Waves splash over the natural lava grotto and cascade like waterfalls into the pool full of tropical fish. Deep-sea caves to explore are to the right of the cove.

- **Kapiolani Park Beach:** In the center of this beach park, a section known as Queen's Beach or Queen's Surf Beach, between the Natatorium and the Waikiki Aquarium, is great for snorkeling. I prefer the reef in front of the Aquarium because it has easy access to the sandy shoreline and the waters are usually calm. Bonus: It's right next door to the Aquarium, in case you see any flora or fauna and would like more information.

4 THE BEST GOLF COURSES

Oahu is golf country, with 5 municipal, 9 military, and 20 private courses to choose from. The courses range from 9-hole municipals, perfect for beginners, to championship courses that stump even the pros. See chapter 6 for complete details.

- **Ko Olina Golf Club** (© **808/676-5309**): *Golf Digest* named this beautiful 6,867-yard, par-72 course one of "America's Top 75 Resort Courses" when it opened in 1992. The rolling fairways and elevated tees and a few too many water features (always where you don't want them) will definitely improve your game or humble your attitude.
- **Turtle Bay Resort** (© **808/293-8574**): Of the two courses to choose from here, we recommend the 18-hole **Arnold Palmer Course** (formerly the Links at Kuilima), designed by Arnold Palmer and Ed Seay. They never meant for golfers to get off too easy—this is a challenging course. The front 9 holes, with rolling terrain, only a few trees, and lots of wind, play like a course on the British Isles. The back 9 holes have narrower, tree-lined fairways and water. In addition to ocean views, the course circles Punahoolapa Marsh, a protected wetland for endangered Hawaiian waterfowl.
- **Makaha Resort Golf Club** (© **808/695-7111** or 808/695-5239): Readers of *Honolulu* magazine named this challenging course Oahu's best. An hour's drive from the crowds of Honolulu, this William Bell–designed course is in Makaha Valley on the island's leeward side. Incredibly beautiful, sheer, 1,500-foot volcanic walls tower over the course, and swaying palm trees and bright bougainvillea surround it; an occasional peacock even struts across the fairways. "I was distracted by the beauty" is a great excuse for your score at day's end.
- **Olomana Golf Links** (© **808/259-7926**): This gorgeous course in Waimanalo is on the other side of the island from Waikiki. The low-handicap golfer may not find this course difficult, but the striking views of the craggy Koolau mountain ridges are worth the greens fees alone. The par-72, 6,326-yard course is popular with local residents and visitors. The course starts off a bit hilly on the front 9, but flattens out by the back 9. The back 9 have their own special surprises, including tricky water hazards.

5 THE BEST WALKS

The weather on Oahu is usually sunny, with trade winds providing cooling breezes—perfect for a walk. Below are our favorites, from city to trail.

- **Diamond Head Crater:** Most everyone can make this moderate walk to the summit of Hawaii's most famous landmark. Kids love the top of the 760-foot volcanic cone, where they have 360-degree views of Oahu, up the leeward coast from Waikiki. The 1.4-mile round-trip takes about an hour. See chapter 6.

- **Makiki–Manoa Cliffs Trails:** A 15-minute drive from downtown, this walk passes through a rainforest and along a ridgetop with nonstop views. The somewhat strenuous loop trail is one you'll never forget, but it's more than 6 miles long, gains 1,260 feet in elevation, and takes about 3 hours to finish. The views of the city and the shoreline are spectacular. See chapter 6.
- **Manoa Falls Trail:** This easy .75-mile (one-way) hike is terrific for families; it takes less than an hour to reach idyllic Manoa Falls. The often-muddy trail

follows Waihi Stream and meanders through the forest reserve past guava and mountain apple trees and wild ginger. The forest is moist and humid and inhabited by nothing more dangerous than giant bloodthirsty mosquitoes. See chapter 6.

- **Chinatown:** Honolulu's Chinatown appeals to the senses: The pungent aroma of Vietnamese *pho* mingles with the sweet scent of burning incense; vendors and shoppers speak noisily in the open market; retired men tell stories over games of mah-jongg; and the constant buzz of traffic all contribute to the cacophony of sounds. No trip to Honolulu is complete without a visit to this exotic, historic district. See chapter 7.

6 THE BEST VIEWS

- **Puu Ualakaa State Park:** Watching the sun set into the Pacific from a 1,048-foot hill named after a sweet potato is actually much more romantic that it sounds. *Puu Ualakaa* translates into "rolling sweet potato hill," which refers to how the early Hawaiians harvested the crop. Don't miss the sweeping panoramic views, which extend from Diamond Head across Waikiki and downtown Honolulu, over the airport and Pearl City, all the way to the Waianae range. Catch great photo ops during the day, romantic sunset views in the evening, and starry skies at night. See chapter 7.
- **Nuuanu Pali Lookout:** Oahu's best-looking side, the Windward Coast, can be seen in its full glory from the Nuuanu Pali Lookout, a gusty perch set amid jagged cliffs piercing the puffy white clouds that go racing by. One thousand feet below, the island is a carpet of green that runs to an azure Pacific dotted by tiny offshore islets.

You'll feel like you're standing on the edge of the world. See chapter 7.

- **Diamond Head Crater:** The view from atop this world-famous 720-foot-tall sleeping volcano is not to be missed. The 360-degree view from Koko Crater to Barbers Point and the Waianae mountains is worth the 560-foot hike. See chapter 6.
- **Lanikai Beach:** This is one of the best places on Oahu to greet the sunrise. Watch the sky slowly move from pitch black to burnt orange as the sun begins to rise over the two tiny offshore islands of Mokulua. This is a five-senses experience: birds singing the sun up; a gentle breeze on your face; the taste of salt in the air; the smell of the ocean, the sand, and the fragrant flowers nearby; and the kaleidoscope of colors as another day dawns. See chapter 6.
- **Puu O Mahuka Heiau:** Once the largest sacrificial temple on Oahu, Puu O Mahuka Heiau is now a state historic site. Located on a 300-foot bluff, the

heiau encompasses some 5 acres. Hawaiians still come here to pray—you may see offerings such as *ti* leaves, flowers, and fruit. Don't disturb the offerings or walk on the stones—it's very disrespectful. The view from this bluff is awe-inspiring, from Waimea Bay all the way to Kaena Point. See chapter 7.

7 THE BEST ADVENTURES FOR THRILL-SEEKERS

See chapter 6 for details on these and many other adventures.

- **Soar in Silence in a Glider:** Soaring through silence on gossamerlike wings, with a panoramic view of Oahu, is an unforgettable experience. Glider rides are available at Dillingham Air Field, in Mokuleia, on Oahu's North Shore. The glider is towed behind a plane; at the right altitude, the tow is dropped, and you (and the glider pilot) are left to soar in the thermals.

- **Surf Waikiki in a Hawaiian Outrigger Canoe:** It's summertime and there's a South Pacific swell rolling into Waikiki from Tahiti; here's your chance to try surfing—in a Hawaiian outrigger canoe. Numerous beach concessions on Waikiki Beach offer the chance to paddle an outrigger canoe and surf back into Waikiki. Not only do you get a great view of the beach from offshore, but the thrill of actually catching a wave and gliding back into shore.

- **Float on the Thermals on a Tandem Hang Glider:** See things from a bird's-eye view (literally) as you and an instructor float high above Oahu on a tandem hang glider.

- **Leap into the Ocean:** Even though all the signs say DANGEROUS, STAY OFF THE ROCKS, a favorite pastime on Oahu is climbing the stone precipice at Waimea Beach Park and leaping into the ocean. This is for experienced swimmers in summer only, as the thundering winter waves drive everyone from the sea, except the professional surfers and the very, very stupid.

- **Venture into the Deep:** It's Hawaii—you have to see what's under the waves. Try scuba diving; you can enjoy a "scuba experience" with absolutely no previous diving experience. Here's your opportunity to glide weightlessly through the ocean while you admire the multicolored marine creatures.

- **Eyeball-to-eyeball with a Shark:** You're 4 miles out from land, which is just a speck on the horizon, with hundreds of feet of open ocean. Suddenly from out of the blue depths a shape emerges: the sleek, pale shadow of a 6-foot-long gray reef shark, followed quickly by a couple of 10-foot-long Galápagos sharks. Within a few heartbeats, you're surrounded by sharks on all sides. Do you panic? No, you are on the North Shore Shark Adventure.

8 THE BEST PLACES TO DISCOVER THE REAL OAHU

Oahu isn't just any other beach destination. It has a wonderfully rich, ancient history and culture, and people who are worth getting to know. If you want to meet the "local" folks who live on Oahu, check out the following:

- **Watch the Ancient Hawaiian Sport of Outrigger Canoe Paddling:** From February to September, on weekday evenings and weekend days, hundreds of canoe paddlers gather at Ala Wai Canal and practice the Hawaiian sport of canoe paddling. Find a comfortable spot at Ala Wai Park, next to the canal, and watch this ancient sport come to life. See the Calendar of Events in chapter 2, "Planning Your Trip to Oahu."

- **Attend a Hawaiian-Language Church Service: Kawaiahao Church** (© 808/ 522-1333) is the Westminster Abbey of Hawaii; the vestibule is lined with portraits of the Hawaiian monarchy, many of whom were coronated in this very building. The coral church is a perfect setting to experience an all-Hawaiian service, held every Sunday at 9am, complete with Hawaiian song. See p. 159.

- **Buy a Lei from Vendors in Chinatown:** A host of cultural sights and experiences are to be had in Honolulu's Chinatown. Wander through this several-square-block area, with its jumble of exotic shops offering herbs, Chinese groceries, and acupuncture services.

Before you leave, be sure to check out the lei sellers on Maunakea Street (near N. Hotel St.), where Hawaii's finest leis go for as little as $3.50. See chapter 7 for neighborhood walking tours and details on where to buy leis.

- **Observe the Fish Auction:** There is nothing else quite like the **Honolulu Fish Auction** at the United Fishing Agency, Pier 38, 1131 N. Nimitz Hwy., Honolulu (© **808/536-2148**). Fishermen bring their fresh catch in at 5:30am (sharp) Monday through Saturday, and the small group of buyers bids on all manner of fish. The auction lasts until all the fish are sold. It is well worth getting up early to enjoy this unique cultural experience. See the Fish Markets section of chapter 8.

- **Get a Bargain at the Aloha Flea Market:** For 50¢ admission, it's an all-day show at the Aloha Stadium parking lot, where more than 1,000 vendors sell everything from junk to jewels. Go early for the best deals. Open Wednesday, Saturday, and Sunday from 6am to 3pm. See the box "Favorite Oahu Experiences," in chapter 6.

9 THE BEST LUXURY HOTELS & RESORTS

- **Halekulani** (© **800/367-2343** or 808/923-2311; www.halekulani.com): Halekulani translates into "House Befitting Heaven," an apt description for this luxury resort spread over 5 acres of prime Waikiki beachfront property. When money is no object, this is the place to stay. The atmosphere of elegance envelops you as soon as you step into the lobby. Even if you don't stay here, drop by at sunset to sip on a mai tai at the gracious House Without a Key and listen to Sonny Kamehele sing Hawaiian songs as a graceful hula dancer sways to the music. See p. 87.

- **Embassy Suites Hotel–Waikiki Beach Walk** (© **800/EMBASSY** [362-2779] or 808/921-2345; www.waikikibeach. embassysuites.com): This ultra-luxurious one- and two-bedroom-suite hotel chain (known for its complimentary, all-you-can-eat, cooked-to-order breakfast and evening manager's cocktail reception) has one of the most central locations in Waikiki and is loaded with amenities. When you pencil it out, it's actually a good "deal" for families. See p. 87.

- **Royal Hawaiian** (© **800/325-3535** or 808/923-7311; www.sheraton.com):

Hidden in the jungle of concrete buildings that make up Waikiki is an oasis of verdant gardens and a shockingly pink building. The Royal Hawaiian Hotel, affectionately called the "pink palace," is known around the world as a symbol of luxury. Since the first day it opened in 1927, the Royal has been the place to stay for celebrities, including Clark Gable, Shirley Temple, President Franklin Roosevelt, the Beatles, Kevin Costner, and others. Its location is one of the best on Waikiki Beach. See p. 89.

- **Moana Surfrider Hotel, A Westin Resort** (℃ 800/325-3535 or 808/922-3111; www.moana-surfrider.com): Step back in time to Old Hawaii at the grand Moana Surfrider Hotel, built in 1901. Entry is through the original colonial porte-cochere, past the highly polished wooden front porch, with white wooden rocking chairs, and into the perfectly restored lobby, with its detailed millwork and intricate plaster detailing on the ceiling. Time seems to slow down here, tropical flowers arranged in huge sprays are everywhere, and everyone in the lobby seems to be smiling. At check-in, guests are greeted with a lei and a glass of fruit juice. This is a hotel not only with class, but also with historic charm. See p. 88.

- **Hilton Hawaiian Village Beach Resort & Spa** (℃ 800/HILTONS [445-8667] or 808/949-4321; www.hiltonhawaiianvillage.com): Waikiki's biggest resort, this place is so big it even has its own post office. Some 3,000 rooms are spread over 20 acres with tropical gardens, thundering waterfalls, exotic wildlife, award-winning restaurants, nightly entertainment, two brand-new state-of-the-art spas, 100 different shops, children's programs, fabulous ocean activities, a secluded lagoon, three swimming pools, Hawaiian cultural activities, two minigolf

courses, and Waikiki Beach. You could spend your entire vacation here and never leave the property. See p. 83.

- **Kahala Hotel & Resort** (℃ 800/367-2525 or 808/739-8888; www.kahalaresort.com): Since 1964, when Conrad Hilton first opened this hotel as a place for rest and relaxation, far from the crowds of Waikiki, the Kahala has always been rated one of Hawaii's premier hotels. A venerable Who's Who of celebrities have stayed at the hotel, including every president since Richard Nixon, a host of rock stars from the Rolling Stones to the Beach Boys, and a range of actors from John Wayne to Bette Midler. The Kahala is a completely up-to-date resort, with exotic Asian touches, but it retains the grace and elegance of a softer, gentler time in the islands. See p. 108.

- **J. W. Marriott Ihilani Resort & Spa at Ko Olina Resort** (℃ 800/626-4446 or 808/679-0079; www.ihilani.com): Located in the quiet of Oahu's west coast, 25 minutes west of Honolulu International Airport—and worlds away from the tourist scene of Waikiki—the Ihilani (which means "heavenly splendor") is the first hotel in the 640-acre Ko Olina Resort. It features a luxury spa and fitness center, plus championship tennis and golf. The plush rooms are spacious, with huge lanais and lagoon or ocean views from some 85% of the units. With luxury like this, who misses Waikiki? See p. 113.

- **Turtle Bay Resort** (Oahu; ℃ 800/203-3650 or 808/293-6000; www.turtlebayresort.com): After a $35-million renovation, this once sterling hotel is back. The resort is spectacular: an hour's drive from Waikiki, but eons away in its country feeling. Sitting on 808 acres, Turtle Bay is loaded with activities and 5 miles of shoreline with secluded white-sand coves. All the rooms have great views, but the separate beach cottages are positioned right on the ocean (the views alone are worth the price). The 42 bungalows have been renovated (hardwood floors, poster beds with feather comforters) and have their own check-in and private concierge. See p. 111.

10 THE BEST BARGAIN ACCOMMODATIONS

It is possible to stay on Oahu without having to take out a second mortgage. Here are some options.

- **The Breakers** (© 800/426-0494 or 808/923-3181; www.breakers-hawaii. com): Full of old-fashioned Hawaiian aloha—and it's only steps from the sands of Waikiki—this two-story hotel has a friendly staff and a loyal following. Each of the tastefully decorated, large rooms comes with a lanai and a kitchenette, with prices starting at $130. See p. 95.
- **Hawaiiana Hotel** (© 800/367-5122 or 808/923-3811; www.hawaiiana hotelatwaikiki.com): "The spirit of Old Hawaii"—The hotel's slogan says it all. This intimate low-rise hotel has guest rooms that feature kitchenettes, two beds (a double and a single, or a queen and a sofa bed), a view of the gardens, two swimming pools, and a location a block from the beach. Rooms start at $125. See p. 95.
- **Royal Grove Hotel** (© 808/923-7691; www.royalgrovehotel.com): This small, family-owned hotel is a great bargain for frugal travelers. What you get here is old-fashioned aloha in cozy accommodations along the lines of Motel 6—basic and clean. And you can't do better for the price—this has to be *the* bargain of Waikiki. For $55 (about the same price a couple would pay to stay in a private room at the hostel in Waikiki), you get a room in the older Mauka Wing, with a double bed or two twins, plus a kitchenette with refrigerator and stove. See p. 105.
- **Ke Iki Beach Bungalows** (© 866/638-8229 or 808/638-8829; www.keiki beach.com): Snuggled on a large lot with its own 200-foot stretch of white-sand beach between two legendary North Shore surf spots (Waimea Bay and Banzai Pipeline), this collection of studio, one-, and two-bedroom cottages offers affordable family bungalows with complete kitchens—if you can live without being right on the ocean, the garden units start at $135. See p. 112.

11 THE BEST RESORT SPAS

- **Abhasa Waikiki Spa in the Royal Hawaiian Hotel** (© 808/922-8200; www.abhasa.com): This contemporary spa, spread out over 7,000 square feet, concentrates on natural, organic treatments in a soothing atmosphere, where the smell of eucalyptus wafts through the air. Experience everything from the latest aromatherapy, to thalassotherapy (soaking in a sweet-smelling hot bath), to shiatsu massages, but their specialty is a cold-laser, antiaging treatment that promises to give you a revitalized face in just 30 minutes. See p. 91.
- **Ihilani Spa at the J. W. Marriott Ihilani** (© 800/626-4446; www. ihilani.com): An oasis by the sea, this 35,000-square-foot facility, filled with

Pampering in Paradise

Spa-goers in Hawaii look for a sense of place, steeped in the culture. They want to hear the sound of the ocean, smell the salt air, and feel the caress of the warm breeze. They want to experience Hawaiian products and traditional treatments that can only be found in the islands. And now they can.

With so much to offer, the spas of Hawaii, once nearly exclusively patronized by women, are now attracting more male clients. Special massages are offered for children and pregnant women, and some spas have programs to nurture and relax brides on their big day.

Today's Hawaiian spas offer a wide diversity of treatments. Forget plain, ordinary massages—now you can try Hawaiian lomilomi, Swedish, aromatherapy (with sweet-smelling oils), craniosacral (massaging the head), shiatsu (no oil, just deep thumb pressure on acupuncture points), Thai (another oil-less massage involving stretching), and hot stone (with heated, and sometimes cold, rocks). There are even side-by-side massages for couples. The truly decadent might try a duo massage—not one, but *two* massage therapists working on you at once.

Massages are just the beginning. Body treatments, for the entire body or for just the face, involve a variety of herbal wraps, masks, or scrubs using a range of ingredients from seaweed to salt to mud, with or without accompanying aromatherapy, lights, and music.

After you have been rubbed and scrubbed, most spas offer an array of water treatments—a sort of hydromassage in a tub with jets and an assortment of colored crystals, oils, and scents.

Those are just the traditional treatments. Most spas also offer a range of alternative health-care procedures, such as acupuncture and chiropractic, and other exotic treatments such as ayurvedic and siddha from India or reiki from Japan. Once your body has been pampered, spas also offer a range of fitness facilities (weight-training equipment, racquetball, tennis, golf) and classes (yoga, aerobics, step, spinning, stretch, tai chi, kickboxing, aquacize). Several even offer adventure fitness packages (from bicycling to snorkeling). For the nonadventurous, most spas have salons, dedicated to hair- and nail-care and makeup.

If all this sounds a bit overwhelming, not to worry, all the spas in Hawaii have individual consultants who will help design an appropriate treatment program to fit your individual needs.

Of course, all this pampering doesn't come cheap. But to banish your tension and stress? The expense may be worth it. Massages are generally $100 to $135 for 50 minutes and $145 to $180 for 80 minutes; body treatments are in the $100 to $180 range; and alternative health-care treatments can be as high as $150 to $220.

floor-to-ceiling windows overlooking lush tropical plants, is truly a spa in the literal sense of the word, meaning "health by water." The modern, multistoried spa combines Hawaiian products with traditional therapies to produce some of the best water treatments in the state. You'll also find a fitness center, tennis courts, and aerobic and stretching classes. See p. 113.

- **Serenity Spa Hawaii** (Outrigger Reef on the Beach (C) **808/926-2882;** www.serenityspahawaii.com): This 5,000-square-foot spa has an extensive menu of treatments from Hawaiian lomilomi to hot lava rock to the very popular "Golden Touch" massage, which helps you get a glowing tan with applications of skin conditioners, tanning accelerators, and SPF sunscreen. See p. 92.

- **Spa Suites at the Kahala** ((C) **808/739-8938**): The Kahala has taken the concept of relaxation to a new level with former garden-view guest rooms converted to individual spas, each with a glass-enclosed shower, private changing area, infinity-edge deep soaking Jacuzzi tub, and personal relaxation area. No detail is overlooked, from the warm foot bath when you arrive to the refreshing tea served on your personal enclosed garden lanai after your treatment. See p. 108.

- **SpaHalekulani,** Halekulani Hotel, Waikiki ((C) **808/923-2311;** www.halekulani.com): Focusing on the healing traditions of the Pacific islands—Samoa, Tonga, and Tahiti, as well as Hawaii—this boutique oasis in Waikiki's most luxurious hotel defines pampered comfort in a nurturing setting designed to relax even the most tense. From the time you step into the elegantly appointed, intimate spa to

the last whiff of fragrant maile, their signature scent, this is truly a "heavenly" experience. Try something unique, like the Polynesian Nonu, a Samoan-inspired massage using stones and the nonu plant, or the Ton Ton Amma, a Japanese amma massage with ton-ton pounders. See p. 87.

- **Turtle Bay Resort** ((C) **800/203-3650;** www.turtlebayresort.com): This Zen-like spa, positioned on the ground floor and facing the ocean, has six treatment rooms, a meditation waiting area, an outdoor workout space, and a complete fitness center and private elevator to rooms on the second floor that are reserved for guests getting spa treatments. For the ultimate in massages, book the oceanside cabana and listen to the gentle lull of the waves as they roll into the North Shore. See p. 111.

- **Waikiki Plantation Spa,** Outrigger Waikiki on the Beach ((C) **808/926-2880;** www.waikikiplantationspa.com): Located in the penthouse of the Outrigger on the Beach hotel and overlooking the heart of Waikiki is this boutique spa with an "island-style" menu of treatments from massages to facials to body wraps and polishes, all using the spa's own private label of lotions and oils. An express elevator zips you up to the 17th floor, where a lanai allows you to relax in total serenity. See p. 89.

12 THE BEST RESTAURANTS

- **Alan Wong's Restaurant** ((C) **808/949-2526**): One of Hawaii's premiere chefs, Alan Wong specializes in absolutely the best Pacific Rim cuisine. His restaurant is always packed, although the ambience is limited and it's located in a shopping mall in the suburbs—but for serious foodies this is heaven. Masterpieces at

this shrine of Hawaii regional cuisine include: warm California rolls made with salmon roe, wasabi, and Kona lobster instead of rice; luau lumpia with butterfish and kalua pig; and ginger-crusted fresh *onaga*. Opihi shooters and day-boat scallops in season are a must, while nori-wrapped tempura ahi is a perennial favorite. The menu changes daily, but the flavors never lose their sizzle. See p. 142.

- **Chef Mavro Restaurant** (© **808/944-4714**): Honolulu is abuzz over the wine pairings and elegant cuisine of George Mavrothalassitis, the culinary wizard from Provence who turned La Mer (at the Halekulani) and Seasons (at the Four Seasons Resort Wailea) into temples of fine dining. He brought his award-winning signature dishes with him and continues to prove his ingenuity with dazzling a la carte and prix-fixe menus. See p. 141.

- **Kaka'ako Kitchen** (© **808/596-7488**): If you're in the market for a quick and healthy breakfast, lunch, or dinner at budget prices, here's the place. It's not fancy; in fact, the trademark Styrofoam plates, warehouse ambience, and home-style cooking are the hallmarks of this local favorite in the Ward Centre. The menu, which changes every 3 to 4 months, includes seared ahi sandwiches with *tobiko* (flying-fish roe) aioli for lunch; and a signature charbroiled ahi steak, beef stew, five-spice shoyu chicken, the very popular meatloaf, and other multi-ethnic entrees for dinner. See p. 134.

- **La Mer** (© **808/923-2311**): This is Hawaii's premier splurge restaurant, the oceanfront bastion of haute cuisine, a romantic, elegant, and expensive place where people dress up—not to be seen, but to match the ambience and food. It's an open-sided room with views of Diamond Head and the sound of trade winds rustling the nearby coconut fronds. Award-winning chef Yves Garnier melds classical French influences with island-fresh ingredients. See p. 120.

- **Ola at Turtle Bay Resort** (© **808/293-0801**; www.turtlebayresort.com): Even if you're staying in Waikiki, plan a day

at the beach on the North Shore and eat here for dinner. You will not regret it. First, the location—literally on the sandy beach next door to the Turtle Bay Resort. Second, the restaurant is an open-air beach pavilion. But the best part is . . . the food! The menu is filled with creative selections (the ahi and lobster *poke* served with a wonton spoon) and some of the best food you will eat in Hawaii. See p. 150.

- **Olive Tree Cafe** (© **808/737-0303**): This temple of Greek and Mediterranean delights is the quintessential neighborhood magnet—casual, bustling, and consistently great. Owner Savas Mojarrad has a following of foodies, hipsters, artists, and all manner of loyalists who appreciate his integrity and generosity. Standards are always high, prices reasonable, the dishes fresh and homemade. Bring your own wine and sit down to fresh fish souvlakia, excellent marinated mussels, and sheep's cheese spanakopita. Mojarrad even makes the yogurt for his famous yogurt-mint-cucumber sauce, the souvlakia's ticket to immortality. Don't miss the chicken saffron, a Tuesday special. See p.147.

- **The Pineapple Room** (© **808/945-6573**): Yes, it's in a department store, but it's Alan Wong, a culinary icon. The food is terrific, particularly anything with ahi (for example, the ahi meatloaf). The room features an open kitchen with a lava-rock wall and abundant natural light, but these are details in a room where food is king. The menu changes regularly, but keep an eye out for the ginger scallion shrimp scampi, nori-wrapped tempura salmon, and superb gazpacho made of yellow and red Waimea tomatoes. See p. 132.

- **Roy's Restaurant** (© **808/396-7697**): Good food still reigns at this busy, noisy flagship Hawaii Kai dining room with the trademark open kitchen. Roy Yamaguchi's deft way with local ingredients, nostalgic ethnic preparations, and fresh fish makes his menu, which changes daily, a novel experience every time. Yamaguchi's special dinners with vintners are a Honolulu staple. See p. 147.

13 THE BEST SHOPPING

Products of Hawaii now merit their own festivals and trade shows throughout the year, and MADE IN HAWAII is a label to be touted. Here are a few places to score some finds.

- **Academy Shop** (in the Honolulu Academy of Arts; ℂ **808/523-8703**): The recent expansion of the Honolulu Academy of Arts made a good thing even better. You'll find a stunning selection of art books, stationery, jewelry, basketry, beadwork, ikats, saris, ethnic fabrics, fiber vessels, accessories, and contemporary gift items representing the art and craft traditions of the world. See p. 241.
- **Avanti Fashion** (ℂ **808/924-1668** and 808/922-2828): In authentic prints from the 1930s and '40s reproduced on silk, Avanti aloha shirts and sportswear elevate tropical garb from high kitsch to high chic. Casual, comfortable, easily cared for, and light as a cloud, the silks look vintage but cost a fraction of collectibles' prices. The nostalgic treasures are available in retail stores statewide, but the best selection is in Waikiki. See p. 233.
- **Bailey's Antiques & Aloha Shirts** (ℂ **808/734-7628**): Bailey's has one of the largest vintage aloha-shirt collections in Honolulu, with prices ranging from inexpensive to sky-high. Old Levi's jeans, mandarin jackets, vintage vases, household items, shawls, purses, and an eye-popping assortment of barkcloth fabrics (the real thing, not repros) are among the mementos in this monumental collection. See p. 233.

- **Contemporary Museum Gift Shop** (ℂ **808/523-3447**): This gets our vote as the most beautiful setting for a gift shop, and its contents are a bonus: extraordinary art-related books, avant-garde jewelry, cards and stationery, home accessories, and gift items made by artists from Hawaii and across the country. Only the best is sold here. See p. 241.
- **Honolulu Chocolate Co.** (ℂ **808/591-2997**): Life's greatest pleasures are dispensed here with abandon: expensive gourmet chocolates made in Honolulu, Italian and Hawaiian biscotti, boulder-size chocolate "turtles," truffles, chocolate-covered coffee beans, and jumbo apricots in white and dark chocolate, to name a few. See p. 236.
- **Mana Hawaii** (ℂ **808/923-2220**): Authentically experience Hawaiian culture in the heart of Waikiki, where five successful Native Hawaiian partners have combined their talents into one mega-culture shop. You will find everything from Hawaiian books to Hawaiian-made gifts, clothing, jewelry, and art, even hula implements and ukuleles, plus healing Hawaiian lotions and oils. See p. 242.
- **Native Books & Beautiful Things** (ℂ **808/596-8885**): Hawaii is the content and context in this shop of books, crafts, and gift items made by island artists and crafters. Musical instruments, calabashes, jewelry, leis, books, fabrics, clothing, home accessories, jams and jellies—they're all high quality and made in Hawaii—a celebration of Hawaiiana. See p. 242.

- **Silver Moon Emporium** (© 808/637-7710): This is an island-wide phenomenon, filled with the terrific finds of owner Lucie Talbot-Holu, who has a gift for discovering fashion treasures. Exquisite clothing and handbags, reasonably priced footwear, hats, jewelry, scarves, and a full gamut of other treasures pepper the attractive boutique. See p. 248.

- **Zuke's Magic & Jokes** (© 808/847-7788): You don't have to be Harry Potter to enter here, but you may feel like him. Amateur and professional magicians stream into this magic store, open only on Saturday, to get the latest "tricks" and learn the art of magic. See p. 242.

14 THE BEST SPOTS FOR SUNSET COCKTAILS

- **Sunset Lanai** (in the New Otani Kaimana Beach Hotel; © 808/923-1555): The hau tree shaded Robert Louis Stevenson as he wrote poems to Princess Kaiulani. Today it frames the ocean view from the Sunset Lanai, next to the Hau Tree Lanai restaurant. Sunset Lanai is the favorite watering hole of Diamond Head–area beachgoers who love Sans Souci Beach, the ocean view, the mai tais and sashimi platters, and the live music during weekend sunset hours. See p. 104.

- **House Without a Key** (in the Halekulani; © 808/923-2311): Oahu's quintessential sunset oasis claims several unbeatable elements: It's outdoors on the ocean, with a view of Diamond Head, it offers great hula and steel guitar music, and it serves one of the best mai tais on the island. You know it's special when even jaded Honoluluans declare it their favorite spot for send-offs, reunions, and gorgeous sunsets. See p. 249.

- **Mai Tai Bar** (in the Royal Hawaiian Hotel; © 808/923-7311): Perched a few feet from the sand, this open-air bar boasts sweeping views of the South Shore and Waianae Mountains and one of the most pleasing views of Waikiki Beach. Surfers and paddlers ride the waves while the light turns golden and crowns Diamond Head with a halo. Sip a mighty mai tai while Carmen and Keith Haugen serenade you. See p. 249.

- **Duke's Canoe Club** (in the Outrigger Waikiki Hotel; © 808/923-0711): It's crowded at sunset, but who can resist listening to the top Hawaiian musicians in this upbeat atmosphere a few feet from the sands of Waikiki? Come in from the beach or from the street—it's always a party at Duke's. Entertainment here is tops, and it reaches a crescendo at sunset. See p. 253.

- **Jameson's by the Sea** (© 808/637-4336): The mai tais here are dubbed the best in Surf City, and the view, although not perfect, doesn't hurt either. Across the street from the harbor, this open-air roadside oasis is a happy stop for North Shore wave watchers and sunset-savvy sightseers. See p. 149.

15 THE BEST OAHU WEBSITES

- **Hawaii Visitors & Convention Bureau** (www.gohawaii.com): An excellent, all-around guide to activities, tours, lodging, and events, plus a huge section on weddings and honeymoons. But keep in mind that only members of the HVCB are listed.

- **Planet Hawaii** (www.planet-hawaii. com): Click on "Island" for an island-by-island guide to activities, lodging, shopping, culture, the surf report, weather, and more. Mostly, you'll find short listings with links to companies' own websites. Click on "Hawaiian Eye" for live images from around the islands.
- **Visit Oahu** (www.visit-oahu.com): An extensive guide to activities, dining, lodging, parks, shopping, and more, from the Oahu chapter of the Hawaii Visitors and Convention Bureau.
- **The Hawaiian Language Website** (www.geocities.com/~olelo/hltableof contents.html): This fabulous site has easy lessons on learning the Hawaiian language.

- **Hawaii Radio & Television Guide** (diallists.hawaiiradiotv.com/hawaiitv. html): A wonderful collection of links to all kinds of Hawaii websites, from radio stations playing Hawaiian music to the daily newspaper to where to find the cheapest gas.
- **State of Hawaii** (www.hawaii.gov): Features information regarding parks, experiences, and activities from hiking and golf to theater, sports, and culture.
- **City and County of Honolulu** (www. co.honolulu.hi.us): Everything you may want to know from the county government, including what to see and do, how to procure camping permits, park information, historical and culture information, beach safety and more.

Planning Your Trip to Oahu

With so many places to explore, things to do, and sights to see in Oahu, where do you start? That's where we come in. In the pages that follow, we'll help you plan your ideal trip, providing information on airlines, seasons, a calendar of events, how to make camping reservations . . . even how to tie the knot.

Oahu is a relatively small island, measuring 26 miles long and some 44 miles across at its widest, totaling 608 square miles of land, with 112 miles of coastline. From outer space, Oahu looks somewhat like a frayed Indian arrowhead with two mountain ridges shoring up each side: the 4,000-foot Waianae Mountains on the leeward (western) coast and the 3,000-foot Koolau Mountains on the windward (eastern) side. At night you can see the lights of suburban Oahu pouring down the mountain valleys and reaching toward the shoreline.

To many, Oahu and its most famous city, Honolulu, are synonymous. In fact, some people think the name of the island is Honolulu, a misnomer further compounded by the island-wide county calling itself the "City and County of Honolulu." Honolulu's best-known neighborhood, Waikiki, is actually quite small, but its spectacular beach and array of resort hotels are what originally put Hawaii on the tourist map.

1 WHEN TO GO

Most visitors don't come to Hawaii when the weather's best in the islands; rather, they come when it's at its worst everywhere else. Thus, the **high season**—when prices are up and resorts are often booked to capacity—is generally from mid-December through March or mid-April. The last 2 weeks of December, in particular, are the prime time for travel to Hawaii. If you're planning a holiday trip, make your reservations as early as possible, expect crowds, and prepare to pay top dollar for accommodations, car rentals, and airfare.

The **off-season,** when the best rates are available and the islands are less crowded, is spring (mid-Apr to mid-June) and fall (Sept to mid-Dec)—a paradox because these are the best seasons to be in Hawaii,

in terms of reliably great weather. If you're looking to save money, or if you just want to avoid the crowds, this is the time to visit. Hotel rates and airfares tend to be significantly lower, and good packages are often available.

Note: If you plan to come to Hawaii between the last week in April and early May, be sure you book your accommodations, interisland air reservations, and car rentals in advance. In Japan, the last week of April is called **Golden Week** because three Japanese holidays take place one after the other. Waikiki is especially busy with Japanese tourists during this time, but the neighboring islands also see dramatic increases.

Due to the large number of families traveling in **summer** (June–Aug), you won't get the fantastic bargains of spring and fall. However, you'll still do much better on packages, airfare, and accommodations than you will in the winter months.

CLIMATE

Because Hawaii lies at the edge of the tropical zone, it technically has only two seasons, both of them warm. There's a dry season that corresponds to **summer** (Apr–Oct) and a rainy season in **winter** (Nov–Mar). It rains every day somewhere in the islands any time of the year, but the rainy season sometimes brings enough gray weather to spoil your tanning opportunities. Fortunately, it seldom rains in one spot for more than 3 days straight.

The **year-round temperature** doesn't vary much. At the beach, the average daytime high in summer is 85°F (29°C), while the average daytime high in winter is 78°F (26°C); nighttime lows are usually about 10°F cooler. But how warm it is on any given day really depends on *where* you are on the island.

Each island has a leeward side (the side sheltered from the wind) and a windward side (the side that gets the wind's full force). The **leeward** sides (the west and south) are usually hot and dry, while the **windward** sides (east and north) are generally cooler and moist. When you want arid, sunbaked, desertlike weather, go leeward. When you want lush, wet, junglelike weather, go windward.

Hawaii is also full of **microclimates,** thanks to its interior valleys, coastal plains, and mountain peaks. So if the weather doesn't suit you, just go to the other side of the island—or head into the hills.

On rare occasions, the weather can be disastrous, as when Hurricane Iniki crushed Kauai in September 1992 with 225-mph winds. Tsunamis have swept Hilo and the south shore of Oahu. But those are extreme exceptions. Mostly, one day follows another here in glorious, sunny procession, each quite like the other.

Waikiki's Average Temperature and Rainy Days

Month	High (°F/°C)	Low (°F/°C)	Water Temp (°F/°C)	Rainy Days
Jan	80/27	70/21	75/24	10
Feb	80/27	66/19	74/23	9
Mar	81/27	66/19	74/23	9
Apr	82/28	69/21	75/24	9
May	84/29	70/21	76/24	7
June	86/30	72/22	77/25	6
July	87/31	73/23	78/26	7
Aug	88/31	74/23	79/26	6
Sept	88/31	74/23	80/27	7
Oct	86/30	72/22	79/26	9
Nov	84/29	70/21	77/25	9
Dec	81/27	67/19	76/24	10

Tips **Travel Tip**

Your best bets for total year-round sun are **Waikiki Beach** and the **Ko Olina** (southwest) coast of Oahu.

HOLIDAYS

When Hawaii observes holidays (especially those over a long weekend), travel between the islands increases, interisland airline seats are fully booked, rental cars are at a premium, and hotels and restaurants are busier.

Federal, state, and county government offices are closed on all federal holidays; for a list, go to "Holidays" in the appendix.

State and county offices are also closed on local holidays, including Prince Kuhio Day (Mar 26), honoring the birthday of Hawaii's first delegate to the U.S. Congress; King Kamehameha Day (June 11), a statewide holiday commemorating Kamehameha the Great, who united the islands and ruled from 1795 to 1819; and Admissions Day (third Fri in Aug), which honors the admittance of Hawaii as the 50th state on August 21, 1959.

Other special days celebrated in Hawaii by many people but which involve no closing of federal, state, and county offices are the Chinese New Year (which can fall in Jan or Feb; in 2010, it's Feb 14), Girls' Day (Mar 3), Buddha's Birthday (Apr 8), Father Damien's Day (Apr 15), Boys' Day (May 5), Samoan Flag Day (in Aug), Aloha Festivals (Sept–Oct), and Pearl Harbor Day (Dec 7).

OAHU CALENDAR OF EVENTS

Please note that, as with any schedule of upcoming events, the following information is subject to change; always confirm the details before you plan your trip around an event.

For an exhaustive list of events beyond those listed here, check http://events.frommers.com, where you'll find a searchable, up-to-the-minute roster of what's happening in cities all over the world.

JANUARY

Rockstar Games Pipeline Pro, Banzai Pipeline, North Shore. Competition is judged on the best wave selection and maneuvers on the wave. Call ✆ 732/528-0621 (www.usbatour.com). January or February.

Sony Open, Waialae Country Club. A $1.2-million PGA golf event featuring the top men in golf. Call ✆ 808/792-9300. Early to mid-January.

Pacific Islands Arts Festival at Thomas Square, across from Honolulu Academy of the Arts, Honolulu. More than 100 artists and handicraft artisans, entertainment, food, and demonstrations fill the day. Admission is free. Call ✆ 808/696-6717. Mid-January.

FEBRUARY

Narcissus Festival, Honolulu. Taking place around the Chinese New Year, this cultural festival includes a queen pageant, cooking demonstrations, and a cultural fair. Call ✆ 808/533-3181.

Sand Castle Building Contest, Kailua Beach Park. Students from the University of Hawaii School of Architecture compete against professional architects to see who can build the best, most unusual, and most outrageous sand sculpture. Call ✆ 808/956-3518.

Punahou School Carnival, Punahou School, Honolulu. This event has everything you can imagine in a school carnival, from high-speed rides to homemade jellies. All proceeds go to scholarship funds for Hawaii's most prestigious high school. Call ✆ 808/944-5753. Early to mid-February.

Buffalo's Big Board Classic, Makaha Beach. This contest involves traditional Hawaiian surfing, long boarding, and

> **Tips** **Daylight Saving Time**
>
> Since 1966, most of the United States has observed daylight saving time from the first Sunday in April to the last Sunday in October. In 2007, these dates changed, and now daylight saving time lasts from 2am on the second Sunday in March to 2am on the first Sunday in November. **Note that Hawaii does *not* observe daylight saving time.** So when daylight saving time is in effect in most of the U.S., Hawaii is 3 hours behind the West Coast and 6 hours behind the East Coast. When the U.S. reverts to standard time in November, Hawaii is 2 hours behind the West Coast and 5 hours behind the East Coast.

canoe-surfing. Call ✆ **808/951-7877.** Depending on surf conditions, it can be held in February or March.

MARCH

St. Patrick's Day Parade, Waikiki (Fort DeRussy to Kapiolani Park), Oahu. Bagpipers, bands, clowns, and marching groups parade through the heart of Waikiki, with lots of Irish-style celebrating all day. Call ✆ **808/536-4612** (O'Toole's Pub). March 17.

Prince Kuhio Day Celebrations. On this state holiday, various festivals throughout Hawaii celebrate the birth of Jonah Kuhio Kalanianaole, who was born on March 26, 1871, and elected to Congress in 1902. March 26.

APRIL

Easter Sunrise Service, National Memorial Cemetery of the Pacific, Punchbowl Crater, Honolulu. For a century, people have gathered at this famous cemetery for Easter sunrise services. Call ✆ **808/566-1430.** April 4, 2010.

MAY

Outrigger Canoe Season. From May to September, canoe paddlers across the state participate in outrigger canoe races nearly every weekend. Call ✆ **808/383-7798,** or go to www.y2kanu.com for this year's schedule of events.

Lei Day Celebrations, various locations. May Day is Lei Day in Hawaii, celebrated with lei-making contests, pageantry, arts and crafts, and the real highlight, a Brothers Cazimero concert at the Waikiki Shell (call ✆ **808/597-1888,** ext. 232, for the show). Call ✆ **808/692-5118** or go to www.honolulu.gov/parks/programs/leiday for Oahu events. May 1.

World Fire-Knife Dance Championships & Samoa Festival, Polynesian Cultural Center, Laie. Junior and adult fire-knife dancers from around the world converge on the center for one of the most amazing performances you'll ever see. Authentic Samoan food and cultural festivities round out the fun. Call ✆ **808/293-3333** (www.polynesianculturalcenter.com). Mid-May.

Lantern Floating Hawaii, Magic Island at Ala Moana Beach Park, Honolulu. The Shinnyo-en Temple's ceremonial floating of some 700 lanterns takes place at sunset, representing an appeal for peace and harmony. Hula and music follow the ceremony. Call ✆ **808/947-2814** (www.lanternfloatinghawaii.com). Memorial Day weekend.

Memorial Day, National Memorial Cemetery of the Pacific, Punchbowl Crater, Honolulu. The armed forces hold a ceremony recognizing those who died for their country, beginning at

9am. Call 📞 **808/532-3720.** Memorial Day (last Mon in May).

JUNE

King Kamehameha Celebration. This state holiday (officially June 11, but celebrated on weekend closest to June 11) features a massive floral parade, *hoolaulea* (party), and much more. Call 📞 **808/586-0333** or visit http://hawaii.gov/dags/king_kamehameha_commission. Most events in 2010 will be held June 12 to 13.

King Kamehameha Hula Competition, Neal Blaisdell Center, Honolulu, Oahu. This is one of the top hula competitions in the world, with dancers from as far away as Japan. It's held the third weekend in June. Call 📞 **808/586-0333** (www.hawaii.gov/dags/king_kamehameha_commission). Mid- to late June.

Flavors of Honolulu, Civic Center Grounds, Honolulu. Formerly known as the Taste of Honolulu, Hawaii's premier outdoor food festival features samples from 25 restaurants, entertainment, beer and wine tasting, cooking demos, and a gourmet marketplace. Proceeds go to Abilities Unlimited. Call 📞 **808/532-2115** (www.abilitiesunlimitedhi.org). Late June.

JULY

Fourth of July Fireworks, Desiderio and Sills Field, Schofield Barracks. A free daylong celebration, with entertainment, food, and games, ends with a spectacular fireworks show. Call 📞 **808/655-0110.**

Quiksilver Molokai to Oahu Paddleboard Race, starts on Molokai and finishes on Oahu. Some 70 participants, from an international field, journey to Molokai to compete in this 32-mile race, considered to be the world championship of long-distance paddleboard racing. The race begins at Kaluakoi Beach on Molokai at 7:30am and finishes at Maunaloa Bay on Oahu around 12:30pm. Call 📞 **808/638-8208.** Mid- to late July.

Ukulele Festival, Kapiolani Park Bandstand, Waikiki, Oahu. This free concert features a ukulele orchestra of some 600 students, ages 4 to 92. Hawaii's top musicians all pitch in. Call 📞 **808/732-3739** (www.roysakuma.net). Late July.

Queen Liliuokalani Keiki Hula Competition, Neal Blaisdell Center, Honolulu, Oahu. More than 500 *keiki* (children) representing 22 *halau* (hula schools) from the islands compete in this dance fest. The event is broadcast a week later on KITV-TV. Call 📞 **808/521-6905.** Late July.

Hawaii State Farm Fair, Aloha Stadium, Honolulu. The annual state fair is a great one: It features displays of Hawaii agricultural products (including orchids), educational and cultural exhibits, entertainment, and local-style food. Call 📞 **808/682-5767** (www.ekfernandez.com). Late July or early August.

Transpac Yacht Race. This international yacht race is held during July in odd-numbered years only (2011, 2013, and so on). Sailors from the United States, Japan, Australia, New Zealand, Europe, and Hawaii race from Long Beach to Honolulu. They then participate in a series of races around the state. Call 📞 **808/944-9666** (www.transpacificyc.org).

AUGUST

Hawaii International Jazz Festival, Hawaii Theatre, Honolulu. This festival includes evening concerts and daily jam sessions, plus scholarship giveaways, the University of Southern California jazz band, and many popular jazz and blues artists. Call 📞 **808/941-9974.** Early August.

Duke's OceanFest Hoolaulea, Waikiki. Nine days of water-oriented competitions and festivities celebrate the life of Duke Kahanamoku. Events include the Hawaii Paddleboard Championship, the Pro Surf Longboard Contest, the International Tandem Surfing Championship, the Corona Extra Duke Volleyball Classic, a Surf Polo Tournament, and a Hawaiian luau (the luau is $60 at the door). Call © **808/545-4880** (www.dukefoundation.org). Mid-August.

Admissions Day, Hawaii became the 50th state on August 21, 1959. On the third Friday in August, the state takes a holiday (all state-related facilities are closed).

Hawaiian Slack-Key Guitar Festival Gabby Style, Queen Kapiolani Park Bandstand, Waikiki. The best of Hawaii's folk music—slack-key guitar—performed by the best musicians in Hawaii. It takes place from noon to 6pm and is absolutely free. Call © **808/ 226-2697** (www.slackkeyfestival.com). Third Sunday in August.

SEPTEMBER

Waikiki Roughwater Swim, Waikiki, Oahu. This popular 2.4-mile, open-ocean swim goes from Sans Souci Beach to Duke Kahanamoku Beach in Waikiki. Early registration is encouraged, but last-minute entries on race day are allowed. Visit www.waikikiroughwaterswim.com for more info. Labor Day.

Aloha Festivals, various locations. Parades and other events celebrate Hawaiian culture and friendliness throughout the state. Call © **808/589-1771** (www.alohafestivals.com).

Aloha Festivals' Poke Contest, Hapuna Beach Prince Hotel, Big Island. Top chefs from across Hawaii and the U.S. mainland, as well as local amateurs, compete in making the Hawaiian delicacy poke (pronounced "po-*kay*"): chopped raw fish mixed with seaweed and spices. Here's your chance to sample poke at its best. Call © **808/880-3424**.

OCTOBER

Hana Hoohiwahiwa O Kaiulani, Sheraton Princess Kaiulani, Waikiki. This hotel commemorates the birthday of its namesake, Princess Victoria Kaiulani, with a week of special activities: complimentary hula lessons, lei-making, ukulele lessons, and more. The crowning touch is the Princess Kaiulani Keiki Hula Festival, which showcases performances by more than 200 *keiki* from *halau* on the island of Oahu. Admission is free. Call © **808/931-4524**. Mid-October.

NOVEMBER

Hawaii International Film Festival, various locations throughout the state. This cinema festival with a cross-cultural spin features filmmakers from Asia, the Pacific Islands, and the United States. Call © **808/550-8457** (www.hiff.org). First 2 weeks in November.

Triple Crown of Surfing, North Shore. The world's top professional surfers compete in events for more than $1 million in prize money. Call © **808/ 739-3965** (www.triplecrownofsurfing.com). Held between mid-November and mid-December, whenever conditions are best.

DECEMBER

Festival of Lights, Honolulu Hale, Honolulu. The mayor throws the switch to light up the 40-foot-tall Norfolk pine and other trees in front of Honolulu Hale. Call © **808/523-4385**. Early December.

Honolulu Marathon, Honolulu, Oahu. This is one of the largest marathons in the world, with more than 30,000 competitors. Call © **808/734-7200** (www.honolulumarathon.org). Second Sunday in December.

2 VISITOR INFORMATION

For advance information, contact the **Hawaii Visitors and Convention Bureau (HVCB)**, Ste. 801, Waikiki Business Plaza, 2270 Kalakaua Ave., Honolulu, HI 96815 (© **800/GO-HAWAII** [464-29244] or 808/923-1811; www.gohawaii.com). Among other things, the bureau publishes the helpful *Accommodations and Car Rental Guide* and supplies free brochures, maps, and *Islands of Aloha,* the official HVCB magazine.

The **Oahu Visitors Bureau,** 1001 Bishop St., Pauahi Tower, Ste. 47, Honolulu, HI 96813 (© **800/OAHU-678** [624-8678] or 808/524-0722; www.visitoahu.com), distributes a free 64-page visitors booklet.

A number of free publications, including *This Week* and *Guide to Oahu,* are packed with money-saving coupons offering discounts on dining, shops, and activities around the island; look for them at the airport and around town.

If you want information about working and living in Hawaii, contact **The Chamber of Commerce of Hawaii,** 1132 Bishop St., Ste. 200, Honolulu, HI 96815 (© **808/545-4300**).

For Hawaii on the Web, see chapter 1, "The Best Oahu Websites."

MAPS: ROADS, TRAILS & ACTIVITIES

One of the best general maps of the island is the *Map of Oahu,* cartography by James A. Bier, published by the University of Hawaii Press, available at bookstores or online at www.uhpress.hawaii.edu.

The best street map we have found is *TMK Maps: Oahu Streets and Condos,* published by Hawaii TMK Service, Inc. (© **808/536-0867**).

The best and most detailed maps for activities are published by **Franko's Maps** (www.frankosmaps.com); they feature a host of island maps, plus a terrific "Hawaiian Reef Creatures Guide," for snorkelers curious about what fish they spotted underwater. Free road maps are published by *This Week Magazine,* a free visitor publication available on Oahu, the Big Island, Maui, and Kauai.

For topographic and other maps of the islands, go to the **Hawaii Geographic Society,** 49 S. Hotel St., Honolulu; or contact P.O. Box 1698, Honolulu, HI 96806 (© **800/538-3950** or 808/538-3952).

3 ENTRY REQUIREMENTS

PASSPORTS

Virtually every air traveler entering the U.S. is required to show a passport. All persons, including U.S. citizens, traveling by air between the United States and Canada, Mexico, Central and South America, the Caribbean, and Bermuda are required to present a valid passport. U.S. and Canadian citizens entering the U.S. at land and sea ports of entry from within the western hemisphere will need to present government-issued proof of citizenship, such as a birth certificate, along with a government-issued photo ID, such as a driver's license. A passport is not required for U.S. or Canadian citizens entering by land or sea, but carrying one is highly encouraged.For information on how to obtain a passport, see "Passports" in the "Fast Facts" section of Chapter 10.

VISAS

For information on obtaining a Visa, please visit "Fast Facts," on p. 258.

The U.S. Department of State has a **Visa Waiver Program (VWP)** allowing citizens of the following countries to enter the United States without a visa for stays of up to 90 days: Andorra, Australia, Austria, Belgium, Brunei, Denmark, Finland, France, Germany, Iceland, Ireland, Italy, Japan, Liechtenstein, Luxembourg, Monaco, the Netherlands, New Zealand, Norway, Portugal, San Marino, Singapore, Slovenia, Spain, Sweden, Switzerland, and the United Kingdom. Citizens of Czech Republic, Estonia, Hungary, Latvia, Lithuania, Malta, Republic of Korea, and Slovakia are soon to be admitted to the VWP. (*Note:* This list was accurate at press time; for the most up-to-date list of countries in the VWP, consult http://travel.state.gov/visa.) Even though a visa isn't necessary, in an effort to help U.S. officials check travelers against terror watch lists before they arrive at U.S. borders, visitors from VWP countries must register online through the Electronic System for Travel Authorization (ESTA) before boarding a plane or a boat to the U.S. Travelers will complete an electronic application providing basic personal and travel eligibility information. The Department of Homeland Security recommends filling out the form at least three days before traveling. Authorizations will be valid for up to 2 years or until the traveler's passport expires, whichever comes first. Currently, there is no fee for

the online application. *Note:* Any passport issued on or after October 26, 2006, by a VWP country must be an **e-Passport** for VWP travelers to be eligible to enter the U.S. without a visa. Citizens of these nations also need to present a round-trip air or cruise ticket upon arrival. E-Passports contain computer chips capable of storing biometric information, such as the required digital photograph of the holder. If your passport doesn't have this feature, you can still travel without a visa if it is a valid passport issued before October 26, 2005, and includes a machine-readable zone, or between October 26, 2005, and October 25, 2006, and includes a digital photograph. For more information, go to **http://travel.state.gov/visa**. Canadian citizens may enter the United States without visas; they will need to show passports (if traveling by air) and proof of residence, however.

Citizens of all other countries must have (1) a valid passport that expires at least 6 months later than the scheduled end of their visit to the U.S., and (2) a tourist visa.

CUSTOMS
What You Can Bring Into the U.S.

Every visitor more than 21 years of age may bring in, free of duty, the following: (1) 1 liter of wine or hard liquor; (2) 200 cigarettes, 100 cigars (but not from Cuba), or 3 pounds of smoking tobacco; and (3) $100 worth of gifts. These exemptions are offered to travelers who spend at least 72 hours in the United States and who have not claimed them within the preceding 6 months. It is forbidden to bring into the country almost any meat products (including canned, fresh, and dried meat products such as bullion, soup mixes, etc.). Generally, condiments including vinegars, oils, spices, coffee, tea, and some cheeses and baked goods are permitted. Avoid rice products, as rice can often harbor insects.

Bringing fruits and vegetables is not advised, though not prohibited. Customs will allow produce depending on where you got it and where you're going after you arrive in the U.S. International visitors may carry in or out up to $10,000 in U.S. or foreign currency with no formalities; larger sums must be declared to U.S. Customs on entering or leaving, which includes filing form CM 4790. For details regarding U.S. Customs and Border Protection, consult your nearest U.S. embassy or consulate, or **U.S. Customs** (www.customs.gov).

What You Can Take Home from Hawaii:

For information on what you're allowed to bring home, contact one of the following agencies:

U.S. Citizens: U.S. Customs & Border Protection (CBP), 1300 Pennsylvania Ave., NW, Washington, DC 20229 (© **877/ 287-8667;** www.cbp.gov).

Canadian Citizens: Canada Border Services Agency (© **800/461-9999** in Canada, or 204/983-3500; www.cbsa-asfc.gc.ca).

U.K. Citizens: HM Customs & Excise at © **0845/010-9000** (from outside the U.K., 020/8929-0152), or consult their website at **www.hmce.gov.uk.**

Australian Citizens: Australian Customs Service at © **1300/363-263,** or log on to **www.customs.gov.au.**

New Zealand Citizens: New Zealand Customs, The Customhouse, 17–21 Whitmore St., Box 2218, Wellington (© **04/ 473-6099** or 0800/428-786; www.customs.govt.nz).

MEDICAL REQUIREMENTS

Unless you're arriving from an area known to be suffering from an epidemic (particularly cholera or yellow fever), inoculations or vaccinations are not required for entry into the United States.

4 GETTING THERE & GETTING AROUND

BY PLANE

Most major U.S. and many international carriers fly to Honolulu International Airport.

United Airlines (© **800/225-5825;** www.ual.com) offers the most frequent service from the U.S. mainland. **American Airlines** (© **800/433-7300;** www. americanair.com) offers flights from Dallas, Chicago, San Francisco, San Jose, Los Angeles, and St. Louis to Honolulu. **Continental Airlines** (© **800/231-0856;** www.continental.com) offers the only daily nonstop from the New York area (Newark) to Honolulu. **Delta Air Lines** (© **800/221-1212;** www.delta.com) flies nonstop from the West Coast and from Houston and Cincinnati. **Hawaiian Airlines** (© **800/367-5320;** www. hawaiianair.com) offers nonstop flights to

Honolulu from several West Coast cities (including new service from San Diego). **Northwest Airlines** (© **800/225-2525;** www.nwa.com) has a daily nonstop from Detroit to Honolulu. **Alaska Airlines** (© **800/252-7522;** www.alaskaair.com) has direct flights to Honolulu from Seattle and Anchorage.

Airlines serving Hawaii from places other than the U.S. mainland include **Air Canada** (© **800/776-3000;** www.air canada.ca); **Air New Zealand** (© **0800/ 737-000** in Auckland, 643/379-5200 in Christchurch, 800/926-7255 in the U.S.; www.airnewzealand.com); **Qantas** (© **008/177-767** in Australia, 800/227-4500 in the U.S.; www.qantas.com.au); **Japan Air Lines** (© **03/5489-1111** in Tokyo, 800/525-3663 in the U.S.; www. japanair.com); **All Nippon Airways**

(ANA; ✆ **03/5489-1212** in Tokyo, 800/235-9262 in the U.S.; www.fly-ana. com); **China Airlines** (✆ **02/715-1212** in Taipei, 800/227-5118 in the U.S.; www.china-airlines.com); **Air Pacific** (✆ **800/227-4446;** www.airpacific.com), serving Fiji, Australia, New Zealand, and the South Pacific; **Korean Air** (✆ **02/656-2000** in Seoul, 800/223-1155 on the U.S. East Coast, 800/421-8200 on the U.S. West Coast, 800/438-5000 from Hawaii; www.koreanair.com); and **Philippine Airlines** (✆ **631/816-6691** in Manila, 800/435-9725 in the U.S.; www. philippineair.com).

Operated by the European Travel Network, **www.discount-tickets.com** is a great online source for regular and discounted airfares to destinations around

The Welcoming Lei

The tropical beauty of the delicate garland, the deliciously sweet fragrance of the blossoms, the sensual way the flowers curl softly around your neck— there's no doubt about it: Getting lei'd in Hawaii is a sensuous experience.

Leis are one of the nicest ways to say hello, goodbye, congratulations, I salute you, my sympathies are with you, or I love you. Giving leis is a historic custom: According to chants, the first lei was given by Hiiaka, the sister of the volcano goddess, Pele. Hiiaka presented Pele with a lei of lehua blossoms on a beach in Puna.

During ancient times, leis given to *alii* (royalty) were accompanied by a bow, as it was *kapu* (forbidden) for a commoner to raise his arms higher than the king's head. The presentation of a kiss with a lei didn't come about until World War II; it's generally attributed to an entertainer who kissed an officer on a dare, then quickly presented him with her lei, saying it was an old Hawaiian custom. It wasn't then, but it sure caught on fast.

Lei-making is a tropical art form. All leis are fashioned by hand in a variety of traditional patterns; some are sewn of hundreds of tiny blooms or shells, or bits of ferns and leaves. Some are twisted, some braided, some strung. Every island has its own special flower lei. On Oahu, the choice is *ilima,* a small orange flower. Big Islanders prefer the *lehua,* a large, delicate red puff. Maui likes the *lokelani,* a small rose. On Kauai, it's the *mokihana,* a fragrant green vine and berry. Molokai prefers the *kukui,* the white blossom of a candlenut tree. And Lanai's lei is made of *kaunaoa,* a bright yellow moss, while Niihau uses its abundant seashells to make leis that were once prized by royalty and are now worth a small fortune.

Leis are available at lei stands at Honolulu International Airport. Other places to get creative, inexpensive leis are the half-dozen lei shops on **Maunakea Street** in Honolulu's Chinatown, and **Flowers by Jou & T Jr.,** 2653 S. King St. (near University Ave.), Honolulu (✆ **808/941-2022**). They're also available from florists, and even at supermarkets.

Leis are the perfect symbol of Hawaii: They're given in the moment, their fragrance and beauty are enjoyed in the moment, and when they fade, their spirit of aloha lives on. Welcome to the islands!

(Tips) Coping with Jet Lag

Jet lag is a pitfall of traveling across time zones. If you're flying north–south, your symptoms will be the result of dehydration and the general stress of air travel. When you travel east–west, however, your body becomes disoriented about what time it is, and everything from your digestive system to your brain is knocked for a loop. Traveling east, say from Maui to Boston, is more difficult on your internal clock than traveling west, say from Atlanta to Oahu, because most peoples' bodies are more inclined to stay up late than fall asleep early.

Here are some tips for combating jet lag:

- **Reset your watch** to your destination time before you board the plane.
- **Drink lots of water** before, during, and after your flight. Avoid alcohol.
- **Exercise and sleep well** for a few days before your trip.
- If you have trouble sleeping on planes, **fly eastward on morning flights.**
- **Natural light** resets your body clock. **Outside In** (www.bodyclock.com) can provide a customized plan of when to seek and avoid daylight.

the world. Compare rates and book accommodations, car rentals, and tours.

If you're traveling in the United States beyond Hawaii, some large American airlines—such as **American, Delta, Northwest, TWA,** and **United**—offer travelers on transatlantic or transpacific flights special discount tickets under the name **Visit USA,** allowing travel between U.S. destinations at reduced rates. These tickets must be purchased before you leave your foreign point of departure. This system is the best, easiest, and fastest way to see the United States at low cost. You should obtain information well in advance from your travel agent or the airline office, as the conditions attached to these discount tickets can change without advance notice.

Locally, **Hawaiian Airlines** (© 800/ 367-5320; www.hawaiianair.com) flies nonstop to Sydney, Tahiti, and American Samoa.

AGRICULTURAL SCREENING AT THE AIRPORTS At Honolulu International and the neighbor-island airports, baggage and passengers bound for the mainland must be screened by agricultural

officials. Officials will confiscate local produce, such as fresh avocados, bananas, and mangoes, in the name of fruit-fly control. Pineapples, coconuts, and papayas inspected and certified for export, boxed flowers, leis without seeds, and processed foods (macadamia nuts, coffee, jams, dried fruit, and the like) will pass.

ARRIVAL AT HONOLULU INTERNATIONAL AIRPORT

Honolulu International Airport sits on the south shore of Oahu, west of downtown Honolulu and Waikiki, near Pearl Harbor.

While the airport is large and constantly expanding, the layout is quite simple and easy to navigate. You can walk or take the **Wiki-Wiki Bus,** a free airport shuttle, from your arrival gate to the main terminal and baggage claim, which is on the ground level. After collecting your bags, exit to the palm-lined street, where uniformed attendants flag down taxis, Waikiki shuttles, and rental car vans; they can also direct you to **TheBus** (see "Getting To & From the Airport," below).

Getting To & From the Airport

BY RENTAL CAR All major rental companies have cars available at Honolulu International Airport (see "Getting Around," later). Rental agency vans pick you up at the middle curbside outside baggage claim and take you to their off-site lot.

BY TAXI Oahu's major cab companies offer island-wide, 24-hour radio-dispatched service, with multilingual drivers, air-conditioned cars, limos, vans, and vehicles equipped with wheelchair lifts. Fares are standard for all taxi firms; from the airport, expect to pay about $35 to $45 (plus tip) to Waikiki, about $35 to $40 to downtown, about $70 to $75 to Kailua, about $65 to $70 to Hawaii Kai, and about $95 to $110 to the North Shore. See "Getting Around," later, for a list of cab companies.

For a flat fee of $35, **Star Taxi** (© 800/ 671-2999 or 808/942-STAR [942-7827]) will take up to four passengers from the airport to Waikiki (with no extra charges for baggage); however, you must book in advance. After you have arrived and before you pick up your luggage, call Star to reconfirm that they'll be outside baggage claim waiting for you.

BY AIRPORT SHUTTLE Shuttle vans operate 24 hours a day, every day of the year, between the airport and all 350 hotels and condos in Waikiki. The cheapest shuttle service is **Airport Waikiki Express** (© 808/566-7333; www.airport waikikishuttle.com), with 24-hour service in air-conditioned vans for just $9 from the airport to Waikiki ($15 round-trip). You can board with two pieces of luggage and a carry-on at no extra charge; surfboards and bicycles are prohibited for safety reasons. Tips are welcome.

BY BUS TheBus (© 808/848-5555; www.thebus.org) is by far the cheapest way to get to Waikiki—a one-way fare is $2 (exact change only)—but you've got to be traveling light to use it. You can board TheBus with a carry-on or small suitcase as long as it fits under the seat and doesn't disrupt other passengers. TheBus nos. 19 and 20 (Waikiki Beach and Hotels) run from the airport to downtown Honolulu and Waikiki (travel time: 1 hr.). The first bus from Waikiki to the airport is at 4:50am on weekdays and 5:25am on weekends; the last bus departs the airport for Waikiki at 11:45pm on weekdays, 11:25pm on weekends. Two bus stops are on the main terminal's upper level; a third is on the second level of the interisland terminal.

GETTING AROUND

BY TAXI Oahu residents own 600,000 registered vehicles, but they have only 1,500 miles of mostly two-lane roads. That's 400 cars for every mile, a fact that becomes abundantly clear during morning and evening rush hours. You can avoid the gridlock by driving between 9am and 3pm or after 6pm.

BY RENTAL CAR Hawaii has some of the lowest car-rental rates in the country. The average nondiscounted, unlimited-mileage rate for a 1-day rental for a mid-size car in Honolulu was $50 in 2007; that's one of the lowest rates in the country, compared with the national average of $56 a day. To rent a car in Hawaii, you must be at least 25 years of age and have a valid U.S. or international driver's license and credit card.

At Honolulu International Airport, you'll find most major rental-car agencies, including **Avis** (© 800/321-3712; www. avis.com), **Budget** (© 800/935-6878; www.budget.com), **Dollar** (© 800/ 800-4000; www.dollar.com), **Enterprise** (© 800/325-8007; www.enterprise.com), **Hertz** (© 800/654-3011; www.hertz. com), **National** (© 800/227-7368; www. nationalcar.com), and **Thrifty** (© 800/ 367-2277; www.thrifty.com). It's almost always cheaper to rent a car at the airport than in Waikiki or through your hotel (unless there's one already included in your package deal), however it's best to book in advance.

I no longer recommend **Alamo,** which tends to overbook their cars. Despite confirmed reservations, many loyal Frommer's readers have been forced to wait 1 to 2 hours at the start of their vacation (after sitting on an airplane for 5-plus hours) for cars to be returned.

Hawaii is a no-fault state, which means that if you don't have **collision-damage insurance,** you are required to pay for all damages before you leave the state, whether or not the accident was your fault. Your personal car insurance back home may provide rental-car coverage; read your policy or call your insurer before you leave home. Bring your insurance identification card if you decline the optional insurance, which usually costs from $12 to $20 a day. Obtain the name of your company's local claim representative before you go. Some credit card companies also provide collision-damage insurance to customers; check with yours before you rent.

DRIVING RULES Hawaii state law mandates that all car passengers must wear a **seat belt,** and all infants must be strapped into car seats. The fine is enforced with vigilance, so buckle up—you'll pay a $95 fine if you don't. **Pedestrians** always have the right of way, even if they're not in the crosswalk. You can turn **right on red** from the right lane after a full and complete stop, unless there's a sign forbidding you to do so.

Main Streets & Highways

Navigating around Oahu is actually easy as there are relatively few roads—some circle the perimeter of the island and a handful cut across the island.

TO & FROM THE AIRPORT The main thoroughfare that runs from the airport to Honolulu and Waikiki is the **H-1 Freeway.** The H-1 also runs in the opposite direction to Pearl Harbor and Ewa. The artery that runs from the airport to Honolulu and Waikiki is **Nimitz Highway** (which has stoplights). In downtown Honolulu, Nimitz Highway becomes **Ala Moana Boulevard.**

IN HONOLULU The myriad of one-way streets in Honolulu can be confusing and frustrating. If you want to travel in the Diamond Head direction, **King Street** is one-way going toward Diamond Head. **Beretania Street** is one-way in the opposite direction, toward Ewa. In the *mauka* and *makai* directions: **Punchbowl** and **Bishop streets** run toward the ocean (makai), and **Alakea** and **Bethel streets** run toward the mountains (mauka).

Easy Ridin' on Oahu

If your dream is to go screaming down the highway on the back of a big Harley, here's your chance. **Cruzin Hawaii Motorcycles,** 1980 Kalakaua Ave., at Kuhio Avenue, next to Tony Roma's, Waikiki (© **808/945-9595;** www.cruzinhawaii.com), has a range of bikes starting at $79 (insurance is included in the price). Also try **Big Kahuna Motorcycle Rentals,** 407 Seaside Ave., Waikiki (© **808/924-2736;** www.bigkahunarentals.com), which specializes in Harley-Davidson, BMW, Yamaha, and Honda; or **Coconut Cruisers,** 2301 Kalakaua Ave., across from the International Market Place, Honolulu (© **808/924-1644;** www.coconutcruisers. netfirms.com). You must have a valid motorcycle license to rent a bike.

PLANNING YOUR TRIP TO OAHU

2

GETTING THERE & GETTING AROUND

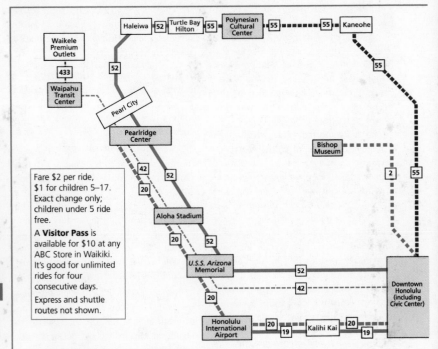

Fare $2 per ride, $1 for children 5–17. Exact change only; children under 5 ride free.

A **Visitor Pass** is available for $10 at any ABC Store in Waikiki. It's good for unlimited rides for four consecutive days.

Express and shuttle routes not shown.

Getting There on TheBus:

Academy of Arts: Take #2 bus (School/Middle St) to Beretania St. and Ward Ave.

Ala Moana Center: Take bus #19 & #20 AIRPORT. Return via #19 WAIKIKI, or cross Ala Moana Blvd. for #20.

Bishop Museum: Take #2 SCHOOL STREET. Get off at Kapalama St., cross School St., walk down Bernice St. Return to School St. and take #2 WAIKIKI.

Byodo-In Temple: Take bus #2 to Hotel-Alakea St. (TRF) to #55 KANEOHE-KAHALUU. Get off at Valley of the Temple cemetery. Also #19 and #20 AIRPORT to King-Alakea St., (TRF) on Alakea St. to #55 KANEOHE-KAHALUU.

Circle Island: Take a bus to ALA MOANA CENTER (TRF) to #52 WAHIAWA CIRCLE ISLAND or #55 KANEOHE CIRCLE ISLAND. This is a 4-hour bus ride.

Chinatown or Downtown: Take any #2 bus going out of Waikiki to Hotel St. Return, take #2 WAIKIKI on Hotel St., or #19 or #20 on King St.

The Contemporary Museum & Punchbowl (National Cemetery of the Pacific): Take #2 bus (TRF) at Alapai St. to #15 MAKIKI-PACIFIC HGTS. Return, take #15 and get off at King St., area (TRF) #2 WAIKIKI.

Diamond Head Crater: Take #22 HAWAII KAI-SEA LIFE PARK to the crater. Take a flashlight. Return to the same area and take #22 WAIKIKI.

Dole Plantation: Take bus to ALA MOANA CENTER (TRF) to #52 WAHIAWA CIRCLE ISLAND.

Foster Botanical Garden: Take #2 bus to Hotel-Riviera St. Walk to Vineyard Blvd. Return to Hotel St. Take #2 WAIKIKI, or take #4 NUUANU and get off at Nuuanu-Vineyard. Cross Nuuanu Ave. and walk one block to the gardens.

Hanauma Bay: Take #22 Beach Bus.

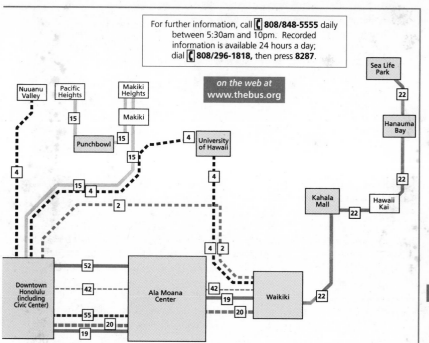

For further information, call ☎ **808/848-5555** daily between 5:30am and 10pm. Recorded information is available 24 hours a day; dial ☎ **808/296-1818**, then press **8287**.

on the web at
www.thebus.org

Aloha Tower Marketplace & Hawaii Maritime Center: Take #19–#20 AIRPORT and get off at Alakea–Ala Moana. Cross the street to the Aloha Tower.

Honolulu Zoo: Take any bus on Kuhio Ave. going DIAMOND HEAD direction to Kapahulu Ave.

Iolani Palace (also **State Capitol, Honolulu Hale, Kawaihao Church, Mission Houses, Queen's Hospital, King Kamehameha Statue, State Judiciary Bldg.**): Take any #2 bus and get off at Punchbowl and Beretania St. Walk to King St. Return #2 WAIKIKI on King St.

Kahala Mall: Take #22 HAWAII KAI–SEA LIFE PARK to Kilauea Ave. Return, #22 WAIKIKI.

Pearl Harbor (*Arizona* **Memorial):** Take #20 AIRPORT. Get off across from Memorial, or take a bus to ALA MOANA CENTER (TRF) to #52.

Polynesian Cultural Center: Take a bus to ALA MOANA CENTER (TRF) to #55 KANEOHE CIRCLE ISLAND. Bus ride takes 2 hours one-way.

Queen Emma's Summer Home: Take #4 NUUANU, or board a bus to ALA MOANA CENTER (TRF) to #55 KANEOHE.

Sea Life Park: Take #22 HAWAII KAI–SEA LIFE PARK. #22 will stop at Hanauma Bay en route to the park.

University of Hawaii: Take #4 NUUANU. The bus will go to the University en route to Nuuanu.

Waimea Valley Audobon Center: Take a bus to ALA MOANA CENTER (TRF) to #52 WAHIAWA CIRCLE ISLAND or #55 KANEOHE CIRCLE ISLAND.

Waikele Premium Outlets: Take bus #42 from Waikiki to Wapahu Transit Center, then bus #433 to Waikele.

Car Rental: To Smoke or Not to Smoke

If you are looking for a non-smoking car, Avis and Budget became the first major rental-car companies to ban smoking in their entire North American fleets in 2009. If you light up in one of Avis or Budget's cars, you can face a clean up fee of up to $250.

Enterprise Holdings, which operates Enterprise Rent-A-Car, Alamo Rent A Car and National Car Rental did not have a smoking ban as we went to press. Instead corporate officials said they left the decision of having cars with no smoking or smoking to each of Hawaii's local rental locations.

There are three parallel main streets in **Waikiki: Kalakaua Avenue** (which is one-way going toward Diamond Head and eventually fronts Waikiki Beach), **Kuhio Avenue** (1 block mauka of Kalakaua Ave., which has two-way traffic), and **Ala Wai Boulevard** (which fronts the Ala Wai Canal and runs one-way in the Ewa direction).

AROUND OAHU From Waikiki, **Highway 72** (the **Kalanianaole Hwy.**) takes you around Makapuu Point into Kailua and Kaneohe. From Kailua and Kaneohe, **Highway 83** (the **Kamehameha Hwy.**) traverses the North Shore to Haleiwa, where it is still called the Kamehameha Highway, but the number of the highway changes to 99, and the highway then cuts through mid-Oahu past Schofield Barracks and Wahiawa, and swings out to Pearl City.

On the leeward coast, H-1 Freeway becomes two-lane **Highway 93** (the **Farrington Hwy.**); after Makaha, the number changes to Highway 930, but it is still called Farrington Highway all the way out to Kaena Point. Although you cannot drive around Kaena Point, Farrington Highway (still called Hwy. 930) picks up on the north side of the point and goes through Mokuleia and Waialua.

ACROSS OAHU Highways that cut across the island are **Highway 99** (see "Around Oahu," above), the **Likelike Highway** (also called Hwy. 63, which goes from Honolulu to Kaneohe), and the **Pali Highway** (also called Hwy. 61, which goes from Honolulu to Kailua). The **H-3 Freeway,** which starts at Pearl Harbor, is the fastest way to get to Kaneohe and Kailua.

One of the best deals anywhere, **TheBus** (ⓒ **808/848-5555,** or 808/296-1818 for recorded information; www.thebus.org) will take you around the whole island for $2. In fact, on a daily basis, more than 260,000 people use the system's 68 lines and 4,000 bus stops.

TheBus goes almost everywhere almost all the time. The most popular route is no. 8 (Waikiki/Ala Moana), which shuttles people between Waikiki and Ala Moana Center every 10 minutes or so (the ride is 15–20 min.). The no. 19 (Airport/Hickam), no. 20 (Airport/Halawa Gate), no. 47 (Waipahu), and no. 58 (Waikiki/Ala Moana) cover the same stretch. Waikiki service begins daily at 5am and runs until midnight; buses run about every 15 minutes during the day and every 30 minutes in the evening.

The Circle Island–North Shore route is no. 52 (Wahiawa/Circle Island); it departs Ala Moana Center every 30 minutes and takes about 4½ hours to circle the island. The Circle Island–South Shore route is no. 55 (Kaneohe/Circle Island); it also

> **Warning!** North Shore Safety
>
> Recently, visitors waiting for a bus along the North Shore were attacked and robbed in broad daylight. You might want to consider splurging on a rental car to visit the North Shore.

leaves Ala Moana every half-hour and takes about 3 to 4½ hours to circle the island.

You can buy a **Visitors Pass** for $20 at any ABC store in Waikiki (ABC stores are literally everywhere in Waikiki). It's good for unlimited rides anywhere on Oahu for 4 days.

BY TROLLEY It's fun to ride the 34-seat, open-air, motorized **Waikiki Trolley** (✆ **800/824-8804** or 808/593-2822; www.waikikitrolley.com), which looks like a San Francisco cable car. It loops around Waikiki and downtown Honolulu, stopping every 40 minutes at 12 key places: Hilton Hawaiian Village, Iolani Palace, Wo Fat's in Chinatown, the State Capitol, King Kamehameha's Statue, the Mission House Museum, Aloha Tower, Honolulu Academy of Arts, Hawaii Maritime Museum, Ward Centre, Fisherman's Wharf, and Restaurant Row. The driver provides commentary along the way. Stops on the new 2-hour, fully narrated Ocean Coast Line (the blue line) of the southeast side of Oahu include Sea Life Park, Diamond Head, and Waikiki Beach. A 1-day trolley pass ($27 for adults, $20 for seniors, and $13 for kids ages 4–11) allows you to jump off all day long (8:30am–

11:35pm). Four-day passes cost $48 for adults, $28 for seniors, and $20 for kids 4 to 11.

BY TAXI Oahu's major cab companies offer islandwide, 24-hour radio-dispatched service, with multilingual drivers, air-conditioned cars, limos, vans, and vehicles equipped with wheelchair lifts. Fares are standard for all taxi firms; from the airport, expect to pay about $35 to $45 (plus tip) to Waikiki, about $35 to $40 to downtown, about $70 to $85 to Kailua, about $65 to $70 to Hawaii Kai, and $95 to $110 to the North Shore.

Try **Aloha State Cab** (✆ 808/847-3566), **Charley's Taxi & Tours** (✆ 808/531-1333), **City Taxi** (✆ 808/524-2121), **Royal Taxi & Tour** (✆ 808/944-5513), **Star Taxi** (✆ 808/942-7827), or **TheCab** (✆ 808/422-2222). **Coast Taxi** (✆ 808/261-3755) serves Windward Oahu; **Hawaii Kai Hui/Koko Head Taxi** (✆ 808/396-6633) serves East Honolulu/Southeast Oahu.

A discount taxi service offers a fixed-price fare of $35 (up to four passengers) to Waikiki, with no additional charge for baggage—call **Star Taxi** (✆ **800/671-2999** or 808/942-STAR [942-7827]). You must book it in advance.

5 MONEY & COSTS

Frommer's lists exact prices in the local currency. The currency conversions quoted above were correct at press time. However, rates fluctuate, so before departing consult a currency exchange website such as **www.**

oanda.com/convert/classic to check up-to-the-minute rates.

Probably the only cities more expensive than Honolulu are New York City, London, and Tokyo. Honolulu is expensive—*very* expensive. Visitors are always shocked

The Value of US$ vs. Other Popular Currencies

US$	Can$	UK£	Euro (€)	Aus$	NZ$
1	C$1.17	£.65	€.74	A$1.32	NZ$1.69

at how much things cost. Think about it: Hawaii is among the most isolated set of islands in the world. It's some 2,500 miles to the nearest continent and nearly everything is shipped in; and if it's not shipped, then it's flown at an even greater cost.

Hotel rooms in Waikiki are second in price to New York City. If you would like to stay on Waikiki Beach, you are looking at rack rates in the $350 and up range (a deal on the Internet can put you in around $250). Hotels off the beach are still expensive; expect to pay $200-plus per day. Then factor in tax (nearly 18%) and/or (very expensive) parking of $18 to $25 a night.

It's always advisable to bring money in a variety of forms on a vacation: a mix of cash, credit cards, and traveler's checks. You should also exchange enough petty cash to cover airport incidentals, tipping, and transportation to your hotel before you leave home, or withdraw money upon arrival at an airport ATM.

ATMS

Nationwide, the easiest and best way to get cash away from home is from an ATM (automated teller machine), sometimes referred to as a "cash machine," or "cashpoint." The **Cirrus** (© **800/424-7787;** www.mastercard.com) and **PLUS** (© **800/ 843-7587;** www.visa.com) networks span the country; you can find them even in remote regions. Go to your bank card's website to find ATM locations at your destination. Be sure you know your daily withdrawal limit before you depart.

ATMs are everywhere in Hawaii—at banks, supermarkets, Longs Drugs, and Honolulu International Airport; and in some resorts and shopping centers.

Note: Many banks impose a fee every time you use a card at another bank's ATM, and that fee is often higher for international transactions (up to $5 or more) than for domestic ones (where they're rarely more than $2). In addition, the bank from which you withdraw cash may charge its own fee. To compare banks' ATM fees within the U.S., use **www. bankrate.com.** Visitors from outside the U.S. should also find out whether their bank assesses a 1% to 3% fee on charges incurred abroad.

CREDIT CARDS & DEBIT CARDS

Credit cards are the most widely used form of payment in the United States: **Visa** (Barclaycard in Britain), **MasterCard** (EuroCard in Europe, Access in Britain, Chargex in Canada), **American Express, Diners Club,** and **Discover.** They also provide a convenient record of all your expenses and offer relatively good exchange rates. You can withdraw cash advances from your credit cards at banks or ATMs, but high fees make credit card cash advances a pricey way to get cash.

It's highly recommended that you travel with at least one major credit card. You must have a credit card to rent a car, and hotels and airlines usually require a credit card imprint as a deposit against expenses.

ATM cards with major credit card backing, known as **debit cards,** are now a commonly acceptable form of payment in most stores and restaurants. Debit cards

What Things Cost in Honolulu	US$
Hamburger at Kua Aina	6.00
Movie ticket (adult)	9.00
Movie ticket (child)	5.50
Entry to Bishop Museum (adult)	16.00
Entry to Bishop Museum (child)	13.00
Entry to Hawaiian Water Adventure Park (adult)	35.00
Entry to Hawaiian Water Adventure Park (child)	25.00
Entry to Honolulu Zoo (adult)	8.00
Entry to Honolulu Zoo (child)	1.00
20-ounce soft drink at drug or convenience store	2.50
16-ounce apple juice	3.50
Cup of coffee	3.00
Taxi from Honolulu Airport to Waikiki	30.00
Bus fare (adult)	2.00
Moderate three-course dinner without alcohol	50.00
Moderately priced double-room in Waikiki	125.00–175.00

draw money directly from your checking account. Some stores enable you to receive cash back on your debit-card purchases as well. The same is true at most U.S. post offices.

TRAVELER'S CHECKS

Though credit cards and debit cards are more often used, traveler's checks are still widely accepted in the U.S. Foreign visitors should make sure that traveler's checks are denominated in U.S. dollars; foreign-currency checks are often difficult to exchange.

You can buy traveler's checks at most banks. Most are offered in denominations of $20, $50, $100, $500, and sometimes $1,000. Generally, you'll pay a service charge ranging from 1% to 4%.

The most popular traveler's checks are offered by **American Express** (© **800/807-6233,** or 800/221-7282 for card holders—this number accepts collect calls, offers service in several foreign languages, and exempts Amex gold and platinum cardholders from the fee); **Visa** (© **800/732-1322**)—AAA members can obtain Visa checks for a $9.95 fee (for checks up to $1,500) at most AAA offices or by calling © 866/339-3378—and **MasterCard** (© 800/223-9920).

Be sure to keep a copy of the traveler's checks' serial numbers separate from your checks in the event that they are stolen or lost. You'll get a refund faster if you know the numbers.

Another option is the new **prepaid traveler's check cards,** reloadable cards that work much like debit cards but aren't linked to your checking account. The **American Express Travelers Cheque Card,** for example, requires a minimum deposit ($300), sets a maximum balance ($2,750), and has a one-time issuance fee of $14.95. You can withdraw money from an ATM ($2.50 per transaction, not including bank fees), and the funds can be purchased in dollars, euros, or pounds. If you lose the card, your available funds will be refunded within 24 hours.

Why Oahu Is More Expensive

No, it's not your imagination—Oahu *is* more expensive than the other Hawaiian Islands. That's the result of the Hawaii State Legislature passing a bill allowing the City and County of Honolulu (which is the entire island of Oahu) to add an additional .5% tax on to the state general excise tax of 4%. Everything you buy on Oahu will have this tax, and so will your hotel bill. The funds from this additional tax are earmarked for mass transit for Oahu.

6 HEALTH

STAYING HEALTHY
Insects & Scorpions

Like any tropical climate, Hawaii is home to lots of bugs. Most of them won't harm you. However, watch out for mosquitoes, centipedes, and scorpions, which do sting and may cause anything from mild annoyance to severe swelling and pain.

MOSQUITOES These pesky insects are not native to Hawaii but arrived as larvae stowed away in water barrels on the ship *Wellington* in 1826, when it anchored in Lahaina. There's not a whole lot you can do about them, except to apply commercial repellent, which you can pick up at any drugstore.

CENTIPEDES These segmented bugs with a jillion legs come in two varieties: 6- to 8-inch-long brown ones and 2- to 3-inch-long blue guys. Both can really pack a wallop with their sting. Centipedes are generally found in damp, wet places, such as under wood piles or compost heaps; wearing closed-toe shoes can help prevent stings. If you're stung, apply ice at once to prevent swelling. See a doctor if you experience extreme pain, swelling, nausea, or any other severe reaction.

SCORPIONS Rarely seen, scorpions are found in arid, warm regions; their stings can be serious. Campers in dry areas should always check their boots before putting them on and shake out sleeping bags and bed rolls. Symptoms of a scorpion sting include shortness of breath, hives, swelling, and nausea. In the unlikely event that you're stung, apply diluted household ammonia and cold compresses to the area of the sting and seek medical help immediately.

Hiking Safety

In addition to taking the appropriate precautions regarding Hawaii's bug population, hikers should always let someone know where they're heading, when they're going, and when they plan to return; too many hikers get lost in Hawaii because they don't let others know their basic plans.

Before you head out, always check weather conditions with the **National Weather Service** (© **808/973-4381** on Oahu; see individual island chapters for local weather information). Hike with a pal, never alone. Wear hiking boots, a sun hat, clothes to protect you from the sun and from getting scratches, and high-SPF sunscreen on all exposed areas of skin. Take water. Stay on the trail. Watch your step. It's easy to slip off precipitous trails and into steep canyons. Many experienced hikers and boaters today pack a cellphone in case of emergency; just dial © **911**.

Vog

The volcanic haze dubbed *vog* is caused by gases released when molten lava—from the continuous eruption of Kilauea volcano on the Big Island—pours into the ocean. Some people claim that long-term exposure to the hazy, smoglike air has caused bronchial ailments, but it's highly unlikely to cause you any harm in the course of your visit.

There actually is a vog season in Hawaii: the fall and winter months, when the trade winds that blow the fumes out to sea die down. The vog is felt not only on the Big Island, but also as far away as Oahu.

One more word of caution: If you're pregnant or have heart or breathing problems, you should avoid exposure to the sulfuric fumes that are ever present in and around the Big Island's Hawaii Volcanoes National Park.

Ocean Safety

Because most people coming to Hawaii are unfamiliar with the ocean environment, they're often unaware of the natural hazards it holds. With just a few precautions, your ocean experience can be a safe and happy one. An excellent book is *All Stings Considered: First Aid and Medical Treatment of Hawaii's Marine Injuries,* by Craig Thomas and Susan Scott (University of Hawaii Press, 1997).

Note that sharks are not a big problem in Hawaii; in fact, they appear so infrequently that locals look forward to seeing them. Since records have been kept, starting in 1779, there have been only about 100 shark attacks in Hawaii, of which 40% have been fatal. Most attacks occurred after someone fell into the ocean from the shore or from a boat; in these cases, the sharks probably attacked after the person was dead. But general rules for avoiding sharks are: Don't swim at sunrise, at sunset, or where the water is murky due to stream runoff—sharks may mistake you for one of their usual meals. And don't swim where there are bloody fish in the water, as sharks become aggressive around blood.

SEASICKNESS The waters in Hawaii can range from as calm as glass (off the Kona Coast on the Big Island) to downright frightening (in storm conditions); they usually fall somewhere in between. In general, expect rougher conditions in winter than in summer. Some 90% of the population tends toward seasickness. If you've never been out on a boat, or if you've been seasick in the past, you might want to heed the following suggestions:

(Tips) Don't Get Burned: Smart Tanning Tips

Hawaii's Caucasian population has the highest incidence of malignant melanoma (deadly skin cancer) in the world. And nobody is completely safe from the sun's harmful rays: All skin types and races can burn. To ensure that your vacation won't be ruined by a painful sunburn, be sure to wear a strong sunscreen that protects against both UVA and UVB rays at all times (look for zinc oxide, benzophenone, oxybenzone, sulisobenzone, titanium dioxide, or avobenzone in the list of ingredients). Wear a wide-brimmed hat and sunglasses. Keep infants under 6 months out of the sun completely, and slather older babies and children with strong sunscreen frequently.

If you do get a burn, aloe vera, cool compresses, cold baths, and benzocaine can help with the pain. Stay out of the sun until the burn is completely gone.

- The day before you go out on the boat, avoid alcohol, caffeine, citrus and other acidic juices, and greasy, spicy, or hard-to-digest foods.
- Get a good night's sleep the night before.
- Take or use whatever seasickness prevention works best for you—medication, an acupressure wristband, gingerroot tea or capsules, or any combination. But do it *before* **you board;** once you set sail, it's generally too late.
- While you're on the boat, stay as low and as near the center of the boat as possible. Avoid the fumes (especially if it's a diesel boat); stay out in the fresh air and watch the horizon. Do not read.
- If you start to feel queasy, drink such clear fluids as water, and eat something bland, such as a soda cracker.

STINGS The most common stings in Hawaii come from jellyfish, particularly Portuguese man-of-war and box jellyfish. Because the poisons they inject are very different, you need to treat each type of sting differently.

A bluish-purple floating bubble with a long tail, the **Portuguese man-of-war** is responsible for some 6,500 stings a year on Oahu alone. These stings, although painful and a nuisance, are rarely harmful; fewer than 1 in 1,000 requires medical treatment. The best prevention is to watch for these floating bubbles as you snorkel (look for the hanging tentacles below the surface). Get out of the water if anyone near you spots these jellyfish.

Reactions to stings range from mild burning and reddening to severe welts and blisters. *All Stings Considered* recommends the following treatment: First, pick off any visible tentacles with a gloved hand, a stick, or anything handy; then rinse the sting with salt- or fresh water, and apply ice to prevent swelling and to help control pain. Avoid folk remedies, such as vinegar, baking soda, or urinating on the wound, which may actually cause further damage. Most Portuguese man-of-war stings will disappear by themselves within 15 to 20 minutes if you do nothing at all to treat them. Still, be sure to see a doctor if pain persists or a rash or other symptoms develop.

Transparent, square-shaped **box jellyfish** are nearly impossible to see in the water. Fortunately, they seem to follow a monthly cycle: 8 to 10 days after the full moon, they appear in the waters on the leeward side of each island and hang around for about 3 days. Also, they seem to sting more in the morning hours, when they're on or near the surface.

The stings can cause anything from no visible marks to hivelike welts, blisters, and pain lasting from 10 minutes to 8 hours. *All Stings Considered* recommends the following treatment: First, pour regular household vinegar on the sting; this will stop additional burning. Do not rub the area. Pick off any vinegar-soaked tentacles with a stick. For pain, apply an ice pack. Seek additional medical treatment if you experience shortness of breath, weakness, palpitations, muscle cramps, or any

---

Everything You've Always Wanted to Know About Sharks

The Hawaii State Department of Land and Natural Resources has launched a website, **www.hawaiisharks.com**, that covers the biology, history, and culture of these carnivores. It also provides safety information and data on shark bites in Hawaii.

> ### (Tips) Enjoying the Ocean & Avoiding Mishaps
>
> The Pacific Whale Foundation has a free brochure called *Enjoying Maui's Unique Ocean Environment* that introduces visitors to Hawaii's ocean, beaches, tide pools, and reefs. Although written for Maui (with maps showing Maui's beaches), it's a great general resource on how to stay safe around the ocean, with hints on how to assess weather before you jump into the water and the best ways to view marine wildlife. To get the brochure, call ✆ **808/244-8390** or visit www.pacific whale.org.

other severe symptoms. Most box jellyfish stings disappear by themselves without any treatment.

PUNCTURES Most sea-related punctures come from stepping on or brushing against the needlelike spines of sea urchins (known locally as *wana*). Be careful when you're in the water; don't put your foot down (even if you have booties or fins on) if you can't clearly see the bottom. Waves can push you into wana in a surge zone in shallow water. The spines can even puncture a wet suit.

A sea urchin puncture can result in burning, aching, swelling, and discoloration (black or purple) around the area where the spines entered your skin. The best thing to do is to pull any protruding spines out. The body will absorb the spines within 24 hours to 3 weeks, or the remainder of the spines will work themselves out. Again, contrary to popular wisdom, do not urinate or pour vinegar on the embedded spines—this will not help.

CUTS All cuts obtained in the marine environment must be taken seriously because the high level of bacteria present in the water can quickly cause the cut to become infected. The best way to prevent cuts is to wear a wet suit, gloves, and reef shoes. Never touch coral; not only can you

get cut, but you can also damage a living organism that took decades to grow.

The symptoms of a coral cut can range from a slight scratch to severe welts and blisters. *All Stings Considered* recommends gently pulling the edges of the skin open and removing any embedded coral or grains of sand with tweezers. Next, scrub the cut well with fresh water. If pressing a clean cloth against the wound doesn't stop the bleeding, or the edges of the injury are jagged or gaping, seek medical treatment.

WHAT TO DO IF YOU GET SICK AWAY FROM HOME

If you suffer from a chronic illness, consult your doctor before your departure. Pack prescription medications in your carry-on luggage, and carry them in their original containers, with pharmacy labels—otherwise, they won't make it through airport security. Visitors from outside the U.S. should carry generic names of prescription drugs. For U.S. travelers, most reliable health-care plans provide coverage if you get sick away from home. Foreign visitors may have to pay all medical costs up front and be reimbursed later. See "Medical Insurance," under "Insurance," in the appendix.

Also see Fast Facts in Chapter 10 for listings of local **doctors, dentists, hospitals,** and **emergency numbers.**

7 SAFETY

GENERAL SAFETY

Although tourist areas are generally safe, visitors should always stay alert, even in laid-back Hawaii (and especially in Waikiki). It's wise to ask the island tourist office if you're in doubt about which neighborhoods are safe. Avoid deserted areas, especially at night. Don't go into any city park at night unless there's an event that attracts crowds—for example, the Waikiki Shell concerts in Kapiolani Park. Generally speaking, you can feel safe in areas where there are many people and open establishments.

Avoid carrying valuables with you on the street, and don't display expensive cameras or electronic equipment. Hold on to your pocketbook, and place your bill-fold in an inside pocket. In theaters, restaurants, and other public places, keep your possessions in sight.

Oahu has seen a series of purse-snatching incidents, in which thieves in slow-moving cars or on foot have snatched handbags from female pedestrians. The Honolulu police department advises women to carry purses on the shoulder away from the street or, better yet, to wear the strap across the chest instead of on one shoulder. Women with clutch bags should hold them close to their chest.

Remember also that hotels are open to the public and that in a large property, security may not be able to screen everyone entering. Always lock your room door—don't assume that once inside your hotel, you're automatically safe.

DRIVING SAFETY

Recently, burglaries of tourists' rental cars in hotel parking structures and at beach parking lots have become more common. Park in well-lighted and well-traveled areas, if possible. Never leave any packages or valuables visible in the car. If someone attempts to rob you or steal your car, do not try to resist the thief or carjacker—report the incident to the police department immediately. Ask your rental agency about personal safety, and get written directions or a map with the route to your destination clearly marked.

WHAT IS ILLEGAL

Generally, Hawaii has the same laws as the mainland United States. Nudity is illegal in Hawaii. There are NO legal nude beaches (I don't care what you have read). If you are nude on a beach (or anywhere) in Hawaii, you can be arrested.

Smoking marijuana also is illegal. Yes, there are lots of "stories" claiming that marijuana is grown in Hawaii, but the drug is illegal; if you attempt to buy it or light up, you can be arrested.

8 SPECIALIZED TRAVEL RESOURCES

GAY & LESBIAN TRAVELERS

Hawaii is known for its acceptance of all groups. The number of gay- or lesbian-specific accommodations on the islands is limited, but most properties welcome gays and lesbians like any other travelers.

Out in Honolulu (www.outin honolulu.com) is a website with gay and lesbian news, blogs, features, shopping, classified and other info.

For more gay and lesbian travel resources, visit frommers.com.

TRAVELERS WITH DISABILITIES

Most disabilities shouldn't stop anyone from traveling in the U.S. Thanks to provisions in the Americans with Disabilities Act, most public places are required to comply with disability-friendly regulations. There are more options and resources out there than ever before.

Travelers with disabilities are made to feel very welcome in Hawaii. There are more than 2,000 ramped curbs in Oahu alone, hotels are usually equipped with wheelchair-accessible rooms, and tour companies provide many special services. The **Hawaii Center for Independent Living,** 414 Kauwili St., Ste. 102, Honolulu, HI 96817 (© **808/522-5400;** fax 808/586-8129), can provide information.

The only travel agency in Hawaii specializing in needs for travelers with disabilities is **Access Aloha Travel** (© **800/ 480-1143;** www.accessalohatravel.com), which can book anything, including rental vans, accommodations, tours, cruises, airfare, and anything else you can think of. For more details on wheelchair transportation and tours around the islands, see "Getting Around" in the individual island chapters.

The **America the Beautiful—National Park and Federal Recreational Lands Pass—Access Pass** (formerly the **Golden Access Passport**) gives visually impaired or permanently disabled persons (regardless of age) free lifetime entrance to federal recreation sites administered by the National Park Service, including the Fish and Wildlife Service, the Forest Service, the Bureau of Land Management, and the Bureau of Reclamation. This may include national parks, monuments, historic sites, recreation areas, and national wildlife refuges.

The America the Beautiful Access Pass can be obtained only in person at any NPS facility that charges an entrance fee. You need to show proof of medically determined disability. Besides free entry, the pass offers a 50% discount on some federal-use fees charged for such facilities as camping, swimming, parking, boat launching, and tours. For more information, go to www.nps.gov/fees_passes.htm or call the United States Geological Survey (USGS), which issues the passes, at © **888/ 275-8747.**

For more on organizations that offer resources to disabled travelers, go to frommers.com.

FAMILY TRAVEL

Hawaii is paradise for children: beaches to run on, water to splash in, and unusual sights to see. To locate accommodations, restaurants, and attractions that are particularly child-friendly, refer to the "Kids" icon throughout this guide, and take a look at the "Family Friendly Hotels" box on p. 90. Be sure to check out the "Especially for Kids" boxes in each island chapter for suggested family activities. And look for *Frommer's Hawaii with Kids* (Wiley Publishing, Inc.).

The larger hotels and resorts offer supervised programs for children and can refer you to qualified babysitters. By state law, hotels can accept only children ages 5 to 12 in supervised activities programs, but they often accommodate younger kids by simply hiring babysitters to watch over them. You can also contact **People Attentive to Children (PATCH),** which can refer you to babysitters who have taken a training course on child care. On Oahu, call © **808/839-1988;** or visit www. patchhawaii.org.

Baby's Away (www.babysaway.com) rents cribs, strollers, highchairs, playpens, infant seats, and the like on Oahu (© **800/496-6386** or 808/222-6041). The staff will deliver whatever you need to wherever you're staying and pick it up when you're done.

Recommended family-travel websites include **Family Travel Forum** (www.familytravelforum.com), a comprehensive site that offers customized trip planning; **Family Travel Network** (www.familytravelnetwork.com), an online magazine providing travel tips; and **TravelWithYour Kids.com** (www.travelwithyourkids.com), a comprehensive site written by parents for parents offering sound advice for long-distance and international travel with children. For a list of more family-friendly travel resources, turn to the experts at frommers.com.

SENIOR TRAVEL

Discounts for seniors are available at almost all of Hawaii's major attractions and occasionally at hotels and restaurants. The Outrigger hotel chain, for instance, offers travelers ages 50 and older a 20% discount off regular published rates—and an additional 5% off for members of AARP. Always ask when making hotel reservations or buying tickets. And always carry identification with proof of your age—it can really pay off.

The U.S. National Park Service offers an **America the Beautiful—National Park and Federal Recreational Lands Pass—Senior Pass** (formerly the **Golden Age Passport**), which gives seniors 62 years or older lifetime entrance to all properties administered by the National Park Service—national parks, monuments, historic sites, recreation areas, and national wildlife refuges—for a one-time processing fee of $10. The pass must be purchased in person at any NPS facility that charges an entrance fee. Besides free entry, the America the Beautiful Senior Pass offers a 50% discount on some federal-use fees charged for such facilities as camping, swimming, parking, boat launching, and tours. For more information, go to www.nps.gov/fees_passes.htm or call the United States Geological Survey (USGS), which issues the passes, at ⓒ **888/275-8747.**

Frommers.com offers more information and resources on travel for seniors.

9 SUSTAINABLE TOURISM

If there is one place on the planet that seems ideally suited for ecotourism and sustainable travel, it's Hawaii, a place people visit because of the ecology—the ocean, the beach, the mountains, and overall beauty of the place. It seems only natural that the maintenance of its environment would be a concern, both to the people who live there and the visitors who come to enjoy all its ecosystem has to offer.

In fact, Hawaii has a long history of environmental stewardship. The ancient Hawaiians not only knew about sustainability, but also practiced it in their daily lives. They had to! When the ancient Hawaiians occupied the islands, they did not have the luxury of "importing" goods from anywhere else. They had to subsist from the land under their feet and the ocean, and those resources had to last not only for their own lifetime, but also for the lifetimes of generations to come. So these ancient people lived in harmony with the land and sea, and had a complex social structure that managed resources and forbid the taking of various resources during certain times of the year, to allow those resources to replenish themselves.

Now fast-forward to the 21st century. Today we, the current stewards of the islands of Hawaii, are just beginning to appreciate how wise and advanced the ancient Hawaiians were. In some ways, the state of Hawaii is a pioneer when it comes to the various ways it protects and saves its natural resources (for example, Hawaii is second only to California in the number of marine reserves in the National System of Marine Protected Areas). And yet in other ways, modern Hawaii still falls short of the ancient Hawaiians, whose unique system sustained, without imports, the entire population.

ONGOING ENVIRONMENTAL INITIATIVES

The State of Hawaii has several excellent programs to preserve the ocean environment and its resources, such as Marine Life Conservation Districts (an ocean version of parks; Kealakekua, on the Big Island of Hawaii, and Hanauma Bay, on Oahu, are two examples), Fishery Management Areas (where what you can take from the ocean is restricted), Fishery Replenishment Areas, and Estuarine Reserves. On land, there are corresponding programs to protect the environment from the Soil and Water Conservation District to Watershed Reserves.

In the visitor industry, the majority of hotels have adopted green practices, not only to save the environment, but also to save them money. Nearly every hotel in the state will have a card in your room asking you to really consider if you need a new towel or if you can hang it up and use it one more day. Various statewide organization have numerous programs recognizing hotels which are helping the environment, such as the Green Business Awards Program, which recently awarded the Maui Price Hotel its top award for the steps the hotel took to modify equipment and work practices to reduce energy by more than 10%, reduce water consumption by some 10 million gallons, and to increase recycling to 560 tons of their total 880 tons of annual waste.

Every island has recycling centers (varying from collection of recyclable bottles only to places that take everything). For a list of recycling centers close to where you will be staying, visit the website of the **Hawaii State Department of Health** (www.hi5deposit.com/redcenters.html).

Restaurants across the state are using more local products and produce than ever. Many proudly tell you that all of their products were grown, grazed, or caught within 100 miles of their restaurant. You can support this effort by ordering local (drink Kona coffee, not a coffee from Central America; eat local fish, not imported seafood), and by asking the restaurant which items on its menu are grown or raised on the island, then ordering the local items.

Below are some helpful hints travelers to Hawaii might want to keep in mind during their adventure to the islands, so that their ecological footprint on Hawaii will be minimal.

What Visitors Can Do in & Around the Ocean

1. Do not touch anything in the ocean. In fact, unless you are standing on the sandy bottom where the waves roll into shore, try not to walk or stand on the ocean floor. The no-touch rule of thumb is not only for your protection—there are plenty of stinging, stabbing things out there that could turn your vacation into a nightmare—but also for the protection of the marine environment. Coral is composed of living things, which take years to grow, and a careless brush of your hand or foot could destroy them. Fragile habitats for marine critters can be damaged forever by your heavy foot.

2. Do not feed the fish, or any other marine creatures. They have their own food and diet, and they can be irreparably harmed by your good intentions if you feed them "people food" or, even worse, some "fish food" you have purchased.

(Tips) **Volunteering on Vacation**

If you are looking for a different type of experience during your next vacation to Hawaii, you might want to consider becoming a volunteer and leaving the islands a little nicer than when you arrived. People interested in volunteering at beach and ocean cleanups can contact the **University of Hawaii Sea Grant College Program** (℃ **808/397-2651,** ext. 256) or **Hawaii Wildlife Fund** (℃ **808/756-1808**). For ecovolunteering on land, contact **Malama Hawaii,** (www.malamahawaii.org/get_involved/volunteer.php), a statewide organization dedicated to *malama* (taking care) of the culture and environment of Hawaii. At this site you will find a range of opportunities on various islands, such as weeding gardens and potting plants in botanical gardens, restoring taro patches, cleaning up mountain streams, bird-watching, and even hanging out at Waikiki Beach helping with a reef project.

3. Leave the ocean and beach area clearer than you found it. If you see trash in the ocean (plastic bags, bottles, and so on) remove it. You may have saved the life of a fish, turtle, marine mammal, or even a seabird by removing that trash, which kills hundreds of marine inhabitants every year. The same thing is true of the beach: Pick up trash, even if it's not yours.

4. The beach is not an ashtray. Do not use the sand for your cigarette butts. How would you like someone using your living room carpet as his ashtray?

5. Look at, but don't approach, turtles or Hawaiian monk seals resting on the shoreline. The good news is that the number of turtles and Hawaiian monk seals on the main Hawaiian Islands is increasing. But while visitors may not know it, both are protected by law. You must stay 100 feet away from them. So take photos, but do not attempt to get close to the resting sea creatures (and no, they are not dead or injured, just resting).

6. If you plan to go fishing, practice catch and release. Let the fish live another day. Ask your charter boat

captain if they practice catch and release; if they say no, book with someone else.

7. If you are environmentally conscious, we do not recommend that you rent jet skis or wave runners, which have significant environmental impact.

What Visitors Can Do on Land

1. Don't litter (this includes throwing a cigarette butt out of your car).

2. Before you go hiking, in addition to the safety tips outlined on p. 38, scrub your hiking shoes (especially the soles) to get rid of seeds and soil.

3. When hiking, carry a garbage bag so you can carry out everything you carried in, including your litter (and if you see other garbage on the trail, carry it out, too).

4. Stay on the trail. Wandering off a trail is not only dangerous to you (you can get lost, fall off overgrown cliffs, or get injured by stepping into a hidden hole), but you could possibly carry invasive species into our native forests.

5. Do not pick flowers or plants along your hike. Just leave the environment the way you found it.

Transportation Concerns

RENTAL CARS Most visitors coming to Hawaii seem to think "convertible" when they think of renting a car, or they think "SUV" for off-road adventures. If you're thinking "hybrid," you'll have to check your budget, because hybrids from car-rental agencies are not only hard to find, but extremely expensive in Hawaii. Car-rental agencies do have a variety of cars to rent, though, and you can make a point of selecting a car that gets the best gas mileage. Also, ask for a white car, as they use less energy to air-condition than a dark-colored car.

INTERISLAND TRANSPORTATION Now that the interisland ferry, Superferry, has declared bankruptcy, the only option for interisland travel between most islands is via air. There are two exceptions, however. If you're traveling between Maui and Lanai, you may want to consider taking the passenger-only Lanai Ferry. If you're traveling between Maui and Molokai, you can take the passenger-only Molokai Princess. Not only are these ferries cheaper than air travel, but their impact on the environment is less, especially when you consider that most airlines will route you from Maui to Honolulu, then from Honolulu on to either Molokai or Lanai.

HAWAIIAN CULTURE

One of Hawaii's most cherished resources is the Hawaiian culture. After years of being ignored, the Hawaiian culture is flourishing more than ever today. Part of the Hawaii school system are the Hawaiian emersion schools, where all children (not just Hawaiians) can attend schools from kindergarten through college taught in the Hawaiian language. And cultural events in Hawaii are very popular.

If you want to support Hawaiian culture, plan to attend such cultural events as Hawaiian music and dance performances (see the Calendar of Events, p. 21).

Search out locally owned establishments (look for our recommendations in this book). Attempt to buy souvenirs made in Hawaii by local residents (we have recommendations in the shopping sections of each island chapter).

If you visit a cultural site, like an ancient *heiau* (temple), the protocol calls for reverence. Be as respectful as you would at a cathedral or church. Never climb or sit on rock walls at a *heiau*. Never take anything from a *heiau*, even rocks, and never pick flowers there. You may see offerings of flowers or fruit—do not disturb them.

Questions to Ponder

One of the toughest questions in Hawaii is "what is the carrying capacity of the islands?" How much can be built before Hawaii becomes overbuilt, or unable to support the increased infrastructure and increased population? How many people can Hawaii hold, and how many visitors, before the beaches are too crowded, the lifestyle is gone, and the islands have more concrete than open green spaces?

Along those same lines, the people of Hawaii are constantly debating cultural issues vs. social issues. For example, currently laws regarding ancient burial sites can stop, reroute, or delay construction projects ranging from building roads to shopping centers. How much do we protect and preserve vs. how much do we allow new infrastructure or buildings to be built to meet modern wants and needs?

General Resources for Green Travel

The following websites provide valuable wide-ranging information on sustainable travel. For a list of even more sustainable resources, as well as tips and explanations on how to travel greener, visit www.frommers.com/planning.

- **Responsible Travel** (www.responsibletravel.com) is a great source of sustainable travel ideas; the site is run by a spokesperson for ethical tourism in the travel industry. **Sustainable Travel International** (www.sustainable travelinternational.org) promotes ethical tourism practices, and manages an extensive directory of sustainable properties and tour operators around the world.
- In the U.K., **Tourism Concern** (www.tourismconcern.org.uk) works to reduce social and environmental problems connected to tourism. The **Association of Independent Tour Operators (AITO)** (www.aito.co.uk) is a group of specialist operators leading the field in making holidays sustainable.
- In Canada, **www.greenlivingonline.com** offers extensive content on how to travel sustainably, including a travel and transport section and profiles of the best green shops and services in Toronto, Vancouver, and Calgary.
- In Australia, the national body that sets guidelines and standards for eco-tourism is **Ecotourism Australia** (www.ecotourism.org.au). **The Green Directory** (www.thegreendirectory.com.au), **Green Pages** (www.thegreen pages.com.au), and **Eco Directory** (www.ecodirectory.com.au) offer sustainable travel tips and directories of green businesses.
- **Carbonfund** (www.carbonfund.org), **TerraPass** (www.terrapass.org), and **Carbon Neutral** (www.carbonneutral.org) provide info on "carbon off-setting," or off-setting the greenhouse gas emitted during flights.
- **Greenhotels** (www.greenhotels.com) recommends green-rated member hotels around the world that fulfill the company's stringent environmental requirements. **Environmentally Friendly Hotels** (www.environmentally friendlyhotels.com) offers more green accommodation ratings. The **Hotel Association of Canada** (www.hacgreenhotels.com) has a Green Key Eco-Rating Program, which audits the environmental performance of Canadian hotels, motels, and resorts.
- **Sustain Lane** (www.sustainlane.com) lists sustainable eating and drinking choices around the U.S.; also visit **www.eatwellguide.org** for tips on eating sustainably in the U.S. and Canada.
- For information on animal-friendly issues throughout the world, visit **Tread Lightly** (www.treadlightly.org). For information about the ethics of swimming with dolphins, visit the **Whale and Dolphin Conservation Society** (www.wdcs.org).
- **Volunteer International** (www.volunteerinternational.org) has a list of questions to help you determine the intentions and the nature of a volunteer program. For general info on volunteer travel, visit **www.volunteer abroad.org** and **www.idealist.org**.

How to Fit in Like a Local

Most visitors to Hawaii want to fit in and be respectful of the local residents. The best way to do that is to be friendly and practice the same common courtesy that you do in your own neighborhood. If you smile and are polite to local residents, chances are they will smile back at you. There are a few things you might want to think about:

1. Be super polite when driving. People in Hawaii do not use their car horn as a comment on other people's driving. Most Hawaii residents use their car horn only as a greeting to a friend.
2. Another driving comment—you may be on vacation, but not everyone here is, so check your rearview mirror. If you are impeding traffic by driving slow, pull off the road. If you want to watch the sunset, pull off the road. If you have a long line of cars behind you, pull off the road.
3. Dress respectfully. Just because it's Hawaii and warm does not mean that it is acceptable to wear your swimwear into a restaurant. A good rule of thumb is to ask yourself: Would I wear this outfit to a restaurant or retail store at home?
4. Remember Hawaii is part of the United States, and is, in fact, a state. A good way to alienate local residents is to say something like "I'm from the States . . . ." Or "Back in the States, we do it this way."

10 PACKAGES FOR THE INDEPENDENT TRAVELER

Package tours are simply a way to buy the airfare, accommodations, and other elements of your trip (such as car rentals, airport transfers, and sometimes even activities) at the same time and often at discounted prices. Before you invest in a package deal, be sure to ask about the cancellation policy and any hidden expenses.

One good source of package deals is the airlines themselves. Most major airlines offer air/land packages, including **American Airlines Vacations** (© 800/321-2121; www.aavacations.com), **Continental Airlines Vacations** (© 800/301-3800; www.covacations.com), **Delta Vacations** (© 800/654-6559; www.deltavacations. com), and **United Vacations** (© 888/854-3899; www.unitedvacations.com). Several big online travel agencies—Expedia, Travelocity, Orbitz, Site59, and Lastminute. com—also do a brisk business in packages.

Some packagers specialize in Hawaiian vacations. **Pleasant Holidays** (© 800/2-HAWAII [242-9244] or 800/242-9244; www.pleasantholidays.com) is by far the biggest and most comprehensive packager to Hawaii; it offers an extensive, high-quality collection of 50 condos and hotels in every price range. **Travelzoo** (www.travelzoo.com) often has package deals to Hawaii as well.

Hawaii's top hotel chains offer package deals and special rates as well. Packages may be available for families, seniors, honeymooners, and golfers, and some offer discounts on rental cars or multinight stays. Check with **Ohana Hotels & Resorts** (© 800/462-6262; www.ohana hotels.com); its more upscale sibling, **Outrigger Hotels & Resorts** (© 800/OUTRIGGER** [688-744437]; www. outrigger.com); and **Castle Resorts & Hotels** (© 800/367-5004; www.castle resorts.com).

Travel packages are also listed in the travel section of your local Sunday newspaper. Or check ads in national travel magazines such as *Arthur Frommer's Budget Travel, Travel + Leisure, National Geographic Traveler,* and *Condé Nast Traveler.*

For more information on package tours and for tips on booking your trip, see Frommers.com.

Tips for Digital Travel Photography

- **Take along a spare camera—or two.** Even if you've been anointed the "official" photographer of your travel group, encourage others in your party to carry their own cameras and provide fresh perspectives—and backup. Your photographic "second unit" may include you in a few shots so you're not the invisible person of the trip.

- **Stock up on digital film cards.** At home, it's easy to copy pictures from your memory cards to your computer as they fill up. During your travels, cards seem to fill up more quickly. Take along enough digital film for your entire trip or, at a minimum, enough for at least a few days of shooting. At intervals, you can copy images to CDs. Many camera stores and souvenir shops offer this service, and a growing number of mass merchandisers have walk-up kiosks you can use to make prints or create CDs while you travel.

- **Share and share alike.** No need to wait until you get home to share your photos. You can upload a gallery's worth to an online photo-sharing service. Just find an Internet cafe where the computers have card readers, or connect your camera to the computer with a cable. You can find online photo-sharing services that cost little or nothing at **www.clickherefree.com**. You can also use America Online's Your Pictures service, or commercial enterprises that give you free or low-cost photo sharing: Kodak's EasyShare gallery (**www.kodak.com**), Flickr (**www.flickr.com**), Snapfish (**www.snap fish.com**), or Shutterfly (**www.shutterfly.com**).

- **Add voice annotations to your photos.** Many digital cameras allow you to add voice annotations to your shots after they're taken. These serve as excellent reminders and documentation. One castle or cathedral may look like another after a long tour; your voice notes will help you distinguish them.

- **Experiment!** Travel is a great time to try out new techniques. Take photos at night, resting your camera on a handy wall or other support as your self-timer trips the shutter for a long exposure. Try close-ups of flowers, crafts, wildlife, or maybe the exotic cuisine you're about to consume. Discover action photography—shoot the countryside from trains, buses, or cars. With a digital camera, you can experiment and then erase your mistakes.

—*From* Travel Photography Digital Field Guide, 1st edition
(Wiley Publishing, Inc.)

If all you want is a fabulous beach and a perfectly mixed mai tai, then Hawaii has what you're looking for. But the islands' wealth of natural wonders is equally hard to resist; the year-round tropical climate and spectacular scenery tend to inspire almost everyone to get outside and explore.

If you don't have your own snorkel gear or other watersports equipment, or if you just don't feel like packing it, don't fret: Everything you'll need is available for rent in the islands. We discuss all kinds of places to rent or buy gear in the chapters that follow.

SETTING OUT ON YOUR OWN VS. USING AN OUTFITTER

There are two ways to go: Plan all the details before you leave and either rent gear or schlep your stuff 2,500 miles across the Pacific, or go with an outfitter or a guide and let someone else worry about the details.

In Hawaii, it's often preferable to go with a local guide who is familiar with the conditions at both sea level and summit peaks, knows the land and its flora and fauna in detail, and has all the gear you'll need. It's also good to go with a guide if time is an issue or if you have specialized interests. If you really want to see native birds, for instance, an experienced guide will take you directly to the best areas for sightings. And many forests and valleys in the interior of the islands are either on private property or in wilderness preserves accessible only on guided tours. The downside? If you go with a guide, plan on spending at least $100 a day per person. I've recommended the best local outfitters and tour-guide operators in chapter 7.

But if you have the time, already own the gear, and love doing the research and planning, try exploring on your own. Each island chapter discusses the best spots to set out on your own, from the top offshore snorkel and dive spots to great daylong hikes, as well as the federal, state, and county agencies that can help you with hikes on public property; I also list references for spotting birds, plants, and sea life. I recommend that you always use the resources available to inquire about weather, trail, or surf conditions; water availability; and other conditions before you take off on your adventure.

For hikers, a great alternative to hiring a private guide is taking a guided hike offered by the **Nature Conservancy of Hawaii,** P.O. Box 96, Honolulu, HI 96759 (© 808/621-2008); or the **Hawaii Chapter of the Sierra Club,** P.O. Box 2577, Honolulu, HI 96813 (© **808/579-9802;** www.hi.sierraclub.org). Both organizations offer guided hikes in preserves and special areas during the year, as well as day- to weeklong work trips to restore habitats and trails and to root out invasive plants. It might not sound like a dream vacation to everyone, but it's a chance to see the "real" Hawaii—including wilderness areas that are ordinarily off-limits.

All Nature Conservancy hikes and work trips are free (donations are appreciated). However, you must reserve a spot for yourself, and a deposit is required for guided hikes to ensure that you'll show up; your deposit is refunded once you do. The hikes are generally twice a month on Oahu.

The Sierra Club offers weekly hikes on Oahu. They are led by certified Sierra Club volunteers and are classified as easy, moderate, or strenuous. These half- or all-day affairs cost $1 for Sierra Club members and $3 for nonmembers (bring exact change). For a copy of the club newsletter, which lists all outings and trail-repair work, send $2 to the address above.

Local ecotourism opportunities are also discussed in the individual island chapters. For more information, contact the **Hawaii Ecotourism Association** (℃ **877/300-7058;** www.hawaiiecotourism.org).Using Activities Desks to Book Your Island Fun If you're unsure of which activity or which outfitter or guide is the right one for you and your family, you might want to consider booking through a discount activities center or activities desk. Not only will they save you money, but good activities centers should also be able to help you find, say, the snorkel cruise that's right for you, or the luau that's most suitable for both you *and* the kids.

Remember, however, that it's in the activities agent's best interest to sign you up with outfitters from which they earn the most commission. Some agents have no qualms about booking you into any activity if it means an extra buck for them. If an agent tries to push a particular outfitter or activity too hard, be skeptical. Conversely, they'll try to steer you away from outfitters who don't offer big commissions. For example, Trilogy, the company that offers Maui's most popular snorkel cruises to Lanai (and the only one with rights to land at Lanai's Hulopoe Beach), offers only minimum commissions to agents and does not allow agents to offer any discounts at all. As a result, most activities desks will automatically try to steer you away from Trilogy.

Another word of warning: Stay away from activities centers that offer discounts as fronts for timeshare sales presentations. Using a free or discounted snorkel cruise or luau tickets as bait, they'll suck you into a 90-minute presentation—and try to get you to buy into a Hawaii timeshare in the process. Because their business is timeshares, not activities, they won't be as interested, or as knowledgeable, about which activities might be right for you.

Finally, you can reserve activities yourself and save the commission by booking via the Internet. Most outfitters offer 10% to 25% off their prices if you book online.

OUTDOOR ACTIVITIES A TO Z

Here's a brief rundown of the many outdoor activities available in Hawaii. For our recommendations on the best places to go, the best shops for renting equipment, and the best outfitters to use, see the individual island chapters later in this book.

BIRDING Many of Hawaii's tropical birds are found nowhere else on earth. There are curved-bill honeycreepers, black-winged red birds, and the rare o'o, whose yellow feathers Hawaiians once plucked to make royal capes. When you go birding, take along *A Field Guide to the Birds of Hawaii and the Tropical Pacific,* by H. Douglas Pratt, Phillip L. Bruner, and Delwyn G. Berett (Princeton University Press, 1987).

BOATING Almost every type of nautical experience is available in the islands, from old-fashioned Polynesian outrigger canoes to America's Cup racing sloops to submarines. You'll find details on all these seafaring experiences in the individual island chapters that follow.

No matter which type of vessel you choose, be sure to see the Hawaiian Islands from offshore if you can afford it. It's easy to combine multiple activities into one cruise: Lots of snorkel boats double as sightseeing cruises and, in winter, whale-watching cruises. The main harbor for visitor activities is Kewalo Basin, in Honolulu.

BODY BOARDING (BOOGIE BOARDING) & BODYSURFING Bodysurfing—riding the waves without a board, becoming one with the rolling water—is a way of life in Hawaii. Some bodysurfers just rely on hands to ride the waves; others use hand boards (flat, paddlelike gloves).

> **Tips** **Travel Tip**
>
> When planning sunset activities, be aware that Hawaii, like other places close to the equator, has a very short (5–10 min.) twilight period after the sun sets. After that, it's dark. If you hike out to watch the sunset, be sure you can make it back quickly, or else take a flashlight.

For additional maneuverability, try a boogie board or body board (also known as belly boards or *paipo* boards). These 3-foot-long boards support the upper part of your body and are very maneuverable in the water. Both bodysurfing and bodyboarding require a pair of open-heeled swim fins to help propel you through the water. The equipment is inexpensive and easy to carry, and both sports can be practiced in the small, gentle waves. See the individual island chapters for details on where to rent boards and where to go.

CAMPING Hawaii's year-round balmy climate makes camping a breeze. However, tropical campers should always be ready for rain, especially in Hawaii's wet winter season, but even in the dry summer season as well. And remember to bring a good mosquito repellent. If you're heading to the top of Hawaii's volcanoes, you'll need a down mummy bag. If you plan to camp on the beach, bring a mosquito net and a rain poncho. Always be prepared to deal with contaminated water (purify it by boiling, filtering, or by using iodine tablets) and the tropical sun (protect yourself with sunscreen, a hat, and a long-sleeved shirt). Also be sure to check out the "Health" section, earlier in this chapter, for hiking and camping tips.

There are many established campgrounds at beach parks, including Malaekahana Beach. For more details on getting regulations and camping information for any of Hawaii's national or state parks, see chapter 4.

Hawaiian Trail and Mountain Club, P.O. Box 2238, Honolulu, HI 96804,

offers an information packet on hiking and camping throughout the islands. Send $2 and a legal-size, self-addressed, stamped envelope for information. Another good source is the *Hiking/Camping Information Packet,* available from **Hawaii Geographic Maps and Books,** 49 S. Hotel St., Honolulu, HI 96813 (② **800/538-3950** or 808/538-3952), for $7. The **University of Hawaii Press,** 2840 Kolowalu St., Honolulu, HI 96822 (② **888/847-7737;** www.uhpress.hawaii.edu), has an excellent selection of hiking, backpacking, and bird-watching guides, especially *The Hiker's Guide to the Hawaiian Islands,* by Stuart M. Ball, Jr.

GOLF Nowhere else on earth can you tee off to whale spouts, putt under rainbows, and play around a live volcano. Hawaii has some of the world's top-rated golf courses. But be forewarned: Each course features hellish natural hazards, such as razor-sharp lava, gusty trade winds, an occasional wild pig, and the tropical heat. And greens fees tend to be very expensive. Still, golfers flock here from around the world and love every minute of it. See the individual island chapters for coverage of the resort courses worth splurging on (with details, where applicable, on money-saving twilight rates), as well as the best budget and municipal courses. Also check out "The Best Golf Courses," in chapter 1.

A few tips on golfing in Hawaii: There's generally wind—10 to 30 mph is not unusual between 10am and 2pm—so you may have to play two to three clubs up or down to compensate. Bring extra balls:

The rough is thick, water hazards are everywhere, and the wind wreaks havoc with your game. On the greens, your putt will *always* break toward the ocean. Hit deeper and more aggressively in the sand because the type of sand used on most Hawaii courses is firmer and more compact than on mainland courses (lighter sand would blow away in the constant wind). And bring a camera—you'll kick yourself if you don't capture those spectacular views.

HIKING Hiking in Hawaii is a breathtaking experience. The islands have hundreds of miles of trails, many of which reward you with a hidden beach, a private waterfall, an Eden-like valley, or simply an unforgettable view. However, rock climbers are out of luck: Most of Hawaii's volcanic cliffs are too steep and brittle to scale.

Hawaiian Trail and Mountain Club, P.O. Box 2238, Honolulu, HI 96804, offers an information packet on hiking and camping in Hawaii; to receive a copy, send $2 and a legal-size, self-addressed, stamped envelope. **Hawaii Geographic Maps and Books,** 49 S. Hotel St., Honolulu, HI 96813 (© **800/538-3950** or 808/538-3952), offers the *Hiking/Camping Information Packet* for $7. Also note that the **Hawaii State Department of Land and Natural Resources,** 1151 Punchbowl St., No. 131, Honolulu, HI 96809 (© **808/587-0300;** www.hawaii. gov), will send you free topographic trail maps.

The **Nature Conservancy of Hawaii** (© **808/537-4508;** www.tnc.org/hawaii) and the **Hawaii Chapter of the Sierra Club,** P.O. Box 2577, Honolulu, HI 96803 (© **808/579-9802;** www.hi.sierra club.org), both offer guided hikes in preserves and special areas during the year. Also see the individual island chapters for complete details on the best hikes for all ability levels.

A couple of terrific books on hiking are *The Hiker's Guide to the Hawaiian Islands* and *The Hiker's Guide to Oahu,* both by Stuart M. Ball, Jr. (both from University of Hawaii Press).

Before you set out on the trail, see "Health," earlier in this chapter, for tips on hiking safety.

HORSEBACK RIDING One of the best ways to see Hawaii is on horseback; riding opportunities are offered for just about every age and level of experience. Be sure to bring a pair of jeans and closed-toe shoes to wear on your ride.

KAYAKING Hawaii is one of the world's most popular destinations for ocean kayaking. Beginners can paddle across a tropical lagoon to two uninhabited islets off Lanikai Beach on Oahu, while more experienced kayakers can take on open ocean. See "Watersports," in chapter 6 for local outfitters and tour guides.

SCUBA DIVING Some people come to the islands solely to take the plunge into the tropical Pacific and explore the underwater world. Hawaii is one of the world's top 10 dive destinations, according to *Rodale's Scuba Diving Magazine.* Here you can see the great variety of tropical marine life (more than 100 endemic species found nowhere else on the planet), explore sea caves, and swim with sea turtles and monk seals in clear, tropical water. If you're not certified, try to take classes before you come to Hawaii so you don't waste time learning and can dive right in.

If you dive, **go early in the morning.** Trade winds often rough up the seas in the afternoon, so most operators schedule early-morning dives that end at noon. To organize a dive on your own, order *The Oahu Snorkelers and Shore Divers Guide,* by Francisco B. de Carvalho, from University of Hawaii Press.

Tip: It's usually worth the extra bucks to go with a good dive operator. Check "Scuba Diving" in the island chapters that follow; I've listed the operators that'll give you the most for your money.

SNORKELING Snorkeling is one of Hawaii's main attractions, and almost anyone can do it. All you need is a mask, a snorkel, fins, and some basic swimming skills. In many places, all you have to do is wade into the water and look down at the magical underwater world.

If you've never snorkeled before, most resorts and excursion boats offer snorkeling equipment and lessons. You don't really need lessons, however; it's plenty easy to figure out for yourself, especially once you're at the beach, where everybody around you will be doing it. If you don't have your own gear, you can rent it from one of dozens of dive shops and activities booths, discussed in the individual island chapters.

While everyone heads for Oahu's Hanauma Bay—the perfect spot for first-timers—other favorite snorkel spots abound all over the island. See "Watersports" in chapter 6.

Some snorkeling tips: Always snorkel with a buddy. Look up every once in a while to see where you are and if there's any boat traffic. Don't touch anything; not only can you damage coral, but camouflaged fish and shells with poisonous spines may also surprise you. Always check with a dive shop, lifeguards, or others on the beach about the area in which you plan to snorkel and ask if there are any dangerous conditions you should know about.

SPORTFISHING You can also try for spearfish, swordfish, various tuna, mahimahi (dorado), rainbow runners, wahoo, barracuda, trevallies, bonefish, and such bottom fish as snappers and groupers, and the biggest catch of them all—marlin. Visiting anglers currently need no license.

Charter fishing boats range widely both in size—from small 24-foot open skiffs to luxurious 50-foot-plus yachts—and in price—from about $100 per person to "share" a boat with other anglers for a half-

day, to $900 a day to book an entire luxury sportfishing yacht on an exclusive basis. Shop around. Prices vary according to the boat, the crowd, and the captain. See the individual island chapters for details. Also, many boat captains tag and release marlin or keep the fish for themselves (sorry, that's Hawaii style). If you want to eat your mahimahi for dinner or have your marlin mounted, tell the captain before you go.

Money-saving tip: Try contacting the charter-boat captain directly and bargaining. Many charter captains pay a 20% to 30% commission to charter-booking agencies and may be willing to give you a discount if you book directly.

SURFING The ancient Hawaiian practice of *hee nalu* (wave sliding) is probably the sport most people picture when they think of Hawaii. Believe it or not, you, too, can do some wave sliding—just sign up at any one of the numerous surfing schools (listed in chapter 6 under "Surfing," in the Watersports section). On world-famous Waikiki Beach, just head over to one of the surf stands that line the sand; these guys say they can get anybody up and standing on a board. If you're already a big kahuna in surfing, check the island chapters for the best deals on rental equipment and the best places to hang ten.

TENNIS Tennis is a popular sport in the islands. Chapter 6 lists details on free municipal courts as well as the best deals on private courts. The etiquette at the free county courts is to play only 45 minutes if someone is waiting.

WHALE-WATCHING Every winter, pods of Pacific humpback whales make the 3,000-mile swim from the chilly waters of Alaska to bask in Hawaii's summery shallows, fluking, spy hopping, spouting, breaching, and having an all-around swell time. About 1,500 to 3,000 humpback whales appear in Hawaiian waters each year.

Not So Close! They Hardly Know You

In the excitement of seeing a whale or a school of dolphins, don't forget that they're protected under the Marine Mammals Protection Act. You must stay at least 300 feet (the length of a football field) away from all whales, dolphins, and other marine mammals. This applies to swimmers, kayakers, and windsurfers. And, yes, visitors have been prosecuted for swimming with dolphins! If you have any questions, call the **National Marine Fisheries Service** (✆ 808/541-2727) or the **Hawaiian Islands Humpback Whale National Marine Sanctuary** (✆ 800/831-4888).

Humpbacks are one of the world's oldest, most impressive inhabitants. Adults grow to be about 45 feet long and weigh a hefty 40 tons. Humpbacks are officially an endangered species; in 1992, the waters around Maui, Molokai, and Lanai were designated a Humpback Whale National Marine Sanctuary. Despite the world's newfound ecological awareness, humpbacks and their habitats and food resources are still under threat from whalers and pollution.

The season's first whale is usually spotted in November, but the best time to see humpback whales in Hawaii is **between January and April.** Just look out to sea. You'll also find a variety of whale-watching cruises, which will bring you up close and personal with the mammoth mammals; see p. 170 for more details.

Money-saving tip: Book a snorkeling cruise during the winter whale-watching months. The captain of the boat will often take you through the best local whale-watching areas on the way, and you'll get two activities for the price of one. It's well worth the money.

WINDSURFING Hawaii is a top windsurfing destination. World-class windsurfers head to the wind and the waves off shore.

Others, especially beginners, set their sails for Oahu's Kailua Bay, where gentle onshore breezes make learning this sport a snap.

See chapter 6 for outfitters and local instructors.

12 STAYING CONNECTED

TELEPHONES

Generally, hotel surcharges on long-distance and local calls are astronomical, so you're better off using your **cellphone** or a **public pay telephone.** Many convenience groceries and packaging services sell **prepaid calling cards** in denominations up to $50; for international visitors these can be the least expensive way to call home. **Local calls** made from pay phones are 50¢.

Most long-distance and international calls can be dialed directly from any phone.

For calls within the United States and to Canada, dial 1 followed by the area code and the seven-digit number. **For other international calls,** dial 011 followed by the country code, city code, and the number you are calling.

Calls to area codes **800, 888, 877,** and **866** are toll-free (not to be confused with Hawaii's area code, 808, which is not free). However, calls to area codes **700** and **900** (chat lines, bulletin boards, "dating" services, and so on) can be very

Frommers.com: The Complete Travel Resource

It should go without saying, but we highly recommend **Frommers.com**, voted Best Travel Site by *PC Magazine*. We think you'll find our expert advice and tips; independent reviews of hotels, restaurants, attractions, and preferred shopping and nightlife venues; vacation giveaways; and an online booking tool indispensable before, during, and after your travels. We publish the complete contents of over 128 travel guides in our **Destinations** section covering nearly 3,600 places worldwide to help you plan your trip. Each weekday, we publish original articles reporting on **Deals and News** via our free **Frommers.com Newsletter** to help you save time and money and travel smarter. We're betting you'll find our new **Events** listings (http://events.frommers.com) an invaluable resource; it's an up-to-the-minute roster of what's happening in cities everywhere—including concerts, festivals, lectures and more. We've also added weekly **podcasts, interactive maps,** and hundreds of new images across the site. Check out our **Travel Talk** area featuring **message boards** where you can join in conversations with thousands of fellow Frommer's travelers and post your trip report once you return.

expensive—usually a charge of 95¢ to $3 or more per minute, and they sometimes have minimum charges that can run as high as $15 or more.

For **reversed-charge or collect calls,** and for person-to-person calls, dial the number 0 then the area code and number; an operator will come on the line, and you should specify whether you are calling collect, person-to-person, or both. If your operator-assisted call is international, ask for the overseas operator.

For **local directory assistance** ("information"), dial 411; for long-distance information, dial 1, then the appropriate area code and 555-1212.

CELLPHONES

Just because your cellphone works at home doesn't mean it'll work everywhere on Oahu. It's a good bet that your phone will work in Honolulu and Waikiki, but take a look at your wireless company's coverage map on its website before heading out. If you need to stay in touch, consider **renting a phone** from **InTouch USA**

(© **800/872-7626;** www.intouchglobal.com) or a rental car location, but be aware that you'll pay $1 a minute or more for airtime.

If you're not from the U.S., you'll be appalled at the poor reach of our **GSM (Global System for Mobile Communications) wireless network,** which is used by much of the rest of the world. Your phone will probably work in most major U.S. cities; it definitely won't work in many rural areas. To see where GSM phones work in the U.S., check out www.t-mobile.com/coverage/national_popup.asp. And you may or may not be able to send text messages home.

INTERNET/E-MAIL WITHOUT YOUR OWN COMPUTER

To find cybercafes in your destination, check **www.cybercaptive.com** and **www.cybercafe.com**. If your hotel doesn't have Web access, head to **Web Site Story Café,** 2555 Cartwright Rd. (in the Hotel

Waikiki), Waikiki (© **808/922-1677**). It's open daily from 7am to 11pm and serves drinks. Or try **Caffé Giovannini,** 1888 Kalakaua Ave. C-106, (© **808/979-2299**).

Aside from formal cybercafes, all **public libraries** on Oahu offer free access if you have a library card, which you can purchase for a $10 fee. The closest library is the **Waikiki-Kapahulu Library,** 400 Kapahulu St. (across from the Ala Wai Golf Course; © **808/733-8488**). Most hotels on Oahu have **in-room dataports** and **business centers,** but the charges can be exorbitant.

WITH YOUR OWN COMPUTER
Every major hotel, even most small B&Bs, have Internet connections, many of them Wi-Fi, but fees can be high (generally $11–$13 per day).

ShakaNet, Hawaii's largest wireless provider, has completed the first phase of its free Wireless Waikiki network. Phase I covers a significant portion of Waikiki and includes an estimated 1,000 hotel rooms, portions of the Honolulu Zoo, Kapiolani Park, Queens Beach, Kuhio Beach, and the adjacent shoreline. The boundaries of Phase I are roughly Kalakaua Avenue, from Liliuokalani Avenue to Queen's Beach in the Diamond Head direction, and Liliuokalani/Kuhio avenues, on the Ewa side, down Kuhio Avenue across Kapiolani Park to Monsarrat Avenue.

As we went to press, Chinatown was about to launch a free wireless service, provided by Earthlink in a 27-block range (bordered by N. Beretania St., Nimitz Hwy., Fort Street Mall, and Nuuanu Stream).

Online Traveler's Toolbox

Veteran travelers usually carry some essential items to make their trips easier. Following is a selection of handy online tools to bookmark and use.

- **Airplane Food** (www.airlinemeals.net)
- **Airplane Seating** (www.seatguru.com and www.airlinequality.com)
- **Hawaii Visitors and Convention Bureau** (www.gohawaii.com)
- **Hawaiian Language** (www.geocities.com/~olelo)
- **Helpful Hawaii Websites and Links** (www.hawaiiradiotv.com/puka.html)
- **Honolulu Daily Newspaper** (www.honoluluadvertiser.com)
- **Honolulu Weekly Guide to Activities** (www.honoluluweekly.com)
- **Foreign Languages for Travelers** (www.travlang.com)
- **Maps** (www.mapquest.com)
- **Oahu Visitors Bureau** (www.visit-oahu.com)
- **Time and Date** (www.timeanddate.com)
- **Travel Warnings** (http://travel.state.gov, www.fco.gov.uk/travel, www.voyage.gc.ca)
- **Universal Currency Converter** (www.xe.com/ucc)
- **Visa ATM Locator** (www.visa.com), **MasterCard ATM Locator** (www.mastercard.com)
- **Weather** (www.intellicast.com and www.weather.com)

Wherever you go, bring a **connection kit** of the right power adapters, or find out whether your hotel supplies them to guests.

For information on electrical currency conversions, see "Electricity," in the Fast Facts section in chapter 10.

13 TIPS ON ACCOMMODATIONS

Hawaii offers everything from simple rooms in restored plantation homes and quaint cottages on the beach to luxurious oceanview condo units and opulent suites in beachfront resorts. Each has its pluses and minuses, so before you book, make sure you know what you're getting into.

TYPES OF ACCOMMODATIONS

HOTELS In Hawaii "hotel" can indicate a wide range of options, from few or no on-site amenities to enough extras to qualify as a miniresort. Generally, a hotel offers daily maid service and has a restaurant, on-site laundry facilities, a pool, and a sundries/convenience–type shop. Top hotels have activities desks, concierge and valet service, room service, business centers, airport shuttles, bars and/or lounges, and perhaps a few more shops.

The advantages of a hotel stay are privacy and convenience; the disadvantage is generally noise (either thin walls between rooms or loud music from a lobby lounge late into the night). Hotels are often a short walk from the beach rather than right on the beachfront (although there are exceptions).

RESORTS In Hawaii, a resort offers everything a hotel does—and more. You can expect direct beach access, with beach cabanas and lounge chairs; pools and a Jacuzzi; a spa and fitness center; restaurants, bars, and lounges; a 24-hour front desk; concierge, valet, and bellhop services; room service (often round-the-clock); an activities desk; tennis and golf; ocean activities; a business center; kids' programs; and more.

The advantages of a resort are that you have everything you could possibly want in the way of services and things to do; the disadvantage is that the price generally reflects this. And don't be misled by a name—just because a place is called "ABC Resort" doesn't mean it actually *is* a resort. Make sure you're getting what you pay for.

CONDOS The roominess and convenience of a condo—which is usually a fully equipped, multiple-bedroom apartment—makes this a great choice for families. Condominium properties in Hawaii generally consist of several apartments set in either a single high-rise or a cluster of low-rise units. Condos usually have amenities such as some maid service (ranging from daily to weekly; it may or may not be included in your rate), a pool, and an on-site front desk or a live-in property manager. Condos tend to be clustered in resort areas. Some are very high-end, but most are quite affordable, especially if you're traveling in a group.

The advantages of a condo are privacy, space, and conveniences—which usually include a full kitchen, a washer and dryer, and a private phone. Downsides are the lack of an on-site restaurant and the density of the units.

BED & BREAKFASTS Hawaii has a wide range of places that call themselves B&Bs: everything from a traditional B&B—several bedrooms in a home, with breakfast served in the morning—to what is essentially a vacation rental on an owner's property that comes with fixings for you to make your own breakfast. Make sure that the B&B you're booking matches

What If Your Dream Hotel Becomes a Nightmare?

To avoid any unpleasant surprises, find out when you make your reservation exactly what the hotel is offering you: cost, minimum stay, included amenities. Ask if there's any penalty for leaving early. Discuss what the cancellation policy is if the accommodations fail to meet your expectations—and get this policy in writing.

If you're not satisfied with your room, notify the front desk or booking agency immediately. Approach the management in a calm, reasonable manner and suggest a solution (like moving to another unit). Be willing to compromise. Do not leave; if you do, you may not get your deposit back.

If all else fails, when you get home, write to any association the property may be a member of (such as the Hawaii Visitors and Convention Bureau or a resort association). Describe your complaint and why the issue was not resolved to your satisfaction. And be sure to let us know if you have a problem with a place recommended in chapter 4!

your own mental picture. Note that laundry facilities and private phones are not always available. I've reviewed lots of wonderful B&Bs in chapter 4. If you have to share a bathroom, I've spelled it out in the listings; otherwise, you can assume that you will have your own.

The advantages of a traditional B&B are its individual style and congenial atmosphere, with a host who's often happy to act as your own private concierge. In addition, they're usually an affordable way to go. The disadvantages are lack of privacy, usually a set time for breakfast, few amenities, and generally no maid service. Also, B&B owners usually require a minimum stay of 2 or 3 nights, and it's often a drive to the beach.

VACATION RENTALS This is another great choice for families and for long-term stays. "Vacation rental" usually means that there will be no one on the property where you're staying. The actual accommodations can range from an apartment to an entire fully equipped house. Generally, vacation rentals allow you to settle in and make yourself at home for a while. They

have kitchen facilities (at least a kitchenette), on-site laundry facilities, and phone; some come with such extras as a TV, VCR, and stereo.

The advantages of a vacation rental are complete privacy, your own kitchen (which can save you money on meals), and lots of conveniences. The disadvantages are a lack of an on-site property manager and generally no maid service; often, a minimum stay is required (sometimes as much as a week). If you book a vacation rental, be sure that you have a 24-hour contact to call if the toilet won't flush or you can't figure out how to turn on the air-conditioning.

BARGAINING ON PRICES

Rates can sometimes be bargained down, but it depends on the place. The best bargaining can be had at **hotels** and **resorts.** If business is slow and you book directly, both places may give you at least part of the commission they'd normally pay a travel agent. Most hotels and resorts also have local rates for islanders, which they may extend to visitors during slow periods. It never hurts to ask about discounted or local rates; a host of special rates are available for the military, seniors, members of the travel industry, families, corporate travelers, and long-term stays. Also ask about **package deals,** which might include a car rental or free breakfast for the same price as a room by itself. Hotels and resorts offer packages for everyone: golfers, tennis players, families, honeymooners, and more. I've found that it's worth the extra few cents to make a local call to the hotel; sometimes the local reservations person knows about package deals that the toll-free operators are unaware of. If all else fails, try to get the hotel or resort to upgrade you to a better room for the same price as a budget room, or waive the parking fee or extra fees for children. Persistence and polite inquiries can pay off.

It's harder to bargain at **bed-and-breakfasts.** You may be able to negotiate down the minimum stay or get a discount if you're staying a week or longer. But generally, a B&B owner has only a few rooms and has already priced the property at a competitive rate; expect to pay what's asked.

You have somewhat more leeway to negotiate at **vacation rentals** and **condos.** In addition to asking for a discount on a multinight stay, ask if they can throw in a rental car to sweeten the deal; believe it or not, they often will.

USING A BOOKING AGENCY VS. DOING IT YOURSELF

If you don't have the time to call places yourself, you might consider a booking agency.

A statewide booking agent for B&B is **Bed & Breakfast Hawaii** (© 800/733-1632 or 808/822-7771; fax 808/822-2723; www.bandb-hawaii.com), offering a range of accommodations from vacation homes to B&Bs, starting at $65 a night. For vacation rentals, contact **Hawaii Beachfront Vacation Homes** (© 808/247-3637; fax 808/235-2644). **Hawaii Condo Exchange** (© 800/442-0404; www.hawaiicondoexchange.com) acts as a consolidator for condo and vacation-rental properties.

14 GETTING MARRIED IN THE ISLANDS

Hawaii is a great place for a wedding. The islands exude romance and natural beauty, and after the ceremony, you're already on your honeymoon. And the members of your wedding party will most likely be delighted, as you've given them the perfect excuse for their own island vacation.

More than 20,000 marriages are performed annually on the islands, mostly on Oahu; nearly half are for couples from somewhere else. The booming wedding business has spawned more than 70 companies that can help you organize a long-distance event and stage an unforgettable wedding, Hawaiian-style or your style. However, you can also plan your own

island wedding, even from afar, and not spend a fortune doing it.

THE PAPERWORK

The state of Hawaii has some very minimal procedures for obtaining a marriage license. The first thing you should do is contact the **Honolulu Marriage License Office,** State Department of Health Building, 1250 Punchbowl St., Honolulu, HI 96813 (© **808/586-4545;** www.state.hi.us/doh/records/vr_marri.html), which is open Monday through Friday from 8am to 4pm. The office no longer will mail you the brochure *Getting Married;* you can download it from the website or contact a marriage-licensing agent closest to where you'll be staying in Hawaii (also listed on the website).

Once in Hawaii, the prospective bride and groom must go together to the marriage-licensing agent to get the license, which costs $60 and is good for 30 days. Both parties must be 15 years of age or older (couples 15–17 years old must have proof of age, written consent of both parents, and written approval of the judge of the family court) and not more closely related than first cousins.

Gay couples cannot marry in Hawaii. After a protracted legal battle, and much discussion in the state legislature, the Hawaii Supreme Court ruled that the state will not issue marriage licenses to same-sex couples.

PLANNING THE WEDDING

DOING IT YOURSELF The marriage-licensing agents, who range from state employees to private individuals, are usually friendly, helpful people who can steer you to a nondenominational minister or marriage performer who's licensed by the state of Hawaii. These marriage performers are great sources of information for budget weddings. They usually know wonderful places to have the ceremony for free or for a nominal fee. For the names, addresses, and telephone numbers of marriage agents in the rural and suburban areas of Oahu, call (℗ **808/586-4544.**

If you don't want to use a wedding planner (see below), but you do want to make arrangements before you arrive in Hawaii, our best advice is to get a copy of the daily newspapers on the island where you want to have the wedding. People willing and qualified to conduct weddings advertise in the classifieds. They're great sources of information and know the best ceremony sites, caterers, florists, and so

on. Check out the *Honolulu Advertiser,* P.O. Box 3110, Honolulu, HI 96802 (℗ **808/525-8000;** www.honolulu advertiser.com); and *MidWeek,* 45-525 Luluku Rd., Kaneohe, HI 96744 (℗ **808/235-5881;** www.midweek.com).

USING A WEDDING PLANNER Wedding planners—many of whom are marriage-licensing agents as well—can arrange everything for you, from a small, private, outdoor affair to a full-blown formal ceremony in a tropical setting. They charge anywhere from $95 to a small fortune—it all depends on what you want. The Hawaii Visitors and Convention Bureau (℗ **800/GO-HAWAII** [464-2924] or 808/923-1811; www.gohawaii.com) can supply contact information on wedding coordinators.

If you want to get married at sea, call Capt. Ken Middleton, of **Tradewind Charters,** based in Honolulu (℗ **800/829-4899** or 808/973-0311; www.tradewindcharters.com), for a private wedding and reception on the ocean waves.

If you fantasize about being wed in an exotic setting, such as near a waterfall, on the beach, or in a garden chapel, **AAA Above Heaven's Gate** (℗ **800/800-2WED** [2933] or 808/259-5429; www.hawaiiweddings.com) can arrange it. The company has garnered rave reviews for their attention to detail in putting together the perfect Hawaii wedding.

Other wedding planners include: **Love Hawaii** (contact Rev. Toni Baran and Rev. Jerry Le Lesch at (℗ **808/235-6966;** www.lovehawaii.com); **Affordable Weddings of Hawaii** (℗ **800/942-4554** or 808/923-4876; www.wedhawaii.com); and **Aloha Wedding Planners** (℗ **800/288-8309** or 808/943-2711; www.alohawedding planners.com).

Suggested Honolulu, Waikiki & Oahu Itineraries

First and foremost, yes, it's possible to have a fabulous vacation in Hawaii and not have to take out a second mortgage. The next most common question readers ask me is: "What should I do in Hawaii?"

My response: How much time to you have, and what do you like to do?

The purpose of this chapter is to give you my expert advice on the best things to see and do, and how to do them in an orderly fashion so you're not driving madly from one end of the island to the other.

Here's the best advice I can give you: **Do not plan to see more than one island per week.** This isn't the Caribbean, where islands are so close to each other that you can island-hop. With the exception of the ferry between Maui and Lanai, getting from one island to another is an all-day affair that consists of: packing and checking out of your hotel, driving to the airport (most island airports are a 30- to 60-minute drive from resort areas), dropping off your rental car, checking in (and standing in long lines) 90 minutes before your scheduled flight, flying from one island to the next, waiting for your luggage (sometimes the wait for the luggage is just as long or longer than your interisland flight), getting yet another rental car, driving 30 to 60 minutes to your hotel, checking in, and so on. Don't waste a day of your vacation seeing our interisland air terminals.

Also, don't max out your days. You're in Hawaii—which means you should allow some time to do nothing but relax. Ease into your vacation. Due to jet lag, you'll probably be tired your first day, and hitting the pillow at 8 or 9pm might sound good. Don't be surprised if you wake up your first morning in Hawaii before the sun comes up. Your internal clock might still be set 2 to 6 hours earlier than Hawaii's.

Finally, think of your first trip to Hawaii as a "scouting" trip. Hawaii is too beautiful, too sensual, too enticing to see just once in a lifetime. You'll be back. You don't need to see and do everything on this trip. In fact, if you fall in love with something in the itinerary below, go back again. I've included very general sample itineraries. If you're a golf fan or a scuba diver, check out chapter 1, "The Best of Oahu" (p. 1) to plan your trip around your passion.

One last thing—you'll need a car to get around the islands, so remember to plan for that expense. Oahu has an adequate public transportation service, TheBus, but it's set up for Hawaiian residents, not tourists carrying coolers, beach mats, beach toys, and other things to the beach (all carryons must fit under the bus seat). So plan to rent a car, but also to get out of it as much as possible. Hawaii is not a place to see from your car window. You have to get out to smell the sweet perfume of plumeria, to feel the warm rain on your face, to hear the sound of the wind through a bamboo forest, and to plunge into the gentle waters of the Pacific.

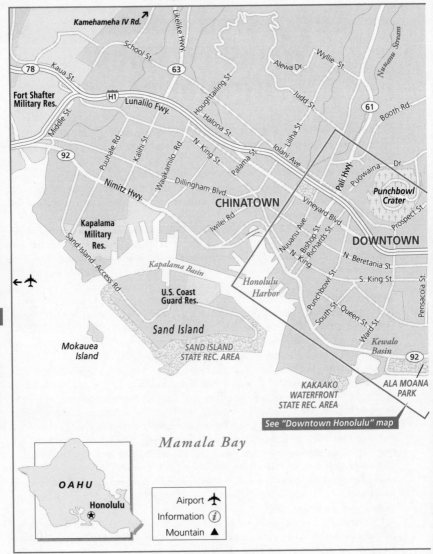

1 THE ISLAND IN BRIEF

HONOLULU

Hawaii's largest city looks like any other big metropolitan center with tall buildings. In fact, some cynics refer to it as "Los Angeles West." But within Honolulu's boundaries, you'll find rainforests, deep canyons, valleys

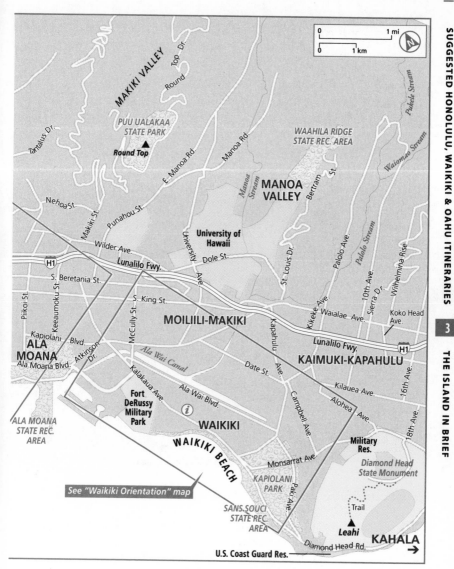

and waterfalls, a nearly mile-high mountain range, coral reefs, and gold-sand beaches. The city proper—where most of Oahu's residents live—is approximately 12 miles wide and 26 miles long, running east to west, roughly between Diamond Head and Pearl Harbor. Within the city are seven hills laced by seven streams that run to Mamala Bay.

Surrounding the central area is a plethora of neighborhoods, ranging from the quiet suburbs of **Hawaii Kai** to *kamaaina*

3

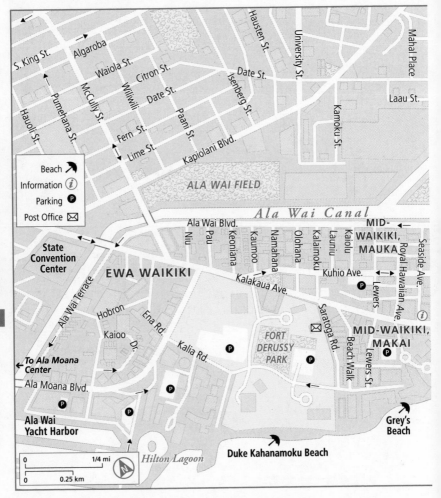

(old-timer) neighborhoods such as **Manoa.** These areas are generally quieter and more residential than Waikiki, but they're still within minutes of beaches, shopping, and all the activities Oahu has to offer.

WAIKIKI Some say that Waikiki is past its prime—that everybody goes to Maui now. If it has fallen out of favor, you couldn't prove it by us. Waikiki is the very

incarnation of Yogi Berra's comment about Toots Shor's famous New York restaurant: "Nobody goes there anymore. It's too crowded."

When King Kalakaua played in Waikiki, it was "a hamlet of plain cottages . . . its excitements caused by the activity of insect tribes and the occasional fall of a coconut." The Merrie Monarch, who gave his name

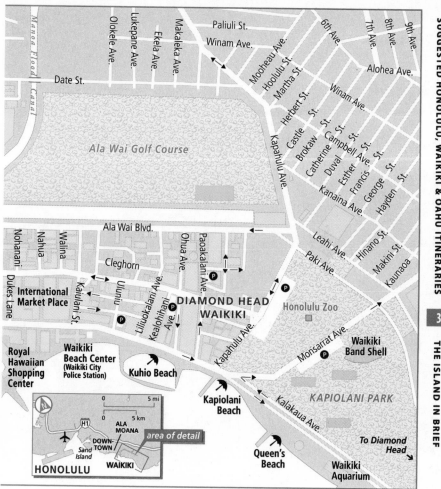

to Waikiki's main street, would love the scene today. Some five million tourists visit Oahu every year, and 9 out of 10 of them stay in Waikiki. This urban beach is where all the action is; it's backed by 175 high-rise hotels with more than 33,000 guest rooms and hundreds of bars and restaurants, all in a 1½-square-mile beach zone. Waikiki means honeymooners and sun seekers,

bikinis and bare buns, a round-the-clock beach party every day of the year—and it's all because of a thin crescent of sand that was shipped over from Molokai. Staying in Waikiki puts you in the heart of it all, but also be aware that this is an on-the-go place with traffic noise 24 hours a day and its share of crime—and it's almost always crowded.

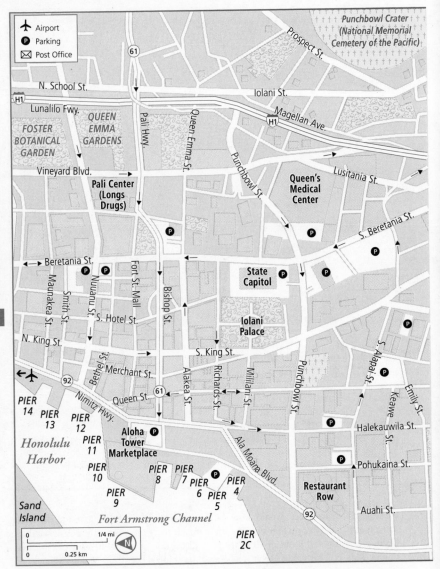

ALA MOANA A great beach as well as a famous shopping mall, Ala Moana is the retail and transportation heart of Honolulu, a place where you can both shop and suntan in one afternoon. All bus routes lead to the open-air **Ala Moana Shopping Center,** across the street from **Ala Moana Beach Park.** This 50-acre, 200-shop behemoth

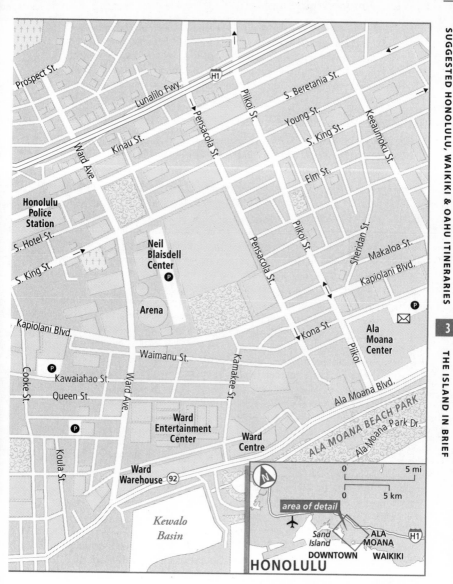

attracts 56 million customers a year (people fly up from Tahiti just to buy their Christmas gifts here). Every European designer from Armani to Vuitton is represented in Honolulu's answer to Beverly Hills's Rodeo Drive. For our purposes, the neighborhood called "Ala Moana" extends along Ala Moana Boulevard from Waikiki in the direction of

Tips **Finding Your Way Around, Oahu Style**

Mainlanders sometimes find the directions given by locals a bit confusing. Seldom will you hear east, west, north, and south; instead, islanders refer to directions as either **makai** (ma-*kae*), meaning toward the sea, or **mauka** (*mow*-kah), toward the mountains. In Honolulu, people use **Diamond Head** as a direction meaning to the east (in the direction of the world-famous crater called Diamond Head), and **Ewa** as a direction meaning to the west (toward the town called Ewa, on the other side of Pearl Harbor).

So, if you ask a local for directions, this is what you're likely to hear: "Drive 2 blocks makai (toward the sea), then turn Diamond Head (east) at the stoplight. Go 1 block and turn mauka (toward the mountains). It's on the Ewa (western) side of the street."

Diamond Head to downtown Honolulu in the Ewa direction (west) and includes the **Ward Centre** and **Ward Warehouse complexes** as well as **Restaurant Row.**

DOWNTOWN A tiny cluster of highrises west of Waikiki, downtown Honolulu is the financial, business, and government center of Hawaii. On the waterfront stands the iconic 1926 Aloha Tower, now the centerpiece of a harborfront shopping and restaurant complex known as the **Aloha Tower Marketplace.** The entire history of Honolulu can be seen in just a few short blocks: Street vendors sell papayas from trucks in skyscraper-lined concrete canyons; joggers and BMWs rush by a lacy palace, where the descendants of the original missionaries (with help from the U.S. Marines) overthrew Hawaii's last queen and stole her kingdom; burly bus drivers sport fragrant white ginger flowers on their dashboards; Methodist churches look like Asian temples; and businessmen wear aloha shirts to billion-dollar meetings.

On the edge of downtown is the **Chinatown Historic District,** the oldest Chinatown in America and still one of Honolulu's liveliest neighborhoods, a nonstop pageant of people, sights, sounds, smells, and tastes—not all Chinese, now

that Southeast Asians, including many Vietnamese, share the old storefronts. Go on Saturday morning, when everyone shops here for fresh goods such as gingerroot, fern fronds, and hogs' heads.

Among the historic buildings and Pan-Pacific corporate headquarters are a few hotels, mainly geared toward business travelers. Most visitors prefer the sun and excitement of Waikiki or choose a quieter neighborhood outside the city.

MANOA VALLEY First inhabited by white settlers, the Manoa Valley, above Waikiki, still has vintage *kamaaina* homes, one of Hawaii's premier botanical gardens in the Lyon Arboretum, the ever-gushing Manoa Falls, and the 320-acre campus of the University of Hawaii, where 50,000 students hit the books when they're not on the beach.

TO THE EAST: KAHALA Except for the estates of world-class millionaires and the luxurious Kahala Hotel & Resort (home of Hoku's, an outstanding beachfront restaurant), there's not much out this way that's of interest to visitors.

EAST OAHU

Beyond Kahala lies East Honolulu and such suburban bedroom communities as Aina Haina, Niu Valley, and Hawaii Kai, among others, all linked by the Kalani-anaole Highway and loaded with homes, condos, fast-food joints, and shopping malls. It looks like Southern California on a good day. A few reasons to come here: to have dinner at **Roy's,** the original and still-outstanding Hawaii regional cuisine restaurant, in Hawaii Kai; to snorkel at **Hanauma Bay** or watch daredevil surfers at **Sandy Beach;** or just to enjoy the natural splendor of the lovely coastline, which might include a hike to **Makapuu Lighthouse.**

THE WINDWARD COAST

The windward side is the opposite side of the island from Waikiki. On this coast, trade winds blow cooling breezes over gorgeous beaches; rain squalls inspire lush, tropical vegetation; and miles of subdivisions dot the landscape. Bed-and-breakfasts, ranging from oceanfront estates to tiny cottages on quiet residential streets, are everywhere. Vacations here are spent enjoying ocean activities and exploring the surrounding areas. Waikiki is just a quick 15-minute drive away.

KAILUA The biggest little beach town in Hawaii, Kailua sits at the foot of the sheer green Koolau Mountains, on a great bay with two of Hawaii's best beaches. The town itself is a funky low-rise cluster of timeworn shops and homes. Kailua has become the B&B capital of Hawaii; it's an affordable alternative to Waikiki, with rooms and vacation rentals from $60 a day and up. With the prevailing trade winds whipping up a cooling breeze, Kailua attracts windsurfers from around the world.

KANEOHE After you clear the trafficky maze of town, Oahu returns to its more natural state. Helter-skelter suburbia sprawls around the edges of Kaneohe, one of the most scenic bays in the Pacific. A handful of B&Bs dot its edge. This great bay beckons you to get out on the water; you can depart from Heeia Boat Harbor

on snorkel or fishing charters and visit Ahu o Laka, the sandbar that appears and disappears in the middle of the bay. From here, you'll have a panoramic view of the Koolau Range.

KUALOA/LAIE The upper northeast shore is one of Oahu's most sacred places, an early Hawaiian landing spot where kings dipped their sails, cliffs hold ancient burial sites, and ghosts still march in the night. Sheer cliffs stab the reef-fringed seacoast, while old fishponds are tucked along the two-lane coast road that winds past empty gold-sand beaches around beautiful Kahana Bay. Thousands "explore" the South Pacific at the **Polynesian Cultural Center,** in Laie, a Mormon settlement with its own Tabernacle Choir of sweet Samoan harmony.

THE NORTH SHORE

Here's the Hawaii of Hollywood—giant waves, surfers galore, tropical jungles, waterfalls, and mysterious Hawaiian temples. If you're looking for a quieter vacation, closer to nature, and filled with swimming, snorkeling, diving, surfing, or just plain hanging out on some of the world's most beautiful beaches, the North Shore is your spot. The artsy little beach town of **Haleiwa** and the surrounding shoreline seem a world away from Waikiki. The North Shore boasts good restaurants, shopping, and cultural activities—but here they come with the quiet of country living. Bed-and-breakfasts are the most common accommodations, but there's one first-class hotel and some vacation rentals as well. *Be forewarned:* It's a long trip—nearly an hour's drive—to Honolulu and Waikiki, and it's about twice as rainy on the North Shore as in Honolulu.

CENTRAL OAHU: THE EWA PLAIN

Flanked by the Koolau and Waianae mountain ranges, the hot, sun-baked Ewa

Plain runs up and down the center of Oahu. Once covered with sandalwood forests (hacked down for the China trade) and later the sugar-cane and pineapple backbone of Hawaii, Ewa today sports a new crop: suburban houses stretching to the sea. But let your eye wander west to the Waianae Range and Mount Kaala, at 4,020 feet the highest summit on Oahu; up there in the misty rainforest, native birds thrive in the hummocky bog. In 1914, the U.S. Army pitched a tent camp on the plain; author James Jones would later call **Schofield Barracks** "the most beautiful army post in the world." Hollywood filmed Jones's *From Here to Eternity* here.

LEEWARD OAHU: THE WAIANAE COAST

The west coast of Oahu is a hot and dry place of dramatic beauty: white-sand beaches bordering the deep blue ocean, steep verdant green cliffs, and miles of Mother Nature's wildness. Except for the luxurious **JW Marriott Ihilani Resort and Spa at Ko Olina, Roy's Ko Olina Restaurant** (a sister of Roy's in Hawaii Kai; see above), and the **Makaha Golf Course,** you'll find virtually no tourist services out here. The funky west coast villages of Nanakuli, Waianae, and Makaha are the last stands of native Hawaiians. This side of Oahu is seldom visited, except by surfers bound for **Yokohama Bay** and those coming to see needle-nose **Kaena Point** (the island's westernmost outpost), which has a coastal wilderness park.

2 OAHU IN 1 WEEK

The island of Oahu is so stunning that the *alii,* the kings of Hawaii, made it the capital of the island nation. You can see all of Oahu's highlights in 1 week, presuming that you're staying in Waikiki; if you're in another location, be sure to factor in travel time. In this itinerary, I've included the all-star things to do and see on this island: Waikiki Beach, Waikiki Aquarium, Pearl Harbor Memorial, Polynesian Cultural Center, Hanauma Bay, Sea Life Park, Bishop Museum, historic downtown Honolulu, Kailua Bay, shopping, art galleries, and a few surprises.

Day ❶: Arrive in Hawaii & Head for Waikiki Beach ★★

Lather up with sunscreen, put on your sunglasses and a hat, and plop down on the most famous beach in the world. If you have kids in tow, or if an hour in Hawaii's intense sun is all you can handle, consider checking out Hawaii's water world by dropping by the **Waikiki Aquarium** (p. 200), or take the children to the **Honolulu Zoo** (p. 197). For insight into Waikiki's past, take the **Waikiki Historic Trail,** a 2-mile trail, marked with bronzed surf boards (p. 189). Try to see the sunset on your first day—just sit anywhere on

Waikiki Beach; if you'd like a liquid libation, all the hotels on the beach can accommodate you—and then get an early dinner.

Day ❷: Pearl Harbor ★★★

Most likely you'll be awake early, so take advantage of it: Drive or take a tour bus to the USS *Arizona* Memorial at Pearl Harbor (p. 194). Entry is free. The best time to go is early in the morning; by the afternoon, the lines are 2 hours long. Next, stop by the USS *Missouri* Memorial (p. 195), the USS *Bowfin* Submarine Museum and Park (p. 195), and the Pacific Aviation

Museum (p. 194). On your way back, either head for the beach at **Ala Moana Beach Park** (p. 153) or embark on a shopping spree across the street at the **Ala Moana Shopping Center** (p. 243). Plan a dinner in Honolulu or surrounding areas.

Day ❸: Polynesian Cultural Center ★★★

You might want to sleep late today. Around or after noon, head for the **Polynesian Cultural Center,** in Laie (p. 226). Allow at least 2 hours (if not the entire afternoon) to tour this mini-glimpse of the Pacific, where you'll walk through various "villages" filled with interactive activities, entertainment, and cultural events. Continue driving down the coast road to the small town of **Kailua,** and eat dinner at **Lucy's Grill 'n Bar** (p. 148) to avoid heavy traffic over the Pali back to Waikiki.

Day ❹: Snorkel in Hanauma Bay & Watch Marine Life at Sea Life Park ★★

If it's not Tuesday (when the park is closed), head out in the morning for spectacular snorkeling at **Hanauma Bay** (p. 156). You could spend the entire day here, but remember that Hawaii's sun is intense, and you don't want sunburn to ruin your vacation. After a couple of hours, wander down the coast to **Sea Life Park** (p. 201). If you have kids, this is a must-stop. Otherwise, you can continue "beach-hopping" along the coastline with stops at **Sandy Beach, Makapuu Point and Makapuu Beach Park,** and **Waimanalo Beach,** before turning back to take the Pali Highway. Be sure to stop at the **Pali Lookout** (p. 202) on your way back to Waikiki.

Day ❺: Historic Honolulu & Hawaiian Culture ★

Head to downtown Honolulu for a historic hike around the old town, and try to visit: **Iolani Palace** (p. 192), **Kawaiahao Church** (p. 193), **Mission Houses Museum**

(p. 193), and the **Hawaii Maritime Center** (p. 192). For a bird's-eye view of where you've been and the whole of Honolulu, go to the top of **Aloha Tower,** at Aloha Tower Marketplace. Stop for lunch either at the Marketplace or at one of the nearby restaurants. Spend the afternoon at the **Bishop Museum** to immerse yourself in Hawaiian culture. Plan dinner outside of Waikiki.

Day ❻: Beach Day at Kailua Beach Park ★

On your last full day on Oahu, travel over the Pali Highway, to the Windward side of the island, to spend a day at **Kailua Beach Park.** This is the perfect beach to relax or snorkel or to try something different such as kayaking or windsurfing. You can spend the entire day here, take an afternoon hike at **Hoomaluhia Botanical Gardens** (p. 225), or venture to another beach park such as **Kahana Bay** or **Malaekahana Bay State Recreation Area.**

Day ❼: Relax, Seek Adventure, Look at Art, or Shop

What you do today depends on how much time you have on your last day here—and how much energy. You might just hang out in **Waikiki** and perhaps take a surfing lesson, ride a surfing canoe, or venture underwater in an **Atlantis Submarine** (p. 169). For the energetic, get up early and climb **Diamond Head** (p. 171). Art lovers should definitely check out the **Honolulu Academy of Arts** (p. 204); the **Contemporary Museum** (p. 203), where you should have lunch; and the **Hawaii State Art Museum** (p. 203). Shoppers can head to Waikiki for the **Ala Moana Shopping Center,** the **DFS Galleria,** and the **Royal Hawaiian Shopping Center;** bargain hunters should make the 45-minute drive out to the **Waikele Premium Outlets.** On your way to the airport, stop on **Maunakea Street in Chinatown** and buy a lei from one of the numerous lei makers (p. 241) to take back as a sweet-smelling memory of your trip.

1 Waikiki

2A Pearl Harbor
2B Ala Moana

3A Polynesian
 Cultural Center
3B Kailua

4A Hanauma Bay
4B Sea Life Park
4C Beaches
4D Pali Lookout

5A Downtown Honolulu
5B Bishop Museum

6A Kailua Beach Park
6B Hoomaluhia Gardens
6C Kahana Bay
6D Malaekahana Bay
 State Recreation Area

7 Waikiki

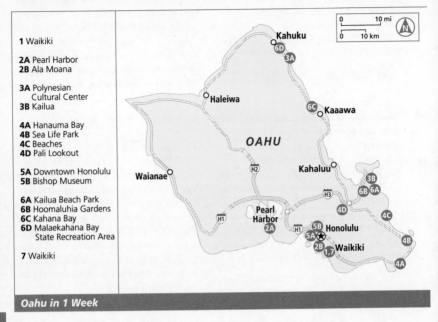

Oahu in 1 Week

8 Chinatown

9A Haleiwa
9B Waimea Beach Park
9C Pupukea Beach Park
9D Kahuku

10A Manoa Falls
10B Diamond Head
10C Makiki-Manoa

11 Waikiki

12A Contemporary
 Museum of Art
12B Hawaii State Art
 Museum & Honolulu
 Academy of Art

13 Shopping in Waikiki

14 Spas in Waikiki

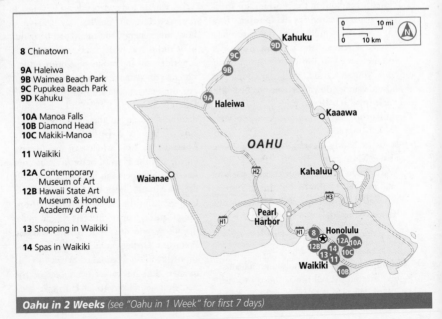

Oahu in 2 Weeks (see "Oahu in 1 Week" for first 7 days)

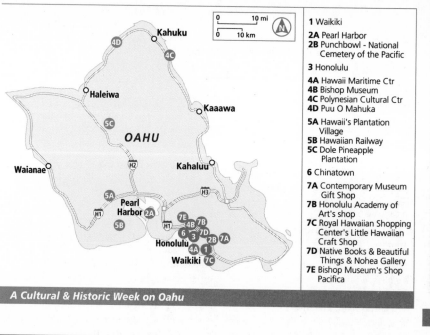

1 Waikiki

2A Pearl Harbor
2B Punchbowl - National Cemetery of the Pacific

3 Honolulu

4A Hawaii Maritime Ctr
4B Bishop Museum
4C Polynesian Cultural Ctr
4D Puu O Mahuka

5A Hawaii's Plantation Village
5B Hawaiian Railway
5C Dole Pineapple Plantation

6 Chinatown

7A Contemporary Museum Gift Shop
7B Honolulu Academy of Art's shop
7C Royal Hawaiian Shopping Center's Little Hawaiian Craft Shop
7D Native Books & Beautiful Things & Nohea Gallery
7E Bishop Museum's Shop Pacifica

A Cultural & Historic Week on Oahu

3

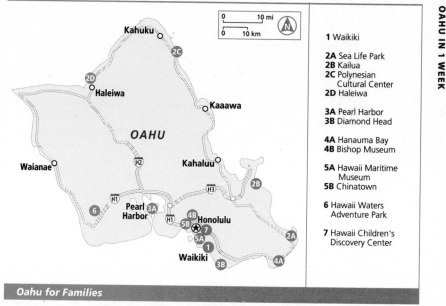

1 Waikiki

2A Sea Life Park
2B Kailua
2C Polynesian Cultural Center
2D Haleiwa

3A Pearl Harbor
3B Diamond Head

4A Hanauma Bay
4B Bishop Museum

5A Hawaii Maritime Museum
5B Chinatown

6 Hawaii Waters Adventure Park

7 Hawaii Children's Discovery Center

Oahu for Families

3 OAHU IN 2 WEEKS

Two weeks really gives you time to discover Oahu. After you check out the highlights mentioned above, visit historic Chinatown, relax on the beaches of the North Shore, take fabulous hikes, explore the waters surrounding the island, check out art galleries and museums, go shopping, relax in spas, or take time to find unique experiences on the island.

Day ❽: Explore Historic Chinatown ★★

See a different side of Hawaii by walking the streets of Honolulu's **Chinatown** (p. 204). You can take a formal tour (offered by the **Chinese Chamber of Commerce** for just $10. Or take the walking tour we recommend on p. 204. Plan to at least have lunch in this exotic part of Oahu (p. 137).

Day ❾: Relax on the Beaches of the North Shore ★★★

Get up early, drive across Oahu, and have breakfast at **Cafe Haleiwa** (p. 150) with the surfers. Wander across the street to the **Paradise Found Cafe** (p. 151) to pick up a picnic lunch, then head out to the beach. Depending on what you want to do and what the weather is like, here are some choices for a day at the beach: In the summer, when the waves are flat, **Waimea Beach Park** is great for swimming, snorkeling, and bodysurfing; in the winter, watch surfers take on huge, 30-foot waves. If you want to go snorkeling or diving, **Pupukea Beach Park** is excellent. On your way home, return to Haleiwa and stop at the **shrimp trucks** (p. 148) for a cheap and delicious meal.

Day ❿: Take a Hike into a Rainforest or Atop an Old Volcano ★★

Spend the day hiking, either into the **rainforest** (see **Manoa Falls Hike** on p. 174) or up to the top of an **old volcano** (see **Diamond Head Hike** on p. 171). Serious hikers might check out the **Makiki-Manoa** series of trails (p. 173). Of course, after all

that exercise, you might want to plan a massage in the afternoon at one of **Hawaii's best spas** (p. 12). You'll deserve it.

Day ⓫: Oahu from the Water ★★

See Hawaii from a different angle—get out on the water for a day. Even if you think you get seasick, take the lunch cruise on *Navatek I.* It's designed with stabilizers to guarantee that you won't get green around the gills. You can enjoy a great lunch and Hawaiian music as you cruise off Waikiki (p. 165). Or plunge underwater with **Atlantis Submarines** (p. 169), where you can view below the ocean blue without getting wet. Plan to eat a fish dinner in Waikiki that night (p. 120).

Day ⓬: Soak up the Culture at Hawaii's Best Art Galleries & Museums ★★

One of Hawaii's best art museums is also a great perch in Honolulu's skyline. Start the day at the **Contemporary Museum of Art** (p. 203) and plan to stay for lunch at the **Cafe** (p. 203). From there, travel into Honolulu to the **Hawaii State Art Museum** (p. 203) and then on to the **Honolulu Academy of Arts** (p. 204). After a day of art, take in a show in Honolulu (p. 254).

Day ⓭: Shop in Paradise ★★

With more than 1,000 stores in Oahu, where's a shopper to begin?! Check out our suggestions for all kinds of shopping (p. 232), ranging from **aloha wear** to **great souvenirs** to the **best discount shopping** spots on the island. You might want to take in a luau on your last night in Hawaii (p. 256).

Day ⑭: A Day of Pampering & Relaxation ★★

Before you board your plane for hours of discomfort, plan a few hours at a **spa.** Oahu has several world-class spas sprinkled throughout the island. Check out our favorites in chapter 1 (p. 12).

4 A CULTURAL & HISTORIC WEEK ON OAHU

Spend a week seeing the sacred sites from ancient Hawaii—where priests once healed people—to the spot where members of royalty were born, to the days of the missionaries and old plantations, to World War II—where Pearl Harbor was attacked. Below are the highlights of Oahu's cultural and historic sights and activities, including: Waikiki, Pearl Harbor, downtown Honolulu, Chinatown, Central Oahu, and other places that give us a vivid reminder of history.

Day ❶: Arrive in Hawaii & Head for Waikiki Beach ★★

To get an overview of Waikiki's history, start off with the 2-mile **Waikiki Historic Trail** (p. 189), marked by a 6-foot-tall surfboard explaining the history of today's favorite resort area. Next, hop on a Segway Personal Transporter with **Glide Ride Tours and Rentals** (p. 188). After a lesson to make sure you are competent, head off for a tour of Waikiki, Kapiolani Park, and Diamond Head. At sunset, wander along the sand at Waikiki Beach and listen to the Hawaiian music coming from every hotel. Plan dinner at either **Hula Grill** or **Duke's** (p. 126).

Day ❷: World War II ★★★

Unfortunately, no trip to Honolulu would be complete without a visit to the **USS Arizona Memorial at Pearl Harbor** (p. 194), where 1,177 U.S. sailors died in a bombing attack by the Japanese on December 7, 1941. Get there early, preferably by the 7:30am opening—otherwise face long lines (waits up to 2 hr.). After spending a couple of hours here, go next door to the **USS Bowfin Submarine Museum and Park** (p. 195), one of just 15 World War II submarines still in existence. If you're ready for more, wander down to the **USS Missouri Memorial**

(p. 195), where the Japanese signed the surrender agreement on September 2, 1945, ending World War II. Definitely take the tour to get the full impact of this historic vessel. Finish with the **Pacific Aviation Museum** (p. 194), where you can sit behind the controls of a simulated plane that flew in World War II. To get a feel for that fateful day in 1941 that propelled the U.S. into the war, sign up for the unforgettable **Island Seaplane Service**'s tour of the entire island (p. 187). Finish the day by wandering through the **(Punchbowl) National Cemetery of the Pacific** (p. 193) to see the true cost of any war.

For an evening activity to cheer you up, try a stand-up comedian (p. 256) or a show in Waikiki (p. 254).

Day ❸: Hawaiian Royalty & Missionaries ★★

If you really want to "understand" Hawaii, take the 45-minute tour of the **Iolani Palace** (p. 192), where you'll see how Hawaiian royalty lived. When sugar planters and descendants of missionaries overthrew the Kingdom of Hawaii on January 17, 1893, Hawaii's last queen, Liliuokalani, was put under house arrest and this palace also became a jail. Next, wander down the street to the crowning achievement of the missionaries, **Kawaiahao**

Church (p. 193), which holds its Sunday service in Hawaiian at 10:30am. To learn more about the missionaries who traveled from New England to Hawaii (via Cape Horn) to spread the gospel, stop by the **Mission Houses Museum** (p. 193). Make one last call at the **Royal Mausoleum,** the final resting place of both royalty and missionaries, and then relax over dinner at **Hau Tree Lanai** (p. 126), which offers ocean views.

Day 4: Hawaii's History on the Land & Sea ★★

If they are open when you arrive in Hawaii, plan to be at the opening of the **Hawaii Maritime Center** at 8:30am, to spend at least an hour wandering through this fascinating reproduction of Hawaii's history, from the ancient journey of Polynesians to the days of the four-masted schooners to today. Next, head out of Honolulu, stopping by Hawaii's premier cultural and historical museum, the **Bishop Museum** (p. 189), where you could spend days but should limit this visit to a couple of hours before heading out to the North Shore via Haleiwa town. Grab a terrific burger or sandwich at **Kua Aina** (p. 134), or sit down for lunch at **Cafe Haleiwa** (p. 150), and then head over to the **Polynesian Cultural Center.** Try to get there as close to the 12:30pm opening time as possible to avoid crowds. Allow at least 2 hours to tour this 42-acre lagoon park (and more time if you have kids). It's pricey to get in (tickets start at $50), so stay as long as you like. At sunset, drive back toward Haleiwa and watch the

sun set behind the mountains at the Hawaiian sacred temple, **Puu O Mahuka.** Plan to enjoy a leisurely dinner at **Haleiwa Joe's** (p. 149).

Day 5: Plantation Days in Hawaii ★

At **Hawaii's Plantation Village** (p. 196), take the hour-long tour of this restored 50-acre village that depicts what life was like on the plantations of 1852 to 1947. The chief mode of transportation at that time was the railroad. You can experience the Old Oahu Railway trains at the **Hawaiian Railway** (p. 196). And to see what a plantation looks like today, stop by the **Dole Pineapple Plantation** (p. 227). Take the afternoon off and go to a beach.

Day 6: Chinese & Asian History in Honolulu ★★

Spend the day seeing a different side of Hawaii by walking the streets of Honolulu's **Chinatown,** take the walking tour we recommend on p. 204. Plan to have lunch in this exotic part of Oahu; try **Little Village Noodle House** (p. 138).

Day 7: Shop ★

Culture hounds will be mesmerized by the **Contemporary Museum Gift Shop** (p. 241), the **Honolulu Academy of Art's Shop** (p. 241), and the **Royal Hawaiian Shopping Center's Little Hawaiian Craft Shop** (p. 241). Artists and collectors could spend an entire day at **Native Books & Beautiful Things** (p. 242), **Nohea Gallery** (p. 242), and **Bishop Museum's Shop Pacifica** (p. 242). So many things to buy and so little time. Start planning your next trip to Hawaii.

5 OAHU FOR FAMILIES

If you have enough trouble getting your kids out of the house in the morning, dragging them thousands of miles away may seem like an insurmountable challenge. But family travel can be immensely rewarding, giving you new ways of seeing the world through smaller pairs of eyes. The following itinerary gives you the nuts and bolts you need to plan an affordable, safe, and fun family vacation.

Day ❶: Arrive in Hawaii & Head for Waikiki Beach ★★

Lather everybody up in sunscreen, take sunglasses and a hat, and plop down on a beach the kids will love—Waikiki. If they get tired of playing in the surf, you might consider a catamaran ride or an outrigger canoe ride (p. 184). After an hour or so on the beach, take the kids to see the marine critters at the **Waikiki Aquarium** (p. 200) or stop by the **Honolulu Zoo** (p. 197). They'll drop off to sleep early.

Day ❷: Drive Around the Island ★★

Most likely, you'll still be on mainland time today—take advantage of it and get up early. Head out for **Sea Life Park,** which opens at 9:30am, and spend a couple of hours on the shows, exhibits, and interactive activities. Grab lunch in Kailua at **Zippy's** (p. 140), and head up the coast to the **Polynesian Cultural Center** (p. 226), in Laie. Plan at least 2 to 3 hours (or as long as the kids will last) here. On the way home, stop at one of the **shrimp trucks in Haleiwa** (p. 148) and have a picnic dinner.

Day ❸: A Sunken Boat, a Submarine & a Volcano ★★

Don't miss the **USS *Arizona* Memorial at Pearl Harbor** (p. 194). Arrive before the 7:30am opening, or lines will be lengthy. After a few hours here, head next door to the **USS *Bowfin* Submarine Museum and Park** (p. 195), one of just 15 World War II submarines still in existence. If energy levels hold out, hit the **USS *Missouri* Memorial** (p. 195), where the Japanese signed the surrender agreement on September 2, 1945, that ended World War II. Finish Pearl Harbor by seeing the **Pacific Aviation Museum** (p. 194), where the kids can sit behind the controls of a simulated plane that flew in World War II. Depending on how tired the kids are at this point, you can head to the beach or hike up to the top of **Diamond Head** (p. 171) to see the sunset view.

Day ❹: Snorkeling, Sharkskin Drumming & Surf Movies Too ★★

If it's not Tuesday (when the park is closed for maintenance), head out for **Hanauma Bay** (p. 156) to snorkel in the clear, warm water. After lunch take the kids to the **Bishop Museum** (p. 189), where they can explore the interior of a volcano and climb to the top to get a bird's-eye view of an erupting caldera, watch a hula, see the skeleton of a whale, and check out war weapons the Hawaiians used.

Day ❺: From the Sea to China ★★

The kids won't want to leave the **Hawaii Maritime Museum** (p. 192), where they can follow the ancient journey of Polynesian voyagers all the way to the nostalgic days of the *Lurline,* which once brought tourists from San Francisco. After a few hours, wander over to **Chinatown** (p. 204) for lunch; the kids will be enthralled with the exotic foodstuffs at the outdoor markets.

Day ❻: A Day at a Water Theme Park ★

Take the kids to **Wet 'n' Wild** (p. 196). They'll love this 29-acre water park; in fact, plan to spend the entire day here. Highlights include a football field–sized wave pool, a 65-foot-high free-fall slide, a water-toboggan bullet slide, inner-tube slides, a body-flume slide, rivers, and a zillion other things that will entertain them for hours. You'll also find restaurants here, along with a few food carts, shops, and Hawaiian performances. Bring plenty of sunscreen.

Day ❼: Final Day or What to do on a Rainy Day ★★

Take the kids to **Hawaii Children's Discovery Center** (p. 197), perfect for ages 2 to 13. This 37,000-square-foot place of color, motion, and activities will entertain them for hours, with hands-on exhibits and interactive stations. Meanwhile, Mom and Dad can get some rest.

6 ONE WEEK OF ADVENTURES ON OAHU

If you're looking for a vacation filled with adventure, Oahu provides plenty of opportunities, from gliding over the rolling surf to plunging under the sea to diving out of a plane, even coming eyeball-to-eyeball with sharks. You can make your entire vacation as thrilling and as heart-pounding as you desire, or you can experience just a couple days of spicy escapades. Below is an itinerary that you can pick and choose from, or—as we say in Hawaii—you can "go for broke."

Day ❶: Arrive in Hawaii & Head for Waikiki Beach ★★

At **Waikiki Beach** (p. 153), learn to surf, ride in a Hawaiian surfing canoe, or snorkel. Ease into your vacation and go to bed early, so you'll be raring to go the next day.

Day ❷: Adventure on the Water: Both Above & Below ★★

Take your pick: Sign up for **scuba diving** (p. 166); dive down in the **Atlantis Submarine** (p. 169), which takes you below the water's surface in the comfort of a high-tech submarine; or get out on the water in a boat. Even if you've gotten seasick in the past, *Navatek I* (p. 165) guarantees a smooth ride.

Day ❸: Hike Through a Tropical Rainforest & Up a Volcano ★★

Spend the day hiking, either into the **rainforest** (see **Manoa Falls Hike** on p. 174) or up to the top of an **old volcano** (see **Diamond Head Hike** on p. 171). Serious hikers might check out the **Makiki-Manoa** series of trails (p. 173). In the afternoon (except Tues, when the park is closed), get a mask, snorkel, and fins at **Snorkel Bob's** (p. 164) and go to **Hanauma Bay** (p. 156).

Day ❹: Up in the Air ★★

Soar through the air on gossamer-like wings via a **glider ride** (p. 182); get a bird's-eye view from a **hang glider** (p. 183); or, for the truly adventurous, leap from a plane in a **sky-diving** venture (p. 183). If these sound a bit too adventurous, take to the air

in the **Island Seaplane Service's** unforgettable tour of the entire island (p. 187). Plan to spend the rest of the day at one of Hawaii's beaches along the **North Shore** (p. 161).

Day ❺: Deep-Sea Fishing or Dolphin Watching ★★

Serious fishermen from around the globe dream of catching a "grander"—a Pacific Blue Marlin weighing a thousand pounds or more. You might try your luck by booking a **sportfishing boat** at Kewalo Basin (p. 168). Or spend the day in the water with **spinner dolphins**—with **Wild Side Tours** (p. 165), you can get up close and personal with these protected marine mammals.

Day ❻: Jaws: Eyeball-to-Eyeball with a Shark ★★

The truly adventurous will actually pay money to come eyeball-to-eyeball with a shark. Of course, a 6-foot×6-foot×10-foot aluminum cage separates the two of you. (You're the one in the cage, as the shark—or sharks!—swim around you.) Call **North Shore Shark Adventure** (p. 168) for this unforgettable experience. If you'd like a little more protection, head over to the **Waikiki Aquarium** (p. 200) and view some sharks through protective glass.

Day ❼: Relax & Be Pampered at a Spa ★★

After a week of adventures, plan a few hours at a **spa**. Oahu has several world-class spas sprinkled throughout the island. Check out my favorites in chapter 1 (p. 12).

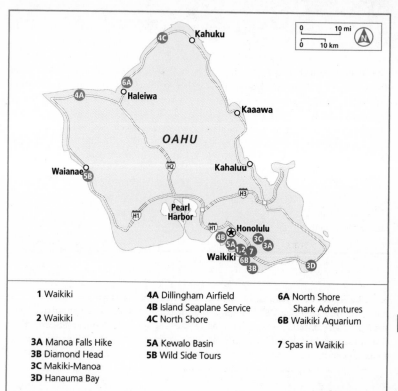

1 Waikiki	**4A** Dillingham Airfield	**6A** North Shore
	4B Island Seaplane Service	Shark Adventures
2 Waikiki	**4C** North Shore	**6B** Waikiki Aquarium
3A Manoa Falls Hike	**5A** Kewalo Basin	**7** Spas in Waikiki
3B Diamond Head	**5B** Wild Side Tours	
3C Makiki-Manoa		
3D Hanauma Bay		

4

Where to Stay

Though the island of Oahu is not the biggest in the Hawaiian chain, it offers the widest variety of accommodations. Should you stay in near-palatial surroundings where kings, heads of state, billionaires, and rock stars have spent the night, or in a quaint bed-and-breakfast on the North Shore where the rolling surf lulls you to sleep? Should you choose the bright lights and action of Waikiki or the quiet comforts of Kahala? Oahu has the perfect place for everyone.

The major **high season** is mid-December to March. At this time of year, rooms are always booked and rates are at the top end. Secondary high season is June to September, when rates are expensive, but bookings are somewhat easier. The **low season,** with fewer tourists, cheaper rates, and possible "deals" on rooms is April to June and September to mid-December.

Be sure to factor in Oahu's 11.962% tax, and don't forget about parking charges—up to $25 a day in Waikiki.

1 WAIKIKI

Some five million tourists visit Oahu every year, and 9 out of 10 of them choose accommodations in Waikiki, a 500-acre beachfront neighborhood of Honolulu. Here's where you'll find all the action—from fast food to fine dining, nightlife including everything from the sweet sounds of Hawaiian melodies to spicy dance music, shopping from bargains to brand names, and every ocean activity you can imagine. Staying here puts you in the heart of it all, but be aware that Waikiki is an on-the-go city with crowds, traffic, noise, and its fair share of crime.

WAIKIKI, EWA END

All the hotels listed below are located from the ocean to Ala Wai Boulevard, and between Ala Wai Terrace, in the Ewa Beach direction (or western side of Waikiki), and Olohana Street and Fort DeRussy Park, in the Diamond Head direction (or eastern side of Waikiki).

Very Expensive

Hawaii Prince Hotel Waikiki ★★ For a vacation with a view (and the feel of a palace), stay in this striking $150-million modern structure—actually, twin 33-story high-tech towers. The high-ceilinged lobby is a mass of pink Italian marble with English slate accents; a grand piano sits in the midst of the raised seating area, where high tea is served every afternoon. A glass-encased elevator with views of Honolulu whisks you up to your room. All bedrooms, which are larger than the average Waikiki hotel room, face the Ala Wai Yacht Harbor, with floor-to-ceiling sliding-glass windows that let you enjoy the view (sorry, no lanais); the higher the floor, the higher the price.

Following Japanese standards, the level of service is impeccable; no detail is ignored, and no request is too small. The outdoor pool is one of the few saltwater pools in Waikiki, with no chemicals or chlorine added. The location is perfect for shopping—Ala

Don't go asking for a balcony in Oahu; you won't find one. Instead, islanders call them lanais. If you're into balcony lounging, be sure to request a lanai with an ocean view.

Moana Center is a 10-minute walk away—and Waikiki's beaches are just a 5-minute walk away (both are also accessible via the hotel's shuttle bus). Culinary options include two great restaurants, one with award-winning Japanese cuisine and one with Euro-Asian buffets (Prince Court, p. 124), plus a lobby cafe coffee bar in the morning and a wine bar in the afternoon.

100 Holomoana St. (just across Ala Wai Canal Bridge, on the ocean side of Ala Moana Blvd.), Honolulu, HI 96815. (C) **800/321-OAHU** [6428] or 808/956-1111. Fax 808/946-0811. www.princeresortshawaii.com. 521 units. $390–$520 double; from $610 suite. Extra person $60. Children 17 and under stay free in parent's room. AE, DC, DISC, MC, V. Valet parking $21, self-parking $15. Bus: 19 or 20. **Amenities:** 2 restaurants; outdoor bar; babysitting; concierge; executive-level rooms; 27-hole golf club a 40-min. shuttle ride away in Ewa Beach; small but newly renovated fitness room; Jacuzzi; outdoor pool; room service; small day spa. *In room:* A/C, TV, fridge, hair dryer, Wi-Fi ($12/day).

Hilton Hawaiian Village Beach Resort & Spa ★★ **Kids** Sprawling over 20 acres on a gorgeous stretch of Waikiki Beach, Waikiki's biggest resort is a minicity unto itself, so big it even has its own post office. You'll find tropical gardens dotted with exotic birds, award-winning restaurants, 100 different shops, a secluded lagoon, and two minigolf courses. This is a great place to stay with the kids: The children's program, one of Waikiki's best, offers a wide range of educational and fun activities, and at three of the resort's restaurants, kids ages 4 to 11 eat free. In 2007, the property underwent a "Village Rejuvenation," with a total revamp of the Duke Kahanamoku Lagoon.

Rooms, which range from simply lovely to ultra-deluxe, are housed in five towers, each with its own restaurants and shopping. This division reduces the chaotic, impersonal feeling you can get from a resort this size. Still, this is the place for a lively, activity-packed vacation; those seeking a more intimate experience might want to look elsewhere. All rooms are large and beautifully furnished (the Tapa Tower rooms were renovated in 2007). If you can afford it, I highly recommend the ones in the Alii Tower, located right on the ocean. Guests in these 348 amenity-laden rooms and suites get the royal treatment, including in-room registration, an exclusive health club and pool, and the full attention of a multilingual staff.

The superluxe **Mandara Spa** ★★ also features a state-of-the-art fitness center. Not that you should plan to do business on your vacation, but for those who must stay in touch, there is a 24-hour hotel business center on property. The latest addition to the village was the recently opened $6-million **Ocean Crystal Chapel**, Waikiki's only freestanding resort wedding chapel, ready for couples to say their "I do's."

2005 Kalia Rd. (at Ala Moana Blvd.), Honolulu, HI 96815. (C) **800/HILTONS** [445-8667] or 808/949-4321. Fax 808/951-5458. www.hiltonhawaiianvillage.com. 2,860 units. $219–$620 double; from $639 suite. Extra person $50. Children 18 and under stay free in parent's room. AE, DC, DISC, MC, V. Valet parking $29, self-parking $24. Bus: 19 or 20. **Amenities:** 16 restaurants (including Bali by the Sea, p. 121); 5 bars; babysitting; children's program; concierge; concierge-level rooms; modern fitness center; 6 outdoor pools; room service; spa; watersports equipment rentals. *In room:* A/C, TV, fridge, hair dryer, high-speed Internet ($15/day).

ccommodations

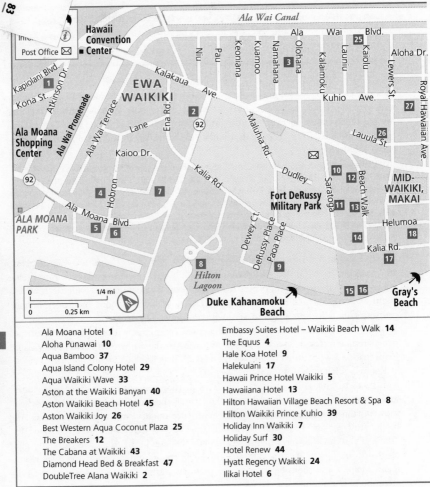

Ala Moana Hotel **1**
Aloha Punawai **10**
Aqua Bamboo **37**
Aqua Island Colony Hotel **29**
Aqua Waikiki Wave **33**
Aston at the Waikiki Banyan **40**
Aston Waikiki Beach Hotel **45**
Aston Waikiki Joy **26**
Best Western Aqua Coconut Plaza **25**
The Breakers **12**
The Cabana at Waikiki **43**
Diamond Head Bed & Breakfast **47**
DoubleTree Alana Waikiki **2**

Embassy Suites Hotel – Waikiki Beach Walk **14**
The Equus **4**
Hale Koa Hotel **9**
Halekulani **17**
Hawaii Prince Hotel Waikiki **5**
Hawaiiana Hotel **13**
Hilton Hawaiian Village Beach Resort & Spa **8**
Hilton Waikiki Prince Kuhio **39**
Holiday Inn Waikiki **7**
Holiday Surf **30**
Hotel Renew **44**
Hyatt Regency Waikiki **24**
Ilikai Hotel **6**

Expensive

The Ilikai Hotel You can't beat the location of the Ilikai Hotel—sitting at the entrance to Waikiki, it overlooks the Ala Wai Harbor and is within walking distance to numerous restaurants and shops. A rooftop pool with cabanas, reflecting pool in the lobby/courtyard, spa, second-floor pool, and cafe in the porte-cochere are some of the features here. Public areas display the spectacular ocean view, and rooms overlook the ocean and mountains. Ownership of these hotel/condo units has been in dispute over the last few years with lots of threats to close them down. Currently that fight seems to have died down. Great deals are offered for seniors, and family packages include rooms

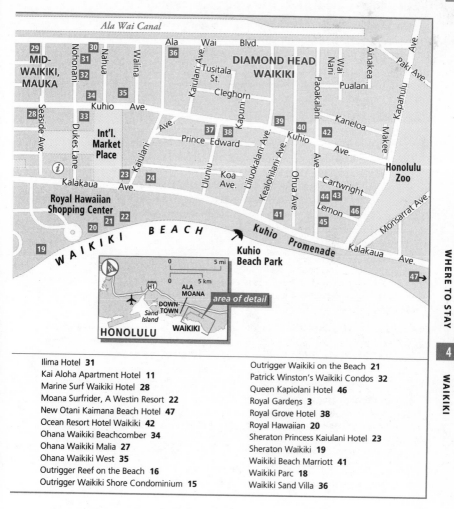

Ilima Hotel **31**
Kai Aloha Apartment Hotel **11**
Marine Surf Waikiki Hotel **28**
Moana Surfrider, A Westin Resort **22**
New Otani Kaimana Beach Hotel **47**
Ocean Resort Hotel Waikiki **42**
Ohana Waikiki Beachcomber **34**
Ohana Waikiki Malia **27**
Ohana Waikiki West **35**
Outrigger Reef on the Beach **16**
Outrigger Waikiki Shore Condominium **15**

Outrigger Waikiki on the Beach **21**
Patrick Winston's Waikiki Condos **32**
Queen Kapiolani Hotel **46**
Royal Gardens **3**
Royal Grove Hotel **38**
Royal Hawaiian **20**
Sheraton Princess Kaiulani Hotel **23**
Sheraton Waikiki **19**
Waikiki Beach Marriott **41**
Waikiki Parc **18**
Waikiki Sand Villa **36**

with full kitchen, midsize car, and free parking. Check the website for online deals, which can make this property very appealing money-wise.

1777 Ala Moana Blvd. (ocean side of Ala Moana Blvd., at Hobron Lane), Honolulu, HI 96815. © **800/367-8434** or 808/949-3811. Fax 808/947-0892. www.ilikaihotel.com. 343 units. $300–$450 double. Extra person $55. AE, DC, DISC, MC, V. Parking $20. Bus: 19 or 20. **Amenities:** Restaurant; bar; concierge; concierge-level rooms; fitness room; Jacuzzi; pool; room service; 4 Plexipave tennis courts. *In room:* A/C, TV, hair dryer; high-speed Internet ($13/day); kitchen (in some units).

Moderate
DoubleTree Alana Hotel Waikiki ★   This boutique hotel operated by the Hilton Hawaiian Village is a welcome oasis of beauty, comfort, and service. It's an intimate

choice, offering the amenities of a much larger, more luxurious hotel at affordable prices. The guest rooms underwent a $2.9-million renovation, with new carpet, wallpaper, woven-palm-frond curtains, refinished and reupholstered furniture, 25-inch TVs, and "Sweet Dream" pillow beds. Some rooms may be small but make good use of the space and offer all the amenities you'd expect from a more expensive hotel. Wireless Internet access is available throughout the hotel, and hard-wired DSL service is on four floors. Many guests are business travelers who expect top-drawer service—and the Alana Waikiki delivers. The staff is attentive to detail and willing to go to great lengths to make you happy. Waikiki Beach is a 10-minute walk away, and the convention center is about a 7-minute walk.

1956 Ala Moana Blvd. (on the Ewa side, near Kalakaua Ave.), Honolulu, HI 96815. (C) **800/222-TREE** [8733] or 808/941-7275. Fax 808/949-0996. www.doubletree.com. 317 units. $139–$349 double; from $259 suite. Extra person $40. Children under 18 stay free in parent's room. AE, DC, DISC, MC, V. Valet parking $25. Bus: 19 or 20. **Amenities:** Bar; concierge; poolside fitness center; outdoor heated pool; room service. *In room:* A/C, TV, fridge, hair dryer, high-speed Internet ($10/day).

Holiday Inn—Waikiki Just 2 blocks from the beach, 2 blocks from Ala Moana Shopping Center, and a 7-minute walk from the convention center, this Holiday Inn has a great location and offers this chain's usual amenities for prices that are quite reasonable for Waikiki. All rooms, which have a modern Japanese look, are equipped with either a king-size bed or two doubles. The property sits back from the street, so noise is minimal. Staff is unbelievably friendly.

1830 Ala Moana Blvd. (btw. Hobron Lane and Kalia Rd.), Honolulu, HI 96815. (C) **888/992-4545** or 808/955-1111. Fax 808/947-1799. www.hnlwaikiki.com. 199 units. $113–$175 double; from $250 suite. Children 19 and under stay free in parent's room. AE, DC, DISC, MC, V. Parking $13. Bus: 19 or 20. **Amenities:** Restaurant; small fitness room; outdoor pool; room service. *In room:* A/C, TV, fridge, hair dryer, Wi-Fi (free).

Royal Gardens (Finds) This quiet, boutique hotel, tucked away on a tree-lined side street is now being managed by Wyndham Hotels, with talk about renovations (no structural changes) in the future. In the interim, rates are very reasonable, but keep in mind that the beach is a few blocks away, about a 10–15 minute walk (worth the walk at these prices).

440 Olohana St. (btw. Kuhio Ave. and Ala Wai Blvd.), Honolulu, HI 96815. (C) **800/367-5666** or 808/943-0202. Fax 808/946-8777. 210 units. www.royalgardens.com. $55–$105 double; from $150 suite. Extra person $25. Children under 12 stay free in parent's room. AE, DC, DISC, MC, V. Parking $18. Bus: 19 or 20. **Amenities:** 2 restaurants; lounge; small fitness room; 2 Jacuzzis; 2 freshwater outdoor pools (1 w/cascading waterfall); 2 saunas. *In room:* A/C, TV, fridge, hair dryer, kitchenette.

Inexpensive

The Equus Formerly the Hawaii Polo Inn, now under the management of Aqua Hotels and Resorts, this small boutique hotel has been renovated and upgraded into a very comfortable inn within walking distance of the Ala Moana Shopping Center,

Waikiki Beach, and the Hawaii Convention Center. All but one of the modest-sized rooms are shower-only, and studio suites are proportionately small but have microwaves and hot plates. A few years ago, the management added additional studio units (with kitchenettes, two-burner stove, dishwasher, and microwave) next door at the Aqua Marina Hotel. *Warning:* Ala Moana Boulevard is very noisy; ask for a room in the back or bring earplugs. Also, the neighborhood can be a little dicey after dark.

1696 Ala Moana Blvd. (btw. Hobron Lane and Ala Wai Canal), Honolulu, HI 96815. ✆ **866/406-2782** or 808/949-0061. Fax 808/949-4906. www.aquaresorts.com/aqua-equus. 68 units (all with shower only). $84–$204 double; $214–$294 suite; from $91 studio with kitchenette in Aqua Waikiki Marina next door. Extra person $25. Children 18 and under stay free in parent's room. AE, DISC, MC, V. Parking $19. Bus: 19 or 20. **Amenities:** Tiny outdoor wading pool. *In room:* A/C, TV, fridge, hair dryer, Internet (free), microwave.

MID-WAIKIKI, MAKAI

All the hotels listed below are between the ocean and Kalakaua Avenue, and between Fort DeRussy in the Ewa (west) direction and Kaiulani Street in the Diamond Head (east) direction.

Very Expensive

Embassy Suites Hotel–Waikiki Beach Walk ★★★ (Kids) This ultra-luxurious outpost of the hotel chain, known for its complimentary, all-you-can-eat, "cooked to order" breakfast and evening manager's cocktail reception, has one of the best central locations in Waikiki. The beach is just a block away from the all-suite-hotel's location amid the shops and restaurants of the newly opened beach walk (see box, "Big Changes in Waikiki: Waikiki Beach Walk," p. 94). The one- and two-bedroom suites feature top-of-the-line furniture, Hawaiian decor (such as bronze hula lamps), plush mattresses, high-quality linen, granite bathroom counters, CD/MP3 players, and views from every window (some are oceanview). The amenities here are numerous; each suite features a separate living room, flat-panel LCD-TV, minifridge, wet bar, microwave, coffeemaker, and lots of entertainment electronics to keep the teenagers happy. The two-towered property is connected via a huge lobby area (with sun deck, swimming pool, waterfall, and covered terrace where those yummy breakfasts are served). At first glance the prices may seem high, but when you add in the included breakfast, evening reception, and amenities, it pencils out to quite a deal for families.

201 Beachwalk St., Honolulu, HI 96815 ✆ **800/EMBASSY** [362-2779] or 808/921-2345. Fax 808/921-2343. www.waikikibeach.embassysuites.com. 421 suites. $249–$329 1-bedroom; $449–$549 2-bedroom. Extra person (over 2 people) in 1-bedroom) $50. AE, DC, DISC, MC, V. Parking $25. Bus: 19 or 20. **Amenities:** Complimentary "cooked to order" breakfast and cocktail party daily; nearby restaurants and bars; bike rentals; children's program in summer and at Christmas; 24-hr. concierge; 24-hour fitness center; outdoor pool and whirlpool spa; room service (lunch and dinner); watersports equipment rentals. *In room:* A/C, TV/DVD, CD/MP3 player, small fridge, hair dryer, microwave, Wi-Fi (free), free local and long-distance calls.

Halekulani ★★★ (Kids) Here's the ultimate heavenly Hawaii vacation. Halekulani translates as "house befitting heaven"—an apt description of this luxury resort spread over 5 acres of prime Waikiki beachfront. Its five buildings are connected by open court-yards and lush, tropical gardens. Upon arrival, you're immediately greeted and escorted to your room, where registration is handled in comfort and privacy. About 90% of the rooms face the ocean, and they're big (averaging 620 sq. ft.), each with a separate sitting area and a large, furnished lanai. Each bathroom features a deep soaking tub, a separate glassed-in shower, and a marble basin. Recent renovations to this luxury property include total refurbishment of the rooms: new entertainment centers with DVD players, a bedside control panel, wireless Internet service, and a new spa.

Other perks include complimentary tickets to any or all of the following: Ihilani Palace, Bishop Museum, Contemporary Art Museum, Honolulu Academy of Arts, and the Honolulu Symphony. A great children's program is offered during the summer and Christmas. The hotel's restaurants (including La Mer, p. 120, and Orchids, p. 123) are outstanding, and the **House Without a Key** ★★ is surely one of the world's most romantic spots for sunset cocktails, light meals, and entertainment. You can't find a better location on Waikiki Beach or a more luxurious hotel.

2199 Kalia Rd. (at the ocean end of Lewers St.), Honolulu, HI 96815. © **800/367-2343** or 808/923-2311. Fax 808/926-8004. www.halekulani.com. 455 units. $425–$750; from $875 suite. Extra person $125. 1 child under 17 stays free in parent's room using existing bedding; additional rollaway bed $40. Maximum 3 people per room. AE, DC, MC, V. Self-parking $24; valet $24. Bus: 19 or 20. **Amenities:** 3 superb restaurants (including La Mer, p. 120, and Orchids, p. 123); 2 bars (including Lewers Lounge, p. 254); babysitting; bike rentals; children's program in summer and at Christmas; 24-hr. concierge; fitness center; gorgeous outdoor pool; room service; spa; watersports equipment rentals. *In room:* A/C, TV/DVD, hair dryer, minibar, Wi-Fi (free).

Moana Surfrider, A Westin Resort ★★ Ⓚⁱᵈˢ This wonderful property was Waikiki's first hotel—it dates from 1901 and is listed on the National Register of Historic Places. The Westin recently completed renovations (with their Heavenly Beds installed, new flatscreen TVs added), added the Westin Kids Club child-care program, and added a new spa, which fills most of the second floor. It's hard to get a bad room here (even before the renovations)—most bedrooms have ocean views and all come with bedside controls, luxury amenities, and comfy plush bathrobes. My pick is the Banyan Wing, where the historic rooms are modern replicas of the hotel's first rooms. They are small and don't have lanais, but they're all reminiscent of Hawaii circa 1901, when steam-ship travel with big trunks was the only way to see Hawaii. Back then, the Moana was considered an innovation in the travel industry: Each guest room featured a private bathroom and a telephone—an unheard-of luxury in the early 20th century. And yesteryear lives on at this grand hotel: The female employees wear traditional Victorian-era muu-muu, and the aloha spirit that pervades this classy and charming hotel is infectious.

ⓘ**Tips** **B&B Etiquette**

In Hawaii, it is traditional and customary to remove your shoes before entering anyone's home. The same is true for most bed-and-breakfast facilities. Most hosts post signs or will politely ask you to remove your shoes before entering the B&B. Not only does this keep the place clean, but you'll also be amazed at how relaxing it is to walk around barefoot. If this custom is unpleasant to you, a B&B may not be for you.

If you've never stayed at a B&B before, here are a few other hints: Generally the hosts live on the property, and their part of the house is off-limits to guests (you do not have the "run of the house"). Most likely there will be a common area that you can use. Don't expect daily maid service. Your host may tidy up, but will not do complete maid service. Also don't expect amenities like little bottles of shampoo and conditioner—this is a B&B, not a resort. Remember you are sharing your accommodations with other guests, so be considerate when you come in late at night.

One of the best reasons to stay here is the hotel's prime stretch of beach, with a lifeguard, beach chairs, towels, and any other service you desire. The Beach Bar and a poolside snack bar are located in an oceanfront courtyard centering on a 100-year-old banyan tree, where live music is featured in the evenings.

2365 Kalakaua Ave. (ocean side of the street, across from Kaiulani St.), Honolulu, HI 96815. (C) **800/325-3535** or 808/922-3111. Fax 808/923-0308. www.moana-surfrider.com or www.starwoodhotelshawaii.com. 793 units. $430–$740 double; from $1,775 suite. Extra person and rollaway bed $85. Children under 18 stay free in parent's room using existing bedding. AE, DC, DISC, MC, V. Valet parking $26; self-parking at sister property $20. Bus: 19 or 20. **Amenities:** 3 restaurants; bar; babysitting; children's program; concierge; nearby fitness room (about a 2-min. walk down the beach at the Sheraton Waikiki); outdoor pool; room service; watersports equipment rentals. *In room:* A/C, TV, fridge, hair dryer, high-speed Internet access ($14/day).

Outrigger Waikiki on the Beach ★ (Kids)   The same value and quality that I've come to expect in every Outrigger hotel are definitely in evidence here, only multiplied by a factor of 10. Even the standard rooms in this 16-story oceanfront hotel are large and comfortable. The prime beachfront location and loads of facilities help make this one of the chain's most attractive properties. Even if you aren't staying here, wander through the renovated lobby, filled with rare and historic Hawaiian artifacts (like a century-old canoe made of koa). The guest rooms all have huge closets, plenty of amenities, and a spacious lanai; the price is entirely dependent on the view. Roomy bathrooms feature granite vanity tops, ceramic floor tiles, and lighted makeup mirrors. Just added: free high-speed Internet connection (most hotels charge $11 a day) and free phone calls to Hawaii and the U.S. mainland. If money is no object, book the Deluxe Oceanfront units, which feature oversize Jacuzzi bathtubs with ocean views of Waikiki Beach. Don't miss the Hula Grill Waikiki (p. 127) and the **Waikiki Plantation Spa** ((C) **808/926-2880;** www.waikikiplantationspa.com), located in the penthouse, which affords fabulous views. Another great amenity is the flight check-in service: Hawaiian Airlines customers can check in and get boarding passes and luggage tags in the lobby (daily 7:30–11:30am) and avoid the lines at the airport.

2335 Kalakaua Ave. (btw. the Royal Hawaiian Shopping Center and the Moana Surfrider), Honolulu, HI 96815. (C) **800/OUTRIGGER** [688-7444] or 808/923-0711. Fax 800/622-4852. www.outrigger.com. 525 units. $213–$779 double; from $679 suite. Ask about package deals, like 5th night free or discount rates for seniors over 50. Extra person $50. Children 17 and under stay free in parent's room using existing bedding. AE, DC, DISC, MC, V. Valet-only parking $25. Bus: 19 or 20. **Amenities:** 3 restaurants (including Hula Grill Waikiki, p. 127, and Duke's Waikiki, p. 126); 3 bars; showroom w/nightly entertainment; babysitting; year-round children's program; concierge; concierge-level rooms; fitness center; Jacuzzi; giant outdoor pool; room service; new Waikiki Plantation Spa; watersports equipment rentals. *In room:* A/C, TV, fridge, hair dryer, high-speed Internet access (free), kitchenette (in some units), free calls to Hawaii and U.S. mainland.

Royal Hawaiian ★★   This flamingo-pink oasis, hidden away among blooming gardens within the concrete jungle of Waikiki, is the height of luxury. Built by Matson steamship lines, the Spanish-Moorish "Pink Palace" opened in 1927 on the same spot where Queen Kaahumanu had her summer palace—on one of the best stretches of Waikiki Beach.

Pass through the lush garden with a spectacular banyan tree, then step into the black terrazzo-marble lobby, which features hand-woven pink carpets and giant floral arrangements. Historic touches include Hawaiian craft displays (quilts, leis, weaving) by local artists every Monday, Wednesday, and Friday, and a new guest activity program with ukulele lessons, lei making, *lauhala* weaving, hula classes, historic tours, and evening

(Kids) Family-Friendly Hotels

If you're traveling with the kids, you'll be welcomed by many of Oahu's resorts, condos, and B&Bs. Our favorite family-friendly accommodations on the island are listed below. If you're looking for a hotel that has supervised activities for your youngster, you might want to consider the **Moana Surfrider, A Westin Resort** (p. 88), which has a great children's program. For a more moderately priced option, try the **Waikiki Sand Villa** (p. 106), in Waikiki, or **Schrader's Windward Country Inn** (p. 110), in Kaneohe. **Embassy Suites Hotel–Waikiki Beach Walk** (p. 87) ain't cheap, but it does give good overall bang for your buck while keeping your kid's social calendar full—they offer children's programs during summer and at Christmas. **Outrigger Waikiki on the Beach** (p. 89) offers children's programs and babysitting services; plus, children stay free in their parents' room at Outrigger Waikiki and its sister hotel, Outrigger Reef on the Beach (p. 92). For full kitchen facilities, look into **Ohana Waikiki Malia** (p. 99) and **ResortQuest at the Waikiki Banyan** (p. 102).

Waikiki:

Hilton Hawaiian Village (p. 83)   The Rainbow Express Keiki Club is Hilton's year-round daily program of activities for children ages 5 to 12. The program costs $80 for a full day, including lunch, and another $6 if you want the excursion, or $50 for a half-day with lunch (add another $3 for an excursion). It offers a wide range of educational and fun activities: Hawaiian arts and crafts, nature walks, wildlife feedings, shell hunting, fishing, and much more. Everything about this hotel is kid-friendly, from the wildlife parading about the grounds to the submarine dives offered just out front.

Halekulani (p. 87)   Between early June and mid-August and during Christmastime, the Halekulani, possibly my favorite hotel in the islands, has a wonderful supervised program for children ages 5 to 12, called the Keikilani (Heavenly Child) Club, normally available Monday to Friday from 9am to 4pm. The $50 fee (the 2nd child in the same family is only $40) includes such goodies as a complimentary backpack with matching water bottle, plus lunch and admission to activities. Daily programs include crafts, games, sightseeing, and excursions to Sea Life Park, the Children's Discovery Center, the Waikiki Aquarium, or the Honolulu Zoo. On-site restaurants House Without A Key and Orchids offer children's menus, with coloring books and crayons to keep youngsters occupied.

Sheraton Waikiki (p. 92)   The Keiki Aloha Program offers year-round activities for children ages 5 to 12 ($50 for one session; winter: morning and afternoon; summer: morning, afternoon, or evening), and supervised meals are available

"talk story" sessions featuring Hawaiian legends. My heart was won over by the Historic Wing's rooms, which contain carved wooden doors, four-poster canopy beds, flowered wallpaper, and period furniture. If you prefer the newer rooms, the latest decor is more Tommy Bahama, with a tropical palm tree motif.

for lunch ($12) and dinner ($12). Activities include boogie boarding, kite flying, sailing on a catamaran, and watching nightly movies. The program is available to all guests of Sheraton and Westin hotels in Waikiki. Just added are Family Days (Sun and Mon), when both parent(s) and child can visit attractions (such as Waikiki Aquarium and the zoo) or participate in activities including hula, lei making, and boogie boarding. Cost is $10 per parent.

Hawaiiana Hotel (p. 95)   This budget hotel in the heart of Waikiki, just a block from the beach, has terrific deals for families of four or less. Starting at $235, a one-bedroom with kitchenette (a big help on the food bill!), has two beds (a double and a single or a queen plus a sofa bed), a view of the gardens, and access to two swimming pools. The friendly staff welcomes families and will happily point out great places to take the kids.

Ilima Hotel (p. 98)   Very popular with locals from neighboring islands, this hotel was designed with families in mind. The units are large, and all have full-size kitchens. Although there's no formal children's program, you'll find free HBO, the Disney Channel, and Nintendo video games in each room—and the coin-op laundry is a big help to Mom and Dad. The beach and the International Market Place are both a short walk away, and TheBus stops just outside.

Beyond Waikiki:

The Kahala Hotel & Resort (p. 108)   The Keiki Club is the year-round activities program for kids ages 5 to 12. Youngsters have a blast dancing the hula, making leis, designing sand sculptures, putting on puppet shows, learning to strum a ukulele, making shell art and fish prints, listening to Hawaiian folk tales and legends, and playing Hawaiian games. The cost is $65 for a full day, 9am to 4pm (including lunch); $45 for a half-day, with lunch; and $35 for a half-day without lunch.

Leeward Oahu:

J.W. Marriott Ihilani Resort & Spa at Ko Olina (p. 113)   The Keiki Beach-comber Club, for children ages 4 to 12, is available daily (9am–3pm) during peak winter, spring, and summer seasons. Activities include kite flying, tide-pool exploration, snorkeling, water games, shave-ice making, beach Olympics, crab hunting, and fishing. Hawaiian cultural activities include lei making, hula dancing, and so many other activities that you're unlikely to even see the kids until you're getting ready for dinner. The cost is $60 per child, which includes all activities, lunch, and a souvenir on their first day at the club; half-day rate is $50 with lunch and $45 without.

One of Waikiki's best spas, **Abhasa** ★★ (© **808/922-8200;** www.abhasa.com), is located on-site. This large contemporary spa concentrates on natural, organic treatments in a soothing atmosphere (the smell of eucalyptus wafts through the air) with everything from the latest aromatherapy thalassotherapy (soaking in a sweet-smelling hot bath of salt water) to shiatsu massages. Its specialty is a cold-laser, anti-aging treatment that promises to give you a refreshed, revitalized face in just 30 minutes.

In the culinary department, the Surf Room is known for its elaborate seafood buffets, while the casual Beach Club features an oceanfront patio that's a great place to start your day. The Royal Hawaiian luau is done in grand style on Monday nights. The hotel's **Mai Tai Bar** ★★ is one of the most popular places in Waikiki for its namesake drink, which supposedly originated here.

2259 Kalakaua Ave. (at Royal Hawaiian Ave., on the ocean side of the Royal Hawaiian Shopping Center), Honolulu, HI 96815. ⓒ **800/325-3535** or 808/923-7311. Fax 808/924-7098. www.royal-hawaiian.com or www.starwoodhotelshawaii.com. 527 units. $370–$630 double; from $440 suite. Extra person $125. Ask about special packages. AE, DC, DISC, MC, V. Valet parking $26; self-parking at Sheraton Waikiki $20. Bus: 19 or 20. **Amenities:** 2 restaurants; landmark bar; babysitting; bike rentals; excellent year-round children's program; multilingual concierge desk; preferential tee times at various golf courses; excellent nearby fitness room (next door at the Sheraton Waikiki); good-size outdoor pool; room service; full-service spa (Abhasa); watersports equipment rentals. *In room:* A/C, TV, fridge, hair dryer, high-speed Internet access ($15/day).

Sheraton Waikiki ★ (Kids) Occupying two 30-story towers, this is by far the biggest of the four beachfront Sheratons. The lobby is immense and filled with shops, travel desks, and people, including loads of conventioneers. If you're not comfortable with crowds, book elsewhere. However, size has its advantages: The Sheraton has everything from a fabulous kids' program (boogie boarding, kite flying, nightly movies) to historical walks and cooking demonstrations for Mom and Dad. Plus, you can "play and charge" (it back to your tab) at Waikiki's other Sheraton hotels.

It's hard to get a bad room here. A whopping 1,200 units have some sort of ocean view, and 650 rooms overlook Diamond Head. Accommodations are spacious, with big lanais for taking it all in. The Sheraton has a minimalist design, and amenities include its trademark "Sweet Sleeper" bed, big LCD flatscreen TVs, and high-speed Internet ($14/day). For the budget-conscious, the Sheraton Manor Hotel occupies a separate adjacent wing and offers all the services and beachfront of the main hotel. The views aren't the best, and the rooms are small and modestly appointed (no lanai), but the price is hard to beat.

2255 Kalakaua Ave. (at Royal Hawaiian Ave., on the ocean side of the Royal Hawaiian Shopping Center and west of the Royal Hawaiian), Honolulu, HI 96815. ⓒ **800/325-3535** or 808/922-4422. Fax 808/923-8785. www.sheraton.com or www.starwoodhotelshawaii.com. 1,852 units. $189–$329 double; from $753 suite. Extra person $80. Children under 18 stay free in parent's room. AE, DC, DISC, MC, V. Valet parking $26; self-parking $20. Bus: 19 or 20. **Amenities:** 4 restaurants; 3 bars; nightclub; babysitting; bike rentals; children's program; concierge; access to Makaha Golf Club's golf and tennis facilities (about 1 hr. away); fitness center; 2 large outdoor pools, including one of the biggest and sunniest along the Waikiki beachfront; room service; watersports equipment rentals. *In room:* A/C, TV, fridge, hair dryer, high-speed Internet access ($13/day), kitchenette, minibar.

Expensive

Outrigger Reef on the Beach ★ (Kids) Location, location, location! This big hotel is right on Waikiki Beach, across from Fort DeRussy, with three towers of beautifully appointed rooms (completely remodeled in 2007–08), excellent service, and a myriad of activities, shops, and restaurants. The $100 million in renovations really was closer to a "rebuild" and the rooms were redesigned and upgraded (with 32-in. LCD TVs). The new porte-cochere, which resembles a traditional A-frame canoe longhouse, in fact houses a 100-year-old Hawaiian fishing canoe. Throughout the lobby are enough shops to qualify as a mini-mall. Off the lobby is an enormous swimming pool, with some 300 chaise lounges surrounding it, three whirlpool spas, and food and cocktail service within hailing distance. And, of course, beautiful Waikiki is in the backyard. The rooms have the usual well-designed, well-appointed Outrigger furnishings and decorations with great views and plenty of extra room for a couple of kids to bed down. Blackout drapes are a nice touch for jet-lagged travelers, as is a hospitality room (with showers) for early check-ins or late checkouts. The on-site Shorebird Beach Broiler is an immensely popular oceanside spot offering buffet breakfasts and broil-your-own dinners. Another great amenity is flight check-in for Hawaiian Airlines customers: Get boarding passes and luggage tags in the lobby (daily 7:30–11:30am) and avoid the lines at the airport.

2335 Kalakaua Ave. (btw. the Royal Hawaiian Shopping Center and the Moana Surfrider), Honolulu, HI 96815. ℂ **800/OUTRIGGER** [688-7444] or 808/923-0711. Fax 800/622-4852. www.outrigger.com. 525 units. $213–$779 double; from $679 suite. Ask about package deals, such as 5th night free or discount rates for seniors over 50. Extra person $50. Children 17 and under stay free in parent's room using existing bedding. AE, DC, DISC, MC, V. Valet-only parking $25. Bus: 19 or 20. **Amenities:** 3 restaurants (including Hula Grill Waikiki, p. 127, and Duke's Waikiki, p. 126); 3 bars; showroom w/nightly entertainment; babysitting; year-round children's program; concierge; concierge-level rooms; fitness center; new Waikiki Plantation Spa; Jacuzzi; giant outdoor pool; room service; watersports equipment rentals. *In room:* A/C, TV, fridge, hair dryer, high-speed Internet access (free), kitchenette (in some units), free calls to Hawaii and U.S. mainland.

Outrigger Waikiki Shore Condominium ★★

As soon as you arrive, you'll see why everyone wants to stay here: the location (right on Waikiki beach, close to restaurants and shopping) and the view (a spectacular panoramic vista of the entire shoreline from Diamond Head to Honolulu). The apartments—which are privately owned and decorated and then rented through Outrigger—range in size from studios to two-bedrooms. Each has a fully equipped kitchen, big lanai, spacious sitting area, washer/dryer, and fabulous views. Full-time residents also live in this complex, so it tends to be quiet and security is tight—entry to the units is through a locked gate and keyed elevators. Because this establishment is part of the Outrigger chain, guests have full access to the Outrigger Reef (right next door), including its pool, exercise room, and business center. Daily maid service, a few on-site shops, and plenty of assistance from the front desk give this condominium stay all the benefits of hotel service with the roominess of your own apartment. As you might expect, reservations are hard to get; book *way* in advance.

2161 Kalia Rd. (on the ocean at Saratoga Rd., across the street from Ft. DeRussy), Honolulu, HI 96815. ℂ **800/OUTRIGGER** [688-7444]. Fax 800/622-4852. www.outrigger.com. 168 units. $355–$355 studio double; $435–$685 1-bedroom apt. (sleeps up to 4); $460–$650 2-bedroom apt. (up to 6). Ask about Outrigger package deals such as free car rental or bed-and-breakfast deals. AE, DC, DISC, MC, V. Valet parking $25; self-parking $18. Bus: 19 or 20. **Amenities:** Outdoor pool; access to all the facilities at the Outrigger Reef next door (including 3 restaurants, 3 bars, babysitting, children's program, concierge, fitness room, Jacuzzi). *In room:* A/C, TV/VCR, fridge, hair dryer, kitchen, washer/dryer.

Waikiki Parc ★★

Recently redesigned and renovated, especially for the 20s-to-30s crowds, this "hidden" hotel offers lots of bonuses: terrifically located, just 100 yards from the beach, it's managed and run by the ultra-luxury Halekulani Hotel (but comes at a more reasonable price). The compact, beautifully appointed rooms have a contemporary, Hawaiian-Zen decor. Rooms are more spacious, and wired Internet access was installed (the thick concrete walls, plus the density of Waikiki buildings, make wireless reception practically impossible). All rooms have lanais with ocean, mountain, or city views. Nice extras include adjustable floor-to-ceiling shutters for those who want to sleep in. The Parc features the same level of service that has made the Halekulani famous and offers an excellent restaurant, Nobu Waikiki, known for its famous chef and cutting-edge Japanese cuisine.

Big Changes in Waikiki: Waikiki Beach Walk

One of Waikiki's biggest projects in decades is the total renovation of an 8-acre area (bound by Saratoga Rd., Kalakaua Ave., Lewers St. and Kalia Rd.) called the "Waikiki Beach Walk." The project, by Outrigger Hotels & Resorts, cost some $460 million.

Phase One, completed in 2007, reconfigured the formerly very congested area (narrow streets, with lots of delivery trucks double-parked, crowded sidewalks, and no vegetation) into an oasis of broad sidewalks, tropical foliage, water features, open space and new, totally renovated hotels. Eleven hotels were razed, upgraded, or changed to suites or condos. Five hotels and one timeshare condominium remains. The bad news for budget travelers is the more-affordable near-oceanfront hotels, neighborhood eateries, and small independent shops have been replaced with luxury (higher-priced) properties with 90,000 square feet of swank shops and trendy restaurants to match, all linked through pedestrian bridges and connecting walkways.

Changes to the hotels in this area include:

- The former 480-room Ohana Reef Towers is now a 193-condominium unit timeshare, operated by Outrigger, and renamed **Wyndham Waikiki Beach Walk.**
- The Ohana Edgewater and Ohana Coral Seas were razed and replaced by **Waikiki Beach Walk,** a 90,000-square-foot retail/entertainment complex with 40 retail shops, four major restaurants, four smaller food and beverage spots, and an open pedestrian plaza.
- The former Ohana Waikiki Village and the Ohana Waikiki Tower hotels, which had a total of 881 rooms, were demolished and an **Embassy Suites-Waikiki Beach Walk,** with a total of 421 suites, was built to replace them.
- The **Outrigger Reef on the Beach** totally refurbished its rooms.
- The **Ohana Islander Waikiki,** on the corner of Kalakaua Avenue and Lewers Street, has renovated its 280 units.

2233 Helumoa Rd. (at Lewers St.), Honolulu, HI 96815. © 800/422-0450 or 808/921-7272. Fax 808/923-1336. www.waikikiparc.com. 297 units. $269–$339 double. Extra person $80. Children 17 and under stay free in parent's room. Ask about room and package deals that start at just $265 a night. AE, DC, MC, V. Valet or self-parking $20. Bus: 19 or 20. **Amenities:** 2 restaurants; weekly wine reception; babysitting; concierge; fitness center; 8th-floor pool deck; room service. *In room:* A/C, TV, fridge, hair dryer, high-speed Internet access ($10/day).

Inexpensive

Aloha Punawai (Value) Here's one of Waikiki's best-kept secrets: a low-profile, family-operated (since 1959) apartment hotel just 2 blocks from the beach and within walking distance of most Waikiki attractions. Waikiki is going upscale and expensive (see "Big Changes in Waikiki: Waikiki Beach Walk," p. 94), so who knows how much longer the old-fashioned accommodations along Saratoga Road and Beach Walk will remain. The Aloha Punawai offers some of the lowest prices in Waikiki; if you stay a week, prices drop even more. And the location is great, just across the street from Fort DeRussy Park and 2 blocks to Grey's Beach, the same great beach shared by the luxury Halekulani and Sheraton Waikiki hotels. The apartments contain a mishmash of furniture and come with full kitchens and lanais. Don't expect the Ritz (or any interior decoration, for that matter), just sparkling-clean accommodations in a great location. Towels and linens are provided. Bathrooms in studios are shower-only.

305 Saratoga Rd. (across from Fort DeRussy and the Waikiki post office, btw. Kalia Rd. and Kalakaua Ave.), Honolulu, HI 96815. © **866/713-9694** or 808/923-5211. Fax 808/923-5211. www.alternative-hawaii. com/alohapunawai. 19 units (studios with shower only). $110–$120 studio double; $125–$150 1-bedroom double (sleeps up to 5). Children 16 and under stay free in parent's room with existing bedding. Extra person $12. Discounts for stays of 1 week or longer. MC, V. Parking $10 (limited). Bus: 19 or 20. *In room:* A/C, TV, fridge, kitchen, no phone.

The Breakers ★ (Value)

Another great buy just a 2-minute walk from numerous restaurants, shopping, and Waikiki Beach, The Breakers is about old-fashioned Hawaiian aloha, comfortable budget accommodations, and family-friendly prices. This two-story 1950s hotel has an accommodating staff and a loyal following. Its six buildings are set around a pool and a tropical garden blooming with brilliant red and yellow hibiscus; wooden jalousies and shoji doors further the tropical ambience. Each of the tastefully decorated, slightly oversize rooms comes with a lanai, kitchenette, and shower-only bathroom. Every Wednesday and Friday, you're invited (as a paying guest) to a formal Japanese tea ceremony from 10am to noon at the Urasenke Tea House next door.

250 Beach Walk (btw. Kalakaua Ave. and Kalia Rd.), Honolulu, HI 96815. © **800/426-0494** or 808/923-3181. Fax 808/923-7174. www.breakers-hawaii.com. 64 units (all with shower only). $130–$150 double; $185 garden studio double. Each additional person $20. AE, DC, MC, V. Limited free parking (just 7 stalls); additional parking across the street $11/day. Bus: 19 or 20. **Amenities:** Restaurant (poolside bar Mon–Fri; grill Fri lunch only); outdoor pool. *In room:* A/C, TV, fridge, hair dryer (on request), kitchenette.

Hawaiiana Hotel ★ (Kids) (Finds)

The hotel's slogan—"The spirit of old Hawaii"—says it all. The lush tropical flowers and carved tiki at the entrance on Beach Walk set the tone for this intimate low-rise hotel. From the moment you arrive, you'll be embraced by the aloha spirit: At check-in, you're given a pineapple, and complimentary Kona coffee and tropical juice are served poolside every morning. The concrete, hollow-tiled guest rooms feature kitchenettes and two beds (a double and a single or a queen-size plus a sofa bed), which makes the Hawaiiana a great choice for families (as does the welcoming, helpful staff). Each room has a view of the gardens and two swimming pools; some bathrooms are shower-only. Hawaiian entertainment is featured every week. The hotel is about a block from the beach and within walking distance of Waikiki shopping and nightlife.

260 Beach Walk (near Kalakaua Ave.), Honolulu, HI 96815. © **800/367-5122** or 808/923-3811. Fax 808/926-5728. www.hawaiianahotelatwaikiki.com. 95 units (some with shower only). $125–$215 double; $235 1-bedroom with kitchenette (sleeps up to 4). Extra person $25. AE, DC, DISC, MC, V. Parking $15. Bus: 19 or 20. **Amenities:** Barbecue; 2 good-size outdoor pools. *In room:* A/C, TV, fridge, high-speed Internet access ($5/day), kitchenette.

Kai Aloha Apartment Hotel (Value)

If you want to experience the Waikiki of 40 years past, stay here. This small apartment hotel just a block from the beach is reminiscent of the low-key hotels that used to line the blocks of Waikiki in the good old days. It offers one-bedroom apartments and studios, all furnished in modest rattan and colorful island prints. Each of the one-bedroom units has a bedroom with either a queen-size bed or two twins, a living room with a couch and two additional twins (Hawaiian houses of 40 years ago all had extra guest beds, called *punee,* in the living room), a full kitchen, a dining table, and even voicemail. Rooms are large enough to accommodate a roll-away bed for a fifth person. Glass jalousies take advantage of the cooling trade winds, and there's air-conditioning for very hot days. Studios have two twin beds, kitchenette, balcony, Plexiglas roof in the bathroom (the forerunner of the skylight), and a screen door for ventilation. The units aren't exactly designer showrooms, but they do offer a homey, comfortable feel and daily maid service. Plus, you're sure to forgive the lack of aesthetics when you're presented with the bill. A large deck on the second floor is a great place to sip early-morning coffee or watch the sun sink into the Pacific.

235 Saratoga Rd. (across from Fort DeRussy and Waikiki post office, btw. Kalakaua Ave. and Kalia Rd.), Honolulu, HI 96815. *C* **808/923-6723.** Fax 808/922-7592. 18 units. $85 studio double; $95 1-bedroom double. Extra person $20. 3-night minimum. AE, MC, V. Parking at separate pay lot across the street for $16. Bus: 19 or 20. *In room:* A/C, TV, fridge, kitchenette.

A Hotel for Military Personnel

Hale Koa Hotel ★★ (Value) We wish we could stay here—but we're not allowed. This is a very exclusive hotel, for active-duty and retired military, reservists, National Guard, and their immediate families only. It's a first-class hotel, right on Waikiki Beach, with the grassy lawns of Fort DeRussy on the other side. The price structure, which depends on military rank (lower ranks get cheaper rates), is 50% to 75% less than what comparable Waikiki hotels charge. The hotel sits on 66 landscaped acres with picnic tables and barbecue grills. The only drawback is that it's usually booked; some guests reserve up to a year in advance.

2055 Kalia Rd. (across from Fort DeRussy, btw. Dewey Way and Saratoga Rd.), Honolulu, HI 96815. *C* **800/367-6027** or 808/955-0555. Fax 800/HALE-FAX [425-3329]. www.halekoa.com. 817 units. Lower ranked enlisted personal rates $87–$162 double, depending on room views; higher rank $148–$277. Extra person $15. AE, DC, DISC, MC, V. Parking $9. Bus: 19 or 20. **Amenities:** 4 restaurants and bars (occasional dinner shows); babysitting; concierge desk; fitness room; Jacuzzi; 2 outdoor pools; room service; sauna; 4 lit tennis courts; racquetball and beach volleyball courts. *In room:* A/C, TV, hair dryer.

MID-WAIKIKI, MAUKA

These mid-Waikiki hotels, on the mountain side of Kalakaua Avenue, are a little farther away from the beach than those listed above. They're all between Kalakaua Avenue and Ala Wai Boulevard, and between Kalaimoku Street in the Ewa direction and Kaiulani Street in the Diamond Head direction.

Expensive

Ohana Waikiki Beachcomber Management of this high-rise property has been taken over by Ohana Hotels & Resorts. One of the pluses to this property is the great location—a block from Waikiki Beach, across the street from the upscale Royal Hawaiian Shopping Center, and next door to bargain shopping at the International Market Place. The rooms feature Berber carpets, contemporary furniture, voicemail, and shower-only bathrooms. Sadly, the passing of Don Ho in 2007 meant the closing of his show, but another awe-inspiring show is in residence here: *The Magic of Polynesia*, with illusionist John Hirokana.

2300 Kalakaua Ave. (at Duke's Lane), Honolulu, HI 96815. *C* **800/462-6262** or 808/922-4646. Fax 808/926-9973. www.ohanahotels.com. 492 units (all with shower only). $139–$389 double; from $509 suite. Extra person from $30. Check the website for special AAA and senior rates. AE, DC, DISC, MC, V. Parking $18. Bus: 19 or 20. **Amenities:** Poolside coffee shop; outdoor pool; free Wi-Fi in lobby. *In room:* A/C, TV, fridge, hair dryer, high-speed Internet access (free), complimentary local and mainland phone calls and newspaper delivery.

Sheraton Princess Kaiulani Hotel ★ This hotel is prized for its excellent location and more moderate rates (for a Sheraton). Portraits of this hotel's eponym, Princess Kaiulani, heir to the throne, who died in 1899 at the age of 24, fill the large open-air lobby. The regal, youthful face looks out on the site that was once her royal estate. A huge swimming pool sits behind a row of restaurants and shops facing Kalakaua Avenue. The lobby connects the three buildings of the Princess Kaiulani: the 11-story original hotel that opened in 1955, the 11-story Kaiulani Wing, and the 29-story Ainahau Tower—the latter two opened in 1960. The rooms, which are perfectly fine if unremarkable, have double-insulated doors with added soundproofing. (We wish every hotel in noisy Waikiki had this feature. You can't hear the blaring sirens or the sound of garbage cans being emptied at 3am.) The hotel's dinner and cocktail show "Creation—A Polynesian Odyssey" is a fun, but touristy, musical-theatrical excursion through the South Pacific. I wouldn't pay the rack rates, but it's often possible to get a good package deal on the Web.

120 Kaiulani Ave. (at Kalakaua Ave., across the street from the Sheraton Moana Surfrider), Honolulu, HI 96815. ℂ **800/325-3535** or 808/922-5811. Fax 808/923-9912. www.sheraton.com. 1,150 units. $250–$440 double; from $360 suite. Extra person $55; children 17 and under stay free in parent's room. Inquire about package deals and Starwood Preferred Guest deals. AE, DC, MC, V. Parking $15. Bus: 19 or 20. **Amenities:** 2 restaurants; 1 bar; concierge; fitness room and good children's program across the street at Sheraton Waikiki; outdoor pool; room service; spa at Royal Hawaiian. *In room:* A/C, TV, fridge, hair dryer.

Moderate

Aqua Island Colony Hotel This off-the-beaten-track property combines the spaciousness of a condominium with the amenities of a hotel. Plus the rates include complimentary continental breakfast. All of the units have private lanais and daily maid service and can sleep up to four. Studios have kitchenettes, and the one-bedrooms—which can sleep up to five—have full kitchens. The views are spectacular: jagged mountains and lush valleys, Diamond Head, or the sparkling Pacific Ocean. The only drawback is the minuscule bathrooms: Ours was so small that the door didn't clear the toilet. The tub/shower combo was also cramped. I found it best to shower with my elbows close to my side to avoid hitting the walls. Access via car (usually tricky on Waikiki's one-way streets) is very convenient from Ala Wai Boulevard.

445 Seaside Ave. (at Ala Wai Blvd.), Honolulu, HI 96815. ℂ **866/406-2782** or 808/923-2345. Fax 808/921-7105. www.aquaresorts.com. 160 units. $190–$210 double; $220–$240 studio with kitchenette; $290–$360 1-bedroom with kitchen (sleeps 4). Includes continental breakfast. Check for Internet specials. Extra person $25. AE, DC, DISC, MC, V. Parking $10. Bus: 19 or 20. **Amenities:** Jacuzzi; outdoor pool; sauna. *In room:* A/C, TV, fridge, hair dryer, full kitchen or kitchenette (some units).

Aqua Waikiki Wave ★ (Finds) It is hard to believe that from the wreck of the old Coral Reef hotel, this sleek, modern oasis has emerged. The result of $7.6 million in renovations is a clean, hip decor with bright white walls, offset by the burnt orange fabric on the bed headboard that extends up to the ceiling. Potted plants and live orchids freshen up the rooms. The 21st century has arrived at this older hotel in the form of flatscreen TVs and free Wi-Fi or high-speed Internet access. About a 10-minute walk from the beach and next door to the International Market Place, rooms at the Wave either have two queen-size beds or a king (with very sleepable mattresses). The decades-old bathrooms have new plumbing, modern fixtures, and resurfaced tiles and tubs. Other pluses for this moderately priced hotel include complimentary daily continental breakfast, fitness center, spa, and small swimming pool.

2299 Kuhio Ave (at Duke's Lane), Honolulu, HI 96817. ℂ **866/406-2782** or 808/922-1262. Fax 808/922-5048. www.aquaresorts.com. 247 units. $121–$132 double; from $135 suite. Extra person $25. AE, DISC,

MC, V. Parking $20. Bus: 19 or 20. **Amenities:** 2 restaurants; babysitting; fitness room; outdoor pool; spa. *In room:* A/C, TV/DVD, fridge, hair dryer, free Wi-Fi.

Aston Waikiki Joy   Tucked away down a narrow path on a side street, this boutique hotel offers outstanding personal service and a Jacuzzi in every room. The Italian marble–accented open-air lobby and the tropical veranda set the scene for the beautifully decorated guest rooms, each with a marble entry, tropical-island decor, and a lanai wide enough for you to sit and enjoy the views. Another plus: All the rooms are soundproof. The suites are even more luxurious: either a king-size bed or two doubles, a fridge, a microwave, a coffeemaker, and a wet bar. Executive suites come with two double beds and a kitchen with microwave and full fridge, and the executive king suites add a separate living room and bedroom. However, a few downsides do exist: The 1960 hotel has had some renovations (new carpet in the rooms, new paint), but it still is an older hotel. The rack rates are on the high side (check the Internet for deals) for a minuscule pool and a 10- to 15-minute walk to the beach. And although there's a sandwich/coffee shop on-site, the food's nothing to brag about. *Hot tip:* Check the website under "e-specials" for rooms starting at $140.

320 Lewers St. (btw. Kuhio and Kalakaua aves.), Honolulu, HI 96815. ℂ **877/997-6667** or 808/923-2300. Fax 808/924-4010. www.astonhotels.com. 94 units. $144–$210 double; $203–$230 double club suite; $244–$270 junior suite with kitchen (sleeps up to 4); $289–$315 1-bedroom executive suite with kitchen (up to 4). Rates include continental breakfast. Extra person $30 for certain rooms. Check the website for special deals and packages. AE, DC, DISC, MC, V. Valet-only parking $19. Bus: 19 or 20. **Amenities:** Restaurant; bar (karaoke); concierge; minuscule outdoor pool w/dry sauna. *In room:* A/C, TV, fridge, hair dryer, Internet access ($10/day), kitchenette (full kitchen in suites).

Holiday Surf ⟨**Value**⟩   Three blocks, or about a 10- to 15-minute walk, from Waikiki Beach lies this 1960s apartment hotel, run since 1964 by the Chun family. Overlooking the Ala Wai Canal, the six-story building can be noisy, but air-conditioning drowns out the street noise and the location is within walking distance of Waikiki attractions, dining, and shopping. The 315-square-foot studios are composed of an immaculately clean bedroom/living room combo, with a bed on one side and a full kitchen across the room. The one-bedroom units are larger and have separate bedrooms (great for families). Some of the rooms have been upgraded, thus the range in prices. *Tip:* If you're on a budget, ask for the "Manager's Special Rates," at $79 for a studio or $89 for a one-bedroom (not deluxe upgraded units, but still clean and very functional). The hotel has also added a spa with massage services and a "floating salon," a chamber that looks like a hot tub with a lid on it; you lie in it, in the dark, in warm water.

2303 Ala Wai Blvd. (corner of Nohonani St.), Honolulu, HI 96815. ℂ **808/923-8488.** Fax 808/923-1475. www.holidaysurfhotel.com. 34 units. $143–$179 studio double; $179–$225 1-bedroom double. Ask about special discounts, such as the Manager Special Rates (20%–30% off). Extra person $15–$20. AE, MC, V. Parking $10. Bus: 19 or 20. **Amenities:** Spa. *In room:* A/C, TV/VCR/DVD, fridge, Internet access ($9/day), kitchen.

Ilima Hotel ★ ⟨**Kids**⟩   The Teruya brothers, former owners of Hawaii's Times Supermarket, wanted to offer comfortable accommodations that Hawaii residents could afford, and they've succeeded. One of Hawaii's small, well-located condo-style hotels, the 17-story, pale-pink Ilima (named for the native orange flower used in royal leis) offers value for your money. Rooms are huge; the location is great (near the International Market Place and the Royal Hawaiian Shopping Center, and 2 blocks from Waikiki Beach); and prices are low. A tasteful koa-wood lobby lined with works by Hawaiian artists greets you upon arrival. Perks include free local phone calls and a full kitchen in every unit; in addition, all the couches fold out into beds, making this a particularly good deal for families. (Kids will appreciate the Nintendo games in each room.) The one-bedroom units now have Jacuzzi tubs. The three sun decks, dry sauna, and truly nice people staffing the front desk help you enjoy your vacation. The only caveat: no ocean views.

445 Nohonani St. (near Ala Wai Blvd.), Honolulu, HI 96815. (✆ **800/801-9366** or 808/923-1877. Fax 808/924-2617. www.hotelwaikiki.com. 99 units. $135–$185 double; $169–$219 1-bedroom (rate for 4); $245–$285 2-bedroom (rate for 4, sleeps up to 6); $375–$395 3-bedroom (rate for 6, sleeps up to 8). Extra person $10. Discounts available for seniors and business travelers. AE, DC, DISC, MC, V. Limited free on-site parking, $18 across the street. Bus: 19 or 20. **Amenities:** Exercise room; outdoor pool w/sauna. *In room:* A/C, TV, fridge, hair dryer, high-speed Internet access (free) in deluxe rooms (floors 10–16), kitchen.

Ohana Waikiki Malia (Kids) This large hotel—part of the cluster of Ohana Hotels on Kuhio and surrounding blocks—offers huge rooms with lanais and either a king-size bed or twins. Recently added are the one-bedroom suites with kitchenettes, great for families. Like those at most Ohana Hotels, the windows have black-out curtains, which not only keep the blaring morning sun out, but also help with the noise from busy Kuhio Avenue. Because a pool isn't on the premises, guests are welcome to use the one at the Ohana Waikiki Surf West across the street. But why bother? One of the most famous beaches in the world is just 3 blocks away. Wheelchair-accessible rooms outfitted with wide doorways and special grips in the bathroom are available.

2211 Kuhio Ave. (btw. Royal Hawaiian Ave. and Lewers St.), Honolulu, HI 96815. (✆ **800/462-6262** or 808/923-7621. Fax 800/622-4852 or 808/921-4804. www.ohanahotels.com. 327 units. $219–$279 double; $309 1-bedroom suite with kitchenette (up to 4 guests). Check the website for specials, discounts (seniors receive up to 45% off and AAA), and packages. Extra person $30. AE, DC, DISC, MC, V. Parking $18. Bus: 19 or 20. **Amenities:** Restaurant (24-hr. coffee shop); children's program; roof-top tennis courts; access to amenities at other Ohana properties (childcare, dining, and more). *In room:* A/C, TV, fridge, hair dryer, kitchenette (some units).

Ohana Waikiki West On the upside, this chain hotel has lots of guest services and facilities, which include a lounge, room service, and lots of shops (even a pharmacy). All of the rooms were redone in 2004 and have refrigerators and shower-only bathrooms; some have kitchenettes. Waikiki Beach is 2 blocks away; restaurants, shopping, and nightlife are all no more than a 10-minute walk, and International Market Place is across the street. The downside is that it's on a very noisy part of Kuhio Avenue. If you are enamored with the budget price and figure a good pair of ear plugs will do the trick, go ahead and book. But if you are a light sleeper, I'd suggest picking another property.

2330 Kuhio Ave. (btw. Nahua and Walina sts.), Honolulu, HI 96815. (✆ **800/462-6262** or 808/922-5022. Fax 800/622-4852 or 808/924-6414. www.ohanahotels.com. 661 units. $119–$209 double; $139–$229 double with kitchenette. Check website for promotions and discounts (seniors and AAA). Extra person $30. AE, DC, DISC, MC, V. Parking $18. Bus: 19 or 20. **Amenities:** 2 restaurants (a branch of Chili's and a bakery/deli); 2 bars (1 poolside, 1 country and western); children's program; outdoor pool; room service (Chili's). *In room:* A/C, TV, fridge, hair dryer, kitchenette (some units).

Inexpensive

Best Western Aqua Coconut Plaza The good news is this property, built in 1962, was totally renovated in 2007 into a fabulous boutique inn with modern decor and amenities (such as free high-speed Internet and flatscreen TVs in every room). Formerly known as the Coconut Plaza, this hotel has been managed by a host of companies, and in 2008, Best Western took over and has made it a very affordable and welcoming place to stay. One of the main reasons to stay here is the price (which includes a continental breakfast) and its location—only a 10-minute walk to the beach and near a bus stop for those without a car. Rooms are comfy and spacious enough for a couple (if you have kids, get a second room). Staff is very friendly and helpful in pointing out things to do and places to eat. It is not on the water, but ask for a room with a mountain view and you'll be just as awe-inspired.

450 Lewers St. (at Ala Wai Blvd.), Honolulu, HI 96815. (C) 808/923-8828. Fax 808/923-3473. www.best westernhawaii.com/hotels/best-western-coconut-waikiki-hotel. 80 units. $115–$195 double; from $225 suite. Rates include continental breakfast. Extra person $25. AE, DC, MC, V. Valet parking $22. Bus: 19 or 20. **Amenities:** Free high-speed Internet access in lobby; tiny outdoor pool w/sun deck. *In room:* A/C, TV, fridge, hair dryer, high-speed Internet access (free), kitchenette.

Marine Surf Waikiki Hotel (Value) Travelers on a budget will like this high-rise hotel in the heart of Waikiki. Part privately owned condo units and part spacious studio apartments, only the studios are available for rent. Each one has a complete kitchen, two extra-long double beds, and a small lanai. The price difference depends on the view. *Tip:* The best views are from floors 17 to 22. The hotel is just a half-block from Kuhio Mall and the International Market Place, and less than 2 blocks from the beach.

364 Seaside Ave. (at Kuhio Ave.), Honolulu, HI 96815. (C) 888/456-SURF [7873] or 808/931-2424. Fax 808/931-2454. 110 units. www.marine-surf.com. $100–$125 double. Check the hotel's website for special Internet rates: $83 at press time. Extra person $10. AE, DC, DISC, MC, V. Parking $5. Bus: 19 or 20. **Ameni-ties:** Restaurant (Italian); bar; outdoor pool. *In room:* A/C, TV, fridge, hair dryer, kitchen.

Patrick Winston's Waikiki Condos (Finds) Looking for a condo priced to fit a tight budget, with a hefty dose of old-fashioned aloha? Try Patrick Winston's rentals, located on a quiet side street. When this five-story condominium hotel was built in 1981, Win-ston bought one unit; he has since acquired 24 more, spent hundreds of thousands of dollars on refurbishment, and put his spacious suites on the market at frugal prices. Stay-ing here is like having a personal concierge; Winston has lots of terrific tips on where to eat, where to shop, and how to get the most for your money, and he can book any activ-ity you want.

Three types of units are available: standard/budget rooms, one-bedroom suites, and ground-floor junior business suites. All have sofa beds, separate bedrooms, lanais with breakfast table and chairs, ceiling fans, full kitchens, and showers in the bathrooms; most have a washer and dryer. All are individually decorated. Eight units are "standard bud-get," which means the carpet has not been replaced or the walls need repainting, but they're otherwise a terrific deal. Waikiki Beach is just a 10- to 15-minute walk away, shopping is a half-block away, and restaurants are within a 5- to 10-minute walk. This area of Waikiki is a little scary at night—not totally safe for a single woman to be wander-ing about by herself. Also be aware there is *no* maid service (you are the maid) and that a one-time cleaning fee increases your total bill by $60.

Hawaiian King Building, 417 Nohonani St., Ste. 409 (btw. Kuhio Ave. and Ala Wai Blvd.), Honolulu, HI 96815. (C) 800/545-1948 or 808/924-3332. Fax 808/922-3894. www.winstonswaikikicondos.com. 24 units (all with shower only). $125–$145 1-bedroom; $145–$165 business suite; $165–$185 1-bedroom with den. Cleaning fee $75–$100. Extra person $10. 7-night minimum. Ask for the Frommer's readers' discount. AE, DC, DISC, MC, V. Limited parking $14. Bus: 19 or 20. **Amenities:** Bar; babysitting; small outdoor pool surrounded by a tropical courtyard. *In room:* A/C, TV, fridge, hair dryer, kitchen, washer/ dryer (in most units).

WAIKIKI, DIAMOND HEAD END

You'll find all these hotels between Ala Wai Boulevard and the ocean, and between Kai-ulani Street (1 block east of the International Marketplace) and Diamond Head itself.

Hilton Waikiki Prince Kuhio In 2007, Hilton took over this 37-floor hotel, several long blocks from the beach and a few blocks from the zoo, and spent $50 million in renovations to make the former moderate Radisson hotel into a high-tech, 21st-century luxury hotel. However, I find the rack rates ridiculously high. This hotel is a 5-minute walk to the beach—but at these rates you could stay on the beach! If you can find a good rate on the Internet (in the $200 range), then go for it; otherwise, you can get a much better deal elsewhere. Each of the sleek, modern rooms has high-speed Internet ($11/day), a flatscreen 42-inch high-def plasma TV with multimedia monitor for a laptop computer, game station console, video/camera, or MP3 player. The contemporary rooms feature Hilton's comfy beds, and the bathrooms feature marble and natural stone and top-end amenities. All rooms are the same; the floor and the view determine the price (from the 18th floor and up, the mountain views overlooking the Ala Wai Canal are spectacular and not as pricey as the oceanview rooms). Hilton has added a 24-hour eatery, MAC 24-7 (p. 125), which comes in handy if you arrive late at night.

2500 Kuhio Ave. (at Liliuokalani Ave.), Honolulu, HI 96815. (*C*) **800/HILTONS** [445-8667] or 808/922-0811. Fax 808/921-5507. www.waikikiprincekuhio.hilton.com. 601 units. $199–$299 double; from $489 suite for 4. Extra person $40. AE, DC, DISC, MC, V. Valet-only parking $25. Bus: 19 or 20. **Amenities:** Restaurant; bar; concierge; concierge-level rooms; small fitness room; Jacuzzi; outdoor pool; room service. *In room:* A/C, TV, fridge, hair dryer, high-speed Internet access ($10/day).

Waikiki Beach Marriott Resort & Spa This 1,310-room hotel has a lot to offer, including a terrific location just across the street from Waikiki Beach, great restaurants (including renowned Maui chef D. K. Kodama's Sansei Seafood Restaurant & Sushi Bar, p. 127, and d.k Steakhouse, p. 126), a terrific spa, and lots of nightly entertainment.

The 5¼-acre property has two towers (one 33 stories, the other 25 stories) and a list of amenities to keep you happy, from an espresso bar to an array of shops. The newly done rooms feature comfortable island-style decor, marble flooring, and granite counters in the bathroom. When the resort opened in 2002 the prices were moderate but have been creeping up every year. With rack rates beginning at $425 (and topping off at $700), we feel you can do better elsewhere in Waikiki. *Hot tip:* Check the Internet for specials in which you can get rooms for half price.

Even if you don't stay here, spa aficionados won't want to miss the **Spa Olakino & Salon ★**. Conceived and managed by Paul Brown, a well-known hair stylist with numerous salons in Hawaii, this boutique spa offers a unique experience: The spa looks directly onto Waikiki Beach (well, actually Kuhio Beach, at the far end of Waikiki). The "menu" of treatments is one of the most enchanting I have seen. I recommend the Na La'au, which starts with a Hawaiian lomilomi massage (using traditional native Hawaiian plants such as kukui nut oil), then goes on to a noni-plant-and-ti-leaf body wrap, and concludes with a trip to a private steam room and shower.

2552 Kalakaua Ave. (entrance on Ohua Ave.), Honolulu, HI 96815. (*C*) **800/367-5370** or 808/922-6611. Fax 808/921-5255. www.marriottwaikiki.com. 1,310 units. $340–$560 double; from $1,500 suite. Extra person $40. Children under 18 stay free in parent's room using existing bedding. AE, DC, DISC, MC, V. Valet parking $29; self-parking $25. Bus: 19 or 20. **Amenities:** 5 restaurants (including Sansei Seafood Restaurant & Sushi Bar, p. 127, and d.k Steakhouse, p. 126); 2 bars; babysitting; concierge; fitness room; Jacuzzi; outdoor pool w/view of Waikiki; room service; elegant spa.; 24-hr. Doctors On Call medical service. *In room:* A/C, TV, hair dryer, Wi-Fi ($14/day).

Hyatt Regency Waikiki ★   This is one of Waikiki's biggest hotels, a $100-million project sporting two 40-story towers and covering nearly an entire city block, just across the street from the Diamond Head end of Waikiki Beach. Some may love the location, but others will find this behemoth too big and impersonal—you can get lost just trying to find the registration desk. The huge second-floor lobby is decorated in koa and wraps around an atrium that rises 40 floors from the ground level. It's filled with the squawks of parrots, tumbling waterfalls, and traffic noise from busy Kalakaua Avenue.

The guest rooms are spacious and luxuriously furnished. But, please—when most rooms go for at least $260, why does the hotel have to charge you an extra couple of bucks for coffee to be used in the "free coffeemaker" in your room? (Not only that, but if you want to empty your minibar to use it as a fridge, the cost is $12!) The deluxe oceanview rooms overlooking Waikiki Beach are fabulous, but can be noisy (traffic on the avenue is constant). You can upgrade to the Regency Club floors, where the rooms are nicer (and the coffee is free); you'll also be entitled to an expedited check-in and entry to a private rooftop sun deck and Jacuzzi and the Regency Club, which has concierge service all day and serves complimentary continental breakfast and afternoon *pupu* (Hawaii-style appetizers).

The 10,000-square-foot, two-story luxury spa offers all the massage services, body treatments, and facials you can imagine.

2424 Kalakaua Ave. (at Kaiulani St., across the street from the beach), Honolulu, HI 96815. ☎ **800/492-8804** or 808/923-1234. Fax 808/926-3415. www.waikiki.hyatt.com. 1,230 units. $299–$499 double; $469–$569 Regency Club double; from $824 suite. Extra person $75 ($125 Regency Club). Children under 18 stay free in parent's room using existing bedding. Check website for special packages. AE, DISC, MC, V. Valet parking $29; self-parking $25. Bus: 19 or 20. **Amenities:** 4 restaurants (including Ciao Mein, p. 125); elegant poolside bar; babysitting; children's program (Fri–Sat evening in winter, daily in summer); concierge; concierge-level rooms; fitness room; Jacuzzi; outdoor pool w/view of Waikiki; room service; spa. *In room:* A/C, TV, fridge, hair dryer, high-speed Internet access ($10/day).

Moderate

Aston at the Waikiki Banyan (Kids)   The one-bedrooms here combine the homey comforts of a condo apartment with the amenities of a hotel. You'll get daily maid service, bellhop service, the assistance of the front desk, and access to an enormous sixth-floor recreation deck with a panoramic mountain view, complete with sauna, barbecue areas, snack bar, and children's play area—a great boon for families (kids 12 and under get a toy when you check in), plus there's a children's library with games and terrific Hawaiian books. The open-air lobby has some impressive lacquer artwork, hand-carved and painted in Hong Kong. All bedrooms have a fully equipped full-size kitchen, a breakfast bar that opens to a comfortably furnished living room (with sofa bed), and a separate bedroom with two double beds or a king-size bed. The one I stayed in had an old-fashioned air conditioner in the wall, but it did the job. Each apartment opens onto a fairly good-size lanai with chairs, a small table, and a partial ocean view, with some buildings blocking the way. *Hot tip:* For apartments starting at $155, check the website, under "e-specials."

201 Ohua Ave. (on mountain side, at Kuhio Ave.), Honolulu, HI 96815. ☎ **866/77-HAWAII** [774-2924] or 808/922-0555. Fax 808/922-0906. www.astonhotels.com. 307 units. $134–$295 for up to 5. Check website for special rates and package deals. AE, DC, DISC, MC, V. Self-parking $8. Bus: 19 or 20. **Amenities:** Barbecue; children's playground; huge outdoor pool; free tennis courts; 2 whirlpools. *In room:* A/C, TV, fridge, hair dryer, high-speed Internet access ($10), kitchen.

Nickel-&-Dime Charges at High-Priced Hotels

Several upscale resorts in Hawaii have begun a practice that I find distasteful and dishonest: charging a so-called "resort fee." This daily fee (generally in the $15-per-day range) is added on to your bill for such "complimentary" items as a daily newspaper, local phone calls, and use of the fitness facilities—amenities that the resort has been happily providing free to its guests for years. In most cases you do not have an option to decline the resort fee—in other words, this is a sneaky way to increase the nightly rate without telling you.

Aston Waikiki Beach Hotel   After a $30-million renovation on a very old and tired hotel, this former Aston resort opened the 717-room property in late 2002. The location, directly across the street from the beach, couldn't be better, but the rooms couldn't be smaller—averaging 225 to 266 square feet (though 85% of them have ocean views). When ResortQuest took over in 2006, they immediately got rid of the Hawaiian "kitschy nostalgia" theme and repainted. The horrible garish colors are gone, replaced with wooden baseboards and bamboo trim over a floral carpet. They installed 32-inch flatscreen TVs, bamboo dressers, and bright floral headboards and accents. One of the traditions ResortQuest maintains is "Breakfast on the Beach"—you get a free breakfast, which you can pack up in an insulated carrying bag and walk across the street to eat. Several food stations offer everything from burritos (veggie, ham, or cheese), pastries, fruit, and cereals to a Japanese breakfast of miso, rice, and fish. Tiki's Grill and Wolfgang Puck Express are other good places to eat here. *Hot tip:* For the best rate, check the website, under "e-specials," or choose one of their package deals.

2570 Kalakaua Ave. (at Paoakalani St.), Honolulu, HI 96815. ℂ **866/77-HAWAII** [774-2924] or 808/922-2511. Fax 808/923-3656. www.astonhotels.com. 717 units. $140–$247 double; from $248 suite. Extra person $45. Check website for special rates and package deals. AE, DC, DISC, MC, V. Valet parking $22. Bus: 19 or 20. **Amenities:** 2 restaurants (including Tiki's Grill & Bar, p. 128); bar; outdoor pool. In room: A/C, TV, fridge, hair dryer, high-speed Internet access ($10/day).

Hotel Renew ★★ ⒻFinds   Once upon a time, this now 70-room boutique hotel was one of the towers to the ResortQuest Waikiki Beach Hotel (see below)—that was the before. The after is an oasis of tranquillity, excellent taste, and high-tech electronic equipment in a sea of schlocky aging Waikiki hotels. After millions in renovations, the renewed hotel offers a quiet, relaxing vacation, just a block from the beach. Guests are seated at the front desks to check in, while their luggage is whisked to their rooms. The new rooms are designed with a clean decor, with black and white walls, discreet lighting, and the slight aroma of scented candles in the air—all similar to the W, but for only a fraction of the price. But it's the electronics that won us over: DVD films that are projected onto a 6-by-4-foot screen (and can work with your computer), a 42-inch high-def flatscreen TV, complimentary high-speed Internet access, a host of 500-plus movies, even an iPod docking station. A daily gourmet breakfast is included, along with free use of the fitness center and access to yoga classes; and when you depart, you'll receive a fresh flower lei to remember your sweet time here.

129 Paoakalani Ave (at Lemon Rd.), Honolulu, HI 96815. ℂ **888/485-7639** or 808/687-7700. Fax 808/687-7701. www.hotelrenew.com. 70 units. $165–$259 double. Extra person $30. AE, DISC, MC, V. Parking $20. Bus: 19 or 20. **Amenities:** Cafe and lounge; complimentary continental breakfast; concierge; fitness

center (including free yoga classes); spa. *In room:* A/C, TV/DVD, CD player, fridge, hair dryer, high-speed Internet access (free).

New Otani Kaimana Beach Hotel ★ (Finds) This is one of Waikiki's best-kept hotel secrets: a boutique hotel nestled right on a lovely stretch of beach at the foot of Diamond Head, with Kapiolani Park just across the street. Robert Louis Stevenson's description of Sans Souci, the beach fronting the hotel, still holds true: "If anyone desires lovely scenery, pure air, clear sea water, good food, and heavenly sunsets, I recommend him cordially to the Sans Souci." The Waikiki-side guest rooms are teeny-tiny, barely with room for two, but tastefully decorated in pale pastels; they open onto lanais with ocean and park views. A good budget buy is the park-view studio with kitchen, which you can stock with provisions from the on-site Mini-Mart, open until 11pm.

Because the hotel overlooks Kapiolani Park, guests have easy access to activities such as golf, tennis, jogging, and bicycling; kayaking and snorkeling are available at the beach. The hotel also arranges for visitors to climb to the top of Diamond Head. The airy lobby opens onto the alfresco Hau Tree Lanai restaurant (p. 126) and features music nightly. The beachfront **Sunset Lanai Lounge** ★ is great for cocktails and has live Hawaiian music at lunch on Friday.

2863 Kalakaua Ave. (ocean side of the street just Diamond Head of the Waikiki Aquarium, across from Kapiolani Park), Honolulu, HI 96815. © 800/356-8264 or 808/923-1555. Fax 808/922-9404. www. kaimana.com. 124 units. $170–$440 double; from $210 studio; from $320 junior suite; from $500 regular suite. Extra person $50. Children 12 and under stay free in parent's room using existing bedding. Check website for special packages. AE, DC, DISC, MC, V. Valet parking $18. Bus: 2 or 14. **Amenities:** 2 restaurants (including the Hau Tree Lanai, p. 126); beachfront bar; babysitting; concierge; fitness room; room service; watersports equipment rentals. *In room:* A/C, TV, fridge, hair dryer, high-speed Internet $12, kitchenette (in some units), minibar (on request).

Inexpensive

Aqua Bamboo and Spa ★ (Value) Formerly a very neglected budget hotel, just a block from Waikiki Beach, Bamboo has been transformed into a contemporary condotel (a condominium/hotel), decorated with an Asian flair. The rooms are stylish and functional with modern furniture, marble bathrooms, and kitchenettes or kitchens. The location is good, too—it's within walking distance to numerous restaurants, shopping, and the Honolulu Zoo, and just 3 minutes to the beach. Because it's small, the staff gives guests personalized attention. As at all the Aqua Resort properties, there's a complimentary continental breakfast every morning, but this hotel has its own spa on property. When booking, be sure to "reserve" a parking space, because the parking lot has a limited number of spaces.

2425 Kuhio Ave. (at Kaiulani Ave.), Honolulu, HI 96815. © 866/406-2782 or 808/922-7777. Fax 808/922-9473. www.aquaresorts.com. 90 units. $130–$145 double; $145–$160 studio double; from $215 1-bedroom; from $385 luxury 2-bedroom suite. AE, DISC, MC, V. Valet parking $22. Bus: 19 or 20. **Amenities:** Complimentary continental breakfast; concierge; fitness center; Jacuzzi; outdoor pool; sauna; spa. *In room:* A/C, TV, fridge, hair dryer, high-speed Internet access (free), kitchenette or kitchen.

Diamond Head Bed & Breakfast ★ (Finds) Hostess Joanne offers a quiet, relaxing place to stay on the far side of Kapiolani Park, away from the hustle and bustle of Waikiki. Staying here is like venturing back 50 years to a time when *kamaaina* (native-born) families built huge houses with airy rooms opening onto big lanais and tropical gardens. The house is filled with family heirlooms and Joanne's artwork. One of the two rooms features the beyond-king-size carved koa bed that once belonged to Princess Ruth, a member of Hawaii's royal family. You'll feel like royalty sleeping in it.

3240 Noela Dr. (at Paki Ave., off Diamond Head Rd.), Honolulu, HI 96815. ©/fax **808/923-3360.** www.
diamondheadbnb.com. 3 units. $130–$145 double. Rates include full breakfast. Extra person $20. 2-night minimum. No credit cards. Free parking. Bus: 2. *In room:* TV, fridge, hair dryer.

Ocean Resort Hotel Waikiki   This large dual-tower hotel on a relatively quiet street is just a short walk from the Honolulu Zoo, Kapiolani Park, and the Waikiki Aquarium, and just 2 minutes from the beach. The property has a bright, clean look. The Diamond Tower houses the budget rooms; at 325 square feet, they boast new carpet, bedspreads, drapes, and other interior redesigns. These rooms have showers only; tub/shower combos are available in the more expensive Pali Tower rooms. All rooms in both towers have refrigerators, and the rooms with kitchenettes have two-burner hot plates and cooking utensils; those from the ninth floor up also have small lanais. Only studios and suites have coffeemakers, so if you want one, ask for it when you reserve. The on-site restaurant offers steak and seafood with live Hawaiian music during dinner. For even more savings on this budget hotel, book on the Internet, for big discounts off rack rates (when we went to press they were offering 52% off).

175 Paoakalani Ave. (near Kuhio Ave.), Honolulu, HI 96815. © **800/367-2317** or 808/922-3861. Fax 808/924-1982. www.oceanresort.com. 450 units. $145–$190 double; $195–$245 studio with kitchenette, suites from $280. Internet specials start at $75. Extra person $25. AE, DC, DISC, MC, V. Parking $15 valet only. Bus: 19 or 20. **Amenities:** Restaurant; bar; babysitting; 2 outdoor pools; currency exchange desk. *In room:* A/C, TV, fridge, hair dryer, kitchenette (studios).

Queen Kapiolani Hotel   This budget property, managed by Castle Resorts, is named for Queen Kapiolani (1834–99), the wife of Hawaii's last king, David Kalakaua (1836–91), and the theme here harks back to the days of the Hawaiian monarchs. The 19th-century flavor of the place reflects that grand era with 10-foot chandeliers in the main dining room and a full-size portrait of the queen in the lobby. The plush decor, however, doesn't extend to the budget rooms, which are quite small. For just a few bucks more, get the superior room. Not only is it double in size, but its shoreline views are vastly improved. The property's location is great—across the street from Kapiolani Park, a half-block to the beach, and within walking distance of the Honolulu Zoo, the Waikiki Aquarium, and the activities of Waikiki, including the municipal tennis courts. For even more savings, book through this hotel's website.

150 Kapahulu Ave. (at Lemon Rd., across from Kapiolani Park), Honolulu, HI 96815. © **800/367-2317** or 808/922-1941. Fax 808/922-1982. www.queenkapiolani.com. 315 units. $140–$195 double; $220–$255 studio with kitchenette; $350–$415 1-bedroom suite with kitchenette (sleeps up to 4). Check for Internet specials, which start at $69. Extra person $25. Children 18 and under stay free in parent's room. AE, DC, DISC, MC, V. Parking $15 self only. Bus: 19 or 20. **Amenities:** Restaurant; bar; babysitting; concierge; large outdoor pool; municipal tennis courts nearby. *In room:* A/C, TV, fridge, hair dryer, some kitchenettes.

Royal Grove Hotel ★ Value   This is a great bargain for frugal travelers. You can't miss the Royal Grove—it's bright pink. Among Waikiki's canyons of corporate-owned high-rises, it's also a rarity in another way: The Royal Grove is a small, family-owned hotel. What you get here is old-fashioned aloha in cozy accommodations along the lines of Motel 6—basic and clean. For years *Frommer's* readers have written in about the aloha spirit of the Fong family; they love the potluck dinners and get-togethers the Fongs have organized so their guests can get to know one another. And you can't do better for the price—this has to be *the* bargain of Waikiki. For $47 (about the same price a couple would pay to stay in a private room at the hostel in Waikiki), you get a clean room in the older Mauka Wing, with two twin beds, plus a kitchenette with refrigerator and stove. I suggest that you spend a few dollars more and go for an air-conditioned room ($64) to

4

help drown out the street noise. Even the most expensive unit, a one-bedroom suite with three beds and kitchenette for $80, is half the price of similar accommodations elsewhere. At these rates, you won't mind that maid service is only twice a week.

The hotel is built around a courtyard pool, and the beach is just a 3-minute walk away. All of Waikiki's attractions are within walking distance. *Tip:* If you book 7 nights or more from April to November, you'll get a discount on the already low rates.

151 Uluniu Ave. (btw. Prince Edward and Kuhio aves.), Honolulu, HI 96815. © **808/923-7691.** Fax 808/922-7508. www.royalgrovehotel.com. 85 units. $55–$60 double (no A/C); $67–$90 standard double; $90–$100 standard 1-bedroom. Extra person $10. Children 5 and under stay free in parent's room. AE, DC, DISC, MC, V. Nearby parking $10. Bus: 19 or 20. **Amenities:** Pool. *In room:* A/C (in most rooms), TV, fridge, kitchen.

Waikiki Sand Villa (Kids) Frugal travelers, take note: This very affordable hotel is located on the quieter side of Waikiki, across the street from the Ala Wai Canal. The 10-story tower has medium-size rooms, most with a double bed plus a single bed (convenient for families) and a lanai with great views of the green mountains. The adjacent three-story building features studio apartments with kitchenettes (fridge, stove, and microwave). For guests arriving early or catching a late flight, there's a hospitality room (complete with shower) for late checkout, and a luggage-storage area.

2375 Ala Wai Blvd. (entrance on Kanekapolei Ave.), Honolulu, HI 96815. © **800/247-1903** or 808/922-4744. Fax 808/926-7587. www.waikikisandvillahotel.com. 214 units. $85–$100 double; $130–$282 studio with kitchenette; from $250 suite. Rates include continental breakfast served poolside every morning. Extra person $28. Children under 17 stay free in parent's room using existing bedding. Internet specials start as low as $81. AE, DC, DISC, MC, V. Valet-only parking $15. Bus: 19 or 20. **Amenities:** 70-ft. outdoor pool w/adjoining whirlpool spa. *In room:* A/C, TV w/Nintendo, fridge (in some units), high-speed Internet access (free), kitchenette (in some units), microwave (in some units).

A Gay-Friendly Hotel

The Cabana at Waikiki Located on a quiet street in Waikiki, this boutique hotel caters to a clientele of gay men and features exquisitely decorated rooms. Each has a queen-size bed and pullout sofa bed, entertainment center with VCR and CD player, lanai, and well-equipped kitchenette. A free continental breakfast is served every morning, and free Internet access is available in the lobby. A giant, eight-person spa is also on the property. The Cabana is within walking distance of gay nightclubs and the gay scene at Queen's Surf Beach.

2551 Cartwright Rd. (btw. Paoakalani and Kapahulu aves.), Honolulu, HI 96815. © **877/902-2121** or 808/926-5555. Fax 808/926-5566. www.cabana-waikiki.com. 15 units. $159–$255 double. Rates include continental breakfast. Extra person $15. Check the website for rates as low as $139. AE, DC, DISC, MC, V. Parking $10. Bus: 19 or 20. **Amenities:** Concierge; complimentary access to nearby (about a 15-min. walk) fitness complex; free Internet access in lobby; Jacuzzi. *In room:* A/C, TV, fridge, hair dryer, kitchenette.

2 HONOLULU BEYOND WAIKIKI

The city of Honolulu extends far beyond the tourist zones of Waikiki. It encompasses a fairly large area, and most of Oahu's population calls it home. Downtown Honolulu is relatively small, occupying only a handful of blocks. The financial, government, and corporate headquarters of businesses are found here. Other neighborhoods range from the quiet suburbs of Hawaii Kai to the *kamaaina* neighborhoods such as Manoa. With the exception of the heart of downtown, these neighborhoods are generally quieter than Waikiki, more residential, yet within minutes of beaches, shopping, and all the activities Oahu has to offer.

ALA MOANA

Ala Moana Hotel   After a multimillion-dollar transformation, this former 1,152-room hotel (on 36 floors) has been converted to a hotel-condominium (sometimes called a condotel), where the units are individually owned, but most are put onto the rental market for guests. Renovations include redone suites and a new pool, sun deck, and fitness center/spa. The Outrigger/Ohana Resort is managing this hotel, so it will run as smoothly as their brand properties. The main advantage of staying here is its proximity to Waikiki, the downtown financial and business district, the new convention center, and Hawaii's largest mall, Ala Moana Shopping Center. The rooms vary in price according to size: The cheaper rooms are small, but all come with two double beds and all the amenities you'll need to make your stay comfortable. The views of Waikiki and Honolulu from the upper floors are spectacular. *Hot tip:* Book on the website and save: Rooms start at $129 ($100 off the rack rate).

410 Atkinson Dr. (at Kona St., next to Ala Moana Center), Honolulu, HI 96814. ℭ **800/367-6025** or 808/955-4811. Fax 808/944-6839. www.alamoanahotel.com. 1,152 units. $149–$329 double; from $299 suite. Extra person $40. Children under 18 stay free in parent's room. AE, DC, DISC, MC, V. Valet parking $20; self-parking $15. Bus: 19 or 20. **Amenities:** 5 restaurants; 2 bars (including Rumours Nightclub, p. 251, plus a Polynesian show); concierge; small fitness room; large outdoor pool; limited room service. *In room:* A/C, TV, fridge, hair dryer, high-speed Internet access (free).

Pagoda Hotel   This is where local residents from neighbor islands stay when they come to Honolulu. Close to shopping and downtown (but *not* close to the beach), the Pagoda has been serving Hawaii's island community for decades. This modest hotel has very plain, motel-like rooms: clean and utilitarian with no extra frills. Ask for a mountain-view room to avoid the street noise. There's easy access to Waikiki via TheBus—the nearest stop is just half a block away. Ask about rental-car packages. Studios and one- and two-bedroom units have kitchenettes. *Tip:* Check the website for Internet rates from $90 and excellent room-car package deals.

1525 Rycroft St. (btw. Keeaumoku and Kaheka sts.), Honolulu, HI 96814. ℭ **800/367-6060** or 808/923-4511. Fax 808/955-5067. www.pagodahotel.com. 361 units. From $140 double hotel room; from $140 studio with kitchenette; from $157 1-bedroom double; from $242 2-bedroom double (sleeps up to 5); lowest rates Sun–Thurs. Extra person $25. Free cribs available. Ask about rental-car packages. AE, DC, DISC, MC, V. Parking $9. Bus: 5 or 6. **Amenities:** Restaurant; bar; babysitting; 2 outdoor pools. *In room:* A/C, TV, fridge, hair dryer, high-speed Internet access ($9/day), kitchenette (in some units).

Downtown

Aston at the Executive Centre Hotel ★   Located in the heart of downtown, this is the perfect hotel for the business traveler. But visitors will not like the long walk to the beach. However business travelers will love not only the location, close to the business and financial center of Honolulu, but they also will appreciate the staff, who are quick to assist in any way. The hotel occupies the top 10 floors of a 40-story, multiuse, glass-walled tower. Every room is a spacious suite, with three phones, a whirlpool bathtub, and unobstructed views of the city, the mountains, and Honolulu Harbor. Executive suites add a full kitchen, washer/dryer, and VCR. All guests awaken to a local newspaper outside their doors. Local phone calls are free. The only downside is that units are privately owned, so quality is inconsistent—some are fantastic, but some need work.

1088 Bishop St. (at S. Hotel St.), Honolulu, HI 96813. ℭ **866/77-HAWAII** [774-2924] or 808/539-3000. Fax 808/523-1088. www.resortquesthawaii.com. 114 suites. $290–$320 suite; $280–$295 1-bedroom. Rates include continental breakfast. Extra person $30. Children under 17 stay free in parent's room. AE, DC, DISC, MC, V. Parking $15. Bus: 1, 2, 3, 9, or 12. **Amenities:** Restaurant; concierge; fitness center w/free weights and aerobic equipment; outdoor pool. *In room:* A/C, TV, fridge, hair dryer, high-speed Internet ($11/day), kitchenette, washer/dryer (some rooms), in-room jet spa.

If you have a late-night flight, a long layover between flights, a delayed flight, or a long period of time between your noon check-out and your flight, consider the services of the hotel choices near the airport (certainly not a place to spend your Hawaiian vacation, but a good overnight resting place): **Best Western—The Plaza Hotel,** 3253 N. Nimitz Hwy., Honolulu (© **800/800-4683** or 808/836-0661; www.bestwestern.com), where rooms go from $99 to $169; and the **Ohana Honolulu Airport Hotel,** 3401 Nimitz Hwy, (© **800/462-6262** or 808/836-0661; www.ohanahotels.com), with rooms from $99 (up to superior rooms with breakfast for $205). Both offer free airport shuttle service.

MANOA
Moderate
Manoa Valley Inn (Overrated)   The 2006 earthquake (in which the entire chimney collapsed), coupled with years of neglect, has left this once–grande dame in a sad state of needing renovations and general sprucing up. As we went to press, the old inn was recently purchased. With any luck, the new owners will restore this B&B back to its original glory. Although once a fabulous place to stay (it's completely off the tourist trail), this historic 1915 gothic home, on a quiet residential street near the University of Hawaii, needs some more work before we can give it our full endorsement. However, if you have your heart set on staying in an inn on the National Register of Historic Places, you will find the rooms charming, complete with antiques, old-fashioned rose wallpaper, and king-size koa beds. The three top-floor rooms share a full bathroom; the others have private bathrooms. Cottage bathrooms feature old-style tubs as well as separate modern showers.

2001 Vancouver Dr. (at University Ave.), Honolulu, HI 96822. © **808/947-6019.** Fax 808/946-6168. www.manoavalleyinn.com. 7 units, 2 with shared bathroom. $99–$125 double with shared bathroom; $140–$170 double with private bathroom (shower only). Rates include continental breakfast. MC, V. Free parking. Bus: 4 or 6. Children 8 and older preferred. *In room:* A/C (in some units), TV (in some units), Wi-Fi (free).

To the East: Kahala
Kahala Hotel & Resort ★★ (Kids)   In one of Oahu's most prestigious residential areas, the Kahala offers the peace and serenity of a neighbor-island vacation, but with the conveniences of Waikiki just a 10-minute drive away. After 11 years under the helm of the Mandarin Oriental Group, this grand old hotel changed management firms in 2006.

All guest rooms currently feature the ultimate in luxury: 19th-century mahogany reproductions, teak parquet floors with hand-loomed Tibetan rugs, overstuffed chairs, canopy beds covered with soft throw pillows, and works by local artists adorning the grass-cloth-covered walls. Views from the floor-to-ceiling sliding-glass doors are of the ocean, Diamond Head, and Koko Head. In-room amenities include two-line phones, 27-inch TVs, large bathrooms with vintage fixtures, free-standing glass showers, large soaking tubs, and "his" and "her" dressing areas.

The lush grounds include an 800-foot crescent-shaped beach and a 26,000-square-foot lagoon (home to two bottle-nosed dolphins, sea turtles, and tropical fish). Other extras that make this property outstanding: Hawaiian cultural programs, shuttle service to Waikiki and major shopping centers, free scuba lessons in the pool, daily dolphin-education talks by a trainer from Sea Life Park, and a great year-round children's program. A must-do indulgence is the recently added spa, which features treatments in former guest rooms redesigned for individualized massages, body scrubs, rubs, wraps, and other pampering therapies.

5000 Kahala Ave. (next to the Waialae Country Club), Honolulu, HI 96816. © **800/367-2525** or 808/739- 8888. Fax 808/739-8800. www.kahalaresort.com. 343 units. $465–$995 double; from $1,600 suite. Extra person $175. Children 17 and under stay free in parent's room. Check the website's "Specials & Packages" for discounts. AE, DC, DISC, MC, V. Parking $25. **Amenities:** 5 restaurants (including Hoku's, p. 146); 4 bars (including Veranda, p. 254); babysitting; complimentary use of bikes; year-round children's program; concierge; nearby golf course; great fitness center w/steam rooms, Jacuzzis, and dry sauna; large outdoor pool; room service; tennis courts; watersports equipment rentals. *In room:* A/C, TV, hair dryer, Wi-Fi ($15/ day), minibar.

HAWAII KAI
Inexpensive
Aloha B&B ★ Perched on a hillside in the residential community of Hawaii Kai is this very affordable B&B, complete with swimming pool, panoramic ocean views, and continental breakfast on the outdoor lanai. Two bedrooms (one with king-size bed, one with twins) share a bathroom and a half (no waiting for the toilet!); the other room has a private bathroom. Hostess Phyllis Young has lots of beach toys and equipment (including coolers and chairs) she will loan you for the day. She'll even do a load of laundry for you for $4. No smoking anywhere on the property, which is just a 10-minute drive to snorkeling in Hanauma Bay and about a 15-minute drive to Waikiki and downtown Honolulu. The inn does not allow smoking.

909 Kahauloa Place, Honolulu, HI 96825. © **808/395-6694.** Fax 808/396-2020. www.home.roadrunner. com/~alohaphyllis. 3 units with shared bathrooms. $85–$100 double. Rates include continental breakfast. 3-night minimum. No credit cards. Free parking. Bus: 22 (stops at the bottom of a steep, uphill climb). **Amenities:** Swimming pool. *In room:* TV, Wi-Fi (free).

J&B's Haven Brits Joan and Barbara Webb have had a successful bed-and-breakfast on Oahu since 1982. Barbara, who has lived in Hawaii since 1970, and her mother Joan, who moved to Hawaii in 1981, are both knowledgeable about Oahu's attractions and love introducing guests to the Hawaii they love. They recently moved to this beautiful house in Hawaii Kai, just 15 minutes east of Waikiki. It's close to Hanauma Bay, Sandy Beach, and Sea Life Park, and is within easy reach of three shopping centers with excellent restaurants. The house features two rooms: the large master bedroom, with private bathroom, king-size bed, minifridge, and microwave; and a smaller room with private bathroom, queen-size bed, small fridge, and microwave. *Note:* This is a smoke-free house. Two very friendly dogs live inside, so if you're allergic to canine housemates, you might look elsewhere.

Kahena St. (at Ainapo St., off Hawaii Kai Dr.), Hawaii Kai. Reservations: P.O. Box 25907, Honolulu, HI 96825. © **808/396-9462.** jnbshaven@hawaii.rr.com. 2 units. $65–$75 double. Rates include expanded continental breakfast. 3-night minimum. No credit cards. Free parking. Bus: 1. *In room:* A/C (room with king-size bed), TV, fridge, microwave.

3 THE WINDWARD COAST

The windward, or eastern, side of the island is where the trade winds blow, rain squalls support lush, tropical vegetation, and subdivisions dot the landscape. The communities of Kailua and Kaneohe dominate here. Bed-and-breakfasts (ranging from oceanfront estates to tiny cottages on quiet residential streets) abound. This is the place for "island" experiences, yet you're still within a 15-minute drive of Waikiki.

Pat O'Malley, of **Pat's Kailua Beach Properties,** 204 S. Kalaheo Ave., Kailua, HI 96734 (© **808/261-1653** or 808/262-4128; fax 808/261-0893; www.patskailua.com), books a wide range of houses and cottages on or near Kailua Beach. Rates start at $100 a day for a studio cottage near the beach and go up to $500 per day for a multimillion-dollar oceanfront home with room to sleep eight. All units are fully furnished, with everything from cooking utensils to telephone and TV, even washer/dryers.

Moderate

Lanikai Bed & Breakfast ★ Finds   This old-time bed-and-breakfast, a *kamaaina* home that reflects the Hawaii of yesteryear, is now into its second generation of owners. The 1,000-square-foot upstairs apartment, which easily accommodates four, is decorated in Old Hawaii bungalow style. There's a king-size bed in one bedroom, twin beds in the other bedroom, a large living/dining room, a big bathroom, a kitchenette, and all the modern conveniences such as DVD players, plus oversize windows to let you enjoy the wonderful views. Or you can follow the ginger- and ti-lined path to a 540-square-foot honeymooner's delight, a quaint studio with a huge patio outside and queen-size bed and sitting area with DVD/VCR combo, cordless phone, answering machine, and recently remodeled full-size kitchen. The units are stocked with breakfast fixings (bagels, juice, fruit, coffee, tea) and all the beach equipment you'll need (towels, mats, chairs, coolers, water jugs). If the B&B is booked, the website lists other accommodations around Lanikai-Kailua.

1277 Mokulua Dr. (btw. Onekea and Aala Dr. in Lanikai), Kailua, HI 96734. © **808/261-7895** or 808/261-1059. www.lanikaibeachrentals.com/vacationrentalsoahu.htm. 2 units. $160 studio double; $175 apt. double or $250 for 3 or 4. Rates include breakfast items in fridge. 5-night minimum. MC, V. Free parking. Bus: 52, 55, or 56. **Amenities:** Washer/dryer, gas grill. *In room:* TV/DVD, fridge, hair dryer, high-speed Internet access (free), kitchenette or kitchen.

Inexpensive

Alii Bluffs Windward Bed & Breakfast   Located on a quiet residential street just 15 minutes from the beach, this traditional B&B is filled with antiques and collectibles, as well as the owners' original art. The guest wing has two rooms, one with a double bed and adjacent bathroom, the other with two extra-long twins and a bathroom across the hall. The yard blooms with tropical plants, and the view of Kaneohe Bay from the pool area is breathtaking. Lots of extras make this B&B stand out from the crowd: daily maid service, a large breakfast served on the poolside lanai, afternoon tea, and sewing kits in the bathroom—they'll even lend you anything you need for the beach.

46-251 Ikiiki St. (off Kamehameha Hwy.), Kaneohe, HI 96744. © **800/235-1151** or 808/235-1124. Fax 808/235-1124. www.hawaiiscene.com/aliibluffs. 2 units. $70–$80 double. Rates include continental breakfast. 3-night minimum. MC, V. Free parking. Bus: 55 or 65. Children must be 16 or older. **Amenities:** Outdoor pool. *In room:* Hair dryer, no phone.

Schrader's Windward Country Inn Kids   Despite the name, the ambience here is more motel than resort, but Schrader's offers a good alternative for families. The property is nestled in a tranquil, tropical setting on Kaneohe Bay, only a 30-minute drive from Waikiki. The complex is made up of cottage-style motels and a collection of older homes. Cottages contain either a kitchenette with refrigerator and microwave or a full kitchen, and a picnic area offers barbecue grills. Prices are based on the views: Depending how much you're willing to pay, you can look out over a Kahuluu fishpond, the Koolau Mountains, or Kaneohe Bay. Watersports are available at an additional cost; don't miss the complimentary 2-hour boat cruise with snorkeling and kayaking. Evening activities include Hawaiian music night and

karaoke night, both with free *pupu*. *Tip:* When booking, ask for a unit with a lanai; that way you'll end up with at least a partial view of the bay.

47–039 Lihikai Dr. (off Kamehameha Hwy.), Kaneohe, HI 96744. 🕐 **800/735-5071** or 808/239-5711. Fax 808/239-6658. www.hawaiiscene.com/schrader. 20 units. $72–$143 1-bedroom double; $127–$215 2-bedroom for 4; $226–$358 3-bedroom for 6; $446–$501 4-bedroom for 8. Rates include continental breakfast. Extra person $7.50. 2-night minimum. AE, DC, DISC, MC, V. Free parking. Bus: 52, 55, or 56. **Amenities:** Outdoor pool; watersports equipment rentals. *In room:* TV, fridge, kitchenette.

Sheffield House (**Kids**)   If you have kids or someone with disabilities needing a room, here's your place in the suburbs of Kailua. Unlike many other B&Bs, Sheffield House welcomes children. The owners, Paul Sheffield and his wife, Rachel, have three kids, so such things as a portable baby bed are no problem. Two units are offered, a one-bedroom and a studio (which is shower-only and fully wheelchair-accessible), each with a private entry (through elaborately landscaped tropical gardens), and a full kitchen. The two spaces can be combined and rented as a two-bedroom/two-bathroom suite.

131 Kuulei Rd. (at Kalaheo Dr.), Kailua, HI 96734. 🕐/fax **808/262-0721.** www.hawaiisheffieldhouse.com. 2 units. $85 double studio; $105 apt. for 4; $200 2-bedroom for 6. Off-season discounts may apply. Rates include 1st day's continental breakfast. 3-night minimum. MC, V. Free parking. Bus: 56 or 57. *In room:* TV, fridge, kitchen.

4 THE NORTH SHORE

Here's the Hawaii of Hollywood: giant waves, surfers galore, tropical jungles, waterfalls, and mysterious Hawaiian temples. If you're looking for a quieter vacation, closer to nature, filled with swimming, snorkeling, diving, surfing, or just plain hanging out on some of the world's most beautiful beaches, the North Shore is for you. It boasts good restaurants, shopping, and cultural activities, along with the quiet of country living. The North Shore doesn't have many accommodations or an abundance of tourist facilities—some say that is its charm. Bed-and-breakfasts are the most common options, but there are some deluxe facilities to consider. *Be forewarned:* The ocean is rough here in winter, and it's nearly an hour's drive from the North Shore to Honolulu and Waikiki.

   Team Real Estate, 66-250 Kamehameha Hwy., Ste. D-103, Haleiwa, HI 96712 (🕐 **800/982-8602** or 808/637-3507; fax 808/637-8881; www.teamrealestate.com), manages vacation rentals on the North Shore. Its units range from $65-a-night condos to $120 one-bedroom apartments to $1,035-per-night 11-bedroom oceanfront luxury homes. A minimum stay of 1 week is required for some properties, but shorter stays are available as well.

Very Expensive

Turtle Bay Resort ★★★   Come here to get out of urban Waikiki, and enjoy the country of Oahu's north shore in a spectacular location on the beach. The resort is located an hour's drive from Waikiki, but it's eons away in its country feeling. It's very private, relaxed and the property is top drawer. Presiding over 808 acres, Turtle Bay is loaded with activities and 5 miles of shoreline with secluded white-sand coves. It's located on Kalaeokaunu Point ("point of the altar"), where ancient Hawaiians built a small altar to the fish gods (the altar's remains are now at the Bishop Museum).

   A recent $35-million renovation to revitalize the 30-year-old resort has made it even more fabulous. The lobby is now open and airy with floor-to-ceiling windows framing the dramatic ocean view. All rooms have ocean views and balconies and now feature marble floors and countertops in the bathroom, and comfy bedding. If you can afford it, book the separate beach cottages. Positioned right on the ocean (the views alone are worth the price), the 42 bungalows boast hardwood floors, four-poster beds with feather comforters, and butler service, even their own private check-in and concierge.

The new soothing Spa Luana offers six treatment rooms, a meditation waiting area, and an outdoor workout area, plus a complete fitness center and a private elevator to the spa's reserved rooms on the second floor. The new restaurant, 21 Degrees North (p. 149), is so good that people drive from all over the island to eat there.

57–091 Kamehameha Hwy. (Hwy. 83), Kahuku, HI 96731. © **800/203-3650** or 808/293-6000. Fax 808/293-9147. www.turtlebayresort.com. 443 units. $232–$300 double; from $527 cottage; from $300 suite; from $662 villa. Extra person $50. Children 17 and under stay free in parent's room. Daily $25 resort fee for self-parking, Internet access, and more. Check website for special packages. AE, DC, DISC, MC, V. Bus: 52 or 55. **Amenities:** 4 restaurants (including 21 Degrees North, p. 149, and Ola, p. 150); 2 bars (live entertainment Fri–Sat at the Bay Club Lounge, plus a poolside bar); babysitting; concierge; 36 holes of golf; 2 Jacuzzis; 2 outdoor heated pools (w/80-ft. water slide); room service; spa w/fitness center; 10 Plexipave tennis courts; watersports equipment rentals; stable w/horseback riding. *In room:* A/C, TV, fridge, hair dryer, high-speed Internet access (included in resort fee).

Moderate

Santa's by the Sea ★ (Finds)   This certainly must be where Santa Claus comes to vacation: St. Nick knows a bargain when he sees it. The location, price, and style make this a must-stay if you plan to visit the North Shore. It's one of the few North Shore B&Bs right on the beach—and not just any beach, but the famous Banzai Pipeline. You can go from your bed to the sand in less than 30 seconds to watch the sun rise over the Pacific. Hosts Gary and Cyndie offer an impeccable one-bedroom unit with finely crafted woodwork, bay windows, and a collection of unique Santa figurines and one-of-a-kind Christmas items. It may sound tacky, but somehow it gives the apartment a country charm. Honeymooners, take note: Privacy abounds here. The unit has its own entrance, a living room with VCR and stereo, a bathroom with shower only, and a full kitchen with everything a cook could need. There's also a barbecue area. Fruit, cereal, bread, coffee, tea, and juice are provided on the first morning, to get you started.

Ke Waena Rd. (off Kamehameha Hwy.), Haleiwa, HI 96712. Reservations c/o Hawaii's Best Bed & Breakfasts, 571 Pauku St., Kailua, HI 96734. © **800/262-9912** or 808/263-3100. Fax 808/62-5030. www.santasbythesea.com. 1 unit (shower only). $225 double. Rates include breakfast items in fridge. Extra person $15. 3-night minimum. No credit cards. Free parking. Bus: 52 or 55. **Amenities:** Washer/dryer; ocean-side gazebo. *In room:* A/C (in bedroom), TV/VCR, fridge, hair dryer, computer with Internet access (free), kitchen.

Inexpensive

Ke Iki Beach Bungalows   This collection of studio, one-, and two-bedroom cottages is located on a beautiful white-sand beach. Snuggled on a large lot with its own 200-foot stretch of white-sand beach between two legendary surf spots (Waimea Bay and Banzai Pipeline), the units are affordable (if you can live without being right on the ocean, the garden units are a great deal). Most units are compact: very small bedrooms with a small kitchen (with all the necessary essentials) and living room. But, hey, with the ocean just outside, how much time are you going to spend inside? The winter waves are too rough for most swimmers, but there's a large lava reef nearby with tide pools to explore and, on the other side, Shark's Cove, a relatively protected snorkeling area. Nearby are tennis courts and a jogging path. All units have full kitchens and their own barbecue areas. *Tip:* Stay on the beach side, where the views are well worth the extra bucks.

59–579 Ke Iki Rd. (off Kamehameha Hwy.), Haleiwa, HI 96712. © **866/638-8229** or 808/638-8229. Fax
808/637-6100. www.keikibeach.com. 11 units. $150 double garden-view studio; $135 double garden-view 1-bedroom; $185–$215 double beachfront 1-bedroom; $155–$185 double garden-view 2-bedroom; $210–$230 double beachfront 2-bedroom. Cleaning fee $55–$100 per week *or* per visit (if less than a week). Extra person stays free. AE, MC, V. Free parking. Bus: 52. **Amenities:** Complimentary watersports equipment and bikes. *In room:* TV, CD player, fridge, kitchen.

Laie Inn   This two-story, plantation-style hotel, within walking distance of the Polynesian Cultural Center, Brigham Young University Hawaii, and the Mormon Temple, has been scheduled (for several years now) to be torn down and replaced with four separate three-story buildings on the 8-acre site. As we went to press, the "latest" discussion no longer had a timeline but was still calling for the old inn to be torn down and rebuilt in "the future." Of course, we've heard this all before. If you would like a place to stay where you can enjoy the nearby Polynesian Cultural Center or get away from urban Waikiki, you will either love or hate this tiny motel. The very old Laie Inn is badly in need of renovation (they recently added new carpets and painted *some* rooms (not all). Generally we found that the bedding and towels are old and worn, the old carpet is dirty, pillows are either lumpy or flat as pancakes, paint is peeling, some bathrooms are moldy and musty, some of the air conditioners sound like they are on their last legs. However, people who love this place all point to the extremely caring staff (as friendly as you will find anywhere in Hawaii), who know that the old place is not up to par, and they make up for it with cheerfulness and helpfulness. The other plus: it is unbelievably cheap! Rates include a small continental breakfast (if you are still hungry, there's a McDonald's nearby). The beach is just across the street.

55-109 Laniloa St. (off Kamehameha Hwy., near the Polynesian Cultural Center), Laie, HI 96762. © **800/526-4562** or 808/293-9282. Fax 808/293-8115. www.laieinnhawaii.com. 49 units. $75–$95 double. Rates include small continental breakfast. Extra person $10. Children under 18 stay free in parent's room. AE, DISC, MC, V. Free parking. Bus: 52 or 55. **Amenities:** Outdoor pool. *In room:* A/C, TV, fridge, free Wi-Fi.

5 LEEWARD OAHU: THE WAIANAE COAST

This area is a new frontier for Oahu visitors. Currently, there is only one exquisite resort in this beach-lined rural section of Oahu, but more are planned. Here's a chance to escape and be far, far away from the hustle and bustle of Waikiki. This is the sunny side of the island, with little rain and lots of sandy beaches. People who love to play golf, enjoy the ocean, and participate in cultural activities will have plenty to do. However, outside the Ko Olina Resort area, there is little in the way of fine dining or interesting shopping.

J. W. Marriott Ihilani Resort & Spa at Ko Olina Resort ★★★ (**Kids**)   When the 640-acre Ko Olina Resort community opened, some 17 miles and 30 minutes west of Honolulu Airport (and worlds away from the tourist scene of Waikiki), critics wondered who would want to stay so far from the city. Lots of people, it turns out. Ihilani ("heavenly splendor") is nestled in a quiet location between the Pacific Ocean and the first of four man-made beach lagoons. Featuring a luxury spa and fitness center, plus tennis and one of Hawaii's premier golf courses, it's a haven of relaxation and well-being. The spa alone is reason enough to come here. Treatments include thalassotherapy, Swiss showers, Vichy showers, Roman pools, and various kinds of massages. You can even have a fitness-and-relaxation program custom-designed.

It's hard to get a bad room in the 15-story building—some 85% of the units enjoy lagoon or ocean views. Accommodations are luxuriously appointed and spacious (680 sq.

ft.), and come with huge lanais outfitted with very comfortable, cushioned teak furniture. A state-of-the-art comfort-control-system panel operates the ceiling fans, air-conditioning, and lights. Luxurious marble bathrooms have deep soaking tubs, separate glass-enclosed showers, and many amenities. Other extras include a daily newspaper, transportation to Waikiki and Ala Moana Shopping Center, a 3-mile coastal fitness trail, and a stretch of four white-sand beaches for ocean activities. The championship 18-hole Ko Olina Golf Course was designed by Ted Robinson.

The Ihilani's children's program puts all others to shame, offering year-round outdoor adventures and indoor learning activities for toddlers and teens alike. Other amenities for the kids include a Computer Learning Center, a 125-gallon fish tank, and an evening lounge for teen-themed parties.

92-1001 Olani St., Kapolei, HI 96707. (©) **800/626-4446** or 808/679-0079. Fax 808/679-0080. www.ihilani. com. 387 units. $249–$439 double; from $850 suite. Extra person $50. Children under 17 (maximum 2) stay free in parent's room using existing bedding. Ask about Paradise Plus package rates, which include a free car rental or daily breakfast for 2 starting at $369. AE, DC, DISC, MC, V. Parking $29. No bus service. Take H-1 west toward Pearl City/Ewa Beach; stay on H-1 until it becomes Hwy. 93 (Farrington Hwy.); look for the exit sign for Ko Olina Resort; turn right on Olani St. **Amenities:** 3 restaurants; 2 bars (w/nightly entertainment poolside); babysitting; excellent children's program; concierge; championship 18-hole Ko Olina Golf Course, designed by Ted Robinson; 2 outdoor pools; room service; world-class spa; tennis club w/pro shop; watersports equipment rentals. *In room:* A/C, TV, hair dryer, minibar, complimentary newspaper delivery, Wi-Fi ($13/day).

6 OAHU'S CAMPGROUNDS & WILDERNESS CABINS

If you plan to camp, you must bring your own gear or buy it here—no one on Oahu rents out gear. If you bring your own equipment, remember that you can't transport fuel (even in a canister) on the plane. If your camping stove requires butane fuel, just leave it at home; butane is very difficult to find in Hawaii.

The best places to camp on Oahu are listed below (for locations, see the "Beaches & Outdoor Pursuits on Oahu" map on p. 154). TheBus's Circle Island route can get you to or near all these sites, but remember: On TheBus, you're allowed only one bag, which has to fit under the seat. If you have more gear, you're going to have to drive or take a cab.

Note: Reservations for all state parks on the island of Oahu cannot be made more than 30 days in advance. To make a reservation, send a letter of request (see contact information, below) stating the park, dates, identification numbers (driver's license, passport, or state ID) for all adults, head count of the minors, and your payment of $18 per night per site for 6 people (each site holds 10 people), if your party is more than six, then an addition fee of $3 per person will be applied for more than six. Payment can be made with a money order, cashier's check, or traveler's check. As we went to press, information is available on the Department of Land and Natural Resources' website, but you cannot apply for permits online. However in 2010, the department promises they will have a Web-based permit system (http://www.hawaiistateparks.org).

HONOLULU

Sand Island State Recreation Area ★

Believe it or not, there is a campground in Honolulu. It's just south of Honolulu Harbor at a waterfront park. Don't be put off by the heavy industrial area you have to drive

Tips on Safety at Hawaii's Parks

Staying at Hawaii's beautiful parks can be a memorable experience. Below are a few safety tips to make sure your stay is safe. Yes, you are in paradise, but don't take unnecessary risks-warnings are posted for your safety, follow them. Be sure to check the weather in advance.

- **Water Safety:** Not all beaches have lifeguards, so know your limits. Poor swimmers must be cautious. If you do not know how to bodysurf or snorkel, do not try it on your own. Always be aware of the ocean, shoreline, and tidal conditions.
- **Emergencies:** In case of an emergency, dial 911 (if you are calling from a pay phone, no coins are required). As a safety rule, always know where the nearest pay phone is to your camp site.
- **Hiking:** Remember that Hawaii has no twilight and we go from daylight to dark FAST! Plan your hike to be back an hour before dark and remember to allow a speed of 1.5 miles per hour when hiking. Always wear proper foot wear (close-toed shoes or hiking shoes) when hiking.
- **Civil Defense Warnings:** Sirens are stationed along the shorelines in Hawaii to alert people of an impending tsunami or other potential hazards. If you hear the siren (a steady tone for 3 minutes, then repeated), immediately get to higher protected ground. (*Note:* the sirens are tested the first Wed of every month at noon)
- **Thefts:** Yes, Virginia, there is theft in Hawaii, and there are particular problems in camping areas. Never leave your personal property in your car or at your campsite unguarded. A thief can get into your locked trunk faster than you can with your keys.

through to reach this 102-acre park with grassy lawns, ironwood trees, and sandy beaches. Campers have great views, better than those of some of the guests in the $400-a-night rooms in Waikiki, of the entire Honolulu coastline all the way to Waikiki. In addition to the scenery, the most popular activity here is shoreline fishing, especially along the western shore of Sand Island. Swimming is an option, but watch out for the rocks along the shoreline bottom; the water quality is occasionally questionable too. The park is also a good base camp for visiting Honolulu attractions; it's just 15 minutes from Waikiki or Pearl Harbor.

Only tent camping is allowed in this park, and only on Friday, Saturday, and Sunday nights. You'll find picnic tables (some under small covered shelters), restrooms with cold showers only, and potable water. You'll need a permit; the fee is $5 per campsite per night. Applications are accepted no earlier than 30 days in advance. Write to the **Department of Land and Natural Resources,** State Parks Division, P.O. Box 621, Honolulu, HI 96809 (© **808/587-0300;** www.hawaiistateparks.org/camping/fees.cfm). Permits are given for a maximum of 5 days in every 30-day period (and because you can only stay on weekends, 5 consecutive days aren't possible). The gates close at 6:45pm in the fall and winter (from the weekend after Labor Day until Mar 31) and 7:45pm in the spring and summer (Apr 1 until the Fri after Labor Day). The gates do not open until 7am the next morning; cars cannot enter or leave during that period. TheBus 19 stops at Nimitz Highway and Puuhale Road; it's just over a mile to walk to the park entrance.

To get here from the Honolulu International Airport, take Nimitz Highway toward Honolulu and Waikiki. Turn right at the Sand Island Access Road (Hwy. 64) and follow it to the end of the road and the park entrance.

CENTRAL OAHU
Keaiwa Heiau State Recreation Area ★
At the southern end of central Oahu, above Halawa Heights, this 385-acre wooded park offers a cool mountain retreat with hiking trails and picnic facilities. This area, in the foothills of the Koolaus, is filled with eucalyptus, ironwood, and Norfolk pines. The remains of the *heiau ho'ola* (temple of treating the sick) are on the grounds, and specimens of Hawaiian medicinal plants are on display. An excellent 5-mile hiking trail, the **Aiea loop,** offers magnificent views of Pearl Harbor and the mountains. There's tent camping only; campers have the choice of flat, open grassy areas or slightly sloping areas with shade trees. Facilities include picnic tables, restrooms with cold showers, outdoor grills, a dishwashing area, a covered pavilion, drinking water, and a public phone. Supplies are available in Aiea, 2 miles away.

You'll need a permit, which cost $5 per campsite per night; applications are accepted no earlier than 30 days in advance. Write to the **Department of Land and Natural Resources** (see "Sand Island State Recreation Area," above, for address and telephone number). Permits are limited to a 5-day stay in every 30-day period. Camping is permitted Friday through Tuesday nights. The gates close at 6:45pm in the fall and winter (from the weekend after Labor Day until Mar 31) and 7:45pm in the spring and summer (Apr 1 until the Fri after Labor Day). The gates do not open until 7am the next morning; cars cannot enter or leave during that period.

From Waikiki, take the H-1 Freeway to Highway 78 and exit at Aiea (Exit 13A). Follow Moanalua Road to Aiea Heights Drive and turn right; the park entrance is at the end of the road. There is no bus service to this area.

THE WINDWARD COAST
Hoomaluhia Botanical Gardens ★
This relatively unknown windward-side camping area, outside Kaneohe, is a real find. *Hoomaluhia* means "peace and tranquillity," an apt description for this 400-acre botanical garden. In the lush garden setting with rare plants and craggy cliffs in the background, it's hard to believe you're just a half-hour from downtown Honolulu. The gardens are laid out with areas devoted to the plants specific to tropical America, native Hawaii, Polynesia, India, Sri Lanka, and Africa. A 32-acre lake sits in the middle of the scenic park (no swimming or boating allowed, though), and there are numerous **hiking trails.** The Visitors Center can suggest a host of activities, ranging from guided walks to demonstrations of ancient Hawaiian plant use. The facilities for this tent-camp area include restrooms, cold showers, dishwashing stations, picnic tables, grills, and water. A public phone is available at the Visitors Center, and shopping and gas are available in Kaneohe, 1 mile away.

Permits are free, but you have to get here on a Friday no later than 3pm, as the office is not open on weekends. Stays are limited to Friday, Saturday, and Sunday nights only. You must apply in person. To get a permit, contact **Parks Permit Section,** Honolulu

Municipal Building, 650 S. King St., Honolulu, HI 96713 (© **808/523-4525;** www. co.honolulu.hi.us/parks/permits.htm), or any Satellite City Halls (www.honolulu.gov/ csd/satellite). For inquiries and reservations, contact **Hoomaluhia Botanical Gardens,** 45-680 Luluku Rd. (at Kamehameha Hwy.), Kaneohe, HI 96744 (© **808/233-7323**). The gate is locked at 4pm; it is open again from 5:30 to 6:30pm, and then closed for the night after that until 9am the next morning. TheBus no. 55 (Circle Island) stops 4 miles from the park entrance.

From Waikiki, take H-1 to the Pali Highway (Hwy. 61) and turn left on Kamehameha Highway (Hwy. 83); at the fourth light, turn left on Luluku Road.

Kualoa Regional Park ★★

This park has a spectacular setting on a peninsula on Kaneohe Bay. The gold-sand beach is excellent for snorkeling, and fishing can be rewarding (p. 160). Two campgrounds are available: Campground A—in a wooded area with a sandy beach and palm, ironwood, kamani, and monkeypod trees—is mainly used for groups, but has a few sites for families, except during the summer, when the Department of Parks and Recreation conducts a children's camping program here. Campground B is on the main beach; it has fewer shade trees, but a great view of Mokolii Island. Facilities at both sites include restrooms, showers, picnic tables, drinking fountains, and a public phone. Campground A also has sinks for dishwashing, a volleyball court, and a kitchen building. Gas and groceries are available in Kaaawa, 2½ miles away. Gate hours are 7am to 8pm; if you're not back by then, you're locked out for the night.

Permits are free but limited to 5 days (no camping Wed–Thurs). Contact the **Honolulu Department of Parks and Recreation,** (see address above in Hoomaluhia Botanical Gardens). Kualoa Regional Park is in the 49-600 area of Kamehameha Highway, across from Mokolii Island. Take the Likelike Highway (Hwy. 63); after the Wilson Tunnel, get in the right lane and turn off on Kahakili Highway (Hwy. 83). Or take TheBus no. 55.

Kahana Bay Beach Park ★★

Under Tahiti-like cliffs, with a beautiful, gold-sand crescent beach framed by pine-needle casuarina trees, Kahana Bay Beach Park is a place of serene beauty. You can swim, bodysurf, fish, hike, picnic, or just sit and listen to the trade winds whistle through the beach pines.

Both tent and vehicle camping are allowed at this oceanside oasis. Facilities include restrooms, picnic tables, drinking water, public phones, and a boat-launching ramp. Note that the restrooms are at the north end of the beach, far away from the camping area, and there are no showers. You'll need a permit; the fee is $5 per campsite per night. There's a 5-night limit, and no camping at all on Wednesday or Thursday nights. You can get a permit from the **Department of Land and Natural Resources,** State Parks Division, P.O. Box 621, Honolulu, HI 96809 (© **808/587-0300;** www.hawaiistate parks.org/camping/fees.cfm).

Kahana Bay Beach Park is in the 52-222 block of Kamehameha Highway (Hwy. 83) in Kahana. From Waikiki, take the H-1 west to the Likelike Highway (Hwy. 63). Continue north on the Likelike, through the Wilson Tunnel, turning left on Highway 83; Kahana Bay is 13 miles down the road on the right. You can also get there via TheBus no. 55.

Waimanalo Bay State Recreation Area ★

Just outside the town of Waimanalo is one of the most beautiful beachfront camping grounds on Oahu: Steep verdant cliffs in the background, a view of Rabbit Island off shore, and miles of white-sand beach complete the picture of Waimanalo Bay State Recreation Area. This campground is close to Sea Life Park and relatively close to Hanauma Bay, Makapuu, and Sandy Beach.

Ocean activities abound: great swimming offshore, good surfing for beginners, and plentiful fishing grounds. There is tent camping only at the 12 sites, which ensures plenty of privacy. The campsites (in numbered slots) are all in the open grassy lawn between the ironwood trees and the shoreline. Each campsite has its own picnic table, barbecue grill, and garbage can. Other facilities in the area include a central restroom with showers, water fountains, and a dishwashing sink. A public telephone is by the caretaker's house.

Permits are free but limited to 5 nights (no camping on Wed or Thurs nights). Contact the **Honolulu Department of Parks and Recreation,** 650 S. King St., Honolulu, HI 96713 (*C* **808/523-4525;** www.co.honolulu.hi.us/parks/permits.htm), for information and permits. Permits are not issued until 2 weeks before your camping dates.

TheBus no. 57 stops on Kalanianaole Highway (Hwy. 72), about a mile's walking distance to the park entrance. From Honolulu, take the H-1 Freeway east until it ends. Continue on Highway 72 into Waimanalo. Turn right on Whiteman Road and then right again on Walker Road, which leads to the park entrance.

THE NORTH SHORE

Malaekahana Bay State Recreation Area ★★★

This beautiful camping site has a mile-long gold-sand beach, with two areas for tent camping. Facilities include picnic tables, restrooms, showers, sinks, drinking water, and a phone. Stays are limited to 5 nights (no camping on Wed or Thurs nights). Camping fees are $5 per campsite per night; permits can be obtained at any state parks office, including the **Department of Land and Natural Resources,** State Parks Division, P.O. Box 621, Honolulu, HI 96809 (*C* **808/587-0300;** www.hawaiistateparks.org/camping/fees.cfm). The park gate is closed between 6:45pm and 7am; vehicles cannot enter or exit during those hours. Groceries and gas are available in Laie and Kahuku, less than a mile away.

The recreation area is on Kamehameha Highway (Hwy. 83) between Laie and Kahuku. To get there, take the H-2 Freeway to Highway 99 to Highway 83 (both roads are called Kamehameha Hwy.); continue on Highway 83 just past Kahuku. Or take TheBus no. 55.

Camp Mokuleia ★★

A quiet, isolated beach on Oahu's North Shore, 4 miles from Kaena Point, is the centerpiece of this 9-acre campground. Camping is available on the beach or in a grassy, wooded area. Activities include swimming, surfing, shore fishing, and beachcombing. Facilities include tent camping, cabins, and lodge accommodations. The tent-camping site has portable chemical toilets, a water spigot, and outdoor showers; there are no picnic tables or barbecue grills, so come prepared. The cabins sleep up to 22 people in bunk beds. The cabins are $190 per night for the 14-bed cabin and $275 per night for the 22-bed cabin. Rooms at the lodge (must have a group of 15 for meal service) are $75 for a shared bathroom and $85 for a private bathroom. Tent camping is $15 per person, per night. Many groups use the camp, but there's a real sense of privacy. Parking is $3 per day. Reservations are required; contact **Camp Mokuleia,** 68-729 Farrington Hwy., Waialua, HI 96791 (*C* **808/637-6241;** www.campmokuleia.org).

Camp Mokuleia is on Farrington Highway, west of Haleiwa. To get here from Waikiki, take the H-1 to the H-2 exit; stay on H-2 until the end. Where the road forks, bear left to Waialua on Highway 803, which turns into Highway 930, to Kaena Point. Look for the green fence on the right, where a small sign at the driveway reads CAMP MOKULEIA, EPISCOPAL CHURCH OF HAWAII.

Where to Dine

You won't go hungry on Oahu. The full range of choices here includes chef-owned glamour restaurants, neighborhood eateries, fast-food joints, ethnic spots, and restaurants and food courts in shopping malls.

The recommendations below are organized by location, beginning with Waikiki, proceeding to neighborhoods west and east of Waikiki, and ending with the Windward Coast and the North Shore.

The culinary scene seems to change each year, and the current trends in Hawaii center on emphasizing organic and locally grown produce (with some restaurants actually naming the farms that grew the lettuce), small plates, sample tastings and even bite-size desserts, interesting and unusual specialty sandwiches on a variety of breads (from spelt to wraps), and exotic salt (in a range of colors and flavors). Hawaii regional cuisine and Pacific regional cuisine still reign supreme in Hawaii, as well as Pan-Asian and Mediterranean.

Whatever you have a hankering for, you'll find it on Oahu. My advice is to be adventurous, try new and different cuisine, and sample foods you've never heard of. It's moments like these that create great memories.

---

1 WAIKIKI

VERY EXPENSIVE

La Mer ★★★ NEOCLASSIC FRENCH This is *the* splurge restaurant of Hawaii, the oceanfront bastion of haute cuisine, where two of the state's finest chefs (George Mavrothalassitis and Philippe Padovani, each with his own eponymous restaurant now) quietly redefined fine dining in Hawaii. La Mer is romantic, elegant, and expensive; dress up not to be seen, but to match the ambience and food. It's the only AAA Five Diamond restaurant in the state, with a second-floor, open-sided room with views of Diamond Head and the sound of trade winds rustling the nearby coconut fronds. Michelin Award–winning chef Yves Garnier melds classical French influences with fresh Island ingredients. Winners include the signature crispy-skin filet of onaga with truffle jus, tomato confit, and fresh basil, and the delightful local fish baked in a rosemary-salt crust. The wine list, desserts, and service—formal without being stiff—complete the dining experience.

At the Halekulani, 2199 Kalia Rd. *C* **808/923-2311.** www.halekulani.com. Reservations recommended. Jackets or long-sleeved shirts required for men. Prix-fixe menus $90 for 2 courses, $120 for 3 courses, $135 for 4 courses; $190 for "Ultimate" dinner with Rémy Martin V.S.O.P., available Nov–Dec only. AE, DC, MC, V. Daily 6–10pm.

Michel's ★★ FRENCH/HAWAIIAN REGIONAL This dining room, on the sand at Sans Souci Beach, has windows that open to the ocean air. One side looks toward the sunset, with torches on the breakwater, and a hula moon above the palm fronds; the Waikiki skyline is visible on the other. All tables have ocean views, and dining here is less stiff and more welcoming than in bygone years. Jackets are no longer required for men, but collared shirts and long pants are preferred. Chef Hardy Kintscher has added his

Well, not totally no smoking, but Hawaii has one of the toughest laws against smoking in the U.S. It's against the law to smoke in public buildings, including airports, shopping malls, grocery stores, retail shops, buses, movie theaters, banks, convention facilities, and all government buildings and facilities. There is no smoking in restaurants, bars, and nightclubs. Most bed-and-breakfasts prohibit smoking indoors; more and more hotels and resorts are becoming nonsmoking, even in public areas. Also, there is no smoking within 20 feet of a doorway, window, or ventilation intake (no hanging around outside a bar to smoke, you must go 20 ft. away). Even some beaches have no-smoking policies (and on those that allow smoking, you'd better pick up your butts and not use the sand as your own private ashtray—or face stiff fines). In Hawaii, breathing fresh clean air is "in" and smoking is "out."

touch to the classics (onion soup, steak tartare, chateaubriand, bouillabaisse) and prepares fresh seafood, vegetarian creations, and rack of lamb with restraint and creativity.

At the Colony Surf Hotel, 2895 Kalakaua Ave. (C) **808/923-6552.** www.michelshawaii.com. Reservations recommended. Collared shirts and long pants preferred for men; no shorts or beachwear permitted. Main courses $36–$49. AE, DC, MC, V. Daily 5:30–9pm; Sun brunch 10am–1pm.

EXPENSIVE

Bali by the Sea ★★ CONTINENTAL/PACIFIC RIM   This is another memorable oceanfront dining room—pale and full of light, with a white grand piano at the entrance and sweeping views of the ocean (ask for a table by the window). The menu merges island cooking styles and ingredients, as in their signature sautéed *opakapaka* (pink snapper) crusted with macadamia nuts and cilantro with ginger-scented jasmine rice and a kaffir lime sauce; the wonderful seafood duo (tempura ahi with orange miso-glazed Kona kampachi) with Molokai sweet potatoes and Big Island hearts of palm salad; or the popular Bali trio, which combines the signature opakapaka with grilled filet mignon and lemongrass prawns in a spicy mango coulis. The menu also features "heart healthy" items like the angel hair pasta with vine-ripened Hawaii tomatoes, Big Island mushrooms, and island-grown asparagus in a basil tomato sauce. Save room for their mouthwatering desserts.

At the Hilton Hawaiian Village, 2005 Kalia Rd. (C) **808/949-4321,** ext. 43. Reservations recommended. Main courses $26–$60. AE, DC, DISC, MC, V. Mon–Sat 6–9:30pm.

Diamond Head Grill ★★ NEW AMERICAN/PACIFIC RIM   New executive chef Eric Sakai has designed a menu that begins with a foie gras torchon with frisée salad and toasted brioche or, for fish fans, cold, smoked hamachi *crudo* with avocado and orange, topped with extra-virgin olive oil. My pick for the best salad is the delightful chicory salad with persimmons, Gorgonzola, and hazelnuts with an apple-cider vinaigrette. Main courses range from house-made pastas (*bruitti ma buni,* a fried ricotta and parmigiano dumpling) to fish (slow-cooked Hawaiian *walu* with braised artichokes and mushrooms) and meat and game (organic chicken with creamy polenta). Suggested wine pairings can accompany each entree. Don't pass up the desserts—the "Way Too Much Chocolate" is a must-try. Fridays and Saturdays after 10pm, the place becomes a very hot nightspot, jammed with beautiful people dancing to music spun by DJs.

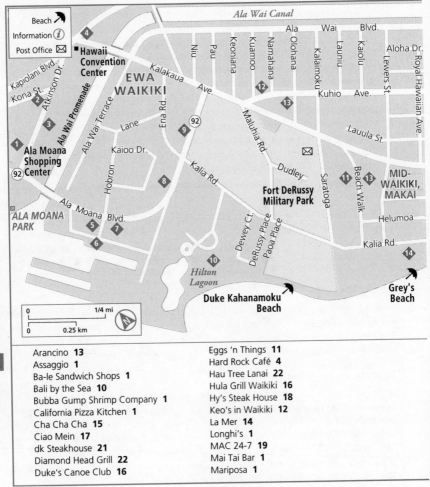

WHERE TO DINE

5

WAIKIKI

Arancino **13**
Assaggio **1**
Ba-le Sandwich Shops **1**
Bali by the Sea **10**
Bubba Gump Shrimp Company **1**
California Pizza Kitchen **1**
Cha Cha Cha **15**
Ciao Mein **17**
dk Steakhouse **21**
Diamond Head Grill **22**
Duke's Canoe Club **16**

Eggs 'n Things **11**
Hard Rock Café **4**
Hau Tree Lanai **22**
Hula Grill Waikiki **16**
Hy's Steak House **18**
Keo's in Waikiki **12**
La Mer **14**
Longhi's **1**
MAC 24-7 **19**
Mai Tai Bar **1**
Mariposa **1**

The Lotus at Diamond Head, 2885 Kalakaua Ave. ℭ **808/922-3734.** www.w-dhg.com. Reservations recommended. Main courses $15–$35. AE, DC, DISC, MC, V. Daily 7–10:30am and 6–10pm; live entertainment Wed–Thurs 5–10pm, DJ Fri–Sat 10pm–2am.

Hy's Steak House STEAKHOUSE This steakhouse is as good as it gets. Think dark, clubby, lots of leather, good Scotch, and filet mignon. This is a great choice for steak lovers with hefty pocketbooks or for those who have tired of Hawaii regional cuisine. Hy's has demonstrated admirable staying power in the cult of low fat, still scoring high among carnivores while offering ample alternatives, such as a grilled vegetable platter and

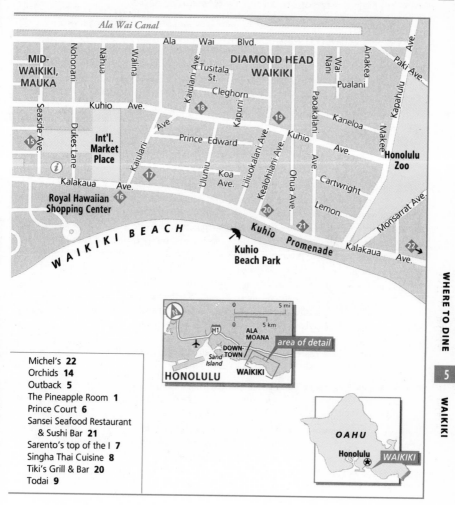

Michel's **22**
Orchids **14**
Outback **5**
The Pineapple Room **1**
Prince Court **6**
Sansei Seafood Restaurant
  & Sushi Bar **21**
Sarento's top of the I **7**
Singha Thai Cuisine **8**
Tiki's Grill & Bar **20**
Todai **9**

excellent salads prepared tableside (the spinach and Caesar are textbook-perfect). "The Only" is its classic best, a kiawe-grilled New York strip steak served with a secret signature sauce. Garlic lovers swear by the "Garlic Steak Diane," a richly endowed rib-eye with sliced mushrooms.

2440 Kuhio Ave. ℂ **808/922-5555.** Reservations recommended. Main courses $21–$60 or market price. AE, DC, DISC, MC, V. Mon–Fri 6–10pm; Sat–Sun 5:30–10pm.

Orchids ★★ INTERNATIONAL/SEAFOOD Orchids highlights fresh local produce and seafood with elegant presentations in a fantasy setting with consummate service. Blinding white linens and a view of Diamond Head from the open oceanfront

Room Service from 50 Different Restaurants

You are not limited to the room service menu in your hotel room; **Room Service in Paradise** (© **808/941-DINE** [3463]; www.941-dine.com) delivers almost a dozen different cuisines (from American/Pacific Rim to Italian to sandwiches and burgers) from oodles of restaurants to your hotel room. All you do is select a restaurant and order what you want (see the online menus or pick up one of the magazines in various Waikiki locations). You are charged for the food, a $7.25 to $8.25 delivery charge in Waikiki (more in outlying areas), and a tip for the driver. Both lunch and dinner are available; call in advance, and your food will be delivered whenever you want. Best of all, you can pay with your credit card.

dining room will start you off with a smile. (The parade of oiled bodies traversing the seawall is part of the entertainment.) At lunch, the seafood and vegetable curries, though pricey, are winners, and the steamed *ehu* (short-tail red snapper) is an Orchids signature. The executive lunch specials are an excellent way to sample this fare without breaking the bank: $22 for two courses and $26 for three. For dinner, onaga is steamed with ginger, Chinese parsley, shiitake mushrooms, and soy sauce, then drizzled with hot sesame oil— delightful. Delicately textured opakapaka is sautéed and presented with wasabi mashed potatoes and wasabi cream, another pleaser with Asian undertones. Lamb, chicken, and beef entrees are offered as well, and the desserts, especially the chocolate hazelnut dacquoise and the Halekulani signature coconut cake, are extraordinary. **Sunday brunch ★★★**, with its outstanding selection of dishes, is one of the best in Hawaii.

At the Halekulani, 2199 Kalia Rd. © **808/923-2311.** Reservations recommended. Dinner main courses $19–$58; 3-course prix-fixe dinner $57; Sun brunch $52 adults, $29 children 5–12. AE, DC, MC, V. Mon–Sat 7:30–11am, 11:30am–2pm, and 6–10pm; Sun 9:30am–2:30pm and 6–10pm.

Prince Court ★ CONTEMPORARY HAWAIIAN   Floor-to-ceiling windows, sunny views of the harbor, and top-notch buffets are Prince Court's attractions, especially at lunch, when locals and visitors line up for the international spread. Chef Khamtan Tanhchaleun keeps the menu fresh and the dining room busy. The harbor view is particularly pleasing at sunset or on Friday nights when fireworks light up the sky. Wednesdays and Thursdays, diners can sample everything from island seafood to Hawaiian regional specialties (such as melt-in-your-mouth ahi carpaccio) and excellent grilled and roasted meats at the buffet. Desserts, too, are legendary, especially the custard-drenched bread pudding and the macadamia nut pie.

At the Hawaii Prince Hotel Waikiki, 100 Holomoana St. © **808/944-4494.** Reservations recommended. Dinner prix fixe and buffet $37–$57 (no a la carte for dinner), breakfast buffet $21, weekend brunch $36, luncheon buffet $25, seafood dinner buffet $43. AE, DC, MC, V. Daily 6–10:30am; Mon–Sat 11am–2pm; Sun brunch 10am–1pm; Mon–Thurs 6–9:30pm; Fri–Sun 5:30–9:30pm.

Sarento's Top of the I ★ ITALIAN   The ride up in the glass elevator at this special-occasion Italian restaurant is an event in itself, and diners rave about the romantic view of the city—but Sarento's is not all show. The stellar Greek salad (a trademark of this restaurant chain), the opakapaka portofino with asparagus in a lemon-dill-butter sauce, and the seafood fra diavolo in marinara sauce prove that Sarento's means business. The

pasta selections include lobster ravioli and the simple (and divine) capellini pomodoro. **125**
Veal lovers come for the osso buco with saffron risotto. Dishes can be buttery, so leave
your inhibitions at the door.

In the Renaissance Ilikai Waikiki, 1777 Ala Moana Blvd. ⓒ **808/955-5559.** Reservations recommended.
Main courses $25–$39. AE, DC, DISC, MC, V. Sun–Thurs 5:30–9pm; Fri–Sat 5:30–9:30pm.

MODERATE

Arancino ITALIAN   When jaded Honolulu residents venture into Waikiki for dinner,
it had better be good. A cheerful cafe with Monet-yellow walls and tile floors, respectable
pastas, wonderful pizzas, fabulous red-pepper salsa and rock-salt focaccia, we-try-harder
service, and reasonable prices, Arancino is worth the hunt. The risotto changes daily, and
you should not miss the Gorgonzola-asparagus pizza if it's on the menu. Expect a line on
the sidewalk to get in, but it's worth the wait.

255 Beach Walk. ⓒ **808/923-5557.** Main courses $10–$35. AE, DC, DISC, MC, V. Daily 11am–2:30pm and
5–10pm.

Ciao Mein ITALIAN/CHINESE   Risotto with chopsticks, fried rice with a fork—
such is the cross-cultural way of Ciao Mein, which is 15 years old and still going strong.
The large, pleasant dining room, efficient service, surprisingly good Chinese food, and
award-winning menu have made this a haven for noodle lovers. The honey-walnut
shrimp, with snap peas and honey-glazed nuts, and the angel-hair pasta with spicy gin-
ger-garlic shrimp, are big hits, and Ciao Mein's tiramisu packs a creamy, ambrosial kick.

WHERE TO DINE

5

WAIKIKI

Dining in Waikiki 24-7

If your flight to Honolulu arrives late and you're starving, your knight in shining
armor in Waikiki is the newly opened **MAC 24-7** (which stands for Modern
American Cooking, 24 hours a day, 7 days a week), at the **Hilton Waikiki Prince
Kuhio Hotel,** 2500 Kuhio Ave. (at Liliuokalani Ave.; ⓒ **808/921-5564**). All day,
every day, the kitchen offers everything from breakfast, lunch, and dinner to
snacks and desserts, and the bar pours drinks all day, except between 4 and
6am. It's not just for late-night dining (although it comes in handy, as Waikiki
eateries shut down by 10–11pm), it's also a great place to get picnic lunches
during the day.

The cuisine is coffee shop/diner "comfort" food, reasonably priced for Waikiki
($4–$28, with most entrees in the $15–$28 range), and plenty of it. Portions
can feed two and, in some cases, three people. My pick for best meal of the
day is breakfast, where the six-pack of buttery cinnamon rolls ($6) will feed
three and the yummy wild blueberry pancakes ($15) are supersized (three
pancakes, each one 14 in. in diameter), plenty for two hungry people. Another
must-try from the menu: the delicious meatloaf with garlic mashed potatoes
and mushroom gravy ($18). The view from the floor-to-ceiling windows is of
the landscaped gardens in the lobby. The decor is sophisticated but sparse
with splashes of bright color, and the waitstaff is friendly and helpful.

The antipasto is Italian, and the seafood fun (as in chow fun) lasagna is a form of Ciao Mein's "collision cuisine"—a mix of Chinese and Italian. Choose from six different pastas and six sauces.

In the Hyatt Regency Waikiki, 2424 Kalakaua Ave. ℭ **808/923-2426.** Reservations recommended. Main courses $25–$40, prix fixe $68–$78. AE, DC, DISC, MC, V. Daily 6–10pm.

d.k Steakhouse ★ STEAK   Attention carnivores: This steakhouse opened in 2004 to rave reviews, giving the national steakhouse chains and the top local steakhouses a run for their money. Locally known chef D. K. Kodama (of Sansei Seafood Restaurant & Sushi Bar, p. 127, and Vino Italian Tapas & Wine Bar, p. 139) and Hawaii's top sommelier Chuck Furuya have created the ultimate steakhouse for the 21st century at very reasonable prices (especially for Waikiki). Purists will love the prime grade and dry-aged (in house for 10 days) New York strip and filet mignon, served unadorned or topped with either three-peppercorn sauce au poivre, blue crab and béarnaise sauce, shiitake mushroom demi-glace, or D.K.'s own sesame seed–miso sauce. The ultimate treat is the 22-ounce, bone-in rib-eye (dry-aged for 15 days): Every bite has a melt-in-your-mouth richness that steak fans will remember forever. I recommend booking a table outside on the lanai and coming early to watch the sun set over Waikiki Beach. The decor is romantic, with dim lighting, intimate wooden booths, and tiny bar lights. Steak alternatives include a fresh catch, lamb chops, and broiled herbed chicken.

Waikiki Beach Marriott Resort, 2552 Kalakaua Ave., 3rd floor. ℭ **808/931-6280.** dksteakhouse.com. Reservations recommended. Main courses $18–$65. AE, DISC, MC, V. Daily 5:30–10pm.

Duke's Waikiki ★ Ⓥalue STEAK/SEAFOOD   Hip, busy, and on the ocean—this is what dining in Waikiki should be. There's hardly a time when the open-air dining room isn't filled with good Hawaiian music. Duke's is popular among singles, but don't dismiss it as a pickup bar—its ambience is stellar. Named after fabled surfer Duke Kahanamoku, this casual, upbeat hotspot buzzes with diners and Hawaiian-music lovers throughout the day. The lunch and Barefoot Bar menus include pizza, sandwiches, burgers, salads, and appetizers such as mac-nut and crab wontons and the ever-popular grilled chicken quesadillas. Dinner fare is steak and seafood, with decent marks for the fresh catch, prepared in your choice of five styles. Live entertainment is featured nightly from 4pm to midnight, with no cover. Be prepared to fight the crowds if you come at sunset.

In the Outrigger Waikiki on the Beach, 2335 Kalakaua Ave. ℭ **808/922-2268.** www.hulapie.com. Reservations recommended for dinner. Main courses $18–$27, breakfast buffet $15. AE, DC, DISC, MC, V. Daily 7am–midnight.

Hau Tree Lanai ★ PACIFIC RIM   Informal and delightful, this Honolulu institution scores higher on ambience than on food. The outdoor setting and earnest menu make it a popular informal dining spot; an ancient hau tree provides shade and charm for diners. A diverse parade of beachgoers at Sans Souci Beach (called "Dig Me Beach" for its eye-candy sunbathers) is part of the scenery. Breakfast here is a must: Choices include salmon Florentine, served with a fresh-baked scone; poi pancakes; Belgian waffles; eggs Benedict; and the Hawaiian platter of miniature poi pancakes, eggs, and a medley of island sausages. Lunchtime offerings include an assortment of burgers, sandwiches, salads, and fresh-fish and pasta specialties. Dinner selections are more ambitious and less reliable: fresh *opah* (moonfish), red snapper, opakapaka, ahi, and chef's specials, in preparations ranging from grilled to stuffed and over-the-top rich.

At the New Otani Kaimana Beach Hotel, 2863 Kalakaua Ave. ℭ **808/921-7066.** Reservations recommended. Breakfast $10–$15, lunch $10–$15, dinner $30–$39. AE, DC, DISC, MC, V. Mon–Sat 7–11am,

11:45am–2pm, and 5:30–9pm; Sun 7–11am, noon–2pm, and 5:30–9pm. Late lunch in the open-air bar
daily 2–4pm.

Hula Grill Waikiki ★★ (**Value**) HAWAIIAN REGIONAL This is the best place for breakfast in Waikiki: Not only does it have a terrific view of all of Waikiki (clear to Diamond Head), but the food is fabulous and a great value. Breakfast is a generous selection of pancakes (banana, mac-nut, pineapple, even coconut) and eggs (from crab cake eggs Benedict to a ham, bacon, and Portuguese sausage omelet with cheddar). Come back for a romantic dinner—the restaurant is decorated in a 1930s Hawaii waterfront home theme, with such touches as an ohia log bar, hula doll collection, slate flooring, and lauhala pine-soffited ceilings. Signature dinner dishes at this beachside bistro include Hawaiian ceviche, fire-grilled *ono* (wahoo), oven-roasted sesame opah, and a nightly collection of specials.

In the Outrigger Waikiki on the Beach, 2335 Kalakaua Ave. ℂ 808/923-HULA [4852]. www.hulagrill waikiki.com. Reservations recommended for dinner. Breakfast $6–$14, main courses $17–$33. AE, DC, MC, V. Daily 6:30–10:45am, 4:30–6pm (happy hour with light menu), and 4:45–10pm.

Keo's in Waikiki ★ THAI With fresh spices, spirited dishes, and a familiar crop of Thai delights, Keo's arrived in Waikiki with a splashy tropical ambience and a menu that islanders and visitors love. Owner Keo Sananikone grows his own herbs, fruits, and vegetables without pesticides on his North Shore farm. Satay shrimp, basil-infused eggplant with tofu, "evil jungle prince" (shrimp, chicken, or vegetables in a basil-coconut-chili sauce), Thai garlic shrimp with mushrooms, pad Thai noodles, and the ever-delectable panang, green, and yellow curries are among his abiding delights.

2028 Kuhio Ave. ℂ 808/951-9355. www.keosthaicuisine.com. Reservations recommended. Main courses $11–$38, prix fixe $30–$50. AE, DC, DISC, MC, V. Daily 7am–2pm; Sun–Thurs 5–10:30pm; Fri–Sat 5–11pm.

Sansei Seafood Restaurant & Sushi Bar ★★ SUSHI/ASIAN/PACIFIC RIM Perpetual award-winner D. K. Kodama, who built Kapalua's Sansei into one of Maui's most popular eateries, has become something of a local legend with his exuberant brand of sushi and fusion cooking. Although some of the flavors (sweet Thai chili sauce with cilantro, for example) may be too fussy for sushi purists, choices abound on the extensive menu: Sansei's award-winning trademark Asian rock shrimp cake and Sansei special sushi (crab, cilantro, cucumber, and avocado with a sweet chili sauce), seared foie gras nigiri sushi (duck liver lightly seared over sushi rice, accompanied by caramelized onion and ripe mango), or the wonderful mango crab salad hand roll with mango, blue crab, greens, and peanuts all wrapped in soybean paper with a sweet Thai chili vinaigrette. More traditional selections range from very fresh yellowtail sushi to Japanese miso eggplant.

Waikiki Beach Marriott Resort, 2552 Kalakaua Ave., 3rd floor. ℂ 808/931-6286. www.sanseihawaii.com. Reservations recommended. Sushi $8–$20, main courses $19–$43. AE, DISC, MC, V. Sat–Wed 5:30–10pm; Thurs–Fri 5:30pm–1am.

Singha Thai Cuisine THAI The Royal Thai dancers arch their graceful fingers nightly in classical Thai dance on the small center stage, but you may be too busy tucking into your blackened ahi summer rolls to notice. Imaginative combination dinners and the use of local organic ingredients are among the special touches of this Thai-Hawaiian fusion restaurant. Complete dinners for two to five cover many tastes and are an ideal way for the uninitiated to sample this cuisine, as well as the elements of Hawaii regional cuisine that have had considerable influence on the chef. Some highlights of a diverse menu: local fresh catch with Thai chili and black-bean sauce; red, green, yellow, and vegetarian curries; and spicy lemongrass soup with shrimp. Such extensive use of fresh

(Moments) Tasty Tours for the Hungry Traveler

See Honolulu—one restaurant at a time. Former Honolulu newspaper food critic and chef Matthew Gray has put together **"Hawaii Food Tours"** to show you a side of Hawaii that you would not discover on your own. He offers three different types of tours, all with transportation from your Waikiki hotel in an air-conditioned van and all with running commentary on Hawaii's history, culture, and architecture. Our favorite was the "Hole-in-the-Wall Tour," a lunch tour from 10am to 2pm for $99 per person, where you visit at least four different ethnic restaurants (Vietnamese, Indian, local food, and dessert). Mathew has already preordered the best dishes from their menus. He also offers the "Hawaiian Feast in Paradise," a three-course feast in contemporary Hawaiian foods for $149, and a "Gourmet Trilogy Tour" of three different restaurants with everything from champagne to a decadent dessert for $199 per person. For information and booking, call © **800/715-2468** or 808/926-FOOD [3663], or go to www.hawaiifoodtours.com.

fish (mahimahi, ono, ahi, opakapaka, onaga, and uku) in traditional Thai preparations is unusual for a Thai restaurant. The entertainment and indoor-outdoor dining add to this first-class experience.

1910 Ala Moana Blvd. (at the Ala Moana end of Waikiki). © **808/941-2898.** www.singhathai.com. Reservations recommended. Main courses $17–$36. AE, DC, DISC, MC, V. Daily 4–11pm.

Tiki's Grill & Bar AMERICAN/PACIFIC RIM   Located on the second floor of the ResortQuest Waikiki Beach Hotel, overlooking Waikiki Beach (grab an outside table on the lanai before sunset), this casual eatery is decorated in palm wood flooring with fish nets hanging from the ceiling and lava-rock walls. A 30-foot volcano is the showpiece in the bar (where you can snack on *pupu,* or appetizers). Chef Ron Villoria's cuisine is good ol' American, with his particular touch of Pacific Rim, apparent in all his fish dishes. Tiki's signature dish is king salmon glazed with lemongrass beurre blanc. Also high on the list is the opah grilled with a spicy seafood salsa. Save room for Tiki's chocolate lava flow, brownie s'mores, and outstanding *lilikoi* (yellow passion fruit) cheesecake with basil syrup. Live Hawaiian music is featured nightly in the bar, plus Saturday and Sunday afternoons.

Aston Waikiki Beach Hotel, 2570 Kalakaua Ave. (at Paoakalani St.). © **808/923-TIKI** [8454]. Main courses $12–$20 lunch, $26–$39 dinner. AE, DC, DISC, MC, V. Daily 10:30am–midnight.

INEXPENSIVE

Cha Cha Cha MEXICAN/CARIBBEAN   Its heroic margaritas, cheap happy-hour beer, *pupu,* excellent homemade chips, and all-around lovable menu make this a Waikiki treasure. From the beans to the salsa to the grilled Jamaican chicken, there's nothing wimpy about the flavors here. The lime, coconut, and Caribbean spices make Cha Cha Cha more than plain old Mex, adding zing to the blackened mahimahi and fresh-fish burritos, the jerk chicken breast, and the grilled veggies in a spinach tortilla. Tacos, tamales, quesadillas, soups, enchiladas, chimichangas, and a host of spicy pork, chicken, and fish ensembles are real pleasers. Blackened swordfish, shrimp fajitas, daily specials, and homemade desserts (including a creamy toasted coconut custard) are some of the highlights.

342 Seaside Ave. ℂ **808/923-7797.** Complete dinners $10–$19. MC, V. Daily 11:30am–11pm; happy hour 4–6pm and 9–11pm.

Eggs 'n Things ★★ BREAKFAST   After a terrible fire a few years ago, this popular breakfast-only eatery reopened just a few blocks from its former location. This eclectic place is famous for its great food served in humongous portions. You'll find the fluffiest omelets (which come with pancakes, potatoes, and toast), melt-in-your-mouth waffles (piled high with fruit and whipped cream), and hot coffee constantly being poured into your cup. It's worth waiting in line for the incredibly reasonable prices.

343 Saratoga Rd. (at Kalakaua Ave.). ℂ **808/949-0820.** www.eggsnthings.com. Breakfast $5–$12. MC, V. Daily 6am–2pm.

---

2 HONOLULU BEYOND WAIKIKI

ALA MOANA & KAKAAKO
Expensive

Longhi's ITALIAN/MEDITERRANEAN   Bob Longhi, who opened Longhi's in Lahaina in 1976, runs this swank, open-air, Italian-Mediterranean restaurant overlooking romantic sunset views of the ocean. It features the family's famous cooking—lobster Longhi over linguine, prawns Amaretto, and *puttana,* a spicy calamari pasta dish with 35 whole garlic cloves. Meals can be pricey, in part because everything comes a la carte, but the view is spectacular and the service is prompt. It also is a great place for breakfast (their French toast, with a "touch" of Grand Marnier, is wickedly divine, and their baked goods are delicious) with moderate prices and that terrific view. Lunch, which can get crowded, features yummy salads, sandwiches, pastas, and excellent fish entrees.

At the Ala Moana Center, 1450 Ala Moana Blvd. ℂ **808/947-9899.** www.longhis.com. Reservations recommended for dinner. Main courses $7.50–$17 breakfast, $12–$20 lunch, $24–$38 dinner. AE, DISC, MC, V. Mon–Fri 8am–10pm; Sat–Sun 7:45am–10pm.

Mariposa ★★ PACIFIC RIM/SOUTHWESTERN   Once you get past the gourmet food department of the new Neiman Marcus, you'll be in Mariposa, a popular lunch spot. High ceilings and tables on the deck with views of Ala Moana Park and its Art Deco bridges add up to a pleasing ambience, with or without the shopping. You'll find cordial service, nearly four dozen reasonably priced wines by the glass, and a menu of Pacific and American (called "heritage cuisine") specialties that include everything from a king crab, shrimp, and mussel risotto to pan-roasted Hawaiian snapper and New York strip loin. Chef Jason Kagihara's creativity emerges with dishes such as the Laksa seafood curry, which is only available at lunch. Another lunchtime favorite is Mariposa's signature starter: the towering, eggy popover with *poha* (cape gooseberry) butter. Save room for my favorite dessert, the Valrhona chocolate fudge cake (four layers of devil's food cake with chocolate ganache and raspberry compote)—heaven on earth!

At Neiman Marcus, Ala Moana Center, 1450 Ala Moana Blvd. ℂ **808/951-3420.** Reservations recommended. Main courses $16–$24 lunch, $27–$39 dinner. AE, DC, MC, V. Sun–Wed 11am–9:30pm; Thurs–Sat 11am–10pm.

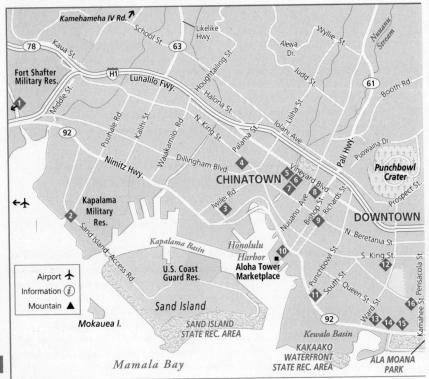

Akasaka **19**
Alan Wongs's Restaurant **22**
Andy's Sandwiches & Smoothies **34**
Angelo Pietro **20**
Assaggio **18**
Buca di Beppo **15**
Café Laufer **37**
Chai's Island Bistro **10**
Che Pasta **9**
Chef Mavro Restaurant **25**
Chiang Mai Thai Cuisine **26**
Contemporary Museum Café **33**
Dream Dinners **41**
Don Ho's Island Grill **10**
Duc's Bistro **6**
Genki Sushi **32**
Gordon Biersch Brewery Restaurant **10**
Hale Vietnam **40**
Hiroshi Eurasian Tapas **11**

Hoku's **41**
I ♥ Country Café **18**
Indigo Eurasian Cuisine **8**
Jimbo's Restaurant **23**
Kaka'ako Kitchen **16**
Kincaid's Fish, Chop and Steakhouse **13**
Kua Aina **15**
La Mariana **2**
Legend Seafood Restaurant **5**
Little Village Noodle House **7**
Longhi's **18**
Maple Garden **27**
Mariposa **18**
Nico's At Pier 38 **1**
Ninniku-Ya Garlic Restaurant **35**
Old Spaghetti Factory **14**
Olive Tree Café **41**
Panda Cuisine **21**
The Pineapple Room at Macy's **18**

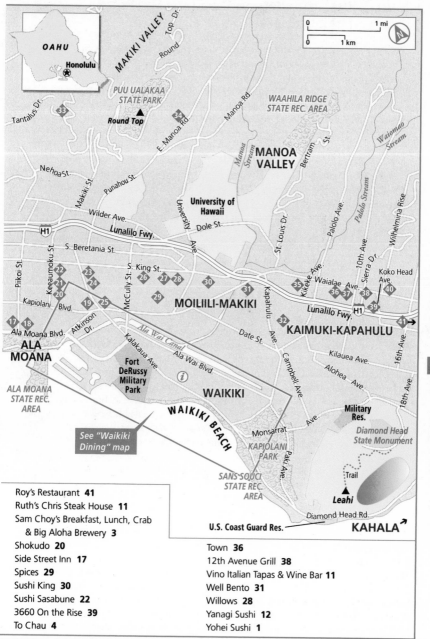

Roy's Restaurant **41**
Ruth's Chris Steak House **11**
Sam Choy's Breakfast, Lunch, Crab
  & Big Aloha Brewery **3**
Shokudo **20**
Side Street Inn **17**
Spices **29**
Sushi King **30**
Sushi Sasabune **22**
3660 On the Rise **39**
To Chau **4**

Town **36**
12th Avenue Grill **38**
Vino Italian Tapas & Wine Bar **11**
Well Bento **31**
Willows **28**
Yanagi Sushi **12**
Yohei Sushi **1**

Value Attention Condo Dwellers: Fix, Freeze & Feed Dinners

If you are staying in a condo or other accommodations with kitchen facilities, there is an alternative to eating out every night or slaving over a stove during your vacation, and its name is Dream Dinners. **Dream Dinners,** Niu Valley Shopping Center, 549 Halemaumau St. (© **808/373-1221;** www.dreamdinners.com), is a "meal assembly kitchen," where you gather all the ingredients for your own heat-and-serve meals, using the recipes and prepared ingredients they provide. After signing up online and booking an appointment, you go through an assembly line choosing various fixings for your entrees. You can freeze or just refrigerate the meals and serve a gourmet dinner for a fraction of the cost of eating out. As we went to press, entrees (which included chicken with honey, garlic, and orange; lemon fish filets; arroz con pollo; lasagna; steakhouse sirloin; and risotto primavera) ranged in price from $4 to $6 per serving. The downsides of this great money-saver are that it's only best for groups or families (you choose 3–6 servings per dinner), it's located in Niu Valley (away from most visitor accommodations), and you need at least 1 to 2 hours to do your "shopping."

The Pineapple Room ★★ HAWAIIAN REGIONAL   Yes, this restaurant is in a department store, but the chef is Alan Wong, a culinary icon. The dishes are culinary masterpieces, particularly anything with fresh island fish or *kalua* pig (such as the kalua pig BLT). The dining room features an open kitchen with a lava-rock wall and abundant natural light, but the food takes center stage. The menu changes regularly, so keep an eye out for the fresh Big Island *moi* (a highly prized Hawaiian fish, in this case served whole and steamed Chinese-style), crispy Asian slaw (with cilantro and mac-nuts), miso-glazed salmon, black-pepper ahi (with risotto), and pineapple barbecued baby back ribs (with garlic mashed potatoes and sautéed corn). We adore the apple curry glazed pork chop with pumpkin and marscapone purée and mango chutney.

At Macy's, 1450 Ala Moana Blvd. © **808/945-6573.** www.alanwongs.com. Reservations recommended for lunch and dinner. Main courses $16–$20 lunch, main courses $28–$38 dinner, sampling dinner $75. AE, DC, MC, V. Mon–Fri 11am–8:30pm; Sat 8–10:30am and 11:30am–8:30pm; Sun 9–10:30am and 11:30am–3pm.

Sushi Sasabune ★★ Finds SUSHI   This elegant sushi restaurant, tucked away among nondescript shops along a very busy street, is one of the marvels of the edible world. If you wish to order from the regular menu, by all means grab a table. But if you sit at the sushi bar, you must submit to the Japanese version of the *Seinfeld* "Soup Nazi," otherwise known as *omakase*. You obey the chef, eat what's served, and God help you if you drop a grain of rice or dip something in wasabi without permission. The payoff is that whatever you eat is freshly shipped in that day and often exotic. Whether it's salmon from Nova Scotia, sea urchin from Japan, halibut from Boston, Louisiana blue crab, or farmed oyster from Washington, Chef Seiji Kumagawa's sushi comes with a strict protocol: Dip only when permitted, and then with restraint. This is an extraordinary experience for sushi aficionados—a journey into new tastes, textures, and sensations. It's expensive but well **133** worth it.

1417 S. King St. Ⓒ **808/947-3800.** Reservations recommended. Sushi $5–$15; *omakase* can run $80–$100 per person. AE, DC, DISC, MC, V. Tues–Fri noon–2pm; Mon–Sat 5:30–10pm.

Moderate

Akasaka ★ JAPANESE/SUSHI BAR Akasaka is difficult to find and you enter through a back door, but this cozy, casual, and always-busy restaurant wins high marks for sushi, sizzling tofu and scallops, miso-clam soup, and the overall quality of its cuisine. Highlights include the *temaki* (spicy tuna) hand-roll, scallop roll with flying-fish roe, hamachi, and soft-shell crab in season. Lunch and dinner specials help ease the bite of the bill, and ordering noodles or other less expensive a la carte items can also reduce the cost considerably. Don't expect geisha girls, or even friendly service—the staff is efficient but not necessarily accommodating.

1646B Kona St. Ⓒ **808/942-4466.** Reservations recommended. Main courses $10–$22. AE, DC, DISC, MC, V. Mon–Sat 11am–2:30pm and 5pm–2am; Sun 5pm–midnight.

Assaggio ★ ITALIAN This wildly popular chain, until recently the toast of suburban Oahu (see p. 147 for the Kailua location), moved into Ala Moana Center to a roar of approval and immediate success. Townies can now enjoy Assaggio's extensive, high-quality Italian offerings—at good prices. The lighter lunch menu features pasta dishes and house specialties (shrimp scampi, rigatoni alla ricotta) at prices around $15 and less. At dinner, a panoply of pastas and specialties streams out of the kitchen: at least nine chicken entrees, pasta dishes ranging from mushroom and clam to linguine primavera, and eight veal choices. One of Assaggio's best features is its prodigious seafood selection: shrimp, scallops, mussels, calamari, and fresh fish in many preparations, ranging from simple garlic and olive oil to spicy tomato and wine sauces. Assaggio's excellent service paired with entrees priced under $20 deserves applause.

At the Ala Moana Center, 1450 Ala Moana Blvd. Ⓒ **808/942-3446.** Reservations recommended. Main courses $10–$18 lunch, $15–$22 dinner. AE, DC, DISC, MC, V. Daily 11am–3pm and 4:30–9:30pm (until 10pm Fri–Sat).

Kincaid's Fish, Chop, and Steakhouse ★ SEAFOOD/STEAKS Kincaid's always wins surveys for one thing or another—best place for a business lunch, best seafood restaurant—because it pleases wide-ranging tastes and budgets. Brisk service, a harbor view, and an extensive seafood menu keep the large dining room full, while fresh-fish sandwiches, seafood chowders, and French onion soups top the menu. They also serve a memorable rack-salted prime rib, pepper-crusted steak and, if you can't make up your mind, a combo plate of center-cut filet mignon with Australian lobster tail. You might want to save room for the true-blue Key lime pie. Kincaid's is also a popular happy-hour rendezvous, with inexpensive beer and appetizers and live entertainment from 8:30 to 11:30pm Friday and Saturday nights.

At Ward Warehouse, 1050 Ala Moana Blvd. Ⓒ **808/591-2005.** Reservations recommended. Lunch $11–$18; dinner main courses $16–$40. AE, DC, DISC, MC, V. Daily 11am–10pm, bar 11am–midnight.

Inexpensive

Angelo Pietro PIZZA/SPAGHETTI This restaurant has a quirky take on Italian food that could come only from Japan. You can order raw potato salad with any of four dressings—shoyu, ginger, *ume* (plum), and sesame-miso—and chase it with one of more than four dozen spaghetti choices, with sauces and toppings ranging from several types each of mushroom, shrimp, chicken, spinach, and sausage to squid ink and eggplant. Pescatore, carbonara with asparagus—everything is grist for the spaghetti mill at the hands of Angelo Pietro. Garlic lovers adore the crisp garlicky chips that are heaped atop some of the selections.

1585 Kapiolani Blvd. ☎ **808/941-0555.** Reservations recommended for groups of 5 or more; not accepted for smaller groups. Main courses $9–$15. AE, DC, DISC, MC, V. Sun–Thurs 11am–10pm; Fri–Sat 11am–11pm.

I ♥ Country Café ⟨Kids⟩ INTERNATIONAL   Give yourself time to peruse the lengthy list of specials posted on the menu board, as well as the prodigious printed menu. Stand in line at the counter, place your order and pay, and find a Formica-topped table; or wait about 10 minutes for your takeout order to appear on a Styrofoam plate heaped with salad and other accompaniments. The small cafe is filled with families, athletes, and bodybuilder types, all in terrific shape. The menu ranges from the virtually fatless vegetarian meal to a regular local-style, gravy-covered lunch special. If you have splurged on a few too many calories, here's the place to make amends.

In Ala Moana Plaza, 451 Piikoi St. ☎ **808/596-8108.** Main courses $6–$10. AE, DC, DISC, MC, V. Daily 8am–9pm.

Kaka'ako Kitchen ★★ ⟨Finds⟩ PLATE LUNCHES   This popular industrial-style, plate-lunch haven in the trendy Ward Centre is busier than ever, with an expanded concept that includes dinner and breakfast service. You'll get excellent home-style cooking (it's owned by chef Russell Siu, of 3660 on the Rise) served on Styrofoam plates, in a warehouse ambience, at budget prices. The menu, which changes every 3 to 4 months, includes a seared ahi sandwich with *tobiko* (flying-fish roe) aioli, sandwiches, beef stew, five-spice shoyu chicken, the very popular meatloaf, and other multiethnic entrees.

At Ward Centre, 1200 Ala Moana Blvd. ☎ **808/596-7488.** Breakfast $5–$8, lunch and dinner main courses $7–$13. AE, MC, V. Mon–Thurs 8am–9pm; Fri–Sat 8am–10pm; Sun 8am–5pm.

Kua Aina ★ ⟨Value⟩ AMERICAN   This popular branch of the ultimate sandwich shop (the original is a North Shore fixture) is in the Ward Centre area (near Borders and Starbucks). Phone in your order if you can. During lunch and dinner hours, people wait patiently in long lines for the famous burgers and sandwiches: the beef burgers with heroic toppings; mahimahi with Ortega chili and cheese (a legend); grilled eggplant and peppers; roast turkey, tuna, and avocado; roast beef and avocado; and about a dozen other selections on kaiser rolls or multigrain wheat or rye breads. The sandwiches and fries are excellent, and the outdoor section with tables has grown (thank goodness)—but there still may be a wait during lunch hour. The takeout business is brisk.

At Ward Village, 1116 Auahi St. ☎ **808/591-9133.** Sandwiches and burgers $7–$9. No credit cards. Mon–Sat 10:30am–9pm; Sun 10:30am–8pm.

Panda Cuisine ★ DIM SUM/SEAFOOD/CHINESE   This is dim-sum heaven, not only for the selection but for the late-night (after 10pm) service, a rare thing for what is a morning and lunchtime tradition in Hong Kong. Panda's dim sum selection—spinach-scallop, chive, taro, shrimp dumplings, pork hash, and some 50-plus others—is a real pleaser. (The spinach-scallop and taro puff varieties are a cut above.) The reckless can spring for the live Maine lobster and Dungeness crab in season, or the king clam and steamed fresh fish, but the steaming bamboo carts yielding toothsome surprises are hard to resist. Noodles and sizzling platters make good accompaniments.

Shokudo ★ ⓕ**inds** JAPANESE/SUSHI   *Shokudo* means "dining room" in Japanese, and this large, beautifully designed but casual dining room is the first U.S. restaurant of this popular Japanese chain. It attracts local families and hip 20-somethings more than

---

ⓚ**ids**   Family-Friendly Restaurants

Honolulu is constantly battling its image as an expensive destination. It's true that accommodations on Oahu are pricey, but the abundance of ethnic restaurants (born of burgeoning new immigrant populations) and the high percentage of working mothers in Hawaii creates an entirely different scenario for dining. Even with a sluggish economy, residents eat out—because they're busy, because they want to, and because many popular ethnic traditions aren't so easy to duplicate at home. What makes a good family restaurant in Hawaii? More than the presence of high chairs, we think it's friendliness, affordability, and menu choices that take into consideration the tastes and preferences of multiple generations. Not including the usual fast-food burger joints that are perennially popular with the kids, here are some suggestions for family-friendly eateries in Honolulu.

Genki Sushi, 900 Kapahulu Ave. (ℂ **808/735-8889**), is part entertainment, part assertiveness training, and part culinary pleasure. Kids love to lunge for their favorites among the freshly made, individually wrapped sushi that parade by on conveyor belts, and the slower ones who miss out the first time around get a chance on the next revolution. Sit with your family around the curvy counters and empty your plates without emptying your pocketbook. See p. 145.

Blockbuster Video outlets are often adjacent to places that kids and teenagers love. And because this may mean less cooking, these places are popular among parents, too. Next to Ala Moana Center, Honolulu's busiest Blockbuster is smack dab next to **I ♥ Country Café,** 451 Piikoi St., Ala Moana Plaza (ℂ **808/596-8108**), which offers everything from meatloaf to shoyu chicken, burgers, vegetarian dishes, and stir-fry, for takeout or dining in—and there's a new branch in Kahala Mall. See p. 134.

In Ward Warehouse, the classic preteen pleaser is the **Old Spaghetti Factory,** 1050 Ala Moana Blvd. (ℂ **808/591-2513**), where kids have been sucking in spaghetti and meatballs for years. Ornate Italianate decor, beveled glass everywhere, and an affordable "Just for Kids" menu for those 12 years old and under (offering a spaghetti with choice of sauce, meatballs, or macaroni and cheese), make this a bonanza for the fun-loving younger set.

Finally, we come to **Zippy's,** the mecca of chili and *saimin* (a popular Hawaiian noodle soup). There are nearly two dozen locations on Oahu alone (call ℂ **808/955-6622** for the one nearest you). All branches feature cheap, tasty chili, burgers, sandwiches, salads, and all-day American fare that's popular among parents and kids. Tasty vegetarian chili and meatless, smoky Boca Burgers are among the healthy choices for non meat-eaters. See p. 140.

tourists. The eatery is a cross between an *izakaya* (Japanese pub where people eat appetizers and have a beer or two) and a sushi bar. The place is huge and looks even bigger with its high ceiling, tiered seating, and central bar. The food comes on small plates, so bring a crowd to taste several items. The 60-item menu (complete with vivid color photos and an English translation of the food, with detailed descriptions of each dish) includes appetizers, tofu, salad, fish and meat, rice, soup, sushi, sashimi, nabe, ishiyaki, noodles, and desserts. Here are my picks: deep-fried battered tofu ($7), grilled herb-spiced chicken ($12), garlic tuna seared on a hot plate ($14), and the honey toast dessert ($7.50), a sumo-size serving of soft, toasted bread drizzled with honey and topped with vanilla ice cream. The waitstaff is extremely knowledgeable, but service suffers during the busy dinner hours.

At the Ala Moana Pacific Center, 1585 Kapiolani Blvd. (at Kaheka St.). ℂ 808/941-3701. www.shokudo japanese.com. Main courses $7.75–$23. MC, V. Sun–Thurs 11:30am–1am; Fri–Sat 11:30am–2am.

Side Street Inn ★ (Finds) LOCAL   After their own fancy kitchens have closed, some of Honolulu's top chefs head to this off-the-beaten-track neighborhood bar with TVs on the walls and a back room with a dartboard and neon beer signs. Very camp. This small side street near Ala Moana Center is noted more for its seedy bars than for pesto-crusted ahi and gourmet Nalo greens, which makes Side Street Inn such a pleasant surprise. The grinds (that's local slang for "eats") are fabulous, with no pretensions and a spirited local feel. The barbecued baby back ribs in *lilikoi* (yellow passion fruit) sauce are tender, flavorful, and a steal at $17. My faves are the blackened ahi, pesto-crusted ahi, shrimp scampi, escargots, and tender fresh-steamed Manila clams in a wine-garlic broth. By the end of the meal, you'll be planning when to return.

1225 Hopaka St. ℂ 808/591-0253. Reservations recommended for groups of 4 or more. Main courses $5–$27. AE, DC, MC, V. Daily 3pm–midnight (bar 2pm–2am).

ALOHA TOWER MARKETPLACE

Chai's Island Bistro PACIFIC RIM/ASIAN   I give Chai's high marks for food but have less enthusiasm for its service and ambience, especially at dinner, when the overamped music can detract from the dining experience (the nightly entertainment, usually live music, can be excruciatingly loud). Also, the dinner entree prices have risen significantly. But the food is generally high quality and creative. The 200-seat restaurant has high ceilings, a good location (though not on the waterfront), indoor-outdoor seating, and a discreetly placed open kitchen. My favorite item on the menu is an appetizer that could be an entree: The sampler for two appears on a boat-size platter—a feast of ahi katsu with yellow curry sauce and wasabi; crisp duck lumpia, tasty and greaseless; macadamia nut–crusted tiger prawns; and Alaskan king crab cakes. Fusion dishes include steamed, fresh, Asian-style moi, and an ample selection of vegetarian dishes.

At the Aloha Tower Marketplace, 1 Aloha Tower Dr. ℂ 808/585-0011. www.chaisislandbistro.com. Reservations recommended. Main courses $13–$32 lunch, $28–$48 dinner. AE, DC, MC, V. Tues–Fri 11am–10pm; Sat–Mon 4–10pm.

Don Ho's Island Grill HAWAIIAN/CONTEMPORARY ISLAND   This shrine to Don Ho, who passed away in 2007, mixes a number of nostalgic interior elements: koa paneling, thatched roof, split-bamboo ceilings, old pictures of Ho with celebrities, faux palm trees, and open sides looking out onto the harbor. It's kitschy and charming, down to the vinyl pareu-printed tablecloths and the flower behind the server's ear. The Hawaiian food is perfectly fine, but people come here more for the atmosphere than the cuisine.

At the Aloha Tower Marketplace, 1 Aloha Tower Dr. ℂ 808/528-0807. www.donho.com. Reservations recommended. Main courses $12–$22 lunch, $15–$27 dinner. AE, DC, DISC, MC, V. Daily 10am–9pm.

Gordon Biersch Brewery Restaurant NEW AMERICAN/PACIFIC RIM Ger-
man-style lagers brewed on the premises would be enough of a draw, but the food is also
a lure at one of Honolulu's liveliest after-work hangouts. Fresh Pacific and Island seafood
highlights the eclectic menu. The lanai bar and the brewery bar—open until 1am—are
the brightest spots in the marketplace, teeming with downtown types who nosh on pot
stickers, grilled steaks, baby back ribs, chicken pizza, garlic fries, and any number of
American classics with deft cross-cultural touches. The stage area for live music is a
popular weekend feature.

At the Aloha Tower Marketplace, 1 Aloha Tower Dr. *C* **808/599-4877.** Reservations recommended. Main
courses $9–$28. AE, DC, DISC, MC, V. Sun–Thurs 10am–midnight; Fri–Sat 10am–1am.

DOWNTOWN

Downtowners love the informal walk-in cafes lining one side of attractive **Bishop Square,**
at 1001 Bishop St. (at King St.), in the middle of the business district, where free entertainment is offered every Friday during lunch hour. The popular **Che Pasta** is a stalwart here,
chic enough for business meetings but not too formal (or expensive) for a spontaneous
rendezvous over pasta and minestrone. Some places in Bishop Square open for breakfast
and lunch, others just for lunch, but most close when business offices empty.

Note: Keep in mind that **Restaurant Row** (Ala Moana Blvd., btw. Punchbowl and
South St.), which features several hot new establishments, offers free validated parking in
the evening.

Duc's Bistro ★★ (Finds) FRENCH/VIETNAMESE Surrounded by lei stands and
marked by a cheery neon sign, this cozy 80-seater stands out at the *mauka* (toward the
mountains) end of Maunakea in Chinatown. Narrow and quietly elegant, the restaurant
has three components: the front room with windows looking out to Maunakea Street,
the windowless back room, and the tiny bar. It has an edgy chic that's more Manhattan
than Honolulu, and the food is beautifully prepared and presented. Sauces for the meats
hint of Grand Marnier (duck supreme), bordeaux (lamb Raymond Oliver), cognac (steak
au poivre), Pernod (prawns and oysters), and fresh herbs and vegetables. From the seafood spring rolls with shrimp, taro, and mushrooms to the excellent "meal in a bowl"
(rice noodles heaped with fresh herbs and julienned vegetables, topped with lime dressing), creative touches abound. Live music is featured nightly and surprise vocalists and
hula dancers have been known to join in the fun.

1188 Maunakea St., Chinatown. *C* **808/531-6325.** www.ducsbistro.com. Reservations recommended.
Main dishes $12–$20. AE, DC, DISC, MC, V. Mon–Fri 11:30am–10pm; Mon–Sat 5–10pm.

Hiroshi Eurasian Tapas ★★ EURO-ASIAN FUSION Star chef Hiroshi Fukui
opened this restaurant along with Hawaii's only master sommelier, Chuck Furuya, and
manager Cheryle Gomez. Part of the *tapas* (appetizers served in Spanish bars) trend,
small plates make up most of the menu here. The result is fabulous, especially for foodies
who want to sample several items off the menu (the staff recommends three dishes per
person). Small plates such as sizzling Koa kampachi carpaccio with ginger, tomato, tofu
and ponzu vinaigrette; foie gras sushi with a teriyaki glaze; Portuguese sausage pot stickers with sweet corn, garlic chili foam, and truffled ponzu sauce; and crab cannelloni with
shiitake mushrooms, dill pesto, mozzarella cheese and miso sauce offer a range of tastes.
Go with a group so you can sample more items. They also serve larger plates such as the
dreamy crab-stuffed mahimahi, crispy skin catch of the day, and an oven-roasted lamb
"T-bone." Try to hold out for the desserts: a delicious green tea crème brûlée, a wicked
chocolate cake with molten chocolate, and a great panna cotta.

On Restaurant Row, 500 Ala Moana Blvd. ℂ **808/533-HIRO** [533-4476]. www.dkrestaurants.com. Reservations recommended. Tapas $8.50–$17, larger plates $22–$37. AE, DISC, MC, V. Daily 5:30–9:30pm.

Indigo Eurasian Cuisine ★★ EURASIAN   Hardwood floors, red brick, wicker, high ceilings, and an overall feeling of Indochine luxury give Indigo a stylish edge. You can dine indoors or in a garden setting on menu offerings such as pot stickers, Buddhist *bao* buns, savory brochettes, tandoori chicken breast, Asian-style noodles and dumplings, plum-glazed baby back ribs, and cleverly named offerings from both East and West. Chef Glenn Chu is popular, but many claim that Indigo is more style than flavor. I disagree—this is a great restaurant.

1121 Nuuanu Ave. ℂ **808/521-2900.** www.indigo-hawaii.com. Reservations recommended. Lunch buffet $16, dinner main dishes $18–$36. AE, DC, DISC, MC, V. Tues–Fri 11:30am–2pm; Tues–Sat 6–9:30pm; martini time in the Green Room Tues–Fri 4–7pm.

Legend Seafood Restaurant ★ DIM SUM/SEAFOOD   This is like a dining room in Hong Kong, with a Chinese-speaking clientele pouring over Chinese newspapers and the clatter of chopsticks punctuating conversations. Excellent dim sum comes in bamboo steamers that beckon seductively from carts. Although dining here is a form of assertiveness training (you must wave madly to catch the server's eye and then point to what you want), the system doesn't deter fans from returning. Among my favorites: deep-fried taro puffs, prawn dumplings, shrimp dim sum, vegetable dumplings, and the open-faced seafood (with shiitake, scallops, and a tofu product called *aburage*). Dim sum is served only at lunch, but dinnertime seafood dishes comfort sufficiently. Not a very elegant restaurant, but the food is serious and great.

At the Chinese Cultural Plaza, 100 N. Beretania St. ℂ **808/532-1868.** Reservations recommended for dinner. Most items under $16. AE, DC, MC, V. Mon–Fri 10:30am–2pm and 5:30–9pm; Sat–Sun 8am–2pm and 5:30–9pm.

Little Village Noodle House CHINESE   Don't let the decor throw you—the interior design here reminds me of a small French bistro in Provence. No matter, the food here is "simple and healthy" (its motto) and authentic Chinese (Northern, Cantonese, and Hong Kong–style). My picks are the Shanghai noodles with stir-fried veggies, the walnut shrimp, and the butterfish in black-bean sauce. The menu is eclectic and offers some interesting selections you don't often see. The service is not only friendly (a rarity in Chinatown), but the waitstaff is quite knowledgeable about the dishes. Even more unique for the area, parking is offered in back! It's BYOB, but the excellent wine store just around the corner (the staff will point it out to you) delivers to the restaurant.

1113 Smith St. ℂ **808/545-3008.** Most items under $14. AE, DISC, MC, V. Sun–Thurs 10:30am–10:30pm; Fri–Sat 10:30am–midnight.

To Chau ★★ Ⓥalue VIETNAMESE PHO   The two stars are strictly for the *pho* (noodle soup), which many think is the best in a city studded with pho (pronounced fur) houses. You'll have to stand in line, ambience is nil, and service can be brusque. But that's all part of the charm at this no-nonsense Formica-style restaurant, located in Chinatown in a stone building along a river and marked, without fail, by a queue of Asian diners. The anticipation is heightened by the view of diners relishing their steaming, long-awaited orders, visible through the windows as you wait your turn on the sidewalk. The menu includes shrimp, spring rolls, and chicken and pork chop plates, but I've never seen anyone order anything but pho. And what a soup this is! The broth is clear, hearty, and marvelously flavored with hints of cinnamon and spice. You can order it with

several choices of steak, and it comes with a heaping platter of fresh bean sprouts, basil, **139**
hot green peppers, and an Asian green called *boke* (bo-*kay*). It's worth the wait, and so
inexpensive.

1007 River St., Chinatown. © **808/533-4549.** Reservations not accepted. Pho $5.25–$7.25. No credit
cards. Daily 8:30am–2:30pm (or until they run out of food).

Vino Italian Tapas & Wine Bar ★ (Finds) ITALIAN Two Japanese guys, D.K.
Kodama (chef and owner of Sansei Seafood Restaurant and Sushi Bar and d.k Steakhouse, reviewed earlier) and Chuck Furuya (Hawaii's top master sommelier) teamed up
to create this culinary adventure for foodies. The cozy room includes murals of a vineyard
and a kitchen with barrels of wine on the walls. Among the mouthwatering Italian creations, I'd recommend any ravioli on the menu. Signature dishes include roasted peppers
with grilled focaccia, tender crispy calamari, seared foie gras, and petite *osso buco*. Don't
pass up the house-made gnocchi or the daily pizza. Furuya has put together an amazing
array of wines by the glass, dispensed from a custom-crafted 20-spigot wine cruvinet.

On Restaurant Row, 500 Ala Moana Blvd. © **808/524-8466.** Reservations recommended. Tapas $8–$23.
AE, DISC, MC, V. Wed–Thurs 5:30–9:30pm; Fri 5:30–12:30am; Sat 5:30–10:30pm.

Yanagi Sushi ★ JAPANESE I love the late-night hours, the sushi bar, and the extensive choices of combination lunches and dinners. But I also love the a la carte Japanese
menu, which covers everything from *chazuke* (a comfort food of rice with tea, salmon,
seaweed, and other condiments) to *shabu-shabu* and other steaming earthenware-pot
dishes. Complete dinners come with choices of sashimi, shrimp tempura, broiled salmon,
New York steak, and many other possibilities. You can dine here affordably or extrava-
gantly, on $7 noodles or a $33 lobster *nabe* (cooked in seasoned broth). Consistently
crisp tempura and fine spicy-ahi hand rolls also make Yanagi worth remembering.

762 Kapiolani Blvd. © **808/597-1525.** Reservations recommended. Main courses $11–$36, complete
dinners $19–$26. AE, DC, DISC, MC, V. Daily 11am–2pm; Mon–Sat 5:30pm–2am; Sun 5:30–10pm.

KALIHI/SAND ISLAND

La Mariana AMERICAN Just try to find a spot more evocative or nostalgic than this
South Seas oasis at lagoon's edge in the bowels of industrial Honolulu, with carved tikis,
glass balls suspended in fishing nets, shell chandeliers, and old tables made from koa
trees. In the back section, the entire ceiling is made of tree limbs. This unique, nearly
50-year-old restaurant is popular for lunch, sunset appetizers, and impromptu Friday-
and Saturday-night singalongs at the piano bar, where a colorful crowd (including some
Don Ho look-alikes) gathers to sing Hawaiian classics like a 1950s high school glee club.
It is delightful. The seared Cajun-style ahi is your best bet as an appetizer or entree; La
Mariana is more about spirit and ambience than food.

50 Sand Island Rd. © **808/848-2800.** Reservations recommended, especially Sat–Sun. Main courses
$6–$12 lunch, $10–$25 dinner. AE, MC, V. Daily 11am–10pm. Turn *makai* (toward the ocean) on Sand
Island Rd. from Nimitz Hwy.; immediately after the first light on Sand Island, take a right and drive toward
the ocean; it's not far from the airport.

Nico's At Pier 38 ★★ (Finds) FRESH FISH This tiny takeout place produces gourmet French cuisine island-style on Styrofoam takeout containers at local plate-lunch
prices. Sit on plastic lanai chairs and tables under a deep green awning to munch on these
delicious entrees at the edge of the pier. French-born chef Nicolas "Nico" Chize has
cooked at such upscale eateries as Michel's and the Bistro At Century Center, but his
small, oddly located eatery is so popular you'll have to stand in line during the crowded

Local Chains & Familiar Names

Todai, 1910 Ala Moana Blvd. (© **808/947-1000**), part of a string of Japanese seafood buffet restaurants with locations ranging from Dallas to Portland to the Beverly Center, is packing 'em in at the gateway to Waikiki with bountiful buffet of sushi (40 kinds), hot entrees (tempura, calamari, fresh fish, gyoza, king crab legs, teppanyaki), and delectable desserts. There's not much ambience, but no one cares; the food is terrific, the selection impressive, the operation as smooth as the green-tea cake, and the prices eye-popping: Lunch is $15 on weekdays and $18 on weekends; dinner is $28 on weekdays and $29 on weekends.

Ala Moana Center's third floor is a mecca for dining and schmoozing. The open-air **Mai Tai Bar** is a popular watering hole. Next door are the boisterous **Bubba Gump Shrimp Company** (© **808/949-4867**) and **California Pizza Kitchen** (© **808/941-7715;** I have to note that on my last visit, it was surprisingly very dirty), which also maintains branches in Waikiki, at 2284 Kalakaua Ave., next door to the Waikiki Beachcomber (© **808/924-2000**); Kahala Mall, 4211 Waialae Ave. (© **808/737-9446**); and Pearlridge, 98-1005 Moanalua Rd. (© **808/487-7741**).

L & L Drive-Inn is a plate-lunch bonanza, with 45 locations in Hawaii—36 on Oahu alone. Meanwhile, **Zippy's Restaurants** ★, the maestros of quick meals, offer a surprisingly good selection of fresh seafood, saimin, chili, and local fare, plus the wholesome new low-fat, vegetarian "Shintani Cuisine" (based on the dietary principles of Hawaiian doctor Terry Shintani). Every restaurant (21 of them on Oahu, at last count) offers a daily Shintani special, and some locations (Kahala, Vineyard, Pearlridge, Kapolei, Waipio) sell cold Shintani items in 2-pound portions to take home and heat up. Call © **808/973-0880** to find the location nearest you.

It's hard to spend more than $7 on the French and Vietnamese specials at the **Ba-Le Sandwich Shops:** pho, croissants as good as the espresso, and wonderful taro/tapioca desserts. Among Ba-Le's 20 locations are those at Ala Moana Center (© **808/944-4752**) and 333 Ward Ave. (© **808/591-0935**).

The ubiquitous **Boston's North End Pizza Bakery** chain claims an enthusiastic following with its reasonable prices and generous toppings. Boston's can be found in Kaimuki, Kaneohe, and Makakilo.

For Italian food, **Buca di Beppo** (© **808/591-0880**) is in the Ward Entertainment Center, 1030 Auahi St. Heaping plates of Italian food, enough to feed a hungry family, make this place quite popular, along with the reasonable prices. Reservations are a must.

In Waikiki, the local **Hard Rock Cafe** is at 1837 Kapiolani Blvd. (© **808/955-7383**). At the Ala Moana end of Waikiki, **Outback Steakhouse**, 1765 Ala Moana Blvd. (© **808/951-6274**), serves great steaks and is always full. In downtown's Restaurant Row, beef eaters can also chow down at swanky **Ruth's Chris Steak House,** 500 Ala Moana Blvd. (© **808/599-3860**).

lunch hour, when you will see commercial fishermen, business executives, and a smattering of tourists (they do take orders over the phone if you want to shorten your wait). My favorite is the furikake pan-seared ahi with the addictive ginger garlic cilantro dip, served with greens or macaroni salad for $8.75. They also have catch-of-the-day specials (grilled swordfish with a fennel-cream sauce was on the menu when I was there), a double cheeseburger to die for, and a mean beef stew. Hearty breakfasts are served till 9:30am weekdays and 10:30am Saturdays.

Pier 38, 1133 N. Nimitz Hwy., Iwilei. (C) 808/540-1377. www.nicospier38.com. Reservations not accepted, but takeout orders accepted by phone. Main courses $6–$10. AE, DC, DISC, MC, V. Mon–Fri 6:30am–5pm; Sat 6:30am–2:30pm.

Sam Choy's Breakfast, Lunch, Crab & Big Aloha Brewery ISLAND CUISINE/SEAFOOD This is a happy, carefree eatery—elegance and cholesterol be damned. Chef/restaurateur Sam Choy's crab house features great fun and gigantic meals (a Choy trademark). Imagine dining in an all-wood *sampan*—a type of boat that is the centerpiece of this 11,000-square-foot restaurant—and washing your hands in an oversize wok that was installed in the center of the room just for kicks. A 2,000-gallon tank containing a live assortment of seasonal crabs (Kona, Maryland, Samoan, Dungeness, Florida stone) lines the open kitchen. Clam chowder, seafood gumbos, oysters from the oyster bar, and assorted *poke* (chunks of marinated raw fish) are also offered at dinner, which comes complete with soup, salad, and entree. Children's menus are an attractive feature for families. Several varieties of Big Aloha beer, brewed on-site, go well with the crab and poke.

580 Nimitz Hwy., Iwilei. (C) 808/545-7979. www.samchoy.com. Reservations recommended for lunch and dinner. Main courses $8–$14 breakfast, $12–$20 lunch, $20–$30 dinner. AE, DC, DISC, MC, V. Sun–Thurs 7am–10pm; Fri–Sat 8am–10pm. Located in the Iwilei industrial area near Honolulu Harbor, across the street from Gentry Pacific Design Center.

Yohei Sushi ★ (Finds) JAPANESE/SUSHI BAR Yohei is difficult to find—tucked away in a small, nondescript complex just before Dillingham Boulevard crosses the bridge into Kalihi, Honolulu's industrial area. But it's well worth the hunt, especially for lovers of authentic Tokyo-style sushi. Try the *amaebi* (sweet shrimp), *akagai* (surf clam), hamachi, *negi toro temaki* (butterfly tuna), *kohada gari chiso temaki* (bluefish), and a wonderful assortment of seafood, fresh as can be.

1111 Dillingham Blvd., across from Honolulu Community College. (C) 808/841-3773. Reservations recommended. Main courses $8–$18 lunch, complete dinners $16–$35. DC, MC, V. Mon–Sat 11am–1:45pm and 5–9:30pm.

MANOA VALLEY/MOILIILI/MAKIKI
Very Expensive
Chef Mavro Restaurant ★★★ PROVENCAL/HAWAIIAN REGIONAL Chef/owner George Mavrothalassitis, a native of Provence, was the winner of the 2003 prestigious James Beard award for Best Chef for Hawaii and the Pacific Northwest. His fans all over the world have admired his creativity since his days at La Mer at Halekulani and at Seasons at the Four Seasons Resort Wailea, making this is a must-do for all serious foodies. His restaurant is the only independently operated AAA Four-Diamond restaurant in Hawaii, in a conveniently accessible, nontouristy neighborhood in McCully where you can order prix fixe or a la carte, with or without dazzling wine pairings. To his list of signature items (filet of moi with crisp scales, sautéed mushrooms, and saffron coulis; or award-winning onaga baked in Hawaiian-salt crust), he's added new favorites:

Keahole lobster in an Asian broth; a Hawaiian/Marseilles bouillabaisse; and cut-it-with-a-fork-tender filet of beef tenderloin crusted with red-wine confit onion. Hints of Tahitian vanilla, lemongrass, *ogo* (seaweed), rosemary, and Madras curry add exotic flavors to the French-inspired cooking and fresh island ingredients. The desserts are extraordinary, especially the all-American apple tart with Hawaiian vanilla ice cream. The split-level room is quietly cordial, and the menu changes monthly to highlight seasonal ingredients.

1969 S. King St. ⓒ **808/944-4714.** www.chefmavro.com. Reservations recommended. Prix-fixe menu $69–$120 ($108–$175 with wine pairings). AE, DC, DISC, MC, V. Tues–Sun 6–9:30pm.

Expensive

Alan Wong's Restaurant ★★★ HAWAII REGIONAL CUISINE Alan Wong is one of Hawaii's most sought-after chefs, but the service at his bustling eatery has often suffered because of his popularity. Long waits in front of the elevator have angered many. Still, worshipful foodies come from all over the state, drawn by the food—which is brilliant—and a menu that is irresistible. The 90-seat room has a glassed-in terrace and open kitchen. Sensitive lighting and curly koa wall panels accent an unobtrusively pleasing environment—casual, but not too much so. The menu's cutting-edge offerings sizzle with the Asian flavors of lemongrass, sweet-and-sour, garlic, and wasabi, deftly melded with the fresh seafood and produce of the islands. The California roll is a triumph, made with salmon roe, wasabi, and Kona lobster instead of rice—served warm. We love the opihi shooters, day-boat scallops, and fresh-fish preparations. But don't get attached to any one item, as the menu changes daily.

1857 S. King St., 3rd floor. ⓒ **808/949-2526.** www.alanwongs.com. Reservations recommended. Main courses $28–$42, 5-course sampling menu $75 ($105 with wine), chef's 7-course tasting menu $95 ($125 with wine). AE, DC, MC, V. Daily 5–10pm.

Moderate

Contemporary Museum Cafe ★ Ⓕⁱⁿᵈˢ HEALTHFUL GOURMET The surroundings are an integral part of the dining experience at this tiny lunchtime cafe, part of an art museum nestled on the slopes of Tantalus amid carefully cultivated Asian gardens, with a breathtaking view of Diamond Head and priceless contemporary artwork displayed indoors and out. The menu is limited to sandwiches, soups, salads, and appetizers, but you won't leave disappointed: They're perfect lunchtime fare. Try the day's crostini, hummus and pita, lentil burger, roasted shallot and tarragon shrimp salad, or fresh-fish specials. Crown your meal with flourless chocolate cake or fresh, locally made gelato. You can also have a Lauhala picnic for two ($30) to enjoy in the gardens.

At The Contemporary Museum (TCM), 2411 Makiki Heights Dr. ⓒ **808/523-3362.** www.tcmhi.org. Reservations recommended. Main courses $10–$12. AE, MC, V. Tues–Sat 11:30am–2:30pm; Sun noon–2:30pm.

Maple Garden SZECHUAN It hums like a top and rarely disappoints. Maple Garden is known for its garlic eggplant, Peking duck, and Chinaman's Hat, a version of mu shu pork, available in vegetarian form as well. The crisp green beans are out of this world. Other hits: braised scallops with Chinese mushrooms, sautéed spinach, and prawns in chili sauce. Vegetarian selections are ample, as are dozens of seafood entrees—everything from sea cucumbers and braised salmon to lobster with black-bean sauce. An ever-expanding visual feast adorns the dining-room walls, covered with original drawings, sketches, and murals by noted artist John Young. The staff is unbelievably friendly, service is top-notch, and most entrees are only $8 to $9.

909 Isenberg St. ⓒ **808/941-6641.** Plates $5–$23 lunch, $8.25–$11 dinner; buffet $11 lunch, $15 dinner. MC, V. Daily 10am–9:30pm.

Spices (Value) SOUTHEAST ASIAN Located in a small building near the university, **143** this tiny Asian bistro specializes in delicious traditional dishes from Vietnam, Laos, Thailand, and Burma (now known as Myanmar), re-created with local Hawaii ingredients. True to the restaurant's name, the smell of pungent spices greets you as you enter the restaurant. Walls are painted in saffron orange, mustard yellow, and green basil trim. A tantalizing cornucopia of Southeast Asian specialties (with plenty of vegetarian dishes) range from curries (green, yellow, Malaysian, and Laotian) to noodles (pad Thai) to soups. But the best is the homemade ice cream with such unusual flavors as durian, pandanus, or chili/lemongrass. Limited parking (about eight spots) behind the restaurant.

2671 S. King St. (at University Ave.) ℂ **808/949-2679.** www.spiceshawaii.com. Curries $14–$18, rice and noodle dishes $12–$14. MC, V. Tues–Fri 11:30am–2pm and 5:30–10pm; Sat 5:30–10pm; Sun 5–9pm. Limited parking (about 8 stalls) behind the restaurant.

Sushi King (Value) JAPANESE This is a top value for lovers of Japanese food. Brusque service can't deter the throngs that arrive for the excellent lunch specials. It's tricky to find, located in a small mini-mall (look for University Flower Shop). Don't pass up the jumbo platters that come with soup, pickles, California roll sushi, and your choice of chicken teriyaki, beef teriyaki, shrimp and vegetable tempura, or calamari and vegetable tempura, all at arrestingly low prices. Other combination lunches offer generous choices that include sashimi, tempura, butterfish, fried oysters, and noodles served hot and cold. Early-bird specials are offered daily from 5:30 to 6:30pm.

2700 S. King St. ℂ **808/947-2836.** Reservations recommended, especially for groups of 5 or more on weekends. Lunch $9–$17, dinner main courses $15–$23. AE, DC, DISC, MC, V. Daily 11:30am–2pm; Wed–Mon 5:30pm–2am; Tues 5:30–10pm.

Willows LOCAL The food is more than adequate, but the ambience is the headliner here. There just aren't many places left in Hawaii with this kind of tropical setting. Shoes click on hardwood floors in rooms surrounded by lush foliage and fountains fed by the area's natural springs. The dining rooms are open-air, with private umbrella-topped tables scattered about. Willows will never regain the charm and nostalgia of its early *kamaaina* (old-time) days, but it has been beautifully restored, and some of its Hawaiian dishes— like *laulau* (meat or fish steamed in taro or ti leaves), lomi lomi salmon ("massaged" salmon, marinated with tomatoes, onion, and salt), and poke—are quite good. Everything is served buffet-style.

817 Hausten St. ℂ **808/952-9200.** www.willowshawaii.com. Reservations recommended. Lunch buffet $20 Mon–Fri, $25 Sat, $35 Sun; dinner buffet $35 daily. AE, DC, DISC, MC, V. Mon–Fri 11am–2pm and 5:30–9pm; Sat–Sun 10am–2:30pm and 5–9pm. No neighborhood parking; valet parking $3, self-parking $3.

Inexpensive

Andy's Sandwiches & Smoothies (Value) GOURMET HEALTH FOOD It started as a health-food restaurant, expanded into a juice bar, and today is a neighborhood fixture for fresh-baked bread, healthy breakfasts and lunches (its mango muffins are famous), and vegetarian fare. Andy's roadside stop always carries fresh papayas, sandwiches, and healthy snacks for folks on the run. The ahi deluxe sandwich is tops, and the fresh roasted turkey sandwiches are an acclaimed favorite.

2904 E. Manoa Rd., opposite Manoa Marketplace. ℂ **808/988-6161.** Most items less than $10. AE, MC, V. Mon–Thurs 7am–5:30pm; Fri 7am–4pm; Sun 7am–2:30pm.

Chiang Mai Thai Cuisine THAI Chiang Mai made sticky rice famous in Honolulu, serving it in bamboo steamers with fish and exotic curries. Menu items include toothsome red, green, and yellow curries; the signature Cornish game hen in lemongrass and spices; and a garlic-infused green papaya salad marinated in tamarind sauce. Spicy shrimp soup, eggplant with basil and tofu, and the vegetarian green curry are favorites.

2239 S. King St. (C) **808/941-1151.** Reservations recommended for dinner. Main courses $9.50–$16. AE, DC, DISC, MC, V. Mon–Fri 11am–2pm; daily 5:30–9:30pm.

Jimbo's Restaurant ★ (Value) JAPANESE Jimbo's is the quintessential neighborhood restaurant—it's small, with a line of regulars outside, serves fantastic house-made noodles and broths, and everything is good and affordable. A must for any noodle lover, Jimbo's serves homemade udon in a flawless broth with a subtly smoky flavor, then tops it with shrimp tempura, chicken, eggs, vegetables, seaweed, roasted *mochi* (Japanese rice bun), and other accompaniments of your choice. Cold noodles (the Tanuki salad is wonderful!), stir-fried noodles, *donburi* (rice dishes with assorted toppings), and combination dinners are other delights. The earthenware pot of noodles, with shiitake mushrooms, vegetables, and udon, plus a platter of tempura on the side, is a top-of-the-line meal. But my favorite is the *nabeyaki* (a clay pot of udon with tempura on top). Owner Jimbo Motojima, a perfectionist, uses only the finest ingredients from Japan.

1936 S. King St. (C) **808/947-2211.** Reservations not accepted. Main courses $8–$20. AE, DC, MC, V. Daily 11am–2:45pm and 5–9:45pm; Fri–Sat 5–10:30pm.

Well Bento (Finds) PLATE LUNCHES We wondered whether such healthy organic food—without the use of eggs, refined sugar, or dairy products—would be satisfying. Countless plate lunches later, we can report that Well Bento will make a guiltless gourmet out of even the fussiest palate. Each plate is aesthetically pleasing, wholesome, and tasty. Louisiana tempeh, salmon grilled over lava rocks or poached with shiitake mushrooms, Cajun-style chicken, and creative vegetarian selections ("plant-based plates") make this a place worth trying. Bean salad, cabbage and seaweed salads, and organic brown rice accompany each plate and are as decorative as they are delicious. This is a good picnic choice, as it's mostly takeout, and only a few seats are provided.

2570 S. Beretania St., 2nd floor. (C) **808/941-5261.** www.wellbento.com. Plate lunches $8–$13. AE, MC, V. Daily 10:30am–9pm.

KAIMUKI/KAPAHULU

Expensive

Ninniku-Ya Garlic Restaurant EURO-ASIAN This is a great restaurant that's a paean to the "stinking rose." Ninniku-Ya is located in a cozy old home, with tables in a split-level dining room and outdoors under venerable trees. The menu titillates with many garlicky surprises and specials. The seasonal specialties are fine but not necessary, as the staples are quite wonderful. The four-mushroom pasta is sublime, the hot-stone filet mignon tender and tasty, and the garlic rice a meal in itself. Every garlic lover should experience the garlic toast and the roasted garlic with blue cheese. Everything contains garlic, even the house-made garlic gelato, which doesn't overpower. Yes, that's garlic gelato—and it gets high marks from me. Look for the festive fairy lights lining the building.

3196 Waialae Ave. (C) **808/735-0784.** Reservations recommended. Main dishes $16–$38. AE, DC, DISC, MC, V. Tues–Thurs and Sun 5:30–8:30pm (last seating); Fri–Sat 5:30–9:30pm.

3660 On the Rise ★★★ EURO-ISLAND Ever since *Wine Spectator* gave this restaurant its "Award of Excellence," it's been packed, and with good reason. In his 200-seat restaurant, Chef Russell Siu adds an Asian or local touch to the basics: rack of lamb with macadamia nuts, filets of catfish in *ponzu* (a Japanese sauce), and seared ahi salad with grilled shiitake mushrooms, a local favorite. The ahi katsu, wrapped in nori and fried medium-rare, is a main attraction in the appetizer department. Diners rave over Chef Gilbert Crisostomo's desserts, especially the warm chocolate cake.

3660 Waialae Ave. (C) **808/737-1177.** www.3660.com. Reservations suggested. Main courses $26–$34, prix-fixe menu $40. AE, DC, DISC, MC, V. Tues–Sun 5:30–9pm.

Moderate

Genki Sushi ★ (Kids) SUSHI   Take your place in line for a seat at one of the U-shaped counters. Conveyor belts parade by with freshly made sushi, usually two pieces per color-coded plate, priced inexpensively. The possibilities are dizzying: spicy tuna topped with scallions, ahi, scallops with mayonnaise, Canadian roll (such as California roll, except with salmon), sea urchin, flavored octopus, sweet shrimp, surf clam, corn, tuna salad, and so on. Genki starts with a Japanese culinary tradition and takes liberties with it, so don't be a purist. By the end of the meal, the piled-high plates are tallied up by color, and presto, your bill appears. Combination platters are available for takeout.

900 Kapahulu Ave. (C) **808/735-7700.** A la carte sushi from $1.50 for 2 pieces; takeout combination platters $26–$46. AE, DC, DISC, MC, V. Sun–Thurs 11am–9pm; Fri–Sat 11am–10pm; takeout available daily 11am–9pm.

Town ★ (Finds) CONTEMPORARY ITALIAN   The latest hip restaurant along Waialae's miracle mile of "in" spots is a surprisingly delicious place to eat (generally the new hot spots, filled with beautiful young diners, tend toward pretense rather than lip-smacking food). Ignore the metro high-tech atmosphere of highly polished concrete floors, stainless steel tables, and incredibly uncomfortable chairs, and ask for a table outside on the lanai (where the noise level will be bearable). The hand-typed (who the heck still has a typewriter these days?), incredibly creative menu changes daily, but promises "local first, organic whenever possible, with aloha always," and delivers. At my last visit, I sampled the ahi tartar on risotto cakes and veggie frito misto, and an Italian tempura of scallops, celery, lemon, and white beans. Entrees range from braised lamb to crispy moi to excellent gnocchi. Desserts (in the $6 range) include the likes of buttermilk panna cotta and chocolate banini (panini of toast, chocolate, and bananas—yum). Lunches are along the lines of sandwiches, salads, and pastas. Breakfast (frittata of the day, eggs, wonderful baked goods) has recently been added.

3435 Waialae Ave. (at 9th St.). (C) **808/735-5900.** Reservations required for dinner. Main courses $5–$9.50 breakfast, $10–$28 lunch, $19–$40 dinner. AE, MC, V. Mon–Thurs 7am–9pm; Fri–Sat 7am–10pm.

12th Avenue Grill ★ (Finds) AMERICAN   This tiny (14 tables) upscale neighborhood diner is packed every night. If you've had your fill of Hawaii regional cuisine and long for some good ol' American food, not quite like mom used to make, Chef Kevin Hanney whips up a gourmet version of macaroni and cheese (with smoked Parmesan), and the restaurant's signature dish is kim-chee steak (beef marinated in a sweet-hot sauce and grilled). A chalkboard menu lists the specials of the night (the smoked trout is a must). Diners are packed in close, so noise is a problem (you can easily find yourself screeching to be heard by your dinner partners). But the food more than makes up for this one flaw. Whatever you order, leave room for the desserts by Chef Samantha Choy (the baker for Sam Choy Restaurants), who always has a fruit crisp of the day on the menu. The most recent upgrade is their full bar.

1145-C 12th Ave. (at Waialae Ave.). (C) **808/732-9469.** Reservations recommended. Small plates $6–$11, large plates $16–$29. MC, V. Mon–Thurs 5:30–9pm; Fri–Sat 5:30–10pm.

Cafe Laufer ★ BAKERY/SANDWICH SHOP This small, cheerful cafe features frilly decor and sublime pastries—from apple scones and Linzer tortes to fruit flan, decadent chocolate mousse, and carrot cake—to accompany the latte and espresso. Fans drop in for simple soups and deli sandwiches on fresh-baked breads; biscotti during coffee break; or a hearty loaf of seven-grain, rye, pumpernickel, or French bread. The place is a solid hit for lunch; the small but satisfying menu includes soup-salad-sandwich specials for a song, a fabulous spinach salad with dried cranberries and Gorgonzola, and gourmet greens with mango-infused, honey-mustard dressing. The orange-seared shrimp salad and the Chinese chicken salad are hits for the light eater, and the smoked Atlantic salmon with fresh pumpernickel bread and cream cheese, Maui onions, and capers is excellent. The special Saturday-night desserts draw a brisk postmovie business.

3565 Waialae Ave. ✆ **808/735-7717**. www.cafelaufer.com. Checks average $14 per person. AE, DC, DISC, MC, V. Sun and Wed–Thurs 10am–9pm; Fri–Sat 10am–10pm.

Hale Vietnam VIETNAMESE Duck into this house of pho and brave the no-frills service for the steaming noodle soups, the house specialty. The stock is simmered and skimmed for many hours and is accompanied by noodles, beef, chicken, and a platter of bean sprouts and fresh herbs. Approach the green chilies with caution. We love the chicken soup and shrimp vermicelli, as well as the seafood pho and spicy chicken with eggplant. Be advised that this restaurant, like most other Vietnamese eateries, uses MSG, and that the pho, although respectable, does not equal that of To Chau in Chinatown, the *ne plus ultra* of pho in Honolulu.

1140 12th Ave. ✆ **808/735-7581**. Reservations recommended for groups. Main courses $12–$26. AE, DISC, MC, V. Daily 10am–10pm.

3 EAST OF WAIKIKI: KAHALA

EXPENSIVE

Hoku's ★★★ HAWAIIAN REGIONAL Elegant without being stuffy, creative without being overwrought, the upscale dining room of the Kahala Hotel & Resort combines European finesse with an Island touch. This is fusion that really works. The setting is stellar, with its ocean view, open kitchen, and astonishing bamboo floor. Reflecting the restaurant's cross-cultural influences, the kitchen is equipped with a kiawe grill and Szechuan woks for the prawn, lobster, tofu, and other stir-fried specialties. The wok-fried whole fresh fish is worthy of a special occasion. The chef's daily selection of appetizers could include pan-seared Hudson Valley foie gras, sashimi, slow-braised pork belly, and other dainty tastings, and is a good choice for the curious. Salt-crusted rack of lamb, sesame ginger black cod and the full range of East-West specialties appeal to many tastes. Sunday brunch is not to be missed. This is one of the few places in Hawaii that has a "dress code"—collared shirts with slacks or evening wear.

At the Kahala Hotel & Resort, 5000 Kahala Ave. ✆ **808/739-8780**. www.kahalaresort.com/dining/hoku. cfm. Reservations recommended. Collared shirts and long pants preferred for men. Main courses $30–$60. AE, DC, DISC, MC, V. Tues–Sat 5:30–10pm; Sun brunch 10:30am–2pm.

Olive Tree Cafe ★★ (**Finds**) GREEK/EASTERN MEDITERRANEAN   Delectables at bargain prices stream out of the tiny open kitchen here. Recently voted "best restaurant in Hawaii under $20" in a local survey, Olive Tree is every neighborhood's dream—a totally hip restaurant with divine fare and friendly prices. The mussel ceviche is broke-the-mouth fabulous, with lemon, lime, capers, herbs, and olive oil—a perfect blend of flavors. The creamy, tender chicken saffron, a frequent special, always elicits groans of pleasure, as does the robust and generous Greek salad, another Olive Tree attraction. I also love the souvlaki, ranging from fresh fish to chicken and lamb, spruced up with the chef's homemade yogurt-dill sauce. First, order and pay at the counter, then grab an umbrella table outside or one of a few seats indoors. Larger parties now have an awning over the sturdy wooden tables on the Koko Head side. It's BYOB, and a group can dine here like sultans without breaking the bank and take in a movie next door, too.

4614 Kilauea Ave., next to Kahala Mall. (**C**) **808/737-0303.** Main courses $8–$15. No credit cards. Daily 5–10pm.

4 EAST OAHU

HAWAII KAI

Roy's Restaurant ★★★ EUROPEAN/ASIAN   This is the first of Roy Yamaguchi's six signature restaurants in Hawaii (he has two dozen all over the world). It is still the flagship and many people's favorite, true to its Euro-Asian roots and Yamaguchi's winning formula: open kitchen, fresh ingredients, ethnic touches, and a good dose of nostalgia mingled with European techniques. The menu changes nightly, but you can generally count on individual pizzas, a varied appetizer menu (Szechuan spiced baby back ribs, blackened ahi), a small pasta selection, and entrees such as garlic-mustard short ribs, hibachi-style salmon in ponzu sauce, and several types of fresh catch. One of Hawaii's most popular restaurants, Roy's is lit up at night with tiki torches outside; the view from within is of scenic Maunalua Bay. Roy's is also renowned for its high-decibel style of dining—it's always full and noisy. Other Roy's restaurants in Hawaii are located in Ko Olina, Oahu; Poipu, Kauai; Waikoloa, Big Island; and Kihei and Napili, Maui. Patrons enjoy live music Friday and Saturday evenings from 7:30 to 10pm and Sunday from 6 to 9pm.

6600 Kalanianaole Hwy., Hawaii Kai. (**C**) **808/396-7697.** www.roysrestaurant.com. Reservations recommended. Main courses $30–$45, 3-course prix-fixe $40. AE, DC, DISC, MC, V. Mon–Fri 5:30–9pm; Sat–Sun 5:30–9:30pm.

5 THE WINDWARD COAST

MODERATE

Assaggio ★ ITALIAN   This was the mother ship of the Assaggio empire before the Ala Moana branch (p. 133) opened. The affordable prices, attentive service, and winning menu items have attracted loyal fans throughout the years. The homemade hot antipasto is a best-seller, with jumbo shrimp, fresh clams, mussels, and calamari in a sauce of cayenne pepper, white wine, and garlic. You can choose linguine, fettuccine, or ziti with 10 different sauces in small or regular portions, or any of nine chicken pastas (the chicken Assaggio, with garlic, peppers, and mushrooms, is especially flavorful). Equally impressive is the extensive list of seafood pastas, including the garlic and olive oil sauté. The half-price, half-portion dinner servings are a plus.

354 Uluniu St., Kailua. ✆ **808/261-2772.** Reservations recommended. Main courses $15–$30. AE, DC, DISC, MC, V. Mon–Fri 11:30am–2:30pm; daily 5–9:30pm.

Buzz's Original Steak House STEAK/SEAFOOD A Lanikai fixture for nearly a half-century, Buzz's is a few feet from Kailua Beach (windsurfing central), just past the bridge that leads into Lanikai. (Though it's on the beach, shirt and shoes are required.) A small deck, varnished koa bar, rattan furniture, and wood walls covered with snapshots and surf pictures will put you immediately at ease. Buzz's has the perfect Gauguinesque tropical ambience to accompany its offerings: great burgers at lunch (including a mushroom garden burger), fresh catch, superb artichoke appetizer, and steak-and-lobster combos, all much-loved by fans. Dinner offerings are pricier, but include Alaskan king crab legs (market price), prime rib, fresh fish, and wonderful items at the soup and salad bar.

413 Kawailoa Rd., Lanikai. ✆ **808/261-4661.** www.buzzssteakhouse.com. Reservations required. Main courses $9–$15 lunch, $16–$33 dinner. No credit cards. Daily 11am–3pm and 4:30–10pm.

Lucy's Grill 'n Bar ★★ HAWAII REGIONAL CUISINE This is one of Kailua's most popular restaurants, not just because of the open-air bar and the outdoor lanai seating, but because of the terrific food. The menu is eclectic Hawaii regional cuisine, with lots of choices and giant portions. The dress is casual, and the clientele is local. Be sure to order the spicy ahi tower with sushi rice, avocado, wasabi cream, and roasted nori to get you started. Any of the fresh fish and seafood is wonderful, especially the Szechuan-spiced

The Shrimp Trucks

The best, sweetest, juiciest shrimp you are ever going to eat will be from a shrimp truck on Oahu's North Shore. Several trucks line up around the entry to Haleiwa, just off the Kamehameha Highway, but here are my two favorites:

Giovanni's Original White Shrimp Truck (✆ **808/293-1839**), which usually parks across the street from the Haleiwa Senior Housing (or McDonald's), claims to be the first shrimp truck to serve the delicious aquaculture shrimp farmed in the surrounding area. The menu is simple: spicy, garlic, or lemon-and-butter shrimp. Skip the lemon-and-butter (boring), and go for the garlic (my fave) or the spicy (but beware—it really packs a punch.) The battered white truck has picnic tables under its awning, so you can munch away right there.

Holy Smokes: Hawaiian Meats and Seafood, the other truck parked in the same area, has a bit more extensive menu; in addition to the famous shrimp, it offers pork spare ribs ($10), smoked chicken ($9), and a steak plate ($12).

The trucks are usually in place before noon and stay until about sunset. Depending on how much shrimp you can down, expect to spend no more than $12 per person.

jumbo tiger prawns with black-bean cream and penne pasta, or the lemongrass-crusted
scallops with yellow Thai curry. Save room for crème brûlée with Tahitian vanilla bean, dark
chocolate soufflé cake, or their "damn fine" apple crisp—a la mode, of course.

33 Aulike St., Kailua. ✆ **808/230-8188.** Reservations recommended. Main courses $14–$28. MC, V. Daily
5–10pm.

6 THE NORTH SHORE

The following restaurants are located in the area shown on the "Oahu's North Shore"
map on p. 231.

Expensive

21 Degrees North ★★★ PACIFIC RIM CUISINE   Foodie alert: It is well worth
the drive from Waikiki (45–60 min.) to the North Shore to enjoy this impressive signature restaurant at Turtle Bay Resort (p. 111). Not only is it visually inspiring, with floor-
to-ceiling windows overlooking the North Shore's famous rolling surf, but chef Hector
Morales' Pacific Rim cuisine is outstanding. The chef has taken contemporary island
cuisine and made it fresh and interesting, and the dishes emerging from the kitchen take
Hawaiian dining to a new level. The ever-changing menu has such unusual combinations
as crab-crusted Hawaiian sea bass with a lemongrass coulis, salmon with Molokai mashed
sweet potatoes and an orange-and-soy glaze, and roasted Peking duck with a vanilla and
plum sweet-and-sour glaze. The five-course tasting menu is a good way to tour numerous
creations.

At Turtle Bay Resort, 57-091 Kamehameha Hwy., Kahuku. ✆ **808/293-8811.** www.turtlebayresort.com.
Reservations required. Main courses $28–$37; 5-course tasting menu $76 without wine, $95 with wine.
AE, DC, DISC, MC, V. Tues–Sat 5:30–9pm.

MODERATE

Haleiwa Joe's AMERICAN/SEAFOOD   There are only two Haleiwa restaurants
close to the ocean, and this is one of them. Next to the Haleiwa bridge, with a great view
of the harbor and sunset, Haleiwa Joe's serves up fresh local seafood such as whole Hawaiian moi, opakapaka, ahi, and whatever comes in fresh that day. This is a steak-and-sea-
food harborside restaurant with indoor-outdoor seating and a surf-and-turf menu that
could include New York steak, coconut shrimp, and black-and-blue sashimi. Sandwiches
and salads make it a great lunch stop, too.

66-011 Kamehameha Hwy., Haleiwa. ✆ **808/637-8005.** Reservations not accepted. Main courses
$9–$18 lunch, $16–$30 dinner. MC, V. Mon–Thurs 11:30am–9:30pm (limited menu 4:15–5:30pm); Fri–Sat
11:30am–10pm (limited menu 4:15–5:30pm, bar until midnight); Sun 11:30am–9:30pm (limited menu
3:45–5pm).

Jameson's by the Sea SEAFOOD   Duck into this roadside watering hole across the
street from the ocean for cocktails, sashimi, and its celebrated salmon pâté, or for other
hot and cold appetizers, salads, and sandwiches. The grilled crab-and-shrimp sandwich
on sourdough bread is a perennial favorite, and it's hard to go wrong with the fresh-fish
sandwich of the day, grilled plain and simple. The dinner menu offers the usual surf-and-
turf choices: fresh *opakapaka ulua* (Hawaiian jackfish), mahimahi, scallops in lemon
butter and capers, lobster tail, and steaks.

62-540 Kamehameha Hwy., Haleiwa. ☏ **808/637-4336.** www.jamesonshawaii.com. Reservations recommended. Main courses $8–$20 lunch, $12–$38 dinner. AE, DC, DISC, MC, V. Mon–Fri 11am–9:30pm; Sat–Sun 9am–9:30pm.

Ola at Turtle Bay Resort ★★ (**Finds**) ISLAND/SEAFOOD   Even if you are staying in Waikiki, plan a day at the beach on the North Shore and eat here for dinner—you will not regret it. First, the location is literally on the beach, next door to the Turtle Bay Resort. Second, the restaurant is an open-air beach pavilion, made from ironwood trees harvested from the surrounding area. The view is of the Pacific waves lapping onto the sand, and the atmosphere when they light the tiki torches at sunset is very, very romantic. But, wait, the best part is . . . the food! Chef Fred DeAngelo named his restaurant Ola, which means "alive" or "healthy" in Hawaiian, and he insists on only the freshest of ingredients. The menu is filled with creative selections (the ahi and lobster poke served with a wonton spoon) and some of the best food you will eat in Hawaii, such as the incredible slow-poached togarashi salmon with a sweet, sugar-cane crust served with Okinawan sweet potato and locally grown corn; the Lawai'a fishermen's stew with lobster, shrimp, scallops, and fresh fish; and a kiawe-smoked beef tenderloin that is so tasty, you'll never forget it.

At Turtle Bay Resort, 57-091 Kamehameha Hwy., Kahuku. ☏ **808/293-0801.** www.turtlebayresort.com. Reservations recommended for dinner. Main courses $9–$16 lunch, $17–$38 dinner. AE, DC, DISC, MC, V. Daily 11am–8:45pm (last seating).

INEXPENSIVE

Cafe Haleiwa BREAKFAST/LUNCH/MEXICAN   Haleiwa's legendary breakfast joint is a big hit with surfers, urban gentry with weekend country homes, reclusive artists, and anyone who loves mahimahi plate lunches and heroic sandwiches. It's a wake-up-and-hit-the-beach kind of place, serving generous omelets with such names as Off the Wall, Off the Lip, and Breakfast in a Barrel. Surf pictures line the walls, and the ambience is Formica casual. Those needing a caffeine fix will appreciate the espresso bar.

66-460 Kamehameha Hwy., Haleiwa. ☏ **808/637-5516.** Reservations not accepted. Main courses $7–$14. AE, MC, V. Daily 7am–1:45pm.

Cholos Homestyle Mexican II (**Value**) MEXICAN   There's usually a wait at this popular eatery, where some of the tables have leather stools without backs, and great home-style Mexican food is presented with so-so service. Still, this is the unhurried North Shore, and the biggest rush for most folks is getting to and from the beach. I recommend the spinach quesadilla, a generous serving filled with black beans, cheese, and fresh vegetables; the chicken fajita plate; and the fish taco plate, a steal at $8 (just $4.75 a la carte). Tables with stools preside outdoors; indoors, it's dark and cavelike, with loud music and Mexican handicrafts.

At the North Shore Marketplace, 66-250 Kamehameha Hwy. ☏ **808/637-3059.** Combination plates $11–$14. AE, DISC, MC, V. Daily 10:30am–9:30pm.

Kua Aina ★ (**Value**) AMERICAN   "What's the name of that sandwich shop on the North Shore?" I hear that often. After 29 years at the same spot, Kua Aina moved a few years ago down the street to a larger, 75-seat eatery. It's as busy as ever, though many diners get their burgers to go and head for the beach. Kua Aina's thin and spindly french fries are renowned islandwide and are the perfect accompaniment to its legendary burgers. Fat, moist, and homemade, the burgers can be ordered with avocado, bacon, and many other

---

(Moments) LUAU!

The sun is setting, the Tiki torches are lit, the pig is taken from the *imu* (an oven in the earth), the drums begin pounding—it's luau time! And now there is a luau on the North Shore, the **Turtle Bay Resort** presents its **Voyages of Polynesia Luau** on the lawn overlooking the ocean. It includes a "Taste of the Islands" luau buffet and a Polynesian revue featuring the songs and dances of the Tuamotu Islands, Samoa, Tahiti, Fiji, and Hawaii. Tickets for the Friday-night dinner and show are $95 for adults and $65 for children ages 4 to 11. To book, call (C) **808/293-6000.**

---

accompaniments, including Ortega chilies and cheese. The tuna/avocado, roast turkey, and mahimahi sandwiches are excellent alternatives to the burgers. Kua Aina is unparalleled on the island and is a North Shore must, eclipsing its fancier competitors at lunch.

66-160 Kamehameha Hwy., Haleiwa. (C) **808/637-6067.** Sandwiches and burgers $7–$8.50. No credit cards. Daily 11am–8pm.

Paradise Found Cafe VEGETARIAN   A tiny cafe behind Celestial Natural Foods, Paradise Found is a bit of a hunt, but stick with it. For more than a few townies, the North Shore sojourn begins at Paradise, the only purely vegetarian restaurant in these parts. Breakfasts feature the "up & at 'em" (scrambled eggs, tempeh, veggies and home fries wrapped in a cheese quesadilla) and the "nanna nutty" (peanut butter, banana, honey, granola, and cinnamon, wrapped in a flour tortilla and grilled). Their smoothies (especially the Waimea Shorebreak) are legendary, and their organic soups, fresh-pressed vegetable juices, sandwiches, and healthy plate lunches are a great launch to a Haleiwa day. Vegan substitutions are willingly made.

66-443 Kamehameha Hwy., Haleiwa. (C) **808/637-4540.** All items under $12. No credit cards. Mon–Sat 9am–5pm; Sun 9am–4pm.

7 LEEWARD OAHU

Roy's Ko Olina ★★★ (Finds) EUROPEAN/ASIAN   The latest in Roy's empire of excellent restaurants opened in 2004 in Ko Olina Resort on the leeward coast of Oahu, some 16 years after the flagship restaurant (p. 147) opened in Hawaii Kai. One of some nearly three dozen locations around the globe, Roy's Ko Olina perches in a peerless location overlooking the lagoon, waterfalls, and 18th hole of the Ko Olina Golf Club. The space, formerly home to the Niblick Restaurant, has been totally transformed to include Roy's famous display kitchen and boasts floor-to-ceiling windows that showcase the view. Roy's usual high-decibel style of dining has been replaced by a relaxing, romantic atmosphere, where you can have a conversation without shouting, while enjoying the incredible cuisine. The menu changes daily, but you can generally count on Roy's classics: blackened ahi, hibachi salmon, and Szechuan baby back ribs. Some great additions include Asian pesto steamed fresh fish, cilantro-dusted *papio* (jack trevally), kiawe-grilled filet mignon, and roasted chicken with *huli-huli* (sort of a Hawaiian barbecue sauce) sauce. Unlike the Hawaii Kai location, Ko Olina is also open for lunch; between lunch-and dinnertime, you can enjoy appetizers at the bar. It's worth the drive to participate in this incredible dining experience.

At the Ko Olina Resort, 92-1220 Aliinui Dr., Kapolei. ℂ **808/676-7697.** www.roysrestaurant.com. Reservations recommended. Lunch $15–$22, appetizers at the bar $9.50–$15, dinner entrees $18–$42. AE, DC, DISC, MC, V. Daily 11am–9:30pm (appetizers only 2–5:30pm).

Fun in the Surf & Sun

Pictures of hotels lining the shores of Waikiki Beach and canyons of tall buildings in downtown Honolulu have given Oahu a bad rap. The island is much more than an urban concrete jungle or a tropical Disneyland blighted by overdevelopment; it's also a haven for the nature lover and outdoor enthusiast. With year-round temperatures in the upper 70s, and miles of verdant unspoiled landscape, Oahu is perfect for outdoor activities of all kinds, including hiking, golf, tennis, biking, and horseback riding. But the island's waters, which also enjoy year-round temperatures in the upper 70s, are where the majority of residents and visitors head for relaxation, rejuvenation, and recreation. Locals don't think of their island or state boundaries as ending at land's edge—rather, they extend beyond the reefs, well out into the ocean.

All the activities in this chapter are organized geographically around the island in a counterclockwise direction.

For camping information, see "Oahu's Campgrounds & Wilderness Cabins," at the end of chapter 4.

1 BEACHES

Oahu has more than 130 beaches of every conceivable kind—from legendary white-sand stretches to secluded rocky bays. Waikiki, of course, is the best known, but there are many others—some more beautiful, all less crowded. The following sample of Oahu's finest beaches was carefully selected to suit every need, taste, and interest, from the sunbather in repose to the most ardent diver.

THE WAIKIKI COAST

Ala Moana Beach Park ★★

Quite possibly America's best urban beach, gold-sand Ala Moana ("by the sea"), on sunny Mamala Bay, stretches for more than a mile along Honolulu's coast between downtown and Waikiki. This 76-acre midtown beach park, with spreading lawns shaded by banyans and palms, is one of the island's most popular playgrounds. It has a man-made beach, created in the 1930s by filling a coral reef with Waianae Coast sand, as well as its own lagoon, yacht harbor, tennis courts, music pavilion, bathhouses, picnic tables, and enough wide-open green spaces to accommodate four million visitors a year. The water is calm almost year-round, protected by black lava rocks set offshore. You can park in the large lot or at metered street parking.

Waikiki Beach ★★★

No beach anywhere is so widely known or so universally sought after as this narrow, 1½-mile-long crescent of imported sand (from Molokai) at the foot of a string of high-rise hotels. Home to the world's longest-running beach party, Waikiki attracts nearly five million visitors a year from every corner of the planet. First-timers are always amazed to discover how small Waikiki Beach actually is, but everyone finds a place for themselves under the tropical sun here.

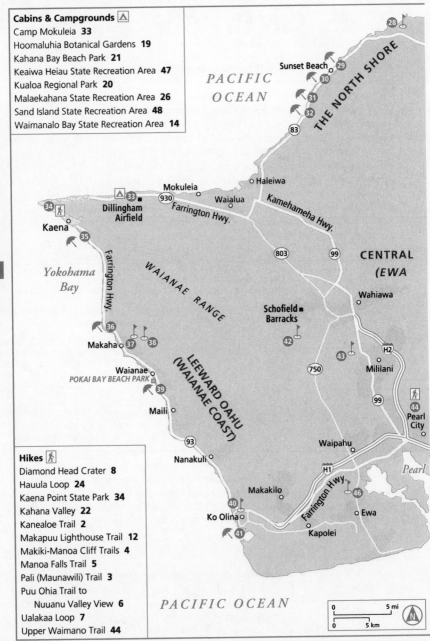

FUN IN THE SURF & SUN

6

BEACHES

Cabins & Campgrounds △
Camp Mokuleia **33**
Hoomaluhia Botanical Gardens **19**
Kahana Bay Beach Park **21**
Keaiwa Heiau State Recreation Area **47**
Kualoa Regional Park **20**
Malaekahana State Recreation Area **26**
Sand Island State Recreation Area **48**
Waimanalo Bay State Recreation Area **14**

PACIFIC OCEAN

THE NORTH SHORE

Sunset Beach

Haleiwa

Mokuleia
△33
Dillingham Airfield
930
Farrington Hwy.
Waialua
Kamehameha Hwy.

34
Kaena
35

Yokohama Bay

Farrington Hwy.

WAIANAE RANGE

803

99

CENTRAL (EWA

Wahiawa

Schofield Barracks
42

36
Makaha 37 38

Waianae
POKAI BAY BEACH PARK
39

Maili

LEEWARD OAHU (WAIANAE COAST)

43

750

H2

Mililani

99

44
Pearl City

Waipahu

93
Nanakuli

Makakilo

H1

Farrington Hwy.
46

Pearl

Ewa

Hikes 🚶
Diamond Head Crater **8**
Hauula Loop **24**
Kaena Point State Park **34**
Kahana Valley **22**
Kanealoe Trail **2**
Makapuu Lighthouse Trail **12**
Makiki-Manoa Cliff Trails **4**
Manoa Falls Trail **5**
Pali (Maunawili) Trail **3**
Puu Ohia Trail to
    Nuuanu Valley View **6**
Ualakaa Loop **7**
Upper Waimano Trail **44**

40
Ko Olina
41

Kapolei

PACIFIC OCEAN

0   5 mi
0   5 km

N

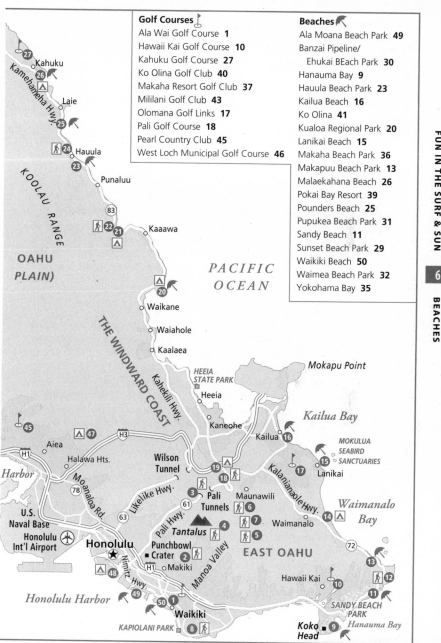

Golf Courses
Ala Wai Golf Course **1**
Hawaii Kai Golf Course **10**
Kahuku Golf Course **27**
Ko Olina Golf Club **40**
Makaha Resort Golf Club **37**
Mililani Golf Club **43**
Olomana Golf Links **17**
Pali Golf Course **18**
Pearl Country Club **45**
West Loch Municipal Golf Course **46**

Beaches
Ala Moana Beach Park **49**
Banzai Pipeline/
 Ehukai BEach Park **30**
Hanauma Bay **9**
Hauula Beach Park **23**
Kailua Beach **16**
Ko Olina **41**
Kualoa Regional Park **20**
Lanikai Beach **15**
Makaha Beach Park **36**
Makapuu Beach Park **13**
Malaekahana Beach **26**
Pokai Bay Resort **39**
Pounders Beach **25**
Pupukea Beach Park **31**
Sandy Beach **11**
Sunset Beach Park **29**
Waikiki Beach **50**
Waimea Beach Park **32**
Yokohama Bay **35**

> **Tips** **A Word of Warning**
>
> Wherever you are on Oahu, remember that you're in an urban area. Never leave valuables in your car. Thefts do occur at Oahu's beaches, and locked cars are not a deterrent.

Waikiki is actually a string of beaches that extends between **Sans Souci State Recreational Area,** near Diamond Head to the east, and **Duke Kahanamoku Beach,** in front of the Hilton Hawaiian Village Beach Resort & Spa, to the west. Great stretches along Waikiki include **Kuhio Beach,** next to the Moana Surfrider, which provides the quickest access to the Waikiki shoreline; the stretch in front of the Royal Hawaiian Hotel known as **Grey's Beach,** which is canted so it catches the rays perfectly; and **Sans Souci,** the small, popular beach in front of the New Otani Kaimana Beach Hotel that's locally known as "Dig Me" Beach because of all the gorgeous bods who strut their stuff here.

Waikiki is fabulous for swimming, board- and bodysurfing, outrigger canoeing, diving, sailing, snorkeling, and pole fishing. Every imaginable type of marine equipment is available for rent here. Facilities include showers, lifeguards, restrooms, grills, picnic tables, and pavilions at the **Queen's Surf** end of the beach (at Kapiolani Park, btw. the zoo and the aquarium). The best place to park is at Kapiolani Park, near Sans Souci.

EAST OAHU

Hanauma Bay ★★

Oahu's most popular snorkeling spot is this volcanic crater with a broken sea wall; its small, curved, 2,000-foot gold-sand beach is packed elbow-to-elbow with people year-round. The bay's shallow shoreline water and abundant marine life are the main attractions, but this good-looking beach is also popular for sunbathing and people-watching. Serious divers shoot "the slot" (a passage through the reef) to gain access to Witch's Brew, a turbulent cove, and then brave strong currents in 70-foot depths at the bay mouth to see coral gardens, turtles, and—that's right—sharks. (Divers: Beware the Molokai Express, a strong current.) Snorkelers hug the safe, shallow (10 ft.) inner bay that, depending on when you go, is either like swimming in a fish-feeding frenzy or like bathing with 300,000 honeymooners. For a real treat, snorkel by moonlight: Every second Saturday, the park stays open until 10pm. Because Hanauma Bay is a conservation district, you may look at but not touch or take any marine life here. Feeding the fish is also prohibited.

In 2004, a $13-million Marine Education Center opened with exhibits and a 7-minute video orienting visitors on this marine life sanctuary. The 10,000-square-foot center includes a training room, gift shop, public restrooms, snack bar, and staging area for the motorized tram, which will take you down the steep road to the beach (tram fees are 50¢ down to the beach, $1 up from the beach to the parking lot, or $2 all-day rides up and down). Facilities include parking, restrooms, a pavilion, a grass volleyball court, lifeguards, barbecue grills, picnic tables, and food concessions. Alcohol is prohibited in the park; no smoking past the visitor center. Expect to pay $1 per vehicle to park and a $5-per-person entrance fee (children 12 and under are free). If you're driving, take Kalanianaole Highway to Koko Head Regional Park. Avoid the crowds by going early, about

8am, on a weekday morning; once the parking lot's full, you're out of luck. Or take TheBus to escape the parking problem: The Hanauma Bay Shuttle runs from Waikiki to Hanauma Bay every half-hour from 8:45am to 1pm; you can catch it at the Ala Moana Hotel, the Ilikai Hotel, or any city bus stop. It returns every hour from noon to 4:30pm. Hanauma Bay is closed on Tuesdays so the fish can have a day off. In the summer, Hanauma Bay stays open until 10pm (night snorkeling!) on the second and fourth Saturdays of each month; during the winter it is open late only on the second Saturday.

Sandy Beach ★

Sandy Beach is one of the best bodysurfing beaches on Oahu; it's also one of the most dangerous. It's better to just stand and watch the daredevils literally risk their necks at this 1,200-foot-long gold-sand beach that's pounded by wild waves and haunted by a dangerous shore break and strong backwash. Weak swimmers and children should definitely stay out of the water here; Sandy Beach's heroic lifeguards make more rescues in a year than those at any other beach on Oahu. Visitors, easily fooled by experienced bodysurfers who make wave-riding look easy, often fall victim to the bone-crunching waves. Lifeguards post flags to alert beachgoers to the day's surf: Green means safe, yellow caution, and red indicates very dangerous water conditions; always check the flags before you dive in.

Facilities include restrooms and parking. Go weekdays to avoid the crowds, weekends to catch the bodysurfers in action. From Waikiki, drive east on the H-1, which becomes Kalanianaole Highway; proceed past Hawaii Kai, up the hill to Hanauma Bay, past the Halona Blow Hole, and along the coast. The next big, gold, sandy beach you see ahead on the right is Sandy Beach. TheBus no. 22 will also get you here.

Makapuu Beach Park ★

Makapuu Beach, the most famous bodysurfing beach in Hawaii, is a beautiful 1,000-foot-long gold-sand beach cupped in the stark black Koolau cliffs on Oahu's easternmost point. Even if you never venture into the water, it's worth a visit just to enjoy the great natural beauty of this classic Hawaiian beach. You've probably already seen it in countless TV shows, from *Hawaii Five-O* to *Magnum, P.I.*

In summer, the ocean here is as gentle as a Jacuzzi, and swimming and diving are perfect; come winter, however, Makapuu is hit with big, pounding waves that are ideal for expert bodysurfers, but too dangerous for regular swimmers. Small boards—3 feet or less with no skeg (bottom fin)—are permitted; regular board surfing is banned by state law.

Facilities include restrooms, lifeguards, barbecue grills, picnic tables, and parking. To get here, follow Kalanianaole Highway toward Waimanalo, or take TheBus no. 57 or 58.

THE WINDWARD COAST

Lanikai Beach ★★

One of Hawaii's best spots for swimming, gold-sand Lanikai's crystal-clear lagoon is like a giant saltwater swimming pool that you're lucky to share with the resident tropical fish and sea turtles. Too gorgeous to be real, this is one of Hawaii's postcard-perfect beaches: It's a mile long and thin in places, but the sand's as soft as talcum powder. Prevailing onshore trade winds make this an excellent place for sailing and windsurfing. Kayakers often paddle out to the two tiny offshore Mokulua islands, which are seabird sanctuaries. Because Lanikai is in a residential neighborhood, it's less crowded than other Oahu beaches, the perfect place to enjoy a quiet day. Sun worshipers should arrive in the morning, though, as the Koolau Range blocks the afternoon rays.

Favorite Outdoor Experiences

Getting a Tan on Waikiki Beach. The best spot for catching the rays on the world-famous beach is in front of the big, pink Royal Hawaiian Hotel—the beach here is set at the perfect angle for sunning. It's also a great spot for people-watching. Get here early; by midday (when the rays are at their peak), it's towel-to-towel out there.

Exploring Oahu's Rainforests. In the misty sunbeams, colorful birds flit among giant ferns and hanging vines, while towering tropical trees form a thick canopy that shelters all below in cool shadows. This emerald world is a true Eden. For the full experience, try Manoa Falls Trail, a walk of less than a mile that ends at a freshwater pool and waterfall.

Snorkeling the Glistening Waters of Hanauma Bay. This underwater park, once a volcanic crater, is teeming with a rainbow of tropical fish. Bordered by a 2,000-foot gold-sand beach, the bay's shallow water (10 ft. in places) is perfect for neophyte snorkelers. Arrive early to beat the crowds—and don't forget that the bay is closed on Tuesday. **Aloha Dive Shop,** Koko Marina Shopping Center (✆ **808/395-5922**), can set you up with fins, mask, and snorkel for just $7 a day.

Hiking to the Top of Diamond Head Crater. Almost everyone can make this easy hike to the top of Hawaii's most famous landmark. The 1.4-mile round-trip goes to the top of the 750-foot volcanic cone, where you have a 360-degree view of Oahu. Allow an hour for the trip up and back, bring $1 for the entry fee, and don't forget your camera.

Heading to Waimea Bay when the Surf's Up. From November to March, monstrous waves—some 30 feet tall—roll into Waimea. When they break on the shore, the ground actually vibrates and everyone on the beach is covered with salt spray mist. The best surfers in the world paddle out to challenge these freight trains. It's amazing to see how small they appear in the lip of the giant waves. And this unforgettable experience won't cost you a dime.

Watching the Ancient Hawaiian Sport of Canoe Paddling. On weekday evenings and weekend days from February to September, hundreds of paddlers gather at Ala Wai Canal and practice taking traditional Hawaiian canoes out to sea. Find a comfortable spot at Ala Wai Park next to the canal and watch the canoe paddlers re-create this centuries-old sport.

Finding a Bargain at the Aloha Flea Market. Just 50¢ will get you into this all-day show at the Aloha Stadium parking lot, where more than 1,000 vendors sell everything from junk to jewels. Go early for the best deals. Open Wednesday, Saturday, and Sunday from 6am to 3pm.

There are no facilities here, just off-street parking. From Waikiki, take the H-1 to the Pali Highway (Hwy. 61) through the Nuuanu Pali Tunnel to Kailua, where the Pali Highway becomes Kailua Road as it proceeds through town. At Kalaheo Avenue, turn right and follow the coast about 2 miles to Kailua Beach Park; just past it, turn left at the

Attending a Hawaiian-Language Church Service. Built in 1842, Kawaiahao Church, 957 Punchbowl St. (near King St.), is the Westminster Abbey of Hawaii; the vestibule is lined with portraits of the Hawaiian monarchy, many of whom were coronated in this very building. The coral church is a perfect setting to experience an all-Hawaiian service, complete with Hawaiian song. Hawaiian-language services are held every Sunday at 9am and admission is free—let your conscience be your guide as to a donation.

Visiting the Lei Sellers in Chinatown. A host of cultural sights and experiences are to be had in Honolulu's Chinatown. Wander through this several-square-block area with its jumble of exotic shops offering herbs, Chinese groceries, and acupuncture services. Be sure to check out the lei sellers on Maunakea Street (near N. Hotel St.), where Hawaii's finest leis go for as little as $3.50.

Experiencing a Turning Point in America's History: The Bombing of Pearl Harbor. Standing on the deck of the USS *Arizona* Memorial at Pearl Harbor is an unforgettable experience. On that fateful day—December 7, 1941—the 608-foot *Arizona* sank in just 9 minutes after being bombed during the Japanese air raid. The 1,177 men on board plunged to a fiery death—and the United States went to war. Go early; you'll wait 2 to 3 hours if you visit at midday. You must wear closed-toe shoes, no flip-flops or sandals.

Watching the Sun Sink into the Pacific from a 1,048-Foot Hill Named after a Sweet Potato. Actually, it's more romantic than it sounds. Puu Ualakaa State Park, at the end of Round Hill Drive, translates into "rolling sweet potato hill" (which was how the early Hawaiians harvested the crop). This majestic view of the sunset is not to be missed.

Ordering a Shave Ice in a Tropical Flavor You Can Hardly Pronounce. In Haleiwa, stop at Matsumoto Shave Ice, 66-087 Kamehameha Hwy., for a snow cone with an exotic flavor poured over the top, such as the local favorite, *li hing mui* (lee hing moo-*ee*, which is sweet, sour, and salty), or with sweet Japanese adzuki beans hidden inside. This taste of tropical paradise goes for just $1.50.

Listening to the Soothing Sounds of Hawaiian Music. Sit under the huge banyan tree at the Sheraton Moana Surfrider's Banyan Veranda in Waikiki, order a cocktail, and sway to live Hawaiian music any night of the week. Another quintessential sunset oasis is the Halekulani's House Without a Key, a sophisticated oceanfront lounge with wonderful hula and steel-guitar music, a great view of Diamond Head, and the best mai tais on the island.

T-intersection and drive uphill on Aalapapa Drive, a one-way street that loops back as Mokulua Drive. Park on Mokulua Drive and walk down any of the eight public-access lanes to the shore. Or, take TheBus no. 56 or 57 (Kailua), and then transfer to the shuttle.

Kailua Beach ★★★

Windward Oahu's premier beach is a 2-mile-long, wide golden strand with dunes, palm trees, panoramic views, and offshore islets that are home to seabirds. The swimming is excellent, and the azure waters are usually decorated with bright sails; this is Oahu's premier windsurfing beach as well. It's also a favorite spot to sail catamarans, bodysurf the gentle waves, or paddle a kayak. Water conditions are quite safe, especially at the mouth of Kaelepulu Stream, where toddlers play in the freshwater shallows at the middle of the beach park. The water's usually about 78°F (26°C), the views are spectacular, and the setting, at the foot of the sheer, green Koolaus, is idyllic. Best of all, the crowds haven't found it yet.

The 35-acre beach park is intersected by a freshwater stream and watched over by lifeguards. Facilities include picnic tables, barbecues, restrooms, a volleyball court, a public boat ramp, free parking, and an open-air cafe. Kailua's new bike path weaves through the park, and windsurfer and kayak rentals are available as well. To get here, take Pali Highway (Hwy. 61) to Kailua, drive through town, turn right on Kalaheo Avenue, and go a mile until you see the beach on your left. Or take TheBus no. 56 or 57 into Kailua, then the no. 70 shuttle.

Kualoa Regional Park ★★

This 150-acre coconut palm–fringed peninsula is the biggest beach park on the windward side and one of Hawaii's most scenic. It's on Kaneohe Bay's north shore, at the foot of the spiky Koolau Ridge. The park has a broad, grassy lawn and a long, narrow, white-sand beach ideal for swimming, walking, beachcombing, kite flying, or sunbathing. Picnic and camping areas are available, too. In ancient Hawaii, this was a very sacred spot where Hawaiian chiefs brought their infant children to be raised and trained as rulers. Today, the park is listed on the National Register of Historic Places. It's easy to see why it was so revered: The curtain of the Koolau Mountains provides a spectacular backdrop in one direction. The waters are shallow and safe for swimming year-round, and at low tide, you can swim or wade out to the islet of Mokolii (popularly known as Chinaman's Hat), which has a small sandy beach and is a bird preserve—so don't spook the red-footed boobies. Lifeguards are on duty.

Because both residents and visitors frequent this huge beach park, it's better to go on a weekday. The park is on Kamehameha Highway (Hwy. 83) in Kualoa; you can get here via TheBus no. 55.

Kahana Bay Beach Park ★★

This white-sand, crescent-shaped beach is backed by a huge, jungle-cloaked valley with dramatic, jagged cliffs and is protected by ironwood and kamani trees. The bay's calm water and shallow, sandy bottom make it a safe swimming area for children. The bay is famous for the *akule* (bigeye scad), which come in seasonally; *papio* (skip jack) and goatfish are also found here. The surrounding park has picnic areas, camping, and hiking trails. The wide sand-bottom channel that runs through the park and out to Kahana Bay is one of the largest on Oahu—it's perfect for kayakers. Locals come here on weekends, so weekdays are less crowded. The beach park is on Kamehameha Highway in Kahana; take TheBus no. 55 (Circle Island) to get here.

Hauula Beach Park

The town of Hauula and nearby Hauula Beach Park were named after the *hau* trees that were once abundant. Although less plentiful now, the trees continue to blossom here every July and August. The blossoms begin as a bright yellow flower in the morning, changing color as the day progresses, until they are reddish gold by dusk and dark red by night, when they fall to the ground. The cycle is repeated the next day.

Hauula Beach Park, which fronts Kamehameha Highway, is a straight and narrow stretch (about 1,000 ft. long), shaded by kamani and ironwood trees. An offshore reef protects the waters off the beach, but the shallow and rocky bottom make the area unsafe for swimming. Snorkeling is good along the edge of the coral reef, and fishing for papio and goatfish can be fruitful. Picnic and camping facilities are available. Weekends tend to be more crowded here, too. TheBus no. 55 (Circle Island) will get you to Hauula Beach.

Pounders Beach

Because of its easy access and its great bodysurfing waves, Pounders is a popular weekend beach. The beach used to be called Pahumoa, after a local fisherman who arranged the local *hukilau* (the catching of fish in a net) and made sure that the elderly living in the area received a portion of the catch. The name change occurred in the 1950s, when a group of students at the Church College of the Pacific (now Brigham Young University–Hawaii) called the beach "Pounders" after the crushing shore break that provided brief but spectacular bodysurfing rides; the nickname stuck.

Pounders is a wide beach, extending a quarter-mile between two points. At the west end of the beach, next to the old landing, the waters usually are calm and safe for swimming. However, at the opposite end, near the limestone cliffs, there's a shore break that can be dangerous for inexperienced bodysurfers; there the bottom drops off abruptly, causing strong rip currents. The weekends and after-school hours are the busiest time for this beach; weekday mornings are the quietest. Park on Kamehameha Highway in Kailua, or take TheBus no. 55 (Circle Island) to get here.

THE NORTH SHORE

Banzai/Pipeline/Ehukai Beach Park ★

Three separate areas are actually here, but because the sandy beach is continuous, with only one sign, EHUKAI BEACH PARK, most people think of it as one beach park. Located near Pupukea, the actual **Ehukai Beach Park** is 1 acre of grass with a parking lot. The long, broad, white-sand beach is known for its winter surfing action. Swimming is good during the spring and summer months, but currents and waves prohibit safe swimming in the winter. The surf in front of Ehukai Beach Park is excellent for body and board surfers.

The park also provides access to Pipeline and Banzai. **Pipeline** is actually about 100 yards to the left of Ehukai Beach Park. When the winter surf rolls in and hits the shallow coral shelf, the waves that quickly form are steep—so steep, in fact, that the crest of the wave falling forward forms a near-perfect tube, or "pipeline." Surfers have tried for years to master Pipeline; many have wiped out, suffering lacerations and broken bones on the shallow reef. The first surfer to ride Pipeline successfully was Phil Edwards in the early 1960s. Even today, Pipeline still causes its share of injuries and fatalities.

Just west of Pipeline is the area surfers call **"Banzai Beach."** The Japanese word *banzai* means "10,000 years"; it's given as a toast or as a battle charge, meaning "go for it." In the late 1950s, filmmaker Bruce Brown was shooting one of the first surf movies ever made, *Surf Safari*, when he saw a bodysurfer ride a huge wave. Brown yelled: "Banzai!" and the name stuck. In the winter, this is a very popular beach with surfers, surf fans, curious residents, and visitors; it's less crowded in the summer months. Again, access is via Ehukai Beach Park, off Kamehameha Highway, on Ke Nui Road in Pupukea. TheBus no. 52 (Circle Island) will drop you on the highway.

> **Impressions**
>
> *The boldness and address with which we saw them perform these difficult and dangerous maneuvers was altogether astonishing.*
> —Capt. James Cook's observations of Hawaiian surfers

Pupukea Beach Park ★

This 80-acre beach park is a Marine Life Conservation District; as such, it has strict rules about taking marine life, sand, coral, shells, and rocks. Two major swimming areas are in the Marine Life Conservation District: **Shark's Cove** and **Three Tables.** Don't worry: Shark's Cove, near the northern end, is *not* named for an abundance of sharks that call this home (in fact, it's relatively uncommon to see a shark here); rather, it's a popular snorkeling and dive site. Diving is best outside the cove, where caves promise interesting night diving. During the calm summer months, this is a popular dive site both day and night.

At the southern end of the Marine Life Conservation District is Three Tables, which is named for the three flat sections of reef visible at low tide. Snorkeling is good around the tables where the water is about 15 feet deep. Diving outside the tables, where the water is 30 to 45 feet deep, is excellent—there are many ledges, arches, lava tubes, and a variety of marine life. Swimming, diving, and snorkeling are best from May to October, when the water is calm; nevertheless, watch out for surges. In the winter, when currents form and waves roll in, this area is very dangerous, even in the tide pools; a lifeguard is never present in this area. Summers find this Marine Life Conservation District brimming with visitors weekdays and weekends; it's a popular site for local dive operators to take their clients. In the winter, it's nearly empty during the week. It's right on Kamehameha Highway in Pupukea and has a small parking lot. TheBus no. 52 (Circle Island) stops at the park.

Malaekahana Bay State Recreation Area ★★★

This almost mile-long white-sand crescent lives up to just about everyone's image of the perfect Hawaiian beach. It's excellent for swimming. On a weekday, you may be the only one here; but should some net fisherman—or kindred soul—intrude upon your delicious privacy, you can swim out to Goat Island (or wade across at low tide) and play Robinson Crusoe. (The islet is a sanctuary for seabirds and turtles, so no chase 'em, brah.) Facilities include restrooms, barbecue grills, picnic tables, outdoor showers, and parking.

To get here, take Kamehameha Highway (Hwy. 83) 2 miles north of the Polynesian Cultural Center; as you enter the main gate, you'll come upon the wooded beach park. Or you can take TheBus no. 52.

Sunset Beach Park ★★

Surfers around the world know this famous site for its spectacular winter surf—the waves can be huge thundering peaks reaching 15 to 20 feet. This surfing spot wasn't really "discovered" until the 1940s; before that, surfers preferred Makaha on the leeward side of the island. During the winter surf season (Sept–Apr) swimming is very dangerous here, due to the alongshore currents and powerful rip currents. The "Sunset rip" has been the site of many rescues and has carried numerous surfboards out to sea. The only safe time to swim at Sunset is during the calm summer months. Sunset also features a huge sandy beach adjacent to the street. This is a great place to people-watch, but don't go too near the water when the lifeguards have posted the red warning flags. One of the most popular beaches on the island, Sunset attracts local surfers, sunbathing beauties, and visitors wanting to get a glimpse of this world-famous surf destination. To avoid the crowds, go during midweek. Because the beach is located right on Kamehameha Highway in Paumalu, TheBus no. 52 (Circle Island) will get you there if you'd rather not drive.

Waimea Beach Park ★★

This deep, sandy bowl has gentle summer waves that are excellent for swimming, snorkeling, and bodysurfing. To one side of the bay is a huge rock that local kids like to climb and dive from. In this placid scene, the only clues of what's to come in winter are those evacuation whistles on poles beside the road. But what a difference a season makes: Winter waves pound the narrow bay, sometimes rising to 50 feet high. When the surf's really up, very strong currents and shore breaks sweep the bay—and it seems like everyone on Oahu drives out to Waimea to get a look at the monster waves and those who ride them. Weekends are great for watching the surfers; to avoid the crowds, go on weekdays. *A safety tip:* Don't get too distracted by the waves and forget to pay attention when parking or crossing the road.

Facilities include lifeguards, restrooms, showers, parking, and nearby restaurants and shops in Haleiwa town. The beach is on Kamehameha Highway (Hwy. 83); from Waikiki, you can take TheBus no. 52.

LEEWARD OAHU/THE WAIANAE COAST

Ko Olina

The developer of the 640-acre Ko Olina Resort has created four white-sand lagoons to make the rocky shoreline more attractive and accessible. Nearly circular, the man-made lagoons offer calm, shallow waters and a powdery white-sand beach bordered by a broad, grassy lawn. No lifeguards are present, but the generally tranquil waters are great for swimming, are perfect for kids, and offer some snorkeling opportunities around the boulders at the entrance to the lagoons. Two lagoons have restrooms, and plenty of public parking is on-hand. Located off H-1 in Kapolei, Ko Olina has no local bus service; the closest bus stop is on Farrington Highway, more than 4 miles away.

Makaha Beach Park

When surf's up here, it's spectacular: Monstrous waves pound the beach from October through April. This is the original home of Hawaii's big-wave surfing championship; surfers today know it as the home of Buffalo's Big Board Surf Classic, where surfers ride the waves on old-Hawaiian-style 10-foot-long wooden boards. Nearly a mile long, this half-moon gold-sand beach is tucked between 231-foot Lahilahi Point, which locals call Black Rock, and Kepuhi Point, a toe of the Waianae mountain range. Summer is the best time to hit this beach—the waves are small, the sand abundant, and the water safe for swimming. Children hug the shore on the north side of the beach, near the lifeguard stand, while surfers dodge the rocks and divers seek an offshore channel full of big fish. *A caveat:* This is a "local" beach; you're welcome, of course, but you can expect "stink eye" (mild approbation) if you are not respectful of the beach and the local residents who use the facility all the time.

Facilities include restrooms, lifeguards, and parking. To get here, take the H-1 freeway to the end of the line, where it becomes Farrington Highway (Hwy. 93), and follow it to the beach; or you can take TheBus no. 51.

Yokohama Bay ★

Where Farrington Highway (Hwy. 93) ends, the wilderness of Kaena Point State Park begins. It's a remote 853-acre coastline park of empty beaches, sand dunes, cliffs, and deep-blue water. This is the last sandy stretch of shore on the northwest coast of Oahu. Sometimes it's known as Keawalua Beach or Puau Beach, but everybody here calls it Yokohama, after the Japanese immigrants who came from that port city to work the cane fields and fish along this shoreline. When the surf's calm—mainly in summer—this is a good area for snorkeling, diving, swimming, shore fishing, and picnicking. When surf's up, board and bodysurfers are out in droves; don't go in the water then unless you're an expert. No lifeguards or facilities are available, except at the park entrance, where a restroom and lifeguard stand are positioned. No bus serves the park.

Pokai Bay Beach Park ★

This wonderful beach, off the beaten path for most visitors, offers excellent swimming year-round, even when the rest of the Waianae shoreline is getting battered by heavy surf. The waters inside this protected bay are calm enough for children and offer excellent snorkeling. The swimming area is marked by buoys. Waianae-area residents have a bit of a reputation for being xenophobic; however, they want the same things most people want. Just go with respect for local customs, be a good steward of the land, and appreciate the local resources. Do what the locals do: Pick up your garbage, don't play loud music, and be courteous and friendly. On weekdays, you can practically have the area to yourself. The beach park is on Waianae Valley Road, off Farrington Highway. TheBus no. 51 will drop you off on the highway, and you can walk the block to the park.

2 WATERSPORTS

Oahu has a wealth of watersports opportunities, whether you're a professional surfer braving giant winter waves on the North Shore, or a recreational water-skier enjoying the calm waters of Hawaii Kai. You can kayak from Lanikai Beach to the Mokulua Islands or float above Waikiki on a parasail as a speedboat tows you blissfully through the air. If you have something of an adventurous spirit, you might scuba dive the walls of Kahuna Canyon, swim with clouds of ta'ape (bluestripe snapper), or view an occasional shark from the comfort of a passenger submarine. No matter what your aquatic interests are, whether you're a beginner or an expert, you can find the right sport on Oahu.

If you want to rent beach toys (such as a mask, snorkel, and fins; boogie boards; surfboards; kayaks; and more), check out the following rental shops: **Snorkel Bob's,** on the way to Hanauma Bay at 700 Kapahulu Ave. (at Date St.), Honolulu (© **808/735-7944;** www.snorkelbob.com); and **Aloha Beach Service,** in the Sheraton Moana Surfrider Hotel, 2365 Kalakaua Ave. (© **808/922-3111,** ext. 2341), in Waikiki. On Oahu's windward side, try **Kailua Sailboards & Kayaks,** 130 Kailua Rd., a block from the Kailua Beach Park (© **808/262-2555;** www.kailuasailboards.com). On the North Shore, get equipment from **Surf-N-Sea,** 62-595 Kamehameha Hwy., Haleiwa (© **808/637-9887;** www.surfnsea.com).

BOATING

A funny thing happens to people when they come to Hawaii: Maybe it's the salt air, the warm tropical nights, or the blue Hawaiian moonlight, but otherwise-rational people who have never set foot on a boat in their life suddenly want to go out to sea. You can opt for a "booze cruise" with a thousand loud, rum-soaked strangers, or you can sail on one of these special yachts, all of which will take you out **whale-watching** in season (roughly Dec–Apr).

For fishing charters, see "Sportfishing," below.

Captain Bob's Adventure Cruises ★ See the majestic Windward Coast the way it should be seen—from a boat. Captain Bob will take you on a 4-hour, lazy-day sail of Kaneohe Bay aboard his 42-foot catamaran, which skims across the almost always calm water above the shallow coral reef, lands at the disappearing sandbar Ahu o Laka, and takes you past two small islands to snorkel spots full of tropical fish and, sometimes, turtles. The color of the water alone is worth the price. This is an all-day affair, but hey, getting out on the water is part of the reason you came to Hawaii, right? A shuttle will pick you up at your Waikiki hotel between 9 and 9:30am and bring you back at about 4pm—it's a lot quicker than taking TheBus.

Kaneohe Bay. © **808/942-5077.** All-day cruise $84 adults, $70 children 3–14. Rates include all-you-can-eat barbecue lunch and transportation from Waikiki hotels. No cruises Sun and holidays. Bus: 55 or 56.

Navatek I ★★ You've never been on a boat, you don't want to be on a boat, but here you are being dragged aboard one. Why are you boarding this weird-looking vessel? It guarantees that you'll be "seasick-free," that's why. The 140-foot-long *Navatek I* isn't even called a boat; it's actually a SWATH (Small Waterplane Area Twin Hull) vessel. That means the ship's superstructure—the part you ride on—rests on twin torpedolike hulls that cut through the water so you don't bob like a cork and spill your mai tai. It's the smoothest ride on Mamala Bay. In fact, *Navatek I* is the only dinner cruise ship to receive U.S. Coast Guard certification to travel beyond Diamond Head.

Sunset dinner cruises leave Pier 6 (across from the Hawaii Maritime Museum) nightly. If you have your heart set on seeing the city lights, take the Royal Sunset Dinner Cruise, which runs from 5:15 to 7:15pm. The best deal is the **lunch cruise,** with full buffet lunch and a great view of Oahu offshore. During the **whale season** (roughly Jan–Apr), you can whale-watch, too. The lunch cruise lasts from 11:30am to 2pm. Both cruises include live Hawaiian music.

Aloha Tower Marketplace, Pier 6, c/o Hawaiian Cruises Ltd. © **808/973-1311.** www.atlantisadventures. com/oahu.cfm. Dinner cruises $141 adults, $89 children 2–12; lunch cruises $65 adults, $33 children 2–11. Validated parking $3 before 4:30pm, flat fee of $2 after 4:30pm. Bus: 8, 19, 20, 55, 56, or 57.

Wild Side Tours Picture this: You're floating in the calm waters off the Waianae coast, where your 42-foot sailing catamaran has just dropped you off; below, in the reef are turtles, when in the distance you see . . . spinner dolphins, taking the high, spinning leaps for which they are known. Happens every day on the 4-hour tours operated by the Cullins family, who have been swimming in these waters for decades. In the winter, you may spot humpback whales on the morning cruise, which includes continental breakfast, refreshments, snorkel gear, instruction, and flotation device. They also have an afternoon/sunset whale-watching sail in the winter for $75 per person, and a sunset/full moon/star-gazing sail for $95.

Waianae Boat Harbor, 87-1286 Farrington Hwy., Waianae. © **808/306-7273**. www.sailhawaii.com. Morning sail/snorkel $105 for ages 6 and up (not recommended for younger children); sunset sail $95. MC, V. Bus: 19 or 20 to Ala Moana Center, then 40 or 40A.

BODYBOARDING (BOOGIE BOARDING) & BODYSURFING

Good places to learn to bodyboard are in the small waves of **Waikiki Beach** and **Kailua Beach,** and **Bellows Field Beach Park,** off Kalanianaole Highway (Hwy. 72) in Waimanalo, which is open to the public on weekends (from noon on Fri to midnight on Sun and holidays). To get here, turn toward the ocean on Hughs Road, then right on Tinker Road, which takes you right to the park. See above for a list of rental shops where you can get a boogie board.

OCEAN KAYAKING

For a wonderful adventure, rent a kayak, arrive at Lanikai Beach just as the sun is appearing, and paddle across the emerald lagoon to the pyramid-shaped islands called Mokulua—it's an experience you won't forget. Kayak equipment rental starts at $10 an hour for a single kayak, $16 an hour for a double. In Waikiki try **Prime Time Sports,** Fort DeRussy Beach (© **808/949-8952**); on the windward side, check out **Kailua Sailboards & Kayaks,** 130 Kailua Rd., a block from Kailua Beach Park (© **808/262-2555;** www. kailuasailboards.com), where a single kayak rents for $39 for a half-day, and a double kayak rents for $49 for a half-day. On the North Shore, **Surf-N-Sea,** 62-595 Kamehameha Hwy., Haleiwa (© **808/637-9887;** fax 808/637-3008; www.surfnsea.com), rents kayaks at $10 for the first hour, or $60 a day.

First-timers should go to **Kailua Sailboards & Kayaks** (see above). The company offers a guided tour ($69 adults and $59 children 8–12 years), with the novice in mind, in a safe, protected environment. Lunch, all equipment, and transportation from Waikiki hotels are included. Kayak lessons and self-guided trips are also available.

SCUBA DIVING

Oahu is a wonderful place to scuba dive, especially for those interested in wreck diving. One of the more famous wrecks in Hawaii is the *Mahi,* a 185-foot former minesweeper easily accessible just south of Waianae. Abundant marine life makes this a great place to shoot photos—schools of lemon butterflyfish and taape are so comfortable with divers and photographers that they practically pose. Eagle rays, green sea turtles, manta rays, and white-tipped sharks occasionally cruise by as well, and eels peer out from the wreck.

For nonwreck diving, one of the best spots in summer is **Kahuna Canyon.** In Hawaiian, *kahuna* means priest, wise man, or sorcerer; this massive amphitheater, near Mokuleia, is a

---

Check Out the Beach before You Leave Home
Before you leave your hotel room, check out the **Hawaii Beach Safety** website, **http://oceansafety.soest.hawaii.edu**, a joint venture among various governmental agencies: City and County of Honolulu, University of Hawaii, and the Hawaii Lifeguard Association, among others. You can view the latest wind and wave conditions and other safety information for the beach you want to visit. The site is updated at 9am, 3pm, and 9pm, or if conditions change.

Impressions

Thousands have daily lined the wharves to witness the carpenter, Mr. Dibble, in his novel suit of India-rubber with a glass helmet, disappear beneath the surface of the water . . .

—1840 Honolulu newspaper article

perfect example of something a sorcerer might conjure up. Walls rising from the ocean floor create the illusion of an underwater Grand Canyon. Inside the amphitheater, crabs, octopuses, slippers, and spiny lobsters abound (be aware that taking them in summer is illegal), and giant trevally, parrotfish, and unicorn fish gather as well. Outside the amphitheater, you might just see an occasional shark in the distance.

Because Oahu's most rewarding dives are offshore, your best bet is to book a two-tank dive from a dive boat. Hawaii's oldest and largest outfitter is **Aaron's Dive Shop,** 307 Hahani St., Kailua (© **808/262-2333;** www.hawaii-scuba.com), which offers boat and beach dive excursions off the coast. Boat dives cost from $125 per person, including two tanks and transportation from the Kailua shop. The beach dive off the North Shore in summer or the Waianae Coast in winter is the same price as a boat dive, including all gear and transportation.

In Waikiki, **Dive Oahu,** 1085 Ala Moana (© **808/922-3483;** www.diveoahu.com), offers everything from shipwreck dives in Waikiki to World War II Corsair plane dives in Hawaii Kai, for just $129 for a two-tank boat dive (friends or family members can tag along for just $35 each to snorkel). Captain Brian, who has a couple of decades under his dive belt, loves to help beginners feel comfortable scuba diving, as well as show experienced scuba divers what the Waikiki coast has to offer. On the North Shore, **Surf-N-Sea,** 62-595 Kamehameha Hwy., Haleiwa (© **808/637-9887;** fax 808/637-3008; www.surfnsea.com), has dive tours from the shore (starting at $75 for one tank), from a boat ($135 for two tanks), and at night ($100 for one tank). Surf-N-Sea also rents equipment and can point you to the best dive sites in the area.

Another great resource for diving on your own is the University of Hawaii Sea Grant's *Dive Hawaii Guide,* which describes 44 dive sites on the various Hawaiian islands, including Oahu. Send $2 to UH/SGES, Attn: Dive Guide, 2525 Correa Rd., HIG 237, Honolulu, HI 96822; or download the guide at www.hawaiiscubadiving.com.

SNORKELING

Some of the best snorkeling in Oahu is at the underwater park at **Hanauma Bay** ★★. It's crowded—sometimes it seems there are more people than fish—but Hanauma has clear, warm, protected waters and an abundance of friendly reef fish—including Moorish idols, scores of butterflyfish, damselfish, and wrasses. Hanauma Bay has two reefs, an inner and an outer—the first for novices, the other for experts. The inner reef is calm and shallow (less than 10 ft.); in some places, you can just wade and put your face in the water. Go early: It's packed by 10am (and closed on Tues). For details, see p. 156.

Braver snorkelers may want to head to **Shark's Cove,** on the North Shore just off Kamehameha Highway, between Haleiwa and Pupukea. Sounds risky, we know, but we've never seen any sharks in this cove, and in summer, this big, lava-edged pool is one of Oahu's best snorkel spots. Waves splash over the natural lava grotto and cascade like

(**Moments**) **Experiencing Jaws: Up Close & Personal**

You're 4 miles out from land, which is just a speck on the horizon, with hundreds of feet of open ocean. Suddenly, from the blue depths, a shape emerges: the sleek, pale shadow of a 6-foot-long gray reef shark, followed quickly by a couple of 10-foot-long Galápagos sharks. Within a few heartbeats, you're surrounded by sharks on all sides. Do you panic? No, you paid $120 to be in the midst of these jaws of the deep. Of course, a 6×6×10-foot aluminum shark cage separates you from all those teeth.

It happens every day on the **North Shore Shark Adventure** ((Ⓒ 808/228-5900;** www.hawaiisharkadventures.com), the dream of Captain Joe Pavsek, who decided, after some 30 years of surfing and diving, to share the experience of seeing a shark with visitors. To make sure that the predators of the deep will show up for the viewing, Captain Pavsek heaves "chum," a not very appetizing concoction of fish parts, over the side of his 32-foot boat, *Kailolo*. It's sort of like ringing the dinner bell, and after a few minutes the sharks (generally gray reef, Galápagos, and sandbars, ranging 5–15 ft.) show up—sometimes just a few, sometimes a few dozen.

Depending on sea conditions and the weather, snorkelers can stay in the cage as long as they wish, with the sharks just inches away. The shark cage, connected to the boat with a line, floats several feet back and a little above the surface, holding two snorkelers comfortably and four snugly. You can stay on the boat and view the sharks from a more respectable distance for just $60. The brave and adventuresome will be down in that cage—it definitely will be a memory you won't forget.

waterfalls into the pool full of tropical fish. To the right of the cove are deep-sea caves to explore. For directions, see p. 162.

SPORTFISHING

Kewalo Basin, between the Honolulu International Airport and Waikiki, is the main location for charter fishing boats on Oahu. From Waikiki, take Kalakaua Ewa (west) beyond Ala Moana Center; Kewalo Basin is on the left, across from Ward Centre. Look for charter boats all in a row in their slips; on lucky days, the captains display the catch of the day in the afternoon. You can also take TheBus no. 19 or 20 (toward the airport).

The best way to book a sportfishing charter is through the experts; the best booking desk in the state is **Sportfish Hawaii** ★ ((Ⓒ **877/388-1376** or 808/396-2607; www. sportfishhawaii.com), which not only books boats on Oahu, but on all islands. These fishing vessels have been inspected and must meet rigorous criteria to guarantee that you will have a great time. Prices range from $812 to $932 for a full-day exclusive charter (you, plus five friends, get the entire boat to yourself), $717 for a half-day exclusive, or from $187 for a full-day shared charter (you share the boat with five other people).

SUBMARINE DIVES

Here's your chance to play Jules Verne and experience the underwater world from the comfort of a submarine, which will take you on an adventure below the surface in high-tech comfort. If swimming's not your thing, this is a great way to see Hawaii's spectacular sea life; the entire trip is narrated as you watch tropical fish and sunken ships just outside the sub. Shuttle boats to the sub leave from Hilton Hawaiian Village Pier. The cost is $95 for adults, $45 for kids 12 and under (children must be at least 36 in. tall). *Tip:* Book online for discount rates of $90 for adults and $41 for kids. Call **Atlantis Submarines** ★ (© **800/548-6262** or 808/973-9811; www.atlantissubmarines.com) to reserve. *Warning:* Skip this if you suffer from claustrophobia.

SURFING

In summer, when the water's warm and there's a soft breeze in the air, the south swell comes up. It's surf season, so—call a fire fighter? Yep, that's the **Hawaiian Fire Surf School** (© **888/955-7873** or 808/737-3473; www.hawaiianfire.com), which is owned and operated by the Honolulu firefighters. The instructors (all firefighters) think safety first and transport their clients from Waikiki to a very safe, remote beach in Kalaeloa on West Oahu, where they can practically have the beach all to themselves. Prices are very reasonable: Two-hour group lessons (one teacher for every three students) are $129 for kids and $179 for adults. Expect to spend about 45 minutes on the beach learning the basics and then about 75 minutes in the water. You couldn't be in safer hands!

Now there's no excuse not to learn to surf in Hawaii: Hans Hedemann, a champion surfer for some 34 years, has opened the **Hans Hedemann Surf School** at the Turtle Bay Resort (© **808/924-7778;** www.hhsurf.com), on the North Shore, or in Waikiki. His classes range from one-on-one private sessions to group lessons (four students to one teacher) and begin at $75 an hour.

If you just want to rent a surfboard in Waikiki, **Clyde Aikau's Pure Hawaiian Surf School,** on the beach fronting the Hilton Hawaiian Village (© **808/951-4088;** www. waikikibeachactivities.com), at one end of Waikiki, and **Aloha Beach Service,** facing the Moana Surfrider Hotel (© **808/922-3111,** ext. 2341), at the other end of Waikiki, both rent surfboards and other ocean toys.

Surfboards are also available for rent on the North Shore at **Surf-N-Sea,** 62-595 Kamehameha Hwy., Haleiwa (© **808/637-9887;** www.surfnsea.com), for $5 to $7 an hour. They offer lessons for $85 for 2 hours. (For the best surf shops, where you can soak in the culture as well as pick up gear, also see "Surf & Sports," in chapter 8.)

On the windward side, call **Kimo's Surf Hut,** 151 Hekili St., across from Don Quijote, in Kailua (© **808/262-1644**). Kimo and his wife, Ruth, couldn't be more friendly and helpful. In addition to surfboards that rent for $30 a day, Kimo has a personal collection of vintage surfboards lovingly displayed on the walls of his shop and will gladly tell you the pedigree and history of each board. Although Kimo doesn't offer formal surfing lessons, he'd be happy to give you pointers.

More experienced surfers should drop in on any surf shop around Oahu, or call the **Surf News Network Surfline** (© **808/596-SURF** [7873]) to get the latest surf conditions. **The Cliffs,** at the base of Diamond Head, is a good spot for advanced surfers; 4- to 6-foot waves churn here, allowing high-performance surfing.

If you're in Hawaii in winter and want to see the serious surfers catch the really big waves, bring your binoculars and grab a front-row seat on the beach near **Kalalua Point.**

To get here from Waikiki, take the H-1 toward the North Shore, veering off at H-2, which becomes Kamehameha Highway (Hwy. 83). Keep going to the funky surf town of Haleiwa and Waimea Bay; the big waves will be on your left, just past Pupukea Beach Park.

SWIMMING

For a quiet, peaceful place to swim, **Malaekahana Bay** ★, near Kahuku, is one of the best Oahu beaches. This mile-long, white-sand, crescent-shaped beach is about a 90-minute drive and a million miles from the crowds at Waikiki. To get there, take Kamehameha Highway past Laie and follow the signs to Malaekahana State Recreational Area. Or take TheBus no. 52 (Circle Island). Another good swimming beach is **Lanikai;** secluded and calm, this beach is great for families. From Waikiki, take TheBus no. 56 or 57 (Kailua), and then transfer to the shuttle.

See also section 1 of this chapter, "Beaches," where each description mentions the relative calmness of the waters.

WATER-SKIING

To learn to water-ski, or to just go out and have a good time, call the oldest water-ski company in Hawaii, **Hawaii Water Sports,** Koko Marina Shopping Center (© **808/395-3773;** www.hawaiiwatersportscenter.com; TheBus no. 58). Lessons and boat rental are $49 for 20 minutes and $69 for a half-hour, including the boat and all equipment rental (maximum of five people).

WHALE-WATCHING

From December to April, 45-foot humpback whales—Hawaii's most impressive visitors—come to spend the winter. They make the journey from Alaska to calve and mate in Hawaii's calm, warm waters. Once nearly hunted to extinction, humpback whales are now protected by federal law. The mammals may not be approached by any individual or watercraft within 300 ft..

Whales can frequently be seen off the island on calm days. If you spot the familiar spout of water—a sign the mammal is exhaling—there's a good chance you'll see the whale on the surface. If you're in a car, please pull over, as many accidents have occurred when visitors try to spot whales and drive at the same time.

For whale-watching cruises, see "Boating," earlier in this chapter.

WINDSURFING

Windward Oahu's **Kailua Beach** is the home of champion and pioneer windsurfer Robbie Naish; it's also the best place to learn to windsurf. The oldest and most established windsurfing business in Hawaii is **Naish Hawaii/Naish Windsurfing Hawaii,** 155-A Hamakua Dr., Kailua (© **800/767-6068** or 808/262-6068; www.naish.com). The company offers everything: sales, rentals, instruction, repair, and free advice on where to go when the wind and waves are happening. Private 90-minute lessons start at $75 for one, $100 for two; beginner equipment rental is $25 for 2 hours and $35 for a full day. Kite-surfing lessons are also available ($125 for 1½ hr.). Kiteboard rentals are $25 a day (boards only). **Kailua Sailboards & Kayaks,** 130 Kailua Rd., a block from the Kailua Beach Park (© **808/262-2555;** www.kailuasailboards.com), offers 3-hour small-group lessons in windsurfing ($129 per person, including all gear, plus lunch) and rentals of kitesurfing boards, windsurfing equipment, surfboards, snorkel gear, and ocean kayaks.

3 NATURE HIKES

People think Oahu is just one big urban island, so they're always surprised to discover that the great outdoors is less than an hour away from downtown Honolulu. Highlights of the island's 33 major hiking trails include razor-thin ridgebacks and deep waterfall valleys.

Check out Stuart Ball's *The Hikers Guide to Oahu* (University of Hawaii Press, 1993) before you go. Another good source of hiking information on Oahu is the state's **Na Ala Hele (Trails to Go On) Program** (*C* **808/973-9782** or 808/587-0058).

For a free Oahu recreation map listing all 33 trails, write to the **Department of Land and Natural Resources,** 1151 Punchbowl St., Rm. 310, Honolulu, HI 96813 (*C* **808/ 587-0166;** www.hawaiitrails.org). The department will also send free topographic trail maps on request and issue camping permits (applications for permits are on the website; allow 10 days' processing time).

Another good source of information is the *Hiking/Camping Information Packet,* which costs $7 (postage included); to order, contact **Hawaii Geographic Maps and Books,** 49 S. Hotel St., Honolulu, HI 96813 (*C* **800/538-3950** or 808/538-3952). This store also carries a full line of United States Geographic Survey topographic maps, very handy for hikers.

Be sure to get a copy of *Hiking on Oahu: The Official Guide,* a hiking safety brochure that includes instructions on hiking preparation, safety procedures, emergency phone numbers, and necessary equipment; for a copy, contact the **Department of Land and Natural Resources** (*C* **808/587-0166**) or download it from www2.hawaii.edu/~turner/ hoo/hoo-main.htm.

The **Hawaiian Trail and Mountain Club,** P.O. Box 2238, Honolulu, HI 96804 (www.htmclub.org), offers regular hikes on Oahu. You bring your own lunch and drinking water and meet up with the club at the Iolani Palace to join them on a hike. The club has an information packet on hiking and camping in Hawaii, as well as a schedule of all upcoming hikes; send $2 plus a legal-size, self-addressed, stamped envelope to the address above.

Other organizations that offer regularly scheduled hikes are the **Sierra Club,** 1040 Richards St., Rm. 306, Honolulu, HI 96813 (www.hi.sierraclub.org); the **Nature Conservancy,** 923 Nu'uanu Ave, Honolulu, HI 96817 (*C* **808/537-4508,** ext. 220; www. nature.org); and the **Hawaii Nature Center,** 2131 Makiki Heights Dr. (*C* **808/955- 0100;** www.hawaiinaturecenter.org).

For camping information, see "Oahu's Campgrounds & Wilderness Cabins," at the end of chapter 4.

HONOLULU AREA HIKES
Diamond Head Crater ★★★

This is a moderate, but steep, walk to the summit of Hawaii's most famous landmark. Kids love to look out from the top of the 750-foot volcanic cone, where they have 360-degree views of Oahu up the leeward coast from Waikiki. The 1.4-mile round-trip takes about 1½ hours and the entry fee is $1.

Diamond Head was created by a volcanic explosion about half a million years ago. The Hawaiians called the crater *Leahi* (meaning the brow of the ahi, or tuna, referring to the shape of the crater). Diamond Head was considered a sacred spot; King Kamehameha

(**Fun Facts**   **Fly Away**

Amelia Earhart was the first woman to fly solo from Hawaii to the U.S. mainland. A plaque on Diamond Head Road memorializes her 12-hour, 50-minute flight in 1935 from Honolulu to Oakland, California.

offered human sacrifices at a *heiau* (temple) on the western slope. It wasn't until the 19th century that Mount Leahi got its current name: A group of sailors found what they thought were diamonds in the crater; it turned out they were calcite crystals, but the Diamond Head moniker stuck.

Before you begin your journey to the top of the crater, put on some decent shoes (rubber-soled tennies are fine) and take a flashlight (you'll walk through several dark tunnels), binoculars (for better viewing at the top), water (very important), a hat to protect you from the sun, and a camera. You might want to put all your gear in a pack to leave your hands free for the climb. If you don't have a flashlight or your hotel can't lend you one, you can buy a small one for a few dollars as part of a Diamond Head climbers' "kit" at the gift shop at the **New Otani Kaimana Beach Hotel,** on the Diamond Head end of Kalakaua Avenue, just past the Waikiki Aquarium and across from Kapiolani Park.

Go early, preferably just after the 6:30am opening, before the midday sun starts beating down. The hike to the summit of Diamond Head starts at Monsarrat and 18th avenues on the crater's inland (or *mauka*) side. To get there, take TheBus no. 58 from the Ala Moana Shopping Center or drive to the intersection of Diamond Head Road and 18th Avenue. Follow the road through the tunnel (which is closed 6pm–6am) and park in the lot. The trail head starts in the parking lot and proceeds along a paved walkway (with handrails) as it climbs up the slope. You'll pass old World War I and II pillboxes, gun emplacements, and tunnels built as part of the Pacific defense network. Several steps take you up to the top observation post on Point Leahi. The views are indescribable.

If you want to go with a guide, the Clean Air Team leads a guided hike to the top of Diamond Head every Saturday. The group gathers at 9am, near the front entrance to the Honolulu Zoo (look for the rainbow windsock). Hikers should bring a flashlight and cash to pay the $5 fee. Each person will be given a bag and asked to help keep the trail clean by picking up litter. For more information, call (**808/948-3299.**

Kanealole Trail

This is the starting place for some of Oahu's best hiking trails; miles of trails converge through the Makiki Valley–Tantalus–Round Top–Nuuanu Valley area. To get a general feel for the hikes in the region, take this 1.5-mile round-trip moderate hike, which climbs some 500 feet and takes less than an hour. If you're interested, stop at the **Hawaii Nature Center,** by the trail head at 2131 Makiki Heights Dr. ((**808/955-0100;** www.hawaiinaturecenter.org; Mon–Fri, 8am–4:30pm), where you can find information on the environmental and conservation needs of Hawaii, displays of plants and animals, hands-on exhibits, and numerous maps and pamphlets about this hiking area. They also sponsor organized hikes on weekends.

To get here, take McCully Avenue north out of Waikiki; cross over the H-1 Freeway and turn left on Wilder Avenue. Make a right turn on Makiki Street and continue until the road forks at the park. Take the left fork past the Makiki Pumping Station; the road is now called Makiki Heights Drive. Follow it up to the hairpin turn and make a right onto the small spur road that goes into Makiki Valley; park just beyond the green trailers that house the Hawaii Nature Center. If you are taking TheBus, it's a little trickier: From Waikiki, take TheBus no. 8, 19, 20, or 58 to the Ala Moana Shopping Center and transfer to TheBus no. 17. Tell your driver where you're going, and he'll let you off near the spur road just off Makiki Heights Drive; you'll have to walk the rest of the way.

After stopping at the Hawaii Nature Center, continue up the path, which wanders beneath the protection of kukui trees and lush vines. The path gets smaller and smaller until it's just a footpath. Along this narrow path, look for the tall, bushy, grasslike plant called Job's tears. It's considered a weed in Hawaii, but this is no ordinary grass; it can grow up to 5 feet high and produces a gray, tear-shaped seed. The trail continues through an abandoned valley where there once was a thriving Hawaiian community. Occasionally, you'll spot the remains of stone walls and even a few coffee plants—Makiki Valley supported a coffee plantation in the 19th century. When you meet the Makiki Valley Trail, you can retrace your steps or choose from the dozens of trails in the area.

Makiki–Manoa Cliffs ★★

From rainforests to ridge-top views, this somewhat strenuous loop trail is one you'll never forget. The hike is just over 6 miles, gains 1,260 feet in elevation, and takes about 3 hours. To get to the trail—part of a labyrinth of trails—follow the directions for the Kanealole Trail (see above).

The trail starts by the restrooms of the Hawaii Nature Center. Look for the paved path that crosses Kanealole Stream via a footbridge (Maunalaha Trail). Stay on the trail, following it up the hill into the forest, where you'll pass bananas, Norfolk and Cook Island pines, ti (pronounced tea) plants, and even a few taro patches. Cross over Moleka Stream and look for the four-way junction with the Makiki Valley and Ualakaa trails; turn right on the **Makiki Valley Trail.** This takes you through a dense forest, past a giant banyan tree, and then joins the Moleka Trail. Turn left on the **Moleka Trail**—now you're in the rainforest: Ancient guava trees reach overhead, maidenhair ferns cling to rocks, and tiny, white-flowered begonias crop up.

Further on, the kukui and koa give way to a bamboo-filled forest, which opens up to a parking lot on Round Top Drive at the end of the Moleka Trail. Cross Round Top Drive to the **Manoa Cliffs Trail,** which emerges on Tantalus Drive. Turn right on Tantalus and walk about 100 yards down the street to the **Nahuina Trail** on the left side of Tantalus. As you walk downhill, you'll have breathtaking views of downtown Honolulu. At the junction of Kanealole Trail, turn right and continue back to where you started.

Tips   Outdoor Etiquette

Carry out what you carry in. Find a trash can for all your litter (including cigarette butts—it's very bad form to throw them out your car window). Observe *kapu* (forbidden) and no trespassing signs. Don't climb on ancient Hawaiian *heiau* walls or carry home rocks, all of which belong to the Hawaiian volcano goddess Pele. Some say it's just a silly superstition or coincidence, but each year the U.S. Park Service gets boxes of lava rocks sent back to Hawaii by visitors who've experienced unusually bad luck.

Manoa Falls Trail ★★

This easy .75-mile (one-way) hike is terrific for families; it takes less than an hour to reach idyllic Manoa Falls. The trail head, marked by a footbridge, is at the end of Manoa Road, past Lyon Arboretum. The staff at the arboretum prefers that hikers do not park in their lot, so the best place to park is in the residential area below Paradise Park; you can also get to the arboretum via TheBus no. 5. The often-muddy trail follows Waihi Stream and meanders through the forest reserve past guavas, mountain apples, and wild ginger. The forest is moist and humid and is inhabited by giant bloodthirsty mosquitoes, so bring repellent. If it has rained recently, stay on the trail and step carefully, as it can be very slippery (and it's a long way down if you slide off the side). As we went to press, the state of Hawaii was still assessing the safety of the trail after a series of landslides. Before you venture out, call ℂ **808/587-0300** to check if the trail is open.

Puu Ohia Trail to Nuuanu Valley View ★

This moderate hike takes you through a rainforest, up to the top of Tantalus (Puu Ohia) cinder cone, and down through Pauoa Flats to view Nuuanu Valley. Plan about 2 hours for this 3.5-mile round-trip hike, which gains about 1,200 feet in altitude.

To get there, follow the directions for the Kanealole Trail, above, but turn to the right at the park fork in Makiki Street. The fork to the right is Round Top Drive. Drive to the top and park in the turnout on the ocean side of the street. Unfortunately, bus service is not available.

The Puu Ohia trail head is across the street from where you parked. As you head up (a series of switchbacks and, at the steepest part, hand-cut stairs in the dirt), you'll pass night-blooming jasmine, ginger, Christmas berry, and avocado trees. After dense guava trees and bamboo, the vegetation parts for a magnificent view of Honolulu and Diamond Head. Just as quickly, as you continue along the trail, the bamboo once again obstructs the view. At the next junction, stay on the main trail by bearing to the left; you'll pass through ginger, koa, and bamboo. At the next junction, bear left again, and climb up the steps around the trunk of an old koa tree. At the top is a paved road; turn right and walk downhill. The road leads to an old telephone relay station and then turns into a footpath. You'll pass through bamboo, koa, ti, and strawberry guava, and turn left onto the Manoa Cliffs Trail. At the next junction, turn right on the Puu Ohia Trail, which leads to Pauoa Flats and the view of the Nuuanu Valley. Retrace your steps for your return.

Ualakaa Loop ★

The same series of volcanic eruptions that produced Diamond Head and Koko Crater also produced the cinder cones of Round Top (Puu Ualakaa), Sugarloaf (Puu Kakea), and Tantalus (Puu Ohia). *Puu,* as you may have already guessed, means "hill"; these three hills overlook Honolulu and offer spectacular views. The easy Ualakaa Loop Trail is a half-hour hike of about a mile that traverses through woods, offering occasional panoramic views of Honolulu.

No bus serves this trail head. Follow the directions for the Puu Ohia hike, above, but instead of driving to the top of Round Top Drive, turn off on the fourth major hairpin turn (look for it after a long stretch of panoramic straightaway). The turn will go through the gate of **Puu Ualakaa State Wayside Park.** Continue a little more than 4 miles inside the park; look for a stand of Norfolk pine trees and park there. The trail head is on the right side of the Norfolk pines. The park is open 7am to 7:45pm from April 1 to Labor Day; in winter, the park closes at 6:45pm.

The loop trail, lined with impatiens, passes through Norfolk pines, palm trees, ironwoods, and Christmas berry trees. The once-native forest now has many foreign intru-
sions—including all of the foregoing—as well as ti, banana, banyan, guava, and
mountain apple. At two points along the trail, you emerge on Round Top Drive; just
walk about 100 feet to continue on the trail on the opposite side of the road. The loop
will bring you back to where you started.

PEARL CITY HIKES
Upper Waimano Trail
This is a strenuous, 14-mile round-trip with an altitude gain of nearly 2,000 feet. The
rewards are worth the effort: magnificent views from the top of windward Oahu's Koolau
Mountains and a chance to see rare native Hawaiian plants. Plan a full day for this 8-hour
hike.

To get here from Waikiki, take H-1 to the Pearl City exit (Exit 10) on Moanalua Road;
head north and turn right on Waimano Home Road; follow it to the end, just over 22
miles. Park on the road. Or take TheBus no. 8, 19, 20, or 58 from Waikiki to the Ala
Moana Shopping Center and transfer to TheBus no. 53. Tell your driver where you are
going, and he will take you as far as he can on Waimano Home Road; you'll have to walk
the rest of the way to the trail head (about 1½ miles).

You'll pick up the trail head at the dirt path to the left of the gate, outside the fence
surrounding the Waimano Home. Follow the trail through swamp mahogany trees to the
first junction; turn right at the junction to stay on the upper Waimano Trail. At the
second junction, turn right again to stay on the upper trail. Cross the streambed and
climb the switchbacks on the eucalyptus-covered ridge. The trail ends on the sometimes
rainy—and nearly always windy—peak of the Koolaus, where you'll have views of Wai-
hee Valley and the entire windward side from Kahaluu to Kaneohe Bay. It's very clear that
this is the end of the trail; retrace your steps to the trail head.

EAST OAHU HIKES
Makapuu Lighthouse Trail ★
You've seen this famous old lighthouse on episodes of *Magnum, P.I.* and *Hawaii Five-O*.
No longer manned by the Coast Guard (it's fully automated now), the lighthouse is the
goal of hikers who risk a precipitous cliff trail to gain an airy perch over the Windward
Coast, Manana (Rabbit) Island, and the azure Pacific. It's about a 45-minute, mile-long
hike from Kalanianaole Highway (Hwy. 72), along a paved road that begins across from
Hawaii Kai Executive Golf Course and winds around the 646-foot-high sea bluff to the
lighthouse lookout.

To get to the trail head from Waikiki, take Kalanianaole Highway (Hwy. 72) past
Hanauma Bay and Sandy Beach to Makapuu Head, the southeastern tip of the island;
you can also take TheBus no. 57 or 58. Look for a sign that says NO VEHICLES ALLOWED
on a gate to the right, a few hundred yards past the entrance to the golf course. The trail
isn't marked, but it's fairly obvious: Just follow the abandoned road that leads gradually
uphill to a trail that wraps around Makapuu Point. It's a little precarious, but anyone in
reasonably good shape can handle it.

Tip: When the south swell is running, usually in summer, a couple of blowholes on
the south side of Makapuu Head put the famous Halona blowhole to shame.

Hauula Loop ★

For one of the best views of the coast and the ocean, follow the Hauula Loop Trail on the windward side of the island. It's an easy, 2.5-mile loop on a well-maintained path that passes through a whispering ironwood forest and a grove of tall Norfolk pines. The trip takes about 3 hours and gains some 600 feet in elevation.

To get to the trail, take TheBus no. 55 or follow Highway 83 to Hauula Beach Park. Turn toward the mountains on Hauula Homestead Road; when it forks to the left at Maakua Road, park on the side of the road. Walk along Maakua Road to the wide, grassy trail that begins the hike into the mountains. The climb is fairly steep for about 300 yards but continues to easier-on-the-calves switchbacks as you go up the ridge. Look where you are stepping as you climb: You'll spot wildflowers and mushrooms among the matted needles. The trail continues up, crossing Waipilopilo Gulch, full of several forms of native plant life. Eventually, you reach the top of the ridge, where the views are spectacular.

Camping is permitted along the trail, but it's difficult to find a place to pitch a tent on the steep slopes or in the dense forest growth. A few places along the ridge, however, are wide enough for a tent. Contact the **Division of Forestry and Wildlife,** 1151 Punchbowl St., Honolulu, HI 96813 (© **808/587-0166**), for information on camping permits.

Kahana Valley

Spectacular views of this verdant valley and some clear swimming holes are the rewards of this 4.5-mile-loop trail. The downsides to this 2- to 3-hour, somewhat ardent adventure are mosquitoes (clouds of them) and some thrashing about in dense forest with a bit of navigation along the not-always-marked trail.

The trail starts behind the Visitor's Center at Kahana Valley State Park. To get there, take H-1 to the Pali Highway over to the windward side of Kailua-Kaneohe. Turn left onto Highway 83 (Kamehameha Hwy.) to Kahana Valley State Park. You can also take TheBus no. 55 and get off at the park entrance. Check in at the Visitor's Center for the latest trail conditions, warnings about stream flooding, and directions for the trail.

Pali (Maunawili) Trail ★

For a million-dollar view of the Windward Coast, take this easy 11-mile (one-way) foothill trail. The trail head is about 6 miles from downtown Honolulu, on the windward side of the Nuuanu Pali Tunnel, at the scenic lookout just beyond the hairpin turn of the Pali Highway (Hwy. 61). Just as you begin the turn, look for the scenic overlook sign, slow down, and pull off the highway into the parking lot (sorry, no bus service available).

The mostly flat, well-marked, easy-to-moderate trail goes through the forest on the lower slopes of the 3,000-foot Koolau Mountain range and ends up in the backyard of the coastal Hawaiian village of Waimanalo. Go halfway to get the view and return to your car, or have someone meet you in 'Nalo.

NORTH SHORE HIKES

Waimea Valley

For nearly 3 decades, this 1,875-acre park has lured visitors with activities from cliff diving and hula performances to kayaking and ATV tours. In 2008, the Office of Hawaiian Affairs took over and formed a new nonprofit corporation, Hiipaka, to run the park, **Waimea Valley,** 59-864 Kamehameha Hwy., Haleiwa (© **808/638-7766,** www.waimea valley.net.) Take TheBus no. 52. Admission is $10 for adults, $5 for seniors and children

4 to 12. Open daily 9am to 5pm. The current emphasis is now on perpetuating and sharing the "living Hawaiian culture." A visit here offers a lush walk into the past. The valley is packed with archaeological sites, including the 600-year-old Hale O Lono, a heiau dedicated to the Hawaiian god Lono, which you'll find to the left of the entrance. The botanical collection has 35 different gardens, including super-rare Hawaiian species such as the endangered *Kokia cookei* hibiscus. The valley is also home to fauna such as the endangered Hawaiian moorhen; look for a black bird with a red face cruising in the ponds. The 150-acre Arboretum and Botanical Garden contains more than 5,000 species of tropical plants. Walk through the gardens (take the paved paths or dirt trails) and wind up at 45-foot-high Waimea Falls—bring your bathing suit and you can dive into the cold, murky water. The public is invited to hike the trails and spend a day in this quiet oasis. There are several free cultural activities such as lei making, kappa demonstrations, hula lessons, Hawaiian games and crafts, music, and story telling.

LEEWARD OAHU HIKES
Kaena Point ★
At the very western tip of Oahu lie the dry, barren lands of Kaena Point State Park; 853 acres consisting of a remote, wild coastline of jagged sea cliffs, deep gulches, sand dunes, endangered plant life, and a wind- and surf-battered coastline. *Kaena* means "red-hot" or "glowing" in Hawaiian; the name refers to the brilliant sunsets visible from the point.

Kaena is steeped in numerous legends. A popular one concerns the demigod Maui: Maui had a famous hook that he used to raise islands from the sea. He decided that he wanted to bring the islands of Oahu and Kauai closer together, so one day he threw his hook across the Kauai Channel and snagged Kauai (which is actually visible from Kaena Point on clear days). Using all his might, Maui was able to pull loose a huge boulder, which fell into the waters very close to the present lighthouse at Kaena. The rock is still called Pohaku o Kauai (the rock from Kauai). Like Black Rock in Kaanapali on Maui, Kaena is thought of as the point on Oahu from which souls depart.

To hike out to the departing place, take the clearly marked trail from the parking lot of Kaena Point State Park. The moderate 5-mile round-trip to the point will take a couple of hours. The trail along the cliff passes tide pools abundant in marine life and rugged protrusions of lava reaching out to the turbulent sea; seabirds circle overhead. There are no sandy beaches, and the water is nearly always turbulent. In winter, when a big north swell is running, the waves at Kaena are the biggest in the state, averaging heights of 30 to 40 feet. Even when the water appears calm, offshore currents are powerful, so don't plan to swim. Go early in the morning to see the schools of porpoises that frequent the area just offshore.

To get to the trail head from Honolulu or Waikiki, take the H-1 west to its end; continue on Highway 93 past Makaha and follow Highway 930 to the end of the road. No bus service runs here.

4 GREAT GOLF

It *is* possible to play top-notch golf in Hawaii without having to take out a second mortgage on your home. Oahu has nearly three dozen golf courses, ranging from bare-bones municipal courses to exclusive country clubs with six-figure annual membership fees.

(Tips) **Avoiding the Crowds & Saving Money**

Oahu's golf courses tend to be crowded, so we suggest that you go during mid-week. Also, most island courses have twilight rates with substantial discounts if you're willing to tee off in the afternoon, usually between 1 and 3pm. Look for this feature in the golf listings that follow.

Golfers unfamiliar with Hawaii's courses will be dazzled by some of the spectacular views—the shimmering ocean and majestic mountains, to name a few.

Golfers will also come to know that the windward golf courses play much differently than the leeward courses. On the windward side, the prevailing winds blow from the ocean to the shore, and the grain direction of the greens tends to run the same way—from the ocean to the mountains. Leeward golf courses have the opposite tendency; the winds usually blow from the mountains to the ocean, and the grain direction on the greens matches. Below are a variety of courses, with greens fees (cart costs included) and notes on scenic views, challenges, and a taste of what golfing in paradise is like.

For last-minute and discount tee times, call **Stand-by Golf** (from Hawaii, call © **888/ 645-BOOK** [2665]; www.stand-bygolf.com), which offers discounted and guaranteed tee times for same-day or next-day golfing. You can call between 7am and 11pm Hawaii Standard Time, to book one of the seven semiprivate and resort courses they handle and get a guaranteed tee time for the next day at a 10% to 40% discount.

TheBus does not allow golf bags onboard. If you don't have another means of transportation, you're going to have to rent clubs at the course.

WAIKIKI

Ala Wai Municipal Golf Course   The *Guinness Book of World Records* lists this as the busiest golf course in the world; some 500 rounds a day are played on this 18-hole municipal course within walking distance of Waikiki's hotels. For years, we've held off recommending this par-70, 6,020-yard course because it was so busy (tee times taken by local retirees), but a recent scandal, involving telephone company employees tapping into the tee-time reservation system to get tee times for themselves and their friends, has shaken up the old system, and visitors now have a better chance of playing here. It still is a challenge to get a tee time, and the computerized tee reservations system for all of Oahu's municipal courses will allow you to book only 3 days in advance, but keep trying. Ala Wai basically is a flat layout, bordered by the Ala Wai Canal on one side and the Manoa-Palolo Stream on the other. It's less windy than most Oahu courses, but pay attention to the 372-yard, par-4 1st hole, which demands a straight and long shot to the very tiny green. If you miss, you can make it up on the 478-yard, par-5 10th hole—the green is reachable in two, so with a two-putt, a birdie is within reach.

404 Kapahulu Ave., Waikiki. © **808/733-7387** (golf course) or 808/296-2000 tee-time reservations. www. co.honolulu.hi.us/des/golf/alawai.htm. Greens fees: $42; twilight half-price. From Waikiki turn left on Kapahulu Ave.; the course is on the *mauka* side of Ala Wai Canal. Bus: 19, 20, or 22.

EAST OAHU

Hawaii Kai Golf Course   This is actually two golf courses in one. The par-72, 6,222-yard **Hawaii Kai Championship Golf Course** is moderately challenging, with scenic vistas. The course is forgiving to high-handicap golfers, although it does have a few surprises. The par-3 **Hawaii Kai Executive Golf Course** is fun for beginners and those just getting back in the game after a few years. The course has lots of hills and valleys, with no water hazards and only a few sand traps. Lockers are available.

8902 Kalanianaole Hwy., Honolulu. ✆ **808/395-2358.** www.hawaiikaigolf.com. Greens fees: Championship Course $100 Mon–Fri, $110 Sat–Sun ($100 when booked online), twilight rates $70; Executive Course $37 Mon–Fri, $42 Sat–Sun. Take H-1 east past Hawaii Kai; it's immediately past Sandy Beach on the left. Bus: 58.

THE WINDWARD COAST

Olomana Golf Links   Low-handicap golfers may not find this gorgeous course difficult, but the striking views of the craggy Koolau mountain ridge are worth the fees alone. The par-72, 6,326-yard course is popular with locals and visitors alike. The course starts off a bit hilly on the front 9, but flattens out by the back 9. The back 9 have their own surprises, including tricky water hazards. The 1st hole, a 384-yard, par-4 that tees downhill and approaches uphill, is definitely a warm-up. The next hole is a 160-yard, par-3 that starts from an elevated tee to an elevated green over a severely banked, V-shaped gully. Shoot long here—it's longer than you think—as short shots tend to roll all the way back down the fairway to the base of the gully. This course is very, very green; the rain gods bless it regularly with brief passing showers. You can spot the regular players here—they all carry umbrellas, wait patiently for the squalls to pass, and then resume play. Reservations are a must. Facilities include a driving range, practice greens, club rental, pro shop, and restaurant.

41-1801 Kalanianaole Hwy., Waimanalo. ✆ **808/259-7926.** www.olomanagolflinks.com. Greens fees: $80; twilight fees $26 Mon–Fri, $28 Sat–Sun. Take H-1 to the Pali Hwy. (Hwy. 61); turn right on Kalanianaole Hwy.; after 5 miles, it will be on the left. Bus: 57.

Pali Golf Course (Value)   This beautiful municipal course sits near Kaneohe, just below the historic spot where King Kamehameha the Great won the battle that united the islands of Hawaii. The par-72, 6,494-yard course, designed by Willard G. Wilkinson and built in 1953, makes use of the natural terrain (hills and valleys make up the majority of the 250 acres). The course does not have man-made traps, but a small stream meanders through it. If you're off-line on the 9th, you'll get to know the stream quite well. The challenge here is the weather—whipping winds and frequent rain squalls. Because of the potential for rain, you might want to pay for 9 holes and then assess the weather before signing up for the back 9. The views include Kaneohe Bay, the towns of Kailua and Kaneohe, and the verdant cliffs of the Koolau Mountains. Facilities include practice greens, club rental, locker rooms, and a restaurant.

45-050 Kamehameha Hwy., Kaneohe, HI 96744. ✆ **808/296-2000.** www.co.honolulu.hi.us/des/golf/pali.htm. Greens fees: $42 ($16 extra for an optional cart, which carries 2 golfers); $21 twilight fees after 4pm (walking only, no carts). From Waikiki, take the H-1 freeway to the Pali Hwy. (Hwy. 61). Turn left at Kamehameha Hwy. at the 1st traffic light after going through the Pali Tunnels. The course is immediately on your left after you turn on Kamehameha Hwy. Bus: 55.

THE NORTH SHORE

Kahuku Golf Course (Finds)   This 9-hole budget golf course is a bit funky. There are no club rentals, no clubhouse, and no facilities other than a few pull carts that disappear with the first handful of golfers. But a round at this scenic oceanside course amid the tranquillity of the North Shore is quite an experience nonetheless. Duffers will love the ease of this recreational course, and weight watchers will be happy to walk the gently sloping greens. Don't forget to bring your camera for the views (especially at holes 3, 4,

7, and 8, which are right on the ocean). No reservations are taken; tee times are first-come, first-served—with plenty of retirees happy to sit and wait, the competition is fierce for early tee times. Bring your own clubs and call ahead to check the weather. The cost for this experience? Ten bucks!

56-501 Kamehameha Hwy., Kahuku. ✆ **808/293-5842.** www.co.honolulu.hi.us/des/golf/kahuku.htm. Greens fees $42. Take H-1 west to H-2; follow H-2 through Wahiawa to Kamehameha Hwy. (Hwy. 99, then Hwy. 83); follow it to Kahuku.

Turtle Bay Resort ★   This North Shore resort is home to two of Hawaii's top golf courses. The 18-hole **Arnold Palmer Course** (formerly the Links at Kuilima) was designed by Arnold Palmer and Ed Seay. Turtle Bay used to be labeled a "wind tunnel"; it still is one, though the *casuarina* (ironwood) trees have matured and dampened the wind somewhat. But Palmer and Seay never meant for golfers to get off too easy; this is a challenging course. The front 9, with rolling terrain, only a few trees, and lots of wind, play like a British Isles course. The back 9 have narrower, tree-lined fairways and water. The course circles Puna-hoolapa Marsh, a protected wetland for endangered Hawaiian waterfowl.

Another option is the **George Fazio Course**—the only one Fazio designed in Hawaii—a par-71, 6,200-yard course. Larry Keil, a pro at Turtle Bay, says that people like the Fazio course because it's more of a forgiving resort course, without the water hazards and bunkers of the more challenging Palmer course. The 6th hole has two greens, so you can play the hole as a par-3 or a par-4. The toughest hole has to be the par-3, 176-yard 2nd hole, where you tee off across a lake with the trade winds creating a mean crosswind. The most scenic hole is the 7th, where the ocean is on your left; if you're lucky, you'll see whales cavorting in the winter months. Facilities include a pro shop, driving range, putting and chipping green, and snack bar. Weekdays are best for tee times.

57-049 Kamehameha Hwy., Kahuku. ✆ **808/293-8574** or 808/293-9094. www.turtlebayresort.com. Greens fees: Palmer Course $175; Fazio Course $175. Take H-1 west past Pearl City; when the freeway splits, take H-2 and follow the signs to Haleiwa; at Haleiwa, take Hwy. 83 to Turtle Bay Resort. Bus: 52 or 55.

LEEWARD OAHU: THE WAIANAE COAST

Ko Olina Golf Club ★★★   *Golf Digest* named this 6,867-yard, par-72 course one of "America's Top 75 Resort Courses" in 1992. The Ted Robinson–designed course has rolling fairways and elevated tee and water features. The signature hole—the 12th, a par-3—has an elevated tee that sits on a rock garden with a cascading waterfall. Wait until you get to the 18th hole, where you'll see and hear water all around you—seven pools begin on the right side of the fairway and slope down to a lake. A waterfall is on your left off the elevated green. You'll have no choice but to play the left and approach the green over the water. Book in advance; this course is crowded all the time. Facilities include a driving range, locker rooms, Jacuzzi, steam rooms, and restaurant and bar. Lessons are available.

92-1220 Aliinui Dr., Kapolei. ✆ **808/676-5300.** www.koolinagolf.com. Greens fees $179 ($159 for Ihilani Resort guests); noon rates $149 ($129 for guests); twilight rates (after 1pm in winter and 2:30pm in summer) $119 ($99 for guests). Ask about transportation package from Waikiki hotels. Collared shirts requested for men and women. Take H-1 west until it becomes Hwy. 93 (Farrington Hwy.); turn off at the Ko Olina exit; take the exit road (Aliinui Dr.) into Ko Olina Resort; turn left into the clubhouse. No bus service.

Makaha Resort Golf Club ★★   This challenging course—once named "The Best Golf Course on Oahu" by *Honolulu* magazine—sits some 45 miles west of Honolulu, in Makaha Valley. Designed by William Bell, the par-72, 7,091-yard course meanders toward the ocean before turning and heading into the valley. Sheer volcanic walls tower

1,500 feet above the course, which is surrounded by swaying palm trees and neon-bright bougainvillea; an occasional peacock will even strut across the fairways. The beauty here could make it difficult to keep your mind on the game if it weren't for the course's many challenges: 8 water hazards, 107 bunkers, and frequent brisk winds. This course is packed on weekends, so it's best to try weekdays. Facilities include a pro shop, bag storage, and snack shop.

84-627 Makaha Valley Rd., Waianae. © **808/695-7111** or 808/695-5239. www.makaharesort.net. Greens fees $65 Mon–Fri and $75 Sat–Sun and holidays. Take H-1 west until it turns into Hwy. 93, which winds through the coastal towns of Nanakuli, Waianae, and Makaha. Turn right on Makaha Valley Rd. and follow it to the fork; the course is on the left. Bus: 51.

West Loch Municipal Golf Course (**Value**) This par-72, 6,615-yard course just 30 minutes from Waikiki, in Ewa Beach, offers golfers a challenge at bargain rates. The difficulties on this municipal course are water (lots of hazards), wind (constant trade winds), and narrow fairways. To help you out, the course features a "water" driving range (with a lake) to practice your drives. After a few practice swings on the driving range, you'll be ready to take on this unusual course, designed by Robin Nelson and Rodney Wright. In addition to the driving range, West Loch has practice greens, a pro shop, and a restaurant.

91-1126 Okupe St., Ewa Beach. © **808/675-6076.** www.co.honolulu.hi.us/des/golf/westloch.htm. Greens fees $42; twilight rates (after 1pm) $21; cart $16. Book a week in advance. Take H-1 west to the Hwy. 76 exit; stay in the left lane and turn left at West Loch Estates, just opposite St. Francis Medical Center. To park, take 2 immediate right turns. Bus: 50.

CENTRAL OAHU

Hawaii Country Club This public course in Wahiawa is a modest course where golfers usually have no trouble getting a tee time. The 5,861-yard, par-71 course is not manicured like the resort courses, but it does offer fair play, with relatively inexpensive greens fees. Located in the middle of former sugar cane and pineapple fields, the greens and fairways tend to be a bit bumpy and you have to shoot around a number of tall monkeypod and pine trees, but the views of Pearl Harbor and Waikiki in the distance are spectacular. A few holes are challenging, such as the 7th (a 252-yard, par-4), which has a lake in the middle of the fairway and slim pickings on either side. With the wind usually blowing in your face, most golfers choose an iron to lay up short of the water and then pitch it over for par. Facilities include a driving range, practice greens, a club rental pro shop, and a restaurant.

98-1211 Kunia Rd., Wahiawa, HI 96786. © **808/621-5654.** www.hawaiicc.com. Fees: $65 Mon–Fri; $75 Sat–Sun (cart included); book on the Internet for rates at $55 Mon–Fri and $65 Sat–Sun. From Waikiki, take the H-1 freeway west for about 20 min. Turn off at the Kunia exit (exit 5B) and follow it to the course. No bus service.

Mililani Golf Club This par-72, 6,455-yard public course is home to the Sports Shinko Rainbow Open, where Hawaii's top professionals compete. Located between the Koolau and Waianae mountain ranges on the Leilehua Plateau, this is one of Oahu's most scenic courses, with views of mountains from every hole. Unfortunately, due to lots of views of trees—especially eucalyptus, Norfolk pine, and coconut palm—it's a lesson in patience to stay on the fairways and away from the trees. The two signature holes, the par-4 number 4 (a classic middle hole with water, flowers, and bunkers) and the par-3 number 12 (a comfortable tee shot over a ravine filled with tropical flowers that jumps to the undulating green with bunkers on each side) are so scenic, you'll forgive the challenges they pose.

95-176 Kuahelani Ave., Mililani. ℂ **808/623-2222.** www.mililanigolf.com. Greens fees: $99; twilight $25. Take H-1 west past Pearl City; when the freeway splits, take H-2. Exit at Mililani (exit 5B) onto Meheula Pkwy.; go to the 3rd stoplight (about 2 miles from the exit) and turn right onto Kuahelani Ave. Bus: 52.

Pearl Country Club   Looking for a challenge? You'll find one at this popular public course, just above Pearl City in Aiea. Sure, the 6,230-yard, par-72 looks harmless enough, and the views of Pearl Harbor and the USS *Arizona* Memorial are gorgeous, but around the 5th hole, you'll start to see what you're in for. That par-5, a blind 472-yard hole, doglegs seriously to the left (with a small margin of error between the tee and the steep out-of-bounds hillside on the entire left side of the fairway). A water hazard and a forest await your next two shots. Suddenly, this nice public course becomes not so nice. Oahu residents can't get enough of it, so don't even try to get a tee time on weekends. Stick to weekdays—Mondays are usually the best bet. Facilities include a driving range, practice greens, club rental, a pro shop, and a restaurant.

98-535 Kaonohi St., Aiea. ℂ **808/487-3802.** www.pearlcc.com. Greens fees: $85 Mon–Fri; $95 Sat–Sun; after 4pm 9 holes are $35. Book at least a week in advance. Take H-1 past Pearl Harbor to the Hwy. 78 (Moanalua Fwy.), exit 13A; stay in the left lane where Hwy. 78 becomes Hwy. 99 (Kamehameha Hwy.); turn right on Kaonohi St., entry on the right. Bus: 32 (stops at Pearlridge Shopping Center at Kaonohi and Moanalua sts.; you'll have to walk about ¹/₂ mile uphill from here).

5 OTHER OUTDOOR ACTIVITIES

BICYCLING

Bicycling is a great way to see Oahu. Most streets here have bike lanes. For information on biking trails, races, and tours, check out **www.bikehawaii.com** or ℂ 877/682-7433. For information on bikeways and maps, contact the **Honolulu City and County Bike Coordinator** (ℂ **808/768-8335**).

If you're in Waikiki, you can rent a bike for as little as $10 for a half-day and $20 for 24 hours at **Big Kahuna Rentals,** 407 Seaside Ave. (ℂ **888/451-5544** or 808/924-2736; www.bigkahunarentals.com).

For a bike-and-hike adventure, call **Bike Hawaii** (ℂ **877/682-7433** or 808/734-4214; www.bikehawaii.com); this company offers a variety of group tours, including the Downhill Coasting Ride, which gives you a bird's-eye view of Oahu from 1,800 feet above Waikiki. The tour includes coasting down 5 miles of paved mountain road with scenic views above Waikiki, Honolulu, and Manoa Valley. Listen to the songs of birds, the wind through the trees, and learn about the culture, plants, and geology of the Hawaiian Islands. After that, leave your bike for a 2-mile round-trip hike to a 200-foot waterfall. The 9am-to-3pm trip includes van transportation from your hotel, lunch, bike, helmet, snacks, water bottle, and guide ($153 adults and $96 children under 14).

If you'd like to join club rides, contact the **Hawaii Bicycle League** (ℂ **808/735-5756**), which offers rides every weekend, as well as several annual events. The league can also provide a schedule of upcoming rides, races, and outings.

GLIDER RIDES

Imagine soaring through silence on gossamerlike wings, a panoramic view of Oahu below you. A glider ride is an unforgettable experience, and it's available at Dillingham Air

Field, in Mokuleia, on Oahu's North Shore. The glider is towed behind a plane; at the proper altitude, the tow is dropped and you (and the glider pilot) are left to soar in the thermals. Three costs are involved in a glider ride: plane rental fee, instructor fee, and towing fee. We recommend Mr. Bill, at **Honolulu Soaring** ★ (© **808/637-0207;** www. honolulusoaring.com); he's been offering piloted glider rides since 1970. Rates start at $79 for 10 minutes for just one passenger (and go up to $215 for 60 min.).

HANG-GLIDING

See things from a bird's-eye view (literally) as you and your instructor float high above Oahu on a tandem hang-glider. **Paradise Air Hawaii,** at the Dillingham Air Field (© **808/497-6033;** www.paradiseairhawaii.com), offers the opportunity to try out this daredevil sport. A tandem lesson of ground school plus 30 minutes in the air costs $135.

HORSEBACK RIDING

You can gallop on the beach at the **Turtle Bay Resort,** 57-091 Kamehameha Hwy., Kahuku (© **808/293-8811;** www.turtlebayresort.com; bus no. 52 or 55), where 45-minute rides along sandy beaches with spectacular ocean views and through a forest of ironwood trees cost $55 for adults and $25 for children 7 to 12 (they must be at least 4 ft., 4 in. tall). Romantic evening rides are $90 per person. Advanced riders can sign up for a 60-minute trot-and-canter ride along Kawela Bay ($100).

SKYDIVING

Everything you need to leap from a plane and float to earth can be obtained from **Sky-Dive Hawaii,** 68-760 Farrington Hwy., Wahiawa (© **808/637-9700;** www.hawaiisky diving.com). A tandem jump (where you're strapped to an expert who wears a chute big enough for the both of you) costs $225 (check the website for a coupon that gives you $75 off this rate). No doubt about it—this is the thrill of a lifetime. (Although, as Sky-Dive's website warns, "Skydiving is extremely dangerous.")

TENNIS

Oahu has 181 free public tennis courts. To get a complete list of all facilities or information on upcoming tournaments, send a self-addressed, stamped envelope to **Department of Parks and Recreation,** Tennis Unit, 650 S. King St., Honolulu, HI 96813. In Waikiki, if you want to check on the Diamond Head courts, 3908 Paki Ave., across from the Kapiolani Park, call © **808/971-7150.** The courts are available on a first-come, first-served basis; playing time is limited to 45 minutes if others are waiting.

If you're staying in Waikiki, try the **Wikiki Tennis Court and Lessons** at the Aqua Marina Hotel, 1700 Ala Moana Blvd. (© **808/551-9438;** bus no. 19 or 20), which has one lighted court (9am–9pm daily), with court rental for $10 per person per hour and racket rental for $5 per person per day. Private lessons are $60 per hour, and semi-private instruction is $75 per hour for two or more persons.

If you're on the North Shore, head to the **Turtle Bay Resort,** 57-091 Kamehameha Hwy., Kahuku (© **808/293-8811;** www.turtlebayresort.com; bus no. 52 or 55), which has 10 courts, four of which are lit for night play. You must reserve the night courts in advance; they're very popular. Court time is $10 per person (complimentary for guests); equipment rental and lessons are also available.

6 FROM THE SIDELINES: SPECTATOR SPORTS

Although there aren't any major league sports teams in Hawaii, there are college teams and a handful of professional exposition games—many of them are immensely popular among the local residents. Check the schedule at the 10-story, 50,000-seat **Aloha Stadium,** near Pearl Harbor, 99-500 Salt Lake Blvd. (© **808/486-9555;** www.aloha stadium.hawaii.gov), where high school and **University of Hawaii Warriors** (© **808/ 944-BOWS** [2697]; www.uhathletics.hawaii.edu) football games are also held from September to December. Other events at the stadium include: baseball, soccer, boxing, religious and music festivals, auto shows, motorcrosses, mud races, tractor pulls, and various concerts, plus the well-known weekly Aloha Swap Meet (see p. 158). Express buses often run to the stadium on game nights; they depart from Ala Moana Shopping Center (TheBus no. 47–50 or 52), or from Monsarrat Avenue near Kapiolani Park (The-Bus no. 20). Call TheBus at © **808/848-5555** for times and fares.

The **Neal Blaisdell Center,** at Kapiolani Boulevard and Ward Avenue (© **808/591-2211** or 808/527-5400; www.blaisdellcenter.com/calendar/index.cfm), features a variety of sporting events, such as professional boxing and Japanese sumo wrestling. In December, the Annual **Rainbow Classic,** a collegiate basketball invitational tournament, takes place at the Blaisdell. For bus information, call TheBus at © **808/848-5555,** or visit www.thebus.org.

At the University of Hawaii, the **Rainbow Stadium,** 1337 Lower Campus Rd., and the **Rainbow Wahine Softball Stadium,** next door, are hosts to college baseball and softball from January through May. Information is available at © **808/944-BOWS** [2697] or www.uhathletics.hawaii.edu. Collegiate volleyball, which is extremely popular in Hawaii, takes place at the **Stan Sheriff Center,** also on the UH campus, 1355 Lower Campus Rd., November through May. Information is available at the UH phone number and website listed above.

It's not the World Series, but in the winter (late Sept/early Oct to the end of Nov) **Hawaii Winter Baseball** (© **808/973-7247;** www.hawaiiwinterbaseball.com), with four teams from Oahu (Waikiki Beach Boys, West Oahu CaneFires, North Shore Honu, and Honolulu Sharks) plays 40 games against other minor league teams from the U.S. mainland and Japan at either the Les Murakami Stadium, in Manoa, or at the Hans L'Orange Field, in Waipahu. Believe it or not, the first baseball game in Hawaii was played on July 4, 1866, with the "natives" (Hawaiians) beating the "haoles" (Caucasians) 2 to 1. In 1993, the Hawaii Winter League launched its inaugural baseball season and has been going ever since. Tickets range from $6 to $8.

With Hawaii's cowboy history, **polo** is a popular sport, played every Sunday, starting in either April or May and lasting through late August or early September in Mokuleia or Waimanalo. Polo was introduced to Hawaii in 1886, but faded away during World War II. The games were revived gain in 1950 and moved out to Mokuleia, on the North Shore in the 1960s. Bring a picnic lunch and enjoy the game. Call © **808/637-8401** or visit www.hawaiipolo.com, for schedule and admission information.

A sport you might not be familiar with is Hawaiian **outrigger canoe racing,** which is very big locally. If Hawaii were to have an "official" team sport, it would be Hawaii outrigger canoe racing, or as local residents call it "paddling." Since the 1970's, Hawaii canoe racing has experienced a resurgence. Paddlers range from teenagers to grandmas, who turn out every year for the summer long series of races. Every weekend from Memorial Day to Labor Day, canoe races are held around Oahu. The canoe played a very big part in the Hawaiian's culture. Not only was it the vehicle that got the Polynesians to Hawaii, but everything from the selection of the tree to carve the canoe to the launch was steeped in religious and cultural activities. When Capt. Cook arrived in Hawaii in 1779, he reported sighting some 1500 canoes. The canoe races keep this aspect of the Hawaiian culture alive today. The races are free and draw huge crowds. Check the local papers for information on race schedules, or contact the Oahu Hawaii Canoe Racing Association (www.ohcra.com).

Some of the other spectator sports scheduled during the year, such as the NFL Pro Bowl, the Rainbow Classic, and major golf and surfing tournaments, are listed in the "Oahu Calendar of Events" on p. 21.

Exploring Oahu

While the rest of the Hawaiian Islands are fairly sleepy, Oahu is loaded with diversions. Honolulu itself is full of sights and activities. You might explore historic Honolulu—from the Queen's Summer Palace to the USS *Arizona* Memorial in Pearl Harbor. Or wander through exotic gardens, come face-to-face with brilliantly colored tropical fish, stand on the deck of a four-masted schooner that sailed 100 years ago, venture into haunted places where ghosts are said to roam, take in the spicy smells and sights of Chinatown, and participate in a host of cultural activities from flower lei making to hula dancing.

You don't need a huge budget to experience Honolulu's best activities, and you don't really need a car. TheBus can get you where you need to go for $2, or you can hop on a moderately priced tour or trolley. Your only obstacle to enjoying all the activities here? Trying to fit everything you want to do into your schedule.

See chapter 6 for complete coverage of Oahu's best beaches and all kinds of outdoor activities.

1 GUIDED TOURS

GUIDED ISLAND TOURS

If your time is limited, you might want to consider a guided tour. These tours are informative, can give you a good overview of Honolulu or Oahu in a limited amount of time, and are surprisingly entertaining.

E Noa Tours, 1141 Waimanu St., Ste. 105, Honolulu (© **800/824-8804** or 808/591-2561; www.enoa.com), offers a range of tours, from island loops to explorations of historic Honolulu. These narrated tours are on air-conditioned, 27-passenger minibuses. The Royal Circle Island tour ($68 for adults, $55 for children 6–11, $48 for children under 6), stops at Diamond Head Crater, Hanauma Bay, Byodo-In Temple, Sunset Beach, Waimea Valley (admission included), and various beach sites along the way. Other tours go to the Pearl Harbor/USS *Arizona* Memorial and the Polynesian Cultural Center.

Waikiki Trolley Tours ★, 1141 Waimanu St., Ste. 105, Honolulu (© **800/824-8804** or 808/596-2199; www.waikikitrolley.com), offers three fun tours of sightseeing, entertainment, dining, and shopping. These tours are a great way to get the lay of the land. You can get on and off the trolley as needed (trolleys come along every 2–20 min.). An all-day pass (8:30am–11:35pm) is $27 for adults, $20 for seniors, and $12 for children (4–11); a 4-day pass is $48 for adults, $28 for seniors, and $20 for children. For the same price, you can experience the 2-hour narrated Ocean Coastline tour of the southeast side of Oahu, an easy way to see the stunning views.

Polynesian Adventure Tours, 1049 Kikowaena Place, Honolulu (© **808/833-3000;** www.polyad.com), offers several excursions. The all-day island tour starts at $30 for adults, $33 for children under 12; the half-day scenic shore and rainforest tour is $25 for adults, $21 for children 3 to 11; the half-day USS *Arizona* Memorial Excursion is $31 for adults and $21 for children 3 to 11.

To understand why Oahu was the island of kings, see it from the air. **Island Seaplane Service** ★★ (© **808/836-6273;** www.islandseaplane.com) operates flights departing from a floating dock in the protected waters of Keehi Lagoon (parallel to Honolulu International Airport's runway) in either a six-passenger DeHavilland Beaver or a four-passenger Cessna 206. There's nothing quite like feeling the slap of the waves as the plane skims across the water and then effortlessly lifts into the air.

Your tour will give you aerial views of Waikiki Beach, Diamond Head Crater, Kahala's luxury estates, and the sparkling waters of Hanauma and Kaneohe bays. The half-hour tour ($135) ends here, while the 1-hour tour ($250) continues on to Chinaman's Hat, the Polynesian Cultural Center, and the rolling surf of the North Shore. The flight returns across the island, flying over Hawaii's historic wartime sites: Schofield Barracks and the USS *Arizona* and *Missouri* memorials in Pearl Harbor.

For those who'd prefer a self-guided driving tour, **TourTalk-Oahu** (© **877/585-7499;** www.tourtalkhawaii.com) offers a complete package of 2½-hour narrated compact discs (or cassettes), driving instructions, and a 72-page booklet containing color maps, photos, cultural and historical information, and Hawaii facts for $25.

WAIKIKI & HONOLULU WALKING TOURS

DOWNTOWN HONOLULU   The **Mission Houses Museum,** 553 S. King St., at Kawaiahao Street (© **808/531-0481;** www.missionhouses.org; TheBus no. 2), offers a guided tour of the Visitors' Center, frame House and Printing Office, Tuesday to Saturday at 11am and 2:45pm. Admission is $10 adults, $8 seniors, and $6 children age 6 and up, age 5 and under free.

The **Hawaii Geographic Society** (© **808/538-3952**) presents numerous interesting and unusual tours, such as "A Temple Tour," which includes Chinese, Japanese, Christian, and Jewish houses of worship; an archaeology tour in and around downtown Honolulu; and others. Each is guided by an expert from the Hawaii Geographic Society and must have a minimum of three people; the cost is $10 per person. The society's brochure, *Historic Downtown Honolulu Walking Tour,* is a fascinating self-guided tour of the 200-year-old city center. If you'd like a copy, send $3 to **Hawaii Geographic Maps and Books,** 49 S. Hotel St. (P.O. Box 1698), Honolulu, HI 96808 (© **808/538-3952**).

For a self-guided tour of the neighborhood, see "Walking Tour 1: Historic Chinatown," on p. 204.

GUIDED ECOTOURS

Oahu isn't just high-rises in Waikiki or urban sprawl in Honolulu; it also has extinct craters, hidden waterfalls, lush rainforests, forgotten coastlines, and rainbow-filled valleys. To experience the other side of Oahu, contact **Oahu Nature Tours** (© **808/924-2473;** www.oahunaturetours.com). It offers seven different eco-tours, starting at $27 per person, and provides everything: expert guides (geologists, historians, archaeologists), round-trip transportation, entrance fees, bottled water, snacks, and use of day packs, binoculars, flashlights, and rain gear.

If you want to explore a hidden, ancient Hawaii that even most lifelong residents have never seen, book a tour with **Mauka Makai Excursions** ★, 350 Ward Ave., Honolulu (© **808/255-2206;** www.hawaiianecotours.net), a Hawaiian-owned and -operated eco-tour company specializing in field trips to off-the-beaten-path (and sometimes hidden in the jungle) ancient temples, sea caves, sacred stones, petroglyphs, and other cultural treasures. Tours range from a half-day ($50 adults, $40 children 6–17) to a full day ($80 adults, $60 children). They provide bottled water, insect repellent, rain gear, beach gear, fishing tackle, and hotel pickup; you bring your imagination.

SPECIALTY TOURS

Below are a couple of little-known, off-the beaten path tours.

Hawaii Coffee Company ★★, 1555 Kalani St. (© **808/847-3600;** www.hicoffeeco. com), has an excellent "behind the scenes" tour of their LION and Royal Kona Coffee facility as well as their Hawaiian Island Tea Company. You will be met in the retail/cafe area of their facility and taken through the 55,000-square-foot plant on a step-by-step tour of how Hawaii's oldest and largest coffee company processes and roasts their dozens of different brands and types of coffee. Allow 15 minutes for the tour, plus extra time to try the various coffees in the cafe. This is one of the best places on the island to stock up on a few bags of coffee or boxes of teas. Not only are the prices competitive, but, in November and December, exclusive specialty Christmas coffee can be purchased at this location. Free tours are given Monday to Saturday, 10 times a day (call for current tour times). The E Noa Trolley no. 10 also stops here.

For those looking for a really different look at Honolulu and the island, **Oahu Ghost Tours** (© **877/597-7325;** www.oahughosttours.com) offers a look at the island's super-natural history. Originally started by Glen Grant (1947–2003), who dedicated his life to exploring stories and sightings of the paranormal, the company has continued his inves-tigations of ghosts, unusual sightings, and the unexplainable. The tours range from

---

(**Moments**) **Rolling through Waikiki on a Segway**

One of my favorite ways to tour Waikiki is on a Segway Personal Transporter, the silly looking two-wheeled machine that looks like a push lawn mower (big wheels and a long upright handle). Amazingly enough, within just a few min-utes you get the hang of this contraption, which works through a series of high-tech stabilization mechanisms that read the motion of your body to turn or go forward or backward, and is propelled forward through twisting the hand throttle). And it's fun—think back to the first time you rode your bicycle: the incredible freedom of zipping along without walking. **Glide Ride Tours and Rentals,** in the Hawaii Tapa Tower of the Hilton Hawaiian Village Beach Resort & Spa, 2005 Kalia Rd. (© **808/941-3151;** www.segwayofhawaii.com), will instruct you on the Segway (they make sure that you are fully competent before you leave their training area), then take you on a series of tours (you must be 16 years of age or over and weigh more than 80 pounds). The tours range from a 40-minute introductory tour for $89 per person to a 2¹/₂-hour tour of Waikiki, Kapiolani Park, and Diamond Head, for $110 per person.

Honolulu City Haunts, a 2-mile walking tour of places where supernatural events still occur today ($29 adults and $22 children 11 and younger), to **Sacred Spirits Tour,** a 5-hour walking tour of the most sacred Native Hawaiian spots on Oahu ($52 adults and $39 children 11 and younger), to **Orbs of O'ahu,** a driving tour that circles the island, stopping at some of the "most haunted" locations ($49 adults and $37 children 11 and younger).

2 HISTORIC HONOLULU

The Waikiki you see today bears no resemblance to the Waikiki of yesteryear, a place of vast taro fields extending from the ocean to deep into Manoa Valley, dotted with numerous fishponds and gardens tended by thousands of people. This picture of old Waikiki can be recaptured by following the emerging **Waikiki Historic Trail** ★ (www.waikiki-historictrail.com), a meandering 2-mile walk with 20 bronze surfboard markers (each standing 6 ft., 5 in. tall—you can't miss 'em), complete with descriptions and archival photos of the historic sites. The markers note everything from Waikiki's ancient fishponds to the history of the Ala Wai Canal. The trail begins at Kuhio Beach and ends at the King Kalakaua statue, at the intersection of Kuhio and Kalakaua avenues.

A hula performance is a popular way for visitors to get a taste of traditional Hawaiian culture. See the real thing at the **Bishop Museum's** hula show (see below), or attend one of the free hula performances put on by the **Waikiki Improvement Association,** every Tuesday, Thursday, Saturday, and Sunday, from 6:30 to 7:30pm, at Kuhio Beach Park.

Bishop Museum ★★★ **Kids** Even if you do not have kids, this is a must-see on your vacation. It's a great rainy-day diversion; plan to spend at least half a day here. The museum was founded by a Hawaiian princess, Bernice Pauahi, who collected priceless artifacts and, in her will, instructed her husband, Charles Reed Bishop, to establish a Hawaiian museum "to enrich and delight" the people of Hawaii. Not only does this multibuilding museum have the world's greatest collection of natural and cultural artifacts from Hawaii and the Pacific, but recently it has added a terrific new 16,500-square-foot Richard T. Mamiya Science Adventure Center, specializing in volcanology, oceanography, and biodiversity. You'll become a kid again in this interactive, fun environment: Walk down a "Hawaiian origins" tunnel into the deep ocean zone, stopping along the way to play with all the cool, high-tech toys, then explore the interior of a volcano and climb to the top to get a bird's-eye view of an erupting caldera that looks like the real thing.

The Hawaiian Hall, the original cut-stone building (which dates from 1889) just completed a massive $20-millon renovation which updated the 19th-century-type displays with computer technology, installed new lighting and surround sound, and added recorded Hawaiian voices and chants. The renovated first floor tells the story of Hawaii before Westerners arrived. The importance of land and nature to Hawaiians is the focus on the middle level, and the top floor will have changing exhibits that center on issues relating to Hawaii.

Other buildings on the grounds are jampacked with acquisitions—from insect specimens and ceremonial spears to calabashes and old photos of topless hula dancers. A visit here will give you a good basis for understanding Hawaiian life and culture. You'll see the great feathered capes of kings, the last grass shack in Hawaii, pre-industrial Polynesian art, even the skeleton of a 50-foot sperm whale.

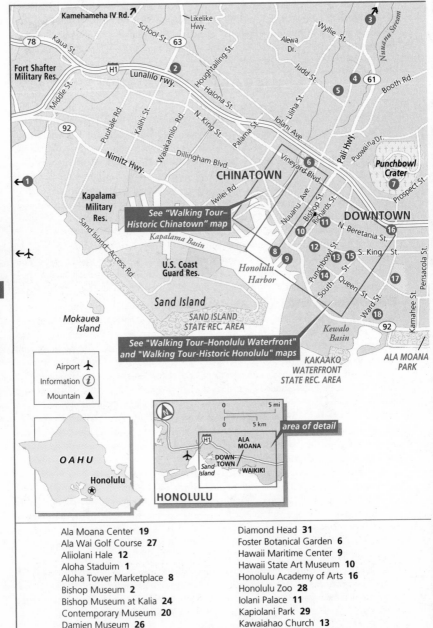

Ala Moana Center **19**
Ala Wai Golf Course **27**
Aliiolani Hale **12**
Aloha Staduim **1**
Aloha Tower Marketplace **8**
Bishop Museum **2**
Bishop Museum at Kalia **24**
Contemporary Museum **20**
Damien Museum **26**

Diamond Head **31**
Foster Botanical Garden **6**
Hawaii Maritime Center **9**
Hawaii State Art Museum **10**
Honolulu Academy of Arts **16**
Honolulu Zoo **28**
Iolani Palace **11**
Kapiolani Park **29**
Kawaiahao Church **13**

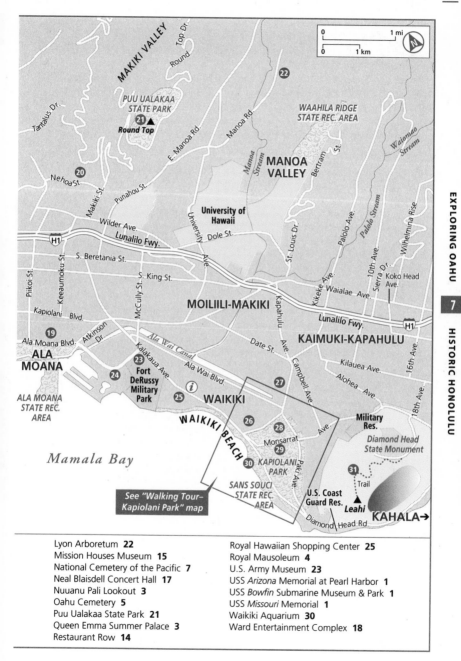

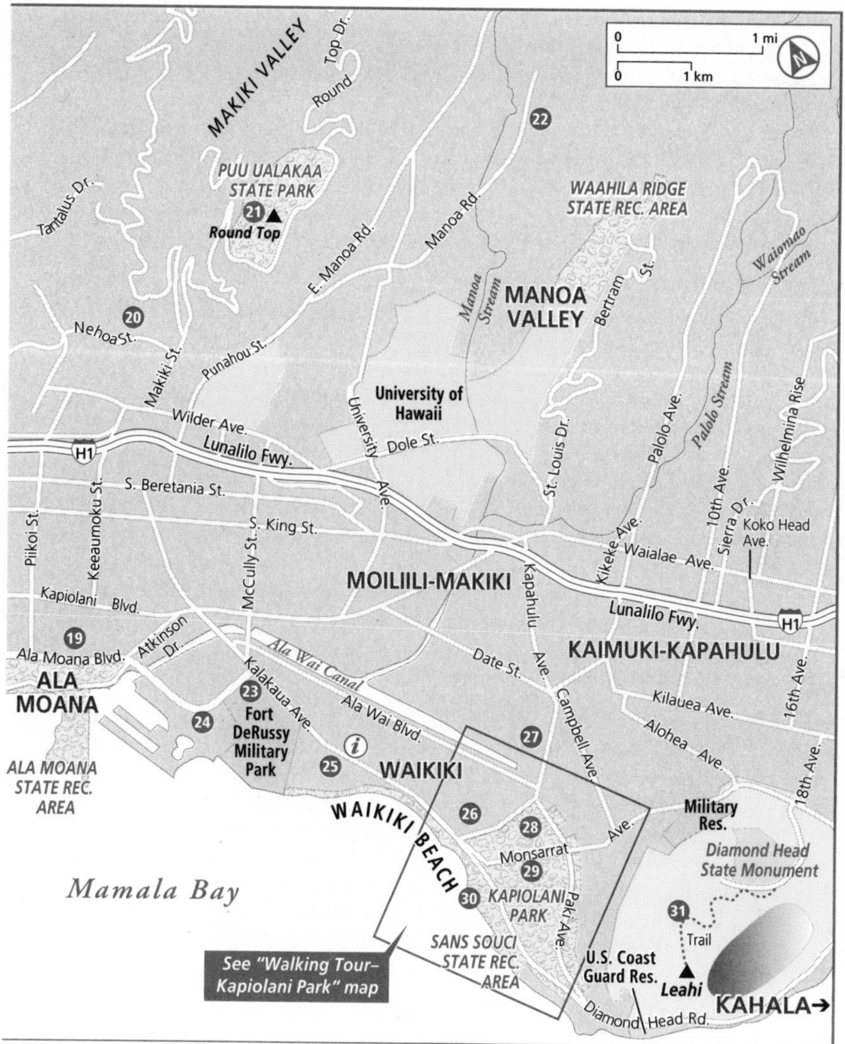
0
1 mi
0
1 km
N
MAKIKI VALLEY
Round Top Dr.
PUU UALAKAA STATE PARK
21
Round Top
Tantalus Dr.
22
WAAHILA RIDGE STATE REC. AREA
E. Manoa Rd.
Manoa Rd.
Manoa Stream
MANOA VALLEY
Bertram St.
Waiomao Stream
20
Nehoa St.
Makiki St.
Punahou St.
University of Hawaii
University Ave.
Palolo Ave.
Palolo Stream
Wilhelmina Rise
Wilder Ave.
H1
Lunalilo Fwy.
Dole St.
St. Louis Dr.
10th Ave.
S. Beretania St.
Sierra Dr.
Koko Head Ave.
Piikoi St.
Keeaumoku St.
S. King St.
McCully St.
Kikeke Ave.
Waialae Ave.
MOILIILI-MAKIKI
Kapahulu Ave.
Kapiolani Blvd.
Lunalilo Fwy.
H1
19
Atkinson Dr.
Ala Moana Blvd.
Ala Wai Canal
Date St.
KAIMUKI-KAPAHULU
16th Ave.
ALA MOANA
23
Kalakaua Ave.
Fort DeRussy Military Park
Ala Wai Blvd.
Kilauea Ave.
Campbell Ave.
24
27
Alohea Ave.
ALA MOANA STATE REC. AREA
25
WAIKIKI
18th Ave.
WAIKIKI BEACH
26
28
Military Res.
Monsarrat Ave.
29
Diamond Head State Monument
Mamala Bay
30
KAPIOLANI PARK
Paki Ave.
31
Trail
See "Walking Tour–Kapiolani Park" map
SANS SOUCI STATE REC. AREA
U.S. Coast Guard Res.
Leahi
KAHALA→
Diamond Head Rd.

Lyon Arboretum **22**
Mission Houses Museum **15**
National Cemetery of the Pacific **7**
Neal Blaisdell Concert Hall **17**
Nuuanu Pali Lookout **3**
Oahu Cemetery **5**
Puu Ualakaa State Park **21**
Queen Emma Summer Palace **3**
Restaurant Row **14**
Royal Hawaiian Shopping Center **25**
Royal Mausoleum **4**
U.S. Army Museum **23**
USS *Arizona* Memorial at Pearl Harbor **1**
USS *Bowfin* Submarine Museum & Park **1**
USS *Missouri* Memorial **1**
Waikiki Aquarium **30**
Ward Entertainment Complex **18**

Hula performances ★ take place weekdays at 11am and 2pm. This daily cultural event is worth making time for. Tours include **Na Mea Makamae,** the story of the creation of the museum and the treasures of Hawaiian culture (12:30pm daily); **Na Hulu Ali'i,** a tour of the elaborate feather artwork of ancient Hawaiians (10:30am and 1:30pm); **Plants of Paradise Garden Tour** (11:30am); and **Meet me at the Hot Spot— Lava Melting Demo** (noon and 2:30pm).

Personally, I would plan my trip around the shows in the planetarium: **The Sky Tonight** (11:30am), **Explorers of Mauna Kea** (1:30pm), and (my fave) **Explorers of Polynesia** (3:30pm).

1525 Bernice St., just off Kalihi St. (aka Likelike Hwy.). ✆ **808/847-3511.** www.bishopmuseum.org. Admission $16 adults, $13 children 4–12 and seniors. Wed–Mon 9am–5pm. Bus: 2.

Hawaii Maritime Center ★ (**Finds**) (**Kids**) As we went to press, this wonderful museum was "temporily closed" due to "economic cut backs." Be sure to call to see if it has reopened when you are in Hawaii. I strongly recommend that you spend a couple of hours here, wandering around and learning the story of Hawaii's rich maritime past, from the ancient journey of Polynesian voyagers to the nostalgic days of the *Lurline,* which once brought tourists from San Francisco on 4-day cruises. Inside the Hawaii Maritime Center's Kalakaua Boat House, patterned after His Majesty King David Kalakaua's own canoe house, are more than 30 exhibits, including Matson cruise ships (which brought the first tourists to Waikiki), flying boats that delivered the mail, and the skeleton of a Pacific humpback whale that beached on Kahoolawe; these latter two are especially interesting to kids. Outside, the *Hokule'a,* a double-hulled sailing canoe that, in 1976, reenacted the Polynesian voyage of discovery, is moored next to the *Falls of Clyde,* a four-masted schooner that once ran tea from China to the West Coast.

Pier 7 (next to Aloha Tower), Honolulu Harbor. ✆ **808/536-6373.** www.bishopmuseum.org. Admission $7.50 adults, $4.50 children 6–17. Daily 8:30am–5pm. Bus: 19 or 20.

Iolani Palace ★ If you want to really "understand" Hawaii, this 45-minute tour is well worth the time. The Iolani Palace was built by King David Kalakaua, who spared no expense. The 3-year project, completed in 1882, cost $360,000—and nearly bankrupted the Hawaiian kingdom. This four-story Italian Renaissance palace was the first electrified building in Honolulu (it had electricity before the White House and Buckingham Palace). Royals lived here for 11 years, until Queen Liliuokalani was deposed and the Hawaiian monarchy fell forever, in a palace coup (led by descendants of the original missionaries and American sugar planters), on January 17, 1893.

Cherished by latter-day royalists, the 10-room palace stands as an architectural statement of the monarchy period. Iolani attracts 60,000 visitors a year in groups of 15; everyone must don denim booties to scoot across the royal floors. Tours are either a comprehensive **guided tour** ★, which offers visitors a brief video about the history of the palace, a docent-guided tour of the inside of the palace, and a self-guided tour of the basement; or an **audio tour** that provides guests with an audio wand for a tour through the first and second floors and concludes with a self-guided tour of the gallery; or the **galleries tour,** a self-guided tour for those with limited time, that includes the palace galleries, complete with crown jewels, the ancient feathered cloaks, the royal china, and more.

364 S. King St. (at Richards St.). ✆ **800/532-1051** or 808/522-0832. www.iolanipalace.org. Grand Tour $20 adults, $5 children 5–12; Audio Tour $13 adults, $5 children 5–12; Gallery Tour $6 adults, $3 children 5–12. Tues–Sat 8:30am–2pm. Call ahead to reserve the Grand Tour. Children under 5 not permitted. Extremely limited parking on palace grounds; try metered parking on the street. Bus: 2.

Kawaiahao Church ★ In 1842, Kawaiahao Church stood complete at last, the crowning achievement of missionaries and Hawaiians working together for the first time on a common project. Designed by Rev. Hiram Bingham and supervised by Kamehameha III, who ordered his people to help build it, the project took 5 years. Workers quarried 14,000 coral blocks weighing 1,000 pounds each from the offshore reefs and cut timber in the forests for the beams.

This proud stone church, complete with bell tower and colonial colonnade, was the first permanent Western house of worship in the islands. It became the church of the Hawaiian royalty and remains in use today. Some fine portraits of Hawaiian royalty hang inside. I recommend seeing this edifice at the **Hawaiian-language services** ★★ (which probably set old Rev. Bingham spinning in his grave), conducted on Sundays at 9am.

957 Punchbowl St. (at King St.). ℂ **808/522-1333.** www.kawaiahao.org. Free admission (donations appreciated). Mon–Fri 8am–4pm; Sun services 9am. Bus: 2.

Mission Houses Museum This museum tells the dramatic story of cultural change in 19th-century Hawaii. American Protestant missionaries established their headquarters here in 1820. Included in the complex are a visitor center and three historic mission buildings, which have been restored and refurnished to reflect the daily life and work of the missionaries.

553 S. King St. (at Kawaiahao St.). ℂ **808/531-0481.** www.missionhouses.org. Admission $10 adults, $8 military personnel and seniors, $6 students (age 6–college), free for children 5 and under. Tues–Sat 9am–4pm. Bus: 2.

Queen Emma Summer Palace Hanaiakamalama, the name of the country estate of Kamehameha IV and Queen Emma, was once in the secluded uplands of Nuuanu Valley. These days it's adjacent to a six-lane highway full of speeding cars. This simple, seven-room New England–style house, built in 1848 and restored by the Daughters of Hawaii, is worth about an hour of your time to see the interesting blend of Victorian furniture and hallmarks of Hawaiian royalty, including feather cloaks and *kahili*, the feathered standards that mark the presence of *alii* (royalty). Other royal treasures include a canoe-shaped cradle for Queen Emma's baby, Prince Albert, who died at the age of 4. (Kauai's ultra-ritzy Princeville Resort is named for the little prince.)

2913 Pali Hwy. (at Old Pali Rd.). ℂ **808/595-3167.** www.daughtersofhawaii.org. Admission $6 adults, $1 children 11 and under. Daily 9am–4pm. Bus: 4, 55, 56, 57, or 65.

Royal Mausoleum In the cool uplands of Nuuanu, on a 3.7-acre patch of sacred land dedicated in 1865—and never surrendered to the United States—stands the Royal Mausoleum, the final resting place of King Kalakaua, Queen Kapiolani, and 16 other Hawaiian royals. Only the Hawaiian flag flies over this grave, a remnant of the kingdom. Allow about an hour for your visit.

2261 Nuuanu Ave. (btw. Wyllie and Judd sts.). ℂ **808/536-7602.** Free admission. Mon–Fri 8am–4:30pm. Bus: 4.

WARTIME HONOLULU

National Cemetery of the Pacific The National Cemetery of the Pacific (also known as "the Punchbowl") is an ash-and-lava tuff cone that exploded about 150,000 years ago—like Diamond Head, only smaller. Early Hawaiians called it Puowaina, or "hill of sacrifice." The old crater is a burial ground for 35,000 victims of three American wars in Asia and the Pacific: World War II, Korea, and Vietnam. Among the graves, you'll find many unmarked ones with the date December 7, 1941, carved in stone. Some will be unknown forever; others are famous, like that of war correspondent Ernie Pyle, killed by a Japanese sniper in April 1945 on Okinawa; still others buried here are remembered only by family and surviving buddies. The white stone tablets, known as the Courts of the Missing, bear the names of 28,788 Americans missing in action in World War II.

Survivors come here often to reflect on the meaning of war and to remember those, like themselves, who stood in harm's way to win peace a half-century ago. Some fight back tears, remembering lost comrades, lost missions, and the sacrifices of those who died.

Punchbowl Crater, 2177 Puowaina Dr. (at the end of the road). ℂ **808/541-1434.** Free admission. Daily 8am–5:30pm (Mar–Sept to 6:30pm). Bus: 15.

Pacific Aviation Museum   Just opened on the 65th anniversary of the bombing of Pearl Harbor, the first phase of this historical museum (in a 42,442-sq.-ft. hangar) tells the story of military aviation in the Pacific during World War II via a collection of original, historical aircraft (Japanese Zero fighter, Navy Wildcat fighter, Army Air corps B-25 Michell bomber, and so on), documentary films, displays (the story of the little-known battle of Niihau, where the Hawaiian residents captured a Japanese pilot on his crash landing on their island), and (my favorite) the interactive simulated aircraft control where you can "experience" what it was like to fly either an American or Japanese plane. They recently have added an "Aviator's Guided Tour," where trained tour guides take you on a journey into aviation history, with stories about the planes and the battles they saw, plus you get a sneak peak into behind the scenes at the Museum with access to parts of the Museum's collection not generally seen by the public (like aircraft being restored, a close up of the F-14 Tomcat, the F-15 Eagle, Bell helicopters and other vintage aircraft).

Pearl Harbor Hangar 37, Ford Island, 319 Lexington Blvd. ℂ **808/441-1000.** www.pacificaviation museum.org. Tickets $14 adults, $7 children ages 4–12; Aviator's Guided Tour $21 adults, $14 children (ages 4-12). Daily 9am–5pm. From Waikiki take H-1 east to the USS *Arizona*/Stadium exit, no. 15A (the 2nd exit after the airport). Continue on H-99 (Kamehameha Hwy.) 1½ miles, at the 4th traffic light, turn left on Kalaloa St and go about 1/10th of a mile. The visitor center will be on your left. Tickets may be purchased at the USS *Bowfin* Ticket Office. Bus: 42, transfer to Bus: 95.

USS Arizona Memorial at Pearl Harbor ★★★   On December 7, 1941, the USS *Arizona*, while moored here in Pearl Harbor, was bombed in a Japanese air raid. The 608-foot battleship sank in 9 minutes without firing a shot, taking 1,177 sailors and Marines to their deaths—and catapulting the United States into World War II.

Nobody who visits the memorial will ever forget it. The deck of the ship lies 6 feet below the surface of the sea. Oil still oozes slowly up from the Arizona's engine room to stain the harbor's calm, blue water; some say the ship still weeps for its lost crew. The memorial is a stark, white, 184-foot rectangle that spans the sunken hull of the ship; it was designed by Alfred Pries, a German architect interned on Sand Island during the war. It contains the ship's bell, recovered from the wreckage, and a shrine room with the names of the dead carved in stone.

Try to arrive at the visitor center, operated by the National Park Service, no later than 1:30pm to avoid the huge crowds; waits of 1 to 3 hours are common, and they don't take reservations at this time. While you're waiting for the free launch (operated by the U.S. Navy) to take you out to the ship—get the **audio tour ★★★**. This will make the trip even more meaningful. The tour (on an MP3 player), which runs about 2½ hours, is like having your own personal park ranger as your guide; the $5 fee is one of Hawaii's best deals. Narrated by Ernest Borgnine, it features stories told by actual Pearl Harbor survivors, both American and Japanese—not to be missed! Plus, while you are waiting for the

boat, the tour guides you step by step through the museum's personal
graphs, and historic documents. You can pause the recording for the
film which precedes your journey to the ship. The tour continues on th
ing the shore line and the memorial itself and continues at the site, g
picture of that fateful day; it continues through your boat ride back. A
least 4 hours for your visit.

Due to increased security measures, visitors cannot carry on purses, handbags, fanny
packs, backpacks, camera bags (but you can carry your camera or video camera with
you), diaper bags, or other items that offer concealment. However, there is a storage
facility to store carry-on-size items (no bigger than 30×30×18 in.), for a fee. Also, you
must wear **closed-toe shoes;** no sandals allowed.

Parents: Note that baby strollers, baby carriages, and baby backpacks are not allowed
in the theater, on the boat, or on the USS *Arizona* Memorial. All babies must be carried.

One last note: Most unfortunately, the USS *Arizona* Memorial is a high-theft area—
leave your valuables in your hotel safe.

Pearl Harbor. © **808/422-0561** (recorded info) or 808/422-2771. www.nps.gov/usar. Free admission.
Daily 7:30am–5pm (programs run 7:45am–3pm). Children under 12 should be accompanied by an adult.
Shirts and closed-toe shoes required; no swimsuits or flip-flops allowed (shorts acceptable). Wheelchairs
gladly accommodated. Drive west on H-1 past the airport; take the USS *Arizona* Memorial exit and follow
the green-and-white signs; there's ample free parking. Bus: 20; or *Arizona* Memorial Shuttle Bus VIP (©
808/839-0911), which picks up at Waikiki hotels 6:50am–1pm ($9 per person round-trip).

USS Bowfin Submarine Museum & Park ★

The USS *Bowfin* is one of only 15
World War II submarines still in existence today. You can go below deck of this famous
submarine—nicknamed the "Pearl Harbor Avenger" for its successful attacks on the
Japanese—and see how the 80-man crew lived during wartime. The *Bowfin* Museum has
an impressive collection of submarine-related artifacts. The Waterfront Memorial honors
submariners lost during World War II.

11 Arizona Memorial Dr. (next to the USS *Arizona* Memorial Visitor Center). © **808/423-1341.** www.
bowfin.org. Admission $10 adults, $7 active-duty military personnel and seniors, $4 children 4–12 (chil-
dren under 4 are not permitted for safety reasons). Daily 8am–5pm. See USS *Arizona* Memorial, above, for
driving, bus, and shuttle directions.

USS Missouri Memorial ★

On the deck of this 58,000-ton battleship (the last one
the navy built), World War II came to an end with the signing of the Japanese surrender
on September 2, 1945. The *Missouri* was part of the force that carried out bombing raids
over Tokyo and provided firepower in the battles of Iwo Jima and Okinawa. In 1955, the
navy decommissioned the ship and placed it in mothballs at the Puget Sound Naval
Shipyard, in Washington State. But the *Missouri* was modernized and called back into
action in 1986, eventually being deployed in the Persian Gulf War, before retiring once
again in 1992. Here it sat until another battle ensued, this time over who would get the
right to keep this living legend. Hawaii won that battle and brought the ship to Pearl
Harbor in 1998. The 887-foot ship is now open to visitors as a museum memorial.

If you have the time, take the 1-hour tour, which begins at the visitor center. Guests
are shuttled to Ford Island on military-style buses while listening to a 1940s-style radio
program (complete with news clips, wartime commercials, and music). Once on the ship,
guests watch an informational film and are then free to explore on their own or take a
guided tour. Highlights of this massive (more than 200-ft. tall) battleship include the
forecastle (or *fo'c'sle,* in Navy talk), where the 30,000-pound anchors are "dropped" on

reet of anchor chain; the 16-inch guns (each 65 ft. long and weighing 116 tons), ...ich can accurately fire a 2,700-pound shell some 23 miles in 50 seconds; and the spot where the Instrument of Surrender was signed as Douglas MacArthur, Chester Nimitz, and "Bull" Halsey looked on.

Battleship Row, Pearl Harbor. ℭ 877/MIGHTY-MO [644-48966]. www.ussmissouri.com. Admission $16 adults, $8 children 4–12. Battleship Guided Tour (60 min.) $7 extra; Explorer's Tour (90 min.) $29 extra. Daily 9am–5pm; guided tours 9:30am–4:30pm. Check in at the USS *Bowfin* Submarine Museum, next to the USS *Arizona* Memorial Visitor Center. Drive west on H-1 past the airport, take the USS *Arizona* Memorial exit, and follow the brown-and-white signs; there's ample free parking. Bus: B, transfer to Bus: 11, transfer to Bus: 20.

JUST BEYOND PEARL HARBOR

Hawaiian Railway Kids   All aboard this train ride back into history! Between 1890 and 1947 the chief mode of transportation for Oahu's sugar mills was the Oahu Railway and Land Co.'s narrow-gauge trains. The line carried not only equipment, raw sugar, and supplies, but also passengers from one side of the island to the other. You can relive those days every Sunday with a 1½-hour narrated ride through Ko Olina Resort and out to Makaha. As an added attraction, on the second Sunday of the month, you can ride on the nearly 100-year-old, custom-built, parlor-observation car belonging to Benjamin F. Dillingham, founder of the Oahu Railway and Land Co. The fare for this treat is $20 (no kids under 13), and you must reserve in advance.

Ewa Station, Ewa Beach. ℭ 808/681-5461. www.hawaiianrailway.com. Admission $10 adults, $7 seniors and children 2–12. Departures Sun at 1pm and 3pm; Mon–Fri by appointment. Take H-1 west to Exit 5A; take Hwy. 76 south for 2½ miles to Tesoro Gas; turn right on Renton Rd. and drive 1½ miles to end of paved section. The station is on the left. Bus: C-Express to Kapalei, then transfer to no. 41, which goes through Ewa and drops you off outside the gate.

Hawaii's Plantation Village   The hour-long tour of this restored 50-acre village offers a glimpse back in time to when sugar planters shaped the land, economy, and culture of Hawaii. From 1852, when the first contract laborers arrived here from China, to 1947, when the plantation era ended, more than 400,000 men, women, and children from China, Japan, Portugal, Puerto Rico, Korea, and the Philippines came to work the sugar cane fields. The "talk story" tour brings the old village alive with 30 faithfully restored camp houses, Chinese and Japanese temples, the Plantation Store, and even a sumo-wrestling ring.

Waipahu Cultural Garden Park, 94-695 Waipahu St. (at Waipahu Depot Rd.), Waipahu. ℭ 808/677-0110. www.hawaiiplantationvillage.org. Admission (including escorted tour) $13 adults; $10 seniors; $7 military personnel; $5 children 4–11; children 3 and under free. Mon–Sat 10am–2pm. Take H-1 west to the Waikele-Waipahu exit (Exit 7); get in the left exit lane and turn left on Paiwa St.; at the 5th light, turn right onto Waipahu St.; after the 2nd light, turn left. Bus: 47.

Wet 'n' Wild ★ Kids   Formerly called the Hawaiian Waters Adventure Park, kids love this 29-acre water-theme amusement park, which opened in 1999 with some $14 million in attractions. Plan to spend the day. Highlights are a football-field-size wave pool for bodysurfing, two 65-foot-high free-fall slides, two water-toboggan bullet slides, inner-tube slides, body-flume slides, a continuous river for floating inner tubes, and separate pools for adults, teens, and children. In addition, there are restaurants, Hawaiian performances, and shops.

400 Farrington Hwy., Kapolei. ℭ 808/674-WAVE [674-9283]. www.hawaiiwetnwild.com. Admission $40 adults, $17 seniors, $30 children 3–11, free for children 2 and under. Hours vary, but generally hours are daily 10:30am–4 or 5pm in peak season (summer); during off-season 10:30am–3:30 or 4pm; closed some weekdays. Take H-1 west to Exit 1 (Campbell Industrial Park). Make an immediate left to Farrington Hwy.; you will see the park on your left.

Rainy Days or Too Much Time in the Sun

If the kids are bored on yet another rainy day or your little darlings are pink from all that sun, take them directly to the **Hawaii Children's Discovery Center,** 111 Ohe St. (across from Kaka'ako Waterfront Park), Honolulu (© **808/524-5437;** www.discoverycenterhawaii.org). Perfect for ages 2 to 13, these 37,000 square feet of color, motion, and activities will entertain them for hours through hands-on exhibits and interactive stations. Where else can they play volleyball with a cyber-robot or put on sparkling costumes from India or dress up as a purple octopus? Lots of summer classes and activities are offered—from playing with clay to painting classes (most of them invite the parents to participate too). Admission $10; $6 seniors; and children under 1 free. Open Tuesday to Friday 9am to 1pm, Saturday to Sunday 10am to 3pm. Take TheBus no. 19, 20, 55, or 57 from Waikiki. Depart the bus in front of Cutter Mazda Volkswagen, on Koula Street. Then walk across Ala Moana Boulevard, toward Pflueger Acura, and follow Ohe Street toward the ocean until you come to a blue and pink concrete building with a smoke stack.

3 FISH, FLORA & FAUNA

Foster Botanical Garden ★★ (Finds) You could spend days in this unique historic garden, a leafy oasis amid the high-rises of downtown Honolulu. Combine a tour of the garden with a trip to Chinatown (just across the street) to maximize your time. The giant trees that tower over the main terrace were planted in the 1850s by William Hillebrand, a German physician and botanist, on royal land leased from Queen Emma. Today this 14-acre public garden, on the north side of Chinatown, is a living museum of plants, some rare and endangered, collected from the tropical regions of the world. Of special interest are 26 "Exceptional Trees" protected by state law, a large palm collection, a primitive cycad garden, and a hybrid orchid collection.

50 N. Vineyard Blvd. (at Nuuanu Ave.). © **808/522-7066.** www.co.honolulu.hi.us/parks/hbg/fbg.htm. Admission $5 adults, $1 children 6–12. Daily 9am–4pm; guided tours Mon–Sat at 1pm (reservations recommended). Bus: 2, 4, or 13.

Honolulu Zoo ★ (Kids) Nobody comes to Hawaii to see an Indian elephant or African lions and zebras. Right? Wrong. This 43-acre municipal zoo in Waikiki attracts visitors in droves. If you've got kids, allot at least half a day. The highlight is the new African Savannah, a 10-acre exhibit with more than 40 African critters roaming around in the open. The zoo also has a rare Hawaiian nene goose, a Hawaiian pig, and mouflon sheep. (Only the goose, an evolved version of the Canadian honker, is considered to be truly Hawaiian; the others are imported from Polynesia, India, and elsewhere.)

For a real treat, take the **Zoo by Twilight Tour** ★, which offers a rare behind-the-scenes look into the lives of the zoo's nocturnal residents. Tours are Saturday from 5:30 to 7:30pm; the cost is $12 for adults and $8 for children ages 4 to 12 years. Other great family programs include: **Snooze in the Zoo,** where kids can discover "who is roaring

(Kids) **Especially for Kids**

See an Erupting Volcano (p. 189)   It looks like the real thing—a real molten-spewing, roaring, rock-launching volcano—only you are standing just a few feet away. It's the Bishop Museum's new 16,500-square-foot Science Adventure Center, specializing in volcanology, oceanography, and biodiversity. Children are spellbound as they wander through the "Hawaiian origins" tunnel into the deep ocean, stopping along the way to play with all the cool, high-tech toys, then exploring the interior of a volcano and climbing to the top to get a bird's-eye view of an erupting caldera.

Take a Walk on the Wild Side (p. 197)   Visit Africa in Hawaii at Waikiki's Kapiolani Park. The lions, giraffes, zebras, and elephants delight youngsters and parents alike. But the great new thrill is the Zoo by Moonlight tour—so kids can see what really goes bump (or roar) in the night.

Shop Aloha Flea Market (p. 158)   Most kids hate to shop. But the Aloha Flea Market, a giant outdoor bazaar at Aloha Stadium every Wednesday, Saturday, and Sunday, is more akin to a carnival, full of strange food, odd goods, and bold barkers. Nobody ever leaves this place empty-handed—or without having had lots of fun.

Fly a Kite at Kapiolani Park (p. 200)   Great open expanses of green and constant trade winds make this urban park one of Hawaii's prime locations for kite flying. Watch the pros fly dragon kites and stage kite-fighting contests, or join in the fun after checking out the convenient kite shop across the street in New Otani's arcade.

Eat Shave Ice at Haleiwa (p. 227)   No visit to Hawaii is complete without an authentic shave ice. You can find shave ice in all kinds of tropical flavors throughout the islands, but for some reason, it tastes better in this funky North Shore surf town.

Beat Bamboo Drums in a Fijian Village (p. 226)   The Polynesian Cultural Center introduces kids to the games played by Polynesian and Melanesian children. The activities, which range from face painting to Hawaiian bowling, go on every day from 12:30 to 5:30pm.

Splash Down at Wet 'n' Wild (p. 196)   This 29-acre water park features a wave pool for bodysurfing, two 65-foot-high free-fall slides, two water-toboggan bullet slides, inner-tube slides, body flume slides, a continuous river for floating inner tubes, and separate pools for adults, teens, and children.

Explore the Bishop Museum (p. 189)   There are some 1,180,000 Polynesian artifacts; 13,500,000 different insect specimens; 6,000,000 marine and land shells; 490,000 plant specimens; 130,000 fish specimens; and 85,000 birds and mammals, all in the Bishop Museum. Kids can explore interactive exhibits, see a 50-foot sperm whale skeleton, and check out a Hawaiian grass hut—the museum has something for everyone.

Walk through a Submarine (p. 195)   At the USS *Bowfin* Submarine Museum Park, an interactive museum offers kids the chance to experience a real submarine—one that served in some of the fiercest naval battles in World War II. Kids can explore the interior of the tightly packed submarine that housed some 90 to 100 men and see the stacked shelves where they slept, the radar and electronics in the command center, and where the torpedoes are stored.

Dream at the Hawaii Maritime Center (p. 192)   Kids will love the Kalakaua Boathouse, the two-story museum of the Maritime Center. Exhibits include such topics as the development of surfing, the art of tattooing, and artifacts from the whaling industry. Next door you'll find the fully rigged, four-masted *Falls of Clyde*, an 1878 cargo and passenger liner. You'll also find the *Hokule'a*, a re-creation of a traditional double-hulled sailing canoe, which in 1976 made the 6,000-mile round-trip voyage to Tahiti using only ancient navigation techniques—the stars, the wind, and the sea.

Watch the Fish and Sharks at the Waikiki Aquarium (p. 200)   Much more than a big fish tank, the Waikiki Aquarium will astound and educate your youngsters. They can probably sit for hours staring at the sharks, turtles, eels, rays, and fish swimming in the main tank. For a few laughs, wander out to the monk seal area and watch the antics of these seagoing clowns.

Snorkel in Hanauma Bay (p. 167)   Kids will be enthralled with the teeming tropical fish and the underwater world at this marine park. The shallow waters near the beach are perfect for neophyte snorkelers, and the long (2,000-ft.) beach has plenty of frolicking room. Get there early; it can get very crowded.

Hike to the Top of Diamond Head Crater (p. 171)   The entire family can make this easy 1.4-mile round-trip walk to the top of the 750-foot volcanic cone with its rewarding view of Oahu. Bring a flashlight for the entry tunnel and a camera for the view.

Explore the Depths in a Submarine Dive (p. 169)   Better than a movie, more exciting than a video game, the *Atlantis* or *Voyager* submarines journey down 100 feet below the water's surface to explore the Neptunian world of tropical reef fish and even an occasional shark or two.

See Sea Creatures at Sea Life Park (p. 201)   Kids love this 62-acre ocean-theme park that features orca whales, dolphins, seals, and penguins. It also offers a Hawaiian reef tank full of native tropical fish, a "touch" pool, and the world's only "wholphin"—a cross between a false killer whale and an Atlantic bottle-nosed dolphin.

and who is snoring" during the night with pizza, tours, and campfire time with s'mores, plus breakfast and a morning stroll ($50 age 4 and up; check website for dates); and **Star Gazing at the Zoo,** an evening tour of the zoo that also explores the night sky above Hawaii with astronomer Dr. Michael Chauvin ($12 adults, $8 children ages 4–12).

151 Kapahulu Ave. (btw. Paki and Kalakaua aves.), at entrance to Kapiolani Park. ⓒ 808/971-7171. www. honoluluzoo.org. Admission $8 adults, $1 children 6–12, family pass $25. Daily 9am–4:30pm. The Zoo parking lot entrance is on Kapahulu Ave. and charges 25¢ per hour. The Shell parking lot across the street on Monsarrat Ave. has free parking. Bus: 2, 8, 19, 20, or 47.

Kapiolani Park ★ (Kids) In 1877, King David Kalakaua gave 130 acres of land to the people of Hawaii and named it after his beloved wife, Queen Kapiolani. This truly royal park has something for just about everyone: tennis courts, soccer and rugby fields, archery, picnic areas, wide-open spaces for kite flying and Frisbee throwing, and a jogging path with aerobic exercise stations. On Sundays in the summer, the Royal Hawaiian Band plays in the bandstand, just as they did during Kalakaua's reign. The Waikiki Shell, located in the park, is host to a variety of musical events, from old Hawaiian songs to rock and roll.

Bordered by Kalakaua Ave. on the ocean side, Monsarrat Ave. on the Ewa side, and Paki Ave. on the mountain side. Bus: 2.

Lyon Arboretum ★ The Lyon Arboretum dates back to 1918, when the Hawaiian Sugar Planters Association wanted to demonstrate the value of watershed for reforestation. In 1953 it became part of the University of Hawaii, where they continued to expand the extensive collection of tropical plants. Six-story-tall breadfruit trees, yellow orchids no bigger than bus tokens, ferns with fuzzy buds as big as human heads . . . these are just a few of the botanical wonders you'll find at the 194-acre Lyon Arboretum. A whole different world opens up to you along the self-guided 20-minute hike through the arboretum to Inspiration Point. You'll pass more than 5,000 exotic tropical plants full of singing birds in this cultivated rainforest (a University of Hawaii research facility) at the head of Manoa Valley.

3860 Manoa Rd. (near the top of the road). ⓒ 808/988-0456. www.hawaii.edu/lyonarboretum. No admission fee, but donations accepted ($5 is suggested). Mon–Fri 9am–4pm. Bus: 5.

Waikiki Aquarium ★★★ (Kids) Do not miss this! Half of Hawaii is its underwater world, so plan to spend at least 2 hours discovering it. Behold the chambered nautilus, nature's submarine and inspiration for Jules Verne's *20,000 Leagues Under the Sea.* You may see this tropical spiral-shelled cephalopod mollusk—the only living one born in captivity—any day of the week here. Its natural habitat is the deep waters of Micronesia, but aquarium director Bruce Carlson not only succeeded in trapping the pearly shell in 1,500 feet of water (by dangling chunks of raw tuna), but also managed to breed this ancient relative of the octopus. Plenty of other fish also inhabit this small but first-class aquarium, located on a live coral reef. The Hawaiian reef habitat features sharks, eels, a touch tank, and habitats for the endangered Hawaiian monk seal and green sea turtle. Recently added: a rotating biodiversity exhibit and interactive displays focusing on corals and coral reefs.

2777 Kalakaua Ave. (across from Kapiolani Park). ⓒ 808/923-9741. www.waquarium.org. Admission $9 adults; $6 active military, seniors, and college students; $4 children 13–17; $2 children 5–12; and free for children 4 and under. Daily 9am–5pm. Bus: 2.

Sea Life Park ★ (**Kids**)   This 62-acre park in East Oahu is one of the island's top attractions. It features whales from Puget Sound, Atlantic bottle-nosed dolphins, California sea lions, and penguins going through their motions to the delight of kids of all ages. With children, allow all day to take in the sights. Also popular are the Hawaiian reef tank full of tropical fish; the "touch" pool, where you can feel a real sea cucumber (commonly found in tide pools); and a bird sanctuary, where you can see such birds as the red-footed booby and the frigate bird. The chief curiosity, though, is the world's only "wholphin"— a cross between a false killer whale and an Atlantic bottle-nosed dolphin. On-site, marine biologists operate a recovery center for endangered marine life; during your visit, you'll be able to see rehabilitated Hawaiian monk seals and seabirds.

41-202 Kalanianaole Hwy. (at Makapuu Point), Honolulu. ✆ **808/259-7933.** www.sealifeparkhawaii. com. Admission $31 adults, $25 children 4–12. Daily 9:30am–5pm. Parking $3. Shuttle buses from Waikiki $5. Bus: 22 or 58.

4 SPECTACULAR VIEWS

Diamond Head ★★★ (**Kids**) (**Moments**)   The 360-degree view from atop Diamond Head Crater is worth the 560-foot ascent and should not be missed. You can see all the way from Koko Crater to Barbers Point and the Waianae Mountains. The 750-foot-tall volcano, which has become the symbol for Hawaii, is about 350,000 years old. The trail to the summit was built in 1910 to service the military installation along the crater; the hike to the top takes about 30 minutes but is quite manageable by anyone of any age. (For additional details, see p. 171.)

Diamond Head has always been considered a "sacred site" by Hawaiians. According to legend, Hi'iaka, the sister to the volcano goddess Pele, named the mountain Leahi (meaning the "brow of the ahi") when she saw the resemblance to the yellowfin tuna (called "ahi" in Hawaiian). Kamehameha the Great built a *luakini heiau* on the top where human sacrifices were made to the god of war, Ku.

The name *Diamond Head* came into use around 1825 when a group of British sailors (some say they were slightly inebriated) found some rocks sparkling in the sun. Absolutely sure they had struck it rich, the sailors brought these "diamonds" back into Honolulu. Alas, the "diamonds" turned out to be calcite crystals. The sailors didn't become fabulously rich, but the name Diamond Head stuck.

Diamond Head Rd. Daily 6am–6pm. Admission $1 for walk-ins, $5 for cars. To get here from Waikiki, take Kalakaua Ave. toward Kapiolani Park. Turn left onto Monsarrat Ave. at the Park. Monsarrat Ave. becomes Diamond Head Rd. after Campbell Ave. Continue on Diamond Head Rd. to turnoff to crater. Turn right into turnoff, follow to parking lot. Bus: 22 or 58.

Lanikai Beach ★★   This is one of the best places on Oahu to greet the sunrise. Watch the sky slowly move from pitch black to wisps of gray to burnt orange as the sun rises over the two tiny offshore islands of Mokulua. Use your five senses for this experience: hear the birds sing, feel the gentle breezes on your face, taste the salt in the air, smell the ocean, and see the kaleidoscope of colors as another day dawns.

Mokulua Dr., Kailua. To get here from Honolulu, take Hwy. 61 (Pali Hwy.) into Kailua. Follow the street (which becomes Kailua Rd., then becomes Kuulei Rd.) until it ends. Turn right on Kalaheo Ave. (which will become Kawailoa Rd. in a few blocks). Follow the road over the canal. At the stop sign, turn left on

Kaneapu Place. At the fork in the road, bear left on one-way Aalapapa Dr. Turn right at any cross street onto Mokulua Dr. No bus service.

Nuuanu Pali Lookout ★ (Moments) Gale-force winds sometimes howl through the mountain pass at this 1,186-foot-high perch guarded by 3,000-foot peaks, so hold onto your hat—and small children. But if you walk up from the parking lot to the precipice, you'll be rewarded with a view that'll blow you away. At the edge, the dizzying panorama of Oahu's windward side is breathtaking: Clouds low enough to pinch scoot by on trade winds; pinnacles of the *pali* (cliffs), green with ferns, often disappear in the mist; the vertical slopes of the Koolaus end in lush green valleys that become the town of Kaneohe; and the Pacific, a magnificent blue, dotted with whitecaps, beckons in the distance. Definitely take a jacket with you; it can be quite misty and cool at the lookout. On very windy days, you'll notice that the waterfalls look as though they are flowing up rather than down.

In 1898, John Wilson built the road up to the lookout using 200 laborers. Even before the road existed, the Nuuanu Pali (which translates as "cool heights") was infamous because legend claims it as the location of Kamehameha the Great's last battle. Although some academic scholars scoff at this, the story alleges that in 1795, Kamehameha pursued Oahu's warriors up Nuuanu to these cliffs and waged a battle in his attempt to unite the Hawaiian islands. Supposedly, the Oahu warriors were driven over the cliffs by Kamehameha's men. Some say the battle never happened, some say it happened but with only a few men fighting, and some say thousands were forced over the cliff, plunging to their deaths. Others say at night you can still hear the cries of these long-dead warriors coming from the valley below.

From on high, the tropical palette of green and blue runs down to the sea. Combine this 10-minute stop with a trip over the Pali to the windward side.

Near the summit of Pali Hwy. (Hwy. 61); take the Nuuanu Pali Lookout turnoff.

Nuuanu Valley Rain Forest (Finds) It's not the same as a peaceful nature walk, but if time is short and hiking isn't your thing, Honolulu has a rainforest you can drive through. It's only a few minutes from downtown Honolulu in verdant Nuuanu Valley, where it rains nearly 300 inches a year. And it's easy to reach: As the Pali Highway leaves residential Nuuanu and begins its climb though the forest, the last stoplight is the Nuuanu Pali Road turnoff; turn right for a junglelike detour of about 2 miles under a thick canopy strung with liana vines, past giant bamboo that creaks in the wind, Norfolk pines, and wild shell ginger. The road rises and the vegetation clears as you drive, blinking in the bright light of day, past a small mountain reservoir.

Soon the road rejoins the Pali Highway. Kailua is to the right and Honolulu to the left—but it can be a hair-raising turn. Instead, turn right, go a half-mile to the Nuuanu Pali Lookout (see above), stop for a panoramic view of Oahu's windward side, and return to the town-bound highway on the other side.

Take the Old Nuuanu Pali Rd. exit off Pali Hwy. (Hwy. 61).

Puu o Mahuka Heiau ★ (Moments) Go around sundown to feel the *mana* (sacred spirit) of this ancient Hawaiian site. The largest sacrificial temple on Oahu, it's associated with the great Kaopulupulu, who sought peace between Oahu and Kauai. This prescient *kahuna* (priest) predicted that the island would be overrun by strangers from a distant land. In 1794, three of Captain George Vancouver's men of the *Daedalus* were sacrificed here. In 1819, the year before New England missionaries landed in Hawaii, King Kamehameha II ordered all idols here to be destroyed.

A national historic landmark, this 18th-century temple, known as the "hill of escape," sits on a 5-acre, 300-foot bluff overlooking Waimea Bay and 25 miles of Oahu's wave-lashed North Coast—all the way to Kaena Point, where the Waianae Range ends in a spirit leap to the other world. The *heiau* (temple) appears as a huge rectangle of rocks twice as big as a football field (170 ft.×575 ft.), with an altar often covered by the flower and fruit offerings left by native Hawaiians.

1 mile past Waimea Bay. Take Pupukea Rd. mauka (inland) off Kamehameha Hwy. at Foodland, and drive ⁷/₁₀ miles up a switchback road. Bus: 52, then walk up Pupukea Rd.

Puu Ualakaa State Park ★ (**Moments**)   The best **sunset view** of Honolulu is from a 1,048-foot-high hill named for sweet potatoes. Actually, the poetic Hawaiian name means "rolling sweet potato hill," which is how early planters used gravity to harvest their crop. The panorama is sweeping and majestic. On a clear day—which is almost always—you can see from Diamond Head to the Waianae Range, almost the length of Oahu. At night, several scenic overlooks provide romantic spots for young lovers who like to smooch under the stars with the city lights at their feet. It's a top-of-the-world experience—the view, that is.

At the end of Round Hill Dr. Daily 7am–6:45pm (to 7:45pm in summer). From Waikiki, take Ala Wai Blvd. to McCully St., turn right, and drive mauka (inland) beyond the H-1 on-ramps to Wilder St.; turn left and go to Makiki St.; turn right, and continue onward and upward about 3 miles.

5 MORE MUSEUMS

Aliiolani Hale   Don't be surprised if this place looks familiar; you probably saw it on *Magnum, P.I.* This gingerbread Italianate building, designed by Australian Thomas Rowe in Renaissance revival style, was built in 1874 and was originally intended to be a palace. Instead, Aliiolani Hale ("chief unto heavens") became the Supreme Court and Parliament government office building. Inside, there's a **Judiciary History Center** ★, which features a multimedia presentation, a restored historic courtroom, and exhibits tracing Hawaii's transition from precontact Hawaiian law to Western law. Allow up to an hour to see it.

417 S. King St. (btw. Mililani and Punchbowl sts.). © **808/539-4999.** Fax 808/539-4996. Free admission. Mon–Fri 9am–4pm; reservations for group tours only. Bus: 1, 2, 3, 4, 8, 11, or 12. Limited meter parking on street.

Contemporary Museum ★   Set on the slopes of Tantalus, one of Honolulu's upscale residential communities, the Contemporary Museum is renowned for its 3 acres of Asian gardens (with reflecting pools, sun-drenched terraces, views of Diamond Head, and stone benches for quiet contemplation). Its Cades Pavilion houses David Hockney's *L'Enfant et les Sortileges,* an environmental installation of his sets and costumes for Ravel's 1925 opera, and six galleries display significant works from the last 4 decades. Equally prominent is the presence of contemporary Hawaiian artists in the museum's programs and exhibitions. Ask about the daily docent-led tours, and look for an excellent cafe and shop. Depending on your passion for art, you could spend an hour to all day here.

2411 Makiki Heights Dr. © **808/526-0232.** www.tcmhi.org. Admission $8 adults, $6 seniors and students, free for children 12 and under; free to all 3rd Thurs of each month. Tues–Sat 10am–4pm; Sun noon–4pm. Docent-guided tours 1:30pm daily. Bus: 15 to Makiki Heights Dr.

Hawaii State Art Museum ★★   Displaying an array of works that reflect a mix of Hawaii's ethnic and cultural traditions, this museum offers a real visual treat. It's housed in the original Royal Hawaiian Hotel built in 1872, during the reign of King Kamehameha V. The works of 284 artists blend Western art forms with traditional forms, most of the pieces dating from the 1960s to the present. Allow at least an hour to view the current exhibit, which depicts Hawaii, its history, culture, and ideals through a variety of mediums.

250 S. Hotel St. (at Richards St.). ℂ **808/586-0900**. www.state.hi.us/sfca. Free admission. Tues–Sat 10am–4pm, and the First Friday of every month 5–9pm. Bus: E.

Honolulu Academy of Arts ★★ This acclaimed museum unveiled its new $28-million Henry R. Luce Pavilion Complex in May 2001 and wowed the state with its new exhibition space, courtyard, expanded outdoor cafe, and gift shop. A magnificent facility got even better, as two 4,000-square-foot galleries were added to the existing 30, and the John Dominis and Patches Damon Holt Gallery displayed the museum's Hawaii regional collection in one space for the first time. Considered Hawaii's premier example of *kamaaina*- (old-time-) style architecture, the Academy is the state's only general fine-arts museum and has expanded steadily over the last decade. It boasts one of the top Asian art collections in the country, including James Michener's collection of Hiroshige's *ukiyo-e* prints. Also on exhibit are American and European masters and prehistoric works of Mayan, Greek, and Hawaiian art. The museum's award-winning architecture is a paragon of graciousness, featuring magnificent courtyards, lily ponds, and sensitively designed galleries. Spend a few hours or linger for a day here.

900 S. Beretania St. ℂ **808/532-8700**, or 808/532-8701 for recorded information. www.honolulu academy.org. Admission $10 adults; $5 students, seniors, and military personnel; free for children under age 12. Free admission on the 1st Wed of the month and 3rd Sun of every month. Tues–Sat 10am–4:30pm; Sun 1–5pm. Bus: 2.

U.S. Army Museum This museum, built in 1909 and used in defense of Honolulu and Pearl Harbor, houses military memorabilia ranging from ancient Hawaiian warfare items to modern-day high-tech munitions. On the upper deck, the Corps of Engineers Pacific Regional Visitors Center shows how the corps works with the civilian community to manage water resources in an island environment. Plan to spend an hour perusing the place.

Fort DeRussy Park, Waikiki. ℂ **808/438-2822**. Free admission. Tues–Sun 10am–4:30pm. Bus: 8.

WALKING TOUR 1   HISTORIC CHINATOWN

GETTING THERE:	From Waikiki, take TheBus no. 2 or 20 toward downtown; get off on North Hotel Street (after Maunakea St.). If you're driving, take Ala Moana Boulevard and turn right on Smith Street; make a left on Beretania Street and a left again at Maunakea. The city parking garage (50¢ per hr.) is on the Ewa (west) side of Maunakea Street, between North Hotel and North King streets.
START & FINISH:	North Hotel and Maunakea streets.
TIME:	1 to 2 hours, depending on how much time you spend browsing.
BEST TIME:	Daylight hours.

Chinese laborers from Guangdong Province first came to work on Hawaii's sugar and pineapple plantations in the 1850s. They quickly figured out that they would never get rich working in the fields; once their contracts were up, a few of the ambitious started small shops and restaurants in the area around River Street.

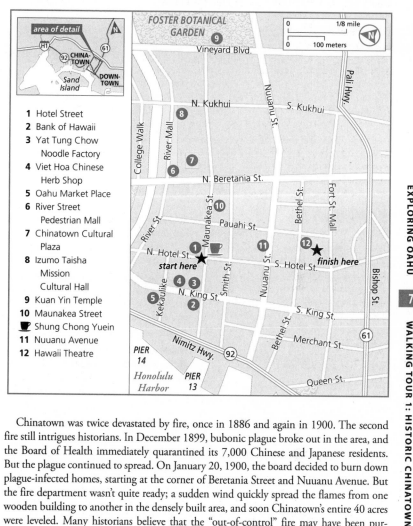

area of detail

FOSTER BOTANICAL GARDEN

Vineyard Blvd.

0 ······ 1/8 mile
0 ······ 100 meters

1 Hotel Street
2 Bank of Hawaii
3 Yat Tung Chow
   Noodle Factory
4 Viet Hoa Chinese
   Herb Shop
5 Oahu Market Place
6 River Street
   Pedestrian Mall
7 Chinatown Cultural
   Plaza
8 Izumo Taisha
   Mission
   Cultural Hall
9 Kuan Yin Temple
10 Maunakea Street
☕ Shung Chong Yuein
11 Nuuanu Avenue
12 Hawaii Theatre

N. Kukhui / S. Kukhui

N. Beretania St.

Pauahi St.

start here / finish here

N. Hotel St. / S. Hotel St.

N. King St. / S. King St.

Merchant St.

PIER 14

Nimitz Hwy.

Honolulu Harbor / PIER 13

Queen St.

Chinatown was twice devastated by fire, once in 1886 and again in 1900. The second fire still intrigues historians. In December 1899, bubonic plague broke out in the area, and the Board of Health immediately quarantined its 7,000 Chinese and Japanese residents. But the plague continued to spread. On January 20, 1900, the board decided to burn down plague-infected homes, starting at the corner of Beretania Street and Nuuanu Avenue. But the fire department wasn't quite ready; a sudden wind quickly spread the flames from one wooden building to another in the densely built area, and soon Chinatown's entire 40 acres were leveled. Many historians believe that the "out-of-control" fire may have been purposely set to drive the Chinese merchants—who were becoming economically powerful and controlled prime real estate—out of Honolulu. If this was indeed the case, it didn't work: The determined merchants built a new Chinatown on the same spot.

Chinatown reached its peak in the 1930s. In the days before air travel, visitors arrived here by cruise ship. Just a block up the street was the pier where they disembarked—and they often headed straight for the shops and restaurants of Chinatown, which mainlanders considered an exotic treat. In the 1940s, military personnel on leave flocked here looking for different kinds of exotic treats—in the form of pool halls, tattoo joints, and brothels.

Today, Chinatown is again rising from the ashes. After deteriorating over the years into a tawdry district of seedy bars, drug dealing, and homeless squatters, the neighborhood recently underwent extensive urban renewal. Just enough sleaze still flourishes on the fringes (a few peep shows and a couple of topless bars) to keep it from being a theme park–style tourist attraction, but Chinatown is poised to relive its glory days.

It's not exactly a microcosm of China, however. What you'll find is a mix of Asian cultures, all packed into a small area where tangy spices rule the cuisine, open-air markets have kept out the mini-malls, and the way to good health is through acupuncture and herbalists. The jumble of streets comes alive every day with bustling residents and visitors from all over the world; a cacophony of sounds, from the high-pitched bleating of vendors in the market to the lyrical dialects of the retired men "talking story" over a game of mah-jongg; and brilliant reds, blues, and greens trimming buildings and goods everywhere you look. No trip to Honolulu is complete without a visit to this exotic, historic district.

Start your walk on the Ewa (west) side of Maunakea Street at:

❶ Hotel Street

During World War II, Hotel Street was synonymous with good times. Pool halls and beer parlors lined the blocks, and prostitutes were plentiful. Nowadays, the more nefarious establishments have been replaced with small shops, from art galleries to specialty boutiques, and urban professionals and recent immigrants look for bargains where the sailors once roamed.

Once you're done wandering through the shops, head to the intersection with Smith Street. On the Diamond Head (east) side of Smith, you'll notice stones in the sidewalk; they were taken from the sandalwood ships, which came to Hawaii empty of cargo except for these stones, which were used as ballast on the trip over. The stones were removed and the ships' hulls were filled with sandalwood for the return to the mainland.

From Hotel Street, turn left on Maunakea and proceed to the corner of King Street to the:

❷ Bank of Hawaii

This unusual-looking bank is not the conservative edifice you'd expect—it's guarded by two fire-breathing dragon statues.

Turn right onto King Street, where you'll pass the shops of various Chinese herbalists. Stop at 150 N. King St., where you'll find the:

❸ Yat Tung Chow Noodle Factory

The delicious, delicate noodles that star in numerous Asian dishes are made here, ranging from threadlike noodles (literally no thicker than embroidery thread) to fat udon noodles. Tours of the factory are not offered, but you can look through the window, past the white cloud of flour that hangs in the air, and watch as dough is fed into rollers at one end of the noodle machines; perfectly cut noodles emerge at the other end.

Proceed to 162 N. King St., to the:

❹ Viet Hoa Chinese Herb Shop

At this location, Chinese herbalists act as both doctors and dispensers of herbs. Patients come in and tell the herbalist what ails them; the herbalist then decides which of the myriad herbs to mix together. Usually, there's a wall of tiny drawers labeled in Chinese characters; the herbalist quickly pulls from the drawers various objects that range from dried flowers and ground-up roots to such exotics as mashed antelope antler. The patient then takes the concoction home to brew into a strong tea.

Cross to the south side of King Street, where, just west of Kekaulike Street, you'll come to the most visited part of Chinatown, the open-air market known as:

❺ Oahu Market Place

Those interested in Asian cooking will find all the necessary ingredients here, including pig's heads, poultry (some still squawking), fresh octopi, salted jellyfish, pungent fish sauce, fresh herbs, and thousand-year-old eggs. The friendly vendors are happy to explain their wares and give instructions on how to prepare these exotic treats. The market, which has been at this spot since 1904, is divided into meats, poultry, fish, vegetables, and fruits. Past the open market are several grocery stores with fresh produce on display on the sidewalk. You're bound to spot some varieties here that you're not used to seeing at your local supermarket.

Follow King Street down to River Street and turn right toward the mountains. A range of inexpensive restaurants lines River Street from King to Beretania. You can get the best Vietnamese and Filipino food in town in these blocks, but go early—lines for lunch start at 11:15am. Beyond Beretania Street is the:

⑥ River Street Pedestrian Mall

Here, River Street ends and the pedestrian mall begins with the **statue of Chinese revolutionary leader Sun Yat-sen.** The wide mall, which borders the Nuuanu Stream, is lined with shade trees, park benches, and tables where seniors gather to play mah-jongg and checkers. Plenty of takeout restaurants are nearby if you'd like to eat lunch outdoors. If you're up early (5:30am in summer and 6am in winter), you'll see senior citizens practicing tai chi.

Along the River Street Mall, extending nearly a block over to Maunakea Street, is the:

⑦ Chinatown Cultural Plaza

This modern complex is filled with shops featuring everything from tailors to calligraphers (most somewhat more expensive than their street-side counterparts), as well as numerous restaurants—a great idea, but in reality, people seem to prefer wandering Chinatown's crowded streets to venturing into a modern mall. A couple of interesting shops here specialize in Asian magazines; there's also a small post office tucked away in a corner of the plaza, for those who want to mail cards home with the "Chinatown" postmark. The best feature of the plaza is the **Moongate Stage** in the center, the site of many cultural presentations, especially around the Chinese New Year.

Bargaining: A Way of Life in Chinatown

In Chinatown, nearly every purchase—from chicken's feet to an 18-carat gold necklace—is made by bargaining. It's the way of life for most Asian countries—and part of the fun and charm of shopping in Chinatown.

The main rule of thumb when negotiating a price is **respect.** The customer must have respect for the merchant and understand that he's in business to make money. This respect is coupled with the understanding that the customer does not want to be taken advantage of and would like the best deal possible.

Keep in mind two rules when bargaining: **cash** and **volume.** Don't even begin haggling if you're not planning to pay cash. The second you pull out a credit card (if the merchant or vendor will even accept it), all deals are off. And remember, the more you buy, the better the deal the merchant will extend to you.

Significant savings can be realized for high-ticket items like jewelry. The price of gold in Chinatown is based on the posted price of the tael (a unit of weight, slightly more than an ounce), which is listed for 14-, 18-, and 24-carat gold, plus the value of the labor. The tael price is non-negotiable, but the cost of the labor is where the bargaining begins.

Continue up the River Street Mall and cross the Nuuanu Stream via the bridge at Kukui Street, which will bring you to the:

8 Izumo Taisha Mission Cultural Hall

This small, wooden Shinto shrine, built in 1923, houses a male deity (look for the X-shaped crosses on the top). Members of the faith ring the bell out front as an act of purification when they come to pray. Inside the temple is a 100-pound sack of rice, symbolizing good health. During World War II, the shrine was confiscated by the city of Honolulu and wasn't returned to the congregation until 1962.

If temples interest you, walk a block toward the mountains to Vineyard Boulevard; cross back over Nuuanu Stream, past the entrance of Foster Botanical Gardens, to:

9 Kuan Yin Temple

This Buddhist temple, painted in a brilliant red with a green ceramic-tiled roof, is dedicated to Kuan Yin Bodhisattva, the goddess of mercy, whose statue towers in the prayer hall. The aroma of burning incense is your clue that the temple is still a house of worship, not an exhibit, so enter with respect and leave your shoes outside. You may see people burning paper "money" for prosperity and good luck, or leaving flowers and fruits at the altar (gifts to the goddess). A common offering is the *pomelo,* a grapefruitlike fruit that's a fertility symbol as well as a gift, indicating a request for the blessing of children.

Continue down Vineyard and then turn right (toward the ocean) on:

10 Maunakea Street

Between Beretania and King streets are numerous **lei shops** (with lei-makers working away right on the premises). The air is heavy with the aroma of flowers being woven into beautiful treasures. Not only is this the best place in all of Hawaii to get a deal on leis, but the size, color, and design of the leis made here are exceptional. Wander through the shops before you decide which lei you want.

TAKE A BREAK

If you have a sweet tooth, stop in at **Shung Chong Yuein** ★, 1027 Maunakea St. (near Hotel St.), for delicious Asian pastries such as moon cakes and almond cookies, all at very reasonable prices. The shop also has a wide selection of dried and sugared candies (such as ginger, pineapple, and lotus root) that you can eat as you stroll or give as an exotic gift to friends back home.

Turn left on Hotel Street and walk in the Diamond Head (east) direction to:

11 Nuuanu Avenue

You may notice that the sidewalks on Nuuanu are made of granite blocks; they came from the ballasts of ships that brought tea from China to Hawaii in the 1800s. On the corner of Nuuanu Avenue and Hotel Street is **Lai Fong Department Store,** a classic Chinatown store owned by the same family for more than 75 years. Walking into Lai Fong is like stepping back in time. The old store sells everything from precious antiques to god-awful knickknacks to rare turn-of-the-century Hawaiian postcards— but it has built its reputation on its fabulous selection of Chinese silks, brocades, and custom dresses.

Between Hotel and Pauahi streets is the **Pegge Hopper Gallery,** 1164 Nuuanu Ave., where you can admire Pegge's well-known paintings of beautiful Hawaiian women.

At Pauahi Street, turn right (toward Diamond Head) and walk up to Bethel Street and the:

12 Hawaii Theatre

This restored 1920 Art Deco theater is a work of art in itself. It hosts a variety of programs, from the Hawaii International Film Festival to beauty pageants (see chapter 9, "Oahu After Dark," for how to find out what's on).

Turn right onto Bethel and walk toward the ocean. Turn right again onto Hotel Street, which will lead you back to where you started.

GETTING THERE: From Waikiki, take Ala Moana Boulevard in the Ewa direction. When Ala Moana ends, turn left on Nimitz Highway. Park on the ocean side of Nimitz at Bishop Street. TheBus: 19 or 20.

START: Aloha Tower, ocean end of Fort Street Mall at Pier 9.

FINISH: Waterfront Plaza and Restaurant Row, Punchbowl Street/Ala Moana Boulevard.

TIME: About 1 to 2 hours, depending on how long you linger in museums and shops.

BEST TIME: Daylight, when the Hawaii Maritime Museum is open (8:30am–5pm daily).

For a look into Honolulu's past when Polynesians first came to Hawaii, take this stroll along the waterfront and the surrounding environs.

Until about 1800, the area around Honolulu Harbor (from Nuuanu Ave. to Alakea St., and from Hotel St. to the ocean) was known as *Koa*. Some scholars say it was named after a dedicated officer to Chief Kakuhihewa of Oahu; others say it comes from the koa tree, which flourishes in this area. In 1793, Captain William Brown, on the British frigate *Butterworth,* sailed the first foreign ship into Honolulu harbor. Like most British explorers, he didn't bother to ask about the name of the harbor; instead, he just called it Fair Haven. Other ships that followed started to call the harbor "Brown's Harbor." Luckily, the name the Hawaiians gave the harbor, Honolulu, which translates into "sheltered bay," became the popular name.

The waterfront area played a vital role in the history of Honolulu. King Kamehameha I moved his royal court here in 1809 to keep an eye on the burgeoning trade from the numerous ships that were coming here. The royal residence was at the makai end of Bethel Street, just 1 block from the start of our tour at the Aloha Tower.

Park in the parking lot on Bishop Street and Nimitz Highway and walk over to Pier 9 to:

❶ Aloha Tower

One of the reasons that the word *aloha* is synonymous with Hawaii is because of the Aloha Tower. Built in 1926 (for the then-outrageous sum of $160,000), this 184-foot, 10-story tower (until 1959, the tallest structure in Hawaii) has clocks on all four of its sides, with the word *aloha* under each clock. Aloha, which has come to mean both "hello" and "farewell," was the first thing steamship passengers saw when they entered Honolulu Harbor. In the days when tourists arrived by steamer, "boat days" were very big occasions. The Royal Hawaiian band would be on hand to play, crowds would gather, flower leis were freely given, and Honolulu came to a standstill to greet the visitors.

Go up the elevator inside the Aloha Tower to the **10th-floor observation deck** for a bird's-eye view that encompasses Diamond Head and Waikiki, the downtown and Chinatown areas, and the harbor coastline to the airport. On the ocean side you can see the harbor mouth, Sand Island, the Honolulu reef runway, and the Pearl Harbor entrance channel. No charge to see the view; the Aloha Tower is open daily 9am to 5pm.

Next to the tower is the:

❷ Aloha Tower Marketplace

In the early 1990s, city officials came up with the idea to renovate and restore the waterfront with shops, restaurants, and bars to bring back the feeling of "boat days." The shops, restaurants, and bars inside the two-story Aloha Tower Marketplace offer an array of cuisines, one-of-a-kind shops, and even a microbrewery. Most shops open at 9am daily and the restaurants and bars don't shut down until the wee hours of the morning.

From the Aloha Tower Marketplace, walk in the Diamond Head direction along the waterfront to Pier 7, where you'll find the:

❸ Hawaii Maritime Center

As we went to press, the Hawaii Maritime Center was a victim of the economy and had temporarily closed. Be sure to call (℃ **808/536-6373**) to see if it has reopened by the time you arrive here. The center is composed of three entities: the museum, which is in the Kalakaua Boathouse; the *Falls of Clyde*, the four-masted ship moored next door; and the *Hokulea*, the 60-foot Polynesian sailing canoe, also moored at Pier 7. See p. 192 to learn more about the center.

Moored next door to the Boathouse is the:

❹ Falls of Clyde

The world's only remaining fully rigged, four-masted ship is on display as a National Historic Landmark. Still afloat, the 266-foot, iron-hulled ship was built in 1878 in Glasgow, Scotland. Matson Navigation bought the ship in 1899 to carry sugar and passengers between Hilo and San Francisco. When that became economically unfeasible, in 1906 the boat was converted into a sail-driven oil tanker. After 1920, it was dismantled and became a floating oil depot for fishing boats in Alaska.

She was headed for the scrap pile when a group of Hawaiian residents raised the money to bring her back to Hawaii in 1963. Since then she has been totally restored, and now visitors can wander across her decks and through the cargo area below.

After viewing the *Falls of Clyde*, wander over to the:

❺ Hokulea

If you're lucky, the 60-foot Polynesian canoe will be docked, but it's often out on jaunts. In 1976, this reproduction of the traditional double-hulled sailing canoe proved to the world that the Polynesians could have made the 6,000-mile round-trip from Tahiti to Hawaii, navigating only by the stars and the wave patterns. Living on an open deck (9 ft. wide by 40 ft. long), the crew of a dozen, along with a traditional navigator from an island in the Northern Pacific, made the successful voyage. Since then there has been a renaissance in the Pacific among native islanders to relearn this art of navigation.

Next door, at Pier 6, you'll find the:

❻ Navatek I

From ancient Polynesian sailing canoes to today's high-tech boats, *Navatek I* is the latest specimen in naval engineering. The 140-foot-long vessel isn't even called a boat; it's actually a SWATH (Small Waterplane Area Twin Hull) vessel. That means the ship's superstructure—the part you ride on—rests on twin torpedolike hulls that cut through the water so you don't bob like a cork. It's the smoothest ride in town and guarantees you will not get seasick or spill your mai tai.

From Pier 6, walk down Ala Moana Boulevard and turn mauka at Punchbowl, where you'll come to:

❼ Waterfront Plaza & Restaurant Row

Eateries serving an array of cuisines (from gourmet Hawaii regional cuisine to burgers), shops, and theaters fill this block-long complex. This is a great place to stop for lunch or dinner, or for a cool drink at the end of your walk.

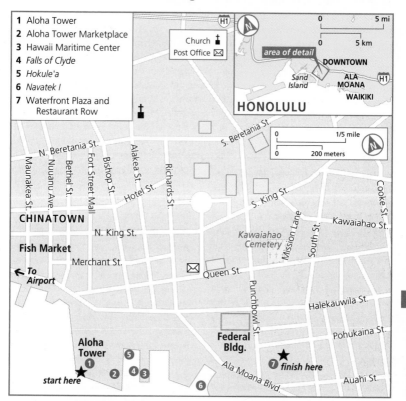

1 Aloha Tower
2 Aloha Tower Marketplace
3 Hawaii Maritime Center
4 *Falls of Clyde*
5 *Hokule'a*
6 *Navatek I*
7 Waterfront Plaza and
Restaurant Row

Church
Post Office

area of detail

DOWNTOWN

Sand
Island

ALA
MOANA

WAIKIKI

HONOLULU

0   1/5 mile
0   200 meters

N. Beretania St.

S. Beretania St.

Maunakea St.
Nuuanu Ave.
Bethel St.
Fort Street Mall
Bishop St.
Alakea St.
Hotel St.
Richards St.
Cooke St.

CHINATOWN

S. King St.

Kawaiahao St.

N. King St.

Fish Market

Kawaiahao
Cemetery

Mission Lane
South St.

Merchant St.

To
Airport

Queen St.

Halekauwila St.

Pohukaina St.

Aloha
Tower

Federal
Bldg.

start here

finish here

Ala Moana Blvd.

Auahi St.

EXPLORING OAHU

7

WALKING TOUR 3: HISTORIC HONOLULU

WALKING TOUR 3   HISTORIC HONOLULU

GETTING THERE:	From Waikiki, take Ala Moana Boulevard in the Ewa direction. Ala Moana Boulevard ends at Nimitz Highway. Turn right on the next street on your right (Alakea St.). Park in the garage across from St. Andrews Church after you cross Beretania Street. TheBus: 1, 2, 3, 4, 11, 12, or 50.
START:	St. Andrew's Church, Beretania and Alakea streets.
FINISH:	Same place.
TIME:	2 to 3 hours, depending on how long you linger in museums.
BEST TIME:	Tuesday through Saturday, daytime, when the Iolani Palace has tours.

The 1800s were a turbulent time in Hawaii. By the end of the 1790s, Kamehameha the Great had united all the islands. Foreigners then began arriving by ship—first explorers, then merchants, and in 1820, missionaries. The rulers of Hawaii were hard-pressed to keep up. By 1840 it was clear that the capital had shifted from Lahaina, Maui, where the Kingdom of Hawaii was actually centered, to Honolulu, where the majority of commerce and trade was taking place. In 1848, the Great Mahele (division) enabled commoners and eventually foreigners to own crown land, and in two generations, more than 80% of all private lands had shifted to foreign ownership. With the introduction of sugar as a crop, the foreigners prospered, and in time they put more and more pressures on the government.

By 1872, the monarchy had run through the Kamehameha line and in 1873 David Kalakaua was elected to the throne. Known as the "Merrie Monarch," Kalakaua redefined the monarchy by going on a world tour, building Iolani Palace, having a European-style coronation, and throwing extravagant parties. By the end of the 1800s, however, the foreign sugar growers and merchants had become extremely powerful in Hawaii. With the assistance of the U.S. Marines, they orchestrated the overthrow of Queen Liliuokalani, Hawaii's last reigning monarch, in 1893. The United States declared Hawaii a territory in 1898.

You can witness the remnants of these turbulent years in just a few short blocks.

Cross the street from the church parking lot and venture back to 1858 when you enter:

❶ St. Andrew's Church

The Hawaiian monarchs were greatly influenced by the royals in Europe. When King Kamehameha IV saw the grandeur of the Church of England, he decided to build his own cathedral. He and Queen Emma founded the Anglican Church of Hawaii in 1858. The king, however, didn't live to see the church completed; he died on St. Andrew's Day, 4 years before King Kamehameha V oversaw the laying of the cornerstone in 1867. The church was named St. Andrew's in honor of King Kamehameha IV's death. This French-Gothic structure was shipped in pieces from England and reassembled here. Even if you aren't fond of visiting churches, you have to see the floor-to-eaves hand-blown stained-glass window that faces the setting sun. In the glass is a mural of Rev. Thomas Staley, the first bishop of Hawaii; King Kamehameha IV; and Queen Emma. The church's excellent thrift shop has some real bargains and is open Monday, Wednesday, and Friday 9:30am to 4pm and Saturday 9am to 1pm.

Next, walk down Beretania Street in the Diamond Head direction to the gates of:

❷ Washington Place

Once the residence of the Governor of Hawaii (sorry, no tours; just peek through the iron fence), it nevertheless occupies a distinguished place in Hawaii's history. The Greek revival–style home, built in 1842 by a U.S. sea captain named John Dominis, got its name from the U.S. ambassador who once stayed there and told so many stories about President George Washington that people started calling the home Washington Place. The sea captain's son, also named John, married a beautiful Hawaiian princess, Lydia Kapaakea, who later became Hawaii's last queen, Liliuokalani. When the queen was overthrown by U.S. businessmen in 1893, she moved out of Iolani Palace and into her husband's inherited home, Washington Place, where she lived until her death in 1917. On the left side of the building, near the sidewalk, is a plaque inscribed with the words to one of the most popular songs written by Queen Liliuokalani, "Aloha Oe" ("Farewell to Thee").

Cross the street and walk to the front of the Hawaii State Capitol, where you'll find the:

❸ Father Damien Statue

The people of Hawaii have never forgotten the sacrifice this Belgian priest made to help the sufferers of leprosy when he volunteered to work with them in exile on the Kalaupapa Peninsula on the island of Molokai. After 16 years of service, Father Damien died of leprosy, at the age of 49. The statue is frequently draped in leis in recognition of Father Damien's humanitarian work.

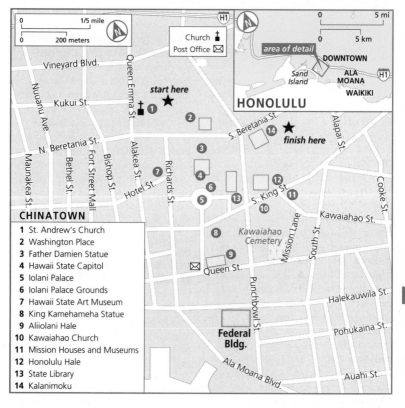

0   1/5 mile

0   200 meters

Church †
Post Office ✉

0   5 mi

0   5 km

area of detail

DOWNTOWN

HONOLULU

Sand Island

ALA MOANA

WAIKIKI

H1

Vineyard Blvd.

Queen Emma St.

Nuuanu Ave.

Kukui St.

start here

❶

❷

N. Beretania St.

S. Beretania St.

❸

❹

❺

❻

❼

❽

❾

❿

⓫

⓬

⓭

⓮

finish here

Alapai St.

Cooke St.

Maunakea St.

Bethel St.

Fort Street Mall

Bishop St.

Alakea St.

Hotel St.

Richards St.

Queen St.

Kawaiahao Cemetery

Mission Lane

South St.

Punchbowl St.

Kawaiahao St.

Federal Bldg.

Halekauwila St.

Pohukaina St.

Ala Moana Blvd.

Auahi St.

S. King St.

CHINATOWN

1 St. Andrew's Church
2 Washington Place
3 Father Damien Statue
4 Hawaii State Capitol
5 Iolani Palace
6 Iolani Palace Grounds
7 Hawaii State Art Museum
8 King Kamehameha Statue
9 Aliiolani Hale
10 Kawaiahao Church
11 Mission Houses and Museums
12 Honolulu Hale
13 State Library
14 Kalanimoku

Behind Father Damien's statue is the:

❹ Hawaii State Capitol

Here's where Hawaii's state legislators work from mid-January to the end of April every year. This is not your typical white dome structure, but a building symbolic of Hawaii. Unfortunately, it symbolizes more of Hawaii than the architect and the state legislature probably bargained for. The building's unusual design has palm-tree-shaped pillars, two cone-shaped chambers (representing volcanoes) for the legislative bodies, and in the inner courtyard, a 600,000-tile mosaic of the sea (Aquarius) created by a local artist. A reflecting pool (representing the sea) surrounds the entire structure. Like a lot of things in Hawaii, it was a great idea, but no one considered the logistics. The reflecting pond also draws brackish water, which rusts the hardware; when it rains, water pours into the rotunda, dampening government business; and the Aquarius floor mosaic became so damaged by the elements that it became a hazard. In the 1990s, the entire building (built in 1969) was closed for a couple of years for renovations, forcing the legislature to set up temporary quarters in several buildings. It's open again, and you are welcome to go into the rotunda and see the woven hangings and murals at the entrance, or take the elevator up to the fifth floor for a spectacular view of the city's historical center.

EXPLORING OAHU

7

WALKING TOUR 3: HISTORIC HONOLULU

Walk down Richards Street toward the ocean and stop at:

❺ Iolani Palace

Hawaii is the only state in the U.S. to have not one, but two royal palaces; one in Kona (on Big Island), where the royals went during the summer, and Iolani Palace (*Iolani* means "royal hawk"). Don't miss the opportunity to see this grande dame of historic buildings. Tours are limited. Admission is $15 for adults, $5 for children ages 5 to 13. Guided tours are offered Tuesday through Saturday 9am to 2:15pm; call ✆ **808/522-0832** for advance reservations.

In ancient times a *heiau* stood in this area. When it became clear to King Kamehameha III that the capital should be transferred from Lahaina to Honolulu, he moved to a modest building here in 1845. The construction of the palace was undertaken by King David Kalakaua and was begun in 1879; it was finished 3 years later at a cost of $350,000. The king spared no expense: You can still see the glass and iron work imported from San Francisco. The palace had all the modern conveniences of its time: Electric lights were installed 4 years before the White House had them; every bedroom had its own full bathroom with hot and cold running water and copper-lined tub, a flush toilet, and a bidet. The king had a telephone line from the palace to his boathouse on the water a year after Alexander Graham Bell introduced it to the world.

It was also in this palace that Queen Liliuokalani was overthrown and placed under house arrest for 9 months. Later, the territorial and then the state government used the palace until it outgrew it. When the legislature left in 1968, the palace was in shambles and has since undergone a $7-million overhaul to restore it to its former glory.

After you visit the palace, spend some time on the:

❻ Iolani Palace Grounds

You can wander around the grounds at no charge. The ticket window to the palace and the gift shop are in the former barracks of the Royal Household Guards. The domed pavilion on the grounds was originally built as a Coronation Stand by King Kalakaua (9 years after he took the throne, he decided to have a formal European-style coronation ceremony where he crowned himself and his queen, Kapiolani). Later he used it as a **Royal Bandstand** for concerts (King Kalakaua, along with Herni Berger, the 1st Royal Hawaiian Bandmaster, wrote "Hawaii Pono'i," the state anthem). Today the Royal Bandstand is still used for concerts by the Royal Hawaiian Band. The more modern building on the grounds is the **State Archives,** built in 1953, which holds records, documents, and photos of Hawaii's people and its history.

From the palace grounds, turn in the Ewa direction, cross Richards Street, and walk to the corner of Richards and Hotel streets to the:

❼ Hawaii State Art Museum

Opened in 2002, the Hawaii State Art Museum is housed in the original Royal Hawaiian Hotel built in 1872, during the reign of King Kamehameha V. All of the 360 works currently displayed were created by artists who live in Hawaii. The pieces were purchased by the state thanks to a 1967 law that says that 1% of the cost of state buildings will be used to acquire works of art. Nearly 4 decades later, the state has amassed some 5,000 pieces. The current exhibit depicts Hawaii, its history, culture, and ideals, through a variety of mediums.

Walk makai down Richards Street and turn left (toward Diamond Head) on S. King Street to the:

❽ King Kamehameha Statue

At the juncture of King, Merchant, and Mililani streets stands a replica of the man who united the Hawaiian Islands. The striking black-and-gold bronze statue is magnificent. The best day to see the statue is on June 11 (King Kamehameha Day), when it is covered with leis in honor of Hawaii's favorite son.

The statue of Kamehameha I was cast by Thomas Gould in 1880 in Paris. However, it was lost at sea somewhere near the Falkland Islands. Subsequently, the insurance money was used to pay for a second statue, but in the meantime, the original statue was recovered. The original was eventually sent to the town of Kapaau on the Big Island, the birthplace of Kamehameha, and the second statue was placed in Honolulu in 1883, as part of King David Kalakaua's coronation ceremony. A third statue (all three are very different, but they were supposedly all cast from the same mold) was sent to Washington, D.C., when Hawaii became a state in 1959.

Right behind King Kamehameha's statue is:

9 Aliiolani Hale

This "House of Heavenly Kings," with its distinctive clock tower, now houses the State Judiciary Building. King Kamehameha V originally wanted to build a palace here and commissioned the Australian architect Thomas Rowe in 1872. However, it ended up as the first major government building for the Hawaiian monarchy. Kamehameha V didn't live to see it completed, and King David Kalakaua dedicated the building in 1874. Ironically, less than 20 years later, on January 17, 1893, Stanford Dole, backed by other prominent sugar planters, stood on the steps to this building and proclaimed the overthrow of the Hawaiian monarchy and the establishment of a provisional government. Tours are conducted Tuesday through Thursday, 10am to 3pm (no charge).

Walk toward Diamond Head on King Street; at the corner of King and Punchbowl, stop in at:

10 Kawaiahao Church

When the missionaries came to Hawaii, the first thing they did was build churches. Four thatched grass churches (one measured 54 ft.×22 ft. and could seat 300 people on lauhala mats; the last thatched church held 4,500 people) had been built

on this site through 1837 before Rev. Hiram Bingham began building what he considered a "real" church—a New England–style congregational structure with Gothic influences. Between 1837 and 1842, the building of the church required some 14,000 giant coral slabs (some weighing more than 1,000 lb.). Hawaiian divers literally raped the reefs, digging out huge chunks of coral and causing irreparable environmental damage.

Kawaiahao is Hawaii's oldest church, and it has been the site of numerous historical events, such as a speech made by King Kamehameha III in 1843, an excerpt from which became Hawaii's state motto (*"Ua mau ke ea o ka aina i ka pono,"* which translates as "The life of the land is preserved in righteousness").

The clock tower in the church, which was donated by King Kamehameha III and installed in 1850, continues to tick today. The church is open Monday through Saturday, from 8am to 4pm; you'll find it to be very cool in temperature. Don't sit in the pews in the back, marked with kahili feathers and velvet cushions; they are still reserved for the descendants of royalty. Sunday service (in Hawaiian) is at 10:30am.

Cross the street, and you'll see the:

11 Mission Houses & Museums

On the corner of King and Kawaiahao streets stand the original buildings of the Sandwich Islands Mission Headquarters: the **Frame House** (built in 1821), the **Chamberlain House** (1831), and the **Printing Office** (1841). The complex is open Tuesday through Saturday from 10am to 4pm; admission is $10 for adults, $8 for military personnel and seniors, $6 for children ages 6 to college. The tours are often led by descendants of the original missionaries to Hawaii.

Believe it or not, the missionaries brought their own prefab house along with them when they came around Cape

Horn from Boston in 1819. The Frame House was designed for frigid New England winters and had small windows. (It must have been stiflingly hot inside.) Finished in 1921 (the interior frame was left behind and didn't arrive until Christmas 1920), it is Hawaii's oldest wooden structure. The Chamberlain House, built in 1931, was used by the missionaries as a storehouse.

The missionaries believed that the best way to spread the Lord's message to the Hawaiians was to learn their language and then to print literature for them to read. So it was the missionaries who gave the Hawaiians a written language. The Printing House on the grounds was where the lead-type Ramage press (brought from New England, of course) printed the Hawaiian Bible.

Cross King Street and walk in the Ewa direction to the corner of Punchbowl and King to:

⑫ **Honolulu Hale**

The **Honolulu City Hall,** built in 1927, was designed by Honolulu's most famous

architect, C. W. Dickey. His Spanish mission–style building has an open-air courtyard, which is used for art exhibits and concerts. Open weekdays.

Cross Punchbowl Street and walk mauka to the:

⑬ **State Library**

Anything you want to know about Hawaii and the Pacific can be found here, the main branch of the state's library system. Located in a restored historic building, it has an open garden courtyard in the middle, great for stopping for a rest on your walk.

Head mauka up Punchbowl to the corner of Punchbowl and Beretania streets, to:

⑭ **Kalanimoku**

The beautiful name, "Ship of Heaven," has been given to this dour state office building. Here you can get information on hiking and camping (from the Department of Land and Natural Resources) in state parks.

Retrace your steps in the Ewa direction down Beretania to Alakea back to the parking garage.

WALKING TOUR 4   KAPIOLANI PARK

GETTING THERE:	From Waikiki, walk toward Diamond Head on Kalakaua Avenue. If you're coming by car, the cheapest parking is metered street parking on Kalakaua Avenue adjacent to the park. TheBus: 19 or 20.
START:	Waikiki Beach Center, Kalakaua Avenue, Diamond Head side of the Sheraton Moana Hotel, across the street from the Hyatt Regency and Uluniu Avenue.
FINISH:	Kapiolani Beach Park.
TIME:	4 to 5 hours. Allow at least an hour each for walking around the park, wandering around the zoo, and exploring the aquarium, plus all the time you want for the beach.
BEST TIME:	Weekday mornings.

On June 11, 1877, King Kamehameha Day, then-King David Kalakaua donated some 140 acres of land to the people of Hawaii for Hawaii's first park. He asked that the park be named after his beloved wife, Queen Kapiolani, and he celebrated the opening of this vast grassy area with a free concert and "high stakes" horse races (the king loved gambling) on the new horse-racing oval he had built below Diamond Head.

The horse races, and the gambling that accompanied it, were eventually outlawed, but the park—and the free concerts—live on. Just a coconut's throw from the high-rise concrete jungle of Waikiki lies this 133-acre grassy park (the Paki playground and a fire station make up the remaining acreage) dotted with spreading banyans, huge monkeypod trees,

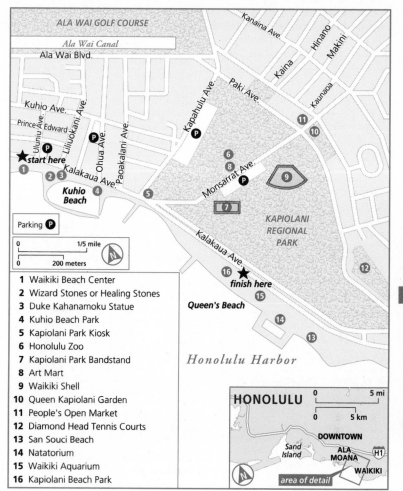

EXPLORING OAHU

7

WALKING TOUR 4: KAPIOLANI PARK

blooming royal poincianas, and swaying ironwoods. Throughout the open spaces are jogging paths, tennis courts, soccer and cricket fields, and even an archery range. People come to the park to listen to music, watch ethnic dancing, exercise, enjoy team sports, take long meditative walks, picnic, buy art, smell the roses, and just relax. The park is the site of international kite-flying contests, the finishing line for the Honolulu marathon, and the home of yearly Scottish highland games, Hawaiian cultural festivals, and about a zillion barbecues and picnics.

Start at the:

❶ Waikiki Beach Center

On the ocean side of Kalakaua Avenue, next to the Sheraton Moana Hotel, is a complex of restrooms, showers, surfboard lockers, rental concessions, and the Waikiki police substation.

On the Diamond Head side of the police substation are the:

❷ Wizard Stones or Healing Stones

These four basalt boulders, which weigh several tons apiece and sit on a lava rock platform, are held sacred by the Hawaiian people.

The story goes that sometime before the 15th century, four powerful healers from Moaulanuiakea, in the Society Islands, named Kapaemahu, Kahaloa, Kapuni, and Kihohi, lived in the Ulukoa area of Waikiki. After years of healing the people and the alii of Oahu, they wished to return home. They asked the people to erect four monuments made of bell stone, a basalt rock that was found in a Kaimuki quarry and that produced a bell-like ringing when struck. The healers spent a ceremonious month transferring their spiritual healing power, or *mana,* to the stones. The great mystery is how the boulders were transported from Kaimuki to the marshland near Kuhio Beach in Waikiki. Over time a bowling alley was built on the spot, and the stones got buried beneath the structure. After the bowling alley was torn down in the 1960s, tourists used the stones for picnicking or drying their wet towels. In 1997, the stones were once again given a place of prominence with the construction of a $75,000 shrine that includes the platform and a wrought-iron fence. Since then the stones have become something of a mecca for students and patients of traditional healing.

Just west of the stones you'll find the:

❸ Duke Kahanamoku Statue

Here, cast in bronze, is Hawaii's most famous athlete, also known as the father of modern surfing. Duke (1890–1968) won Olympic swimming medals in 1912, 1920, 1924, and 1928. He was enshrined in both the Swimming Hall of Fame and the Surfing Hall of Fame. He also traveled around the world promoting surfing. When the city of Honolulu first erected the statue of this lifelong ocean athlete, they placed it with his back to the water. There was public outcry, because no one familiar with the ocean would ever stand with his back to it. To quell the outcry, the city moved the statue closer to the sidewalk.

Continuing in the Diamond Head direction, you'll come to:

❹ Kuhio Beach Park

The two small swimming spots here are great, but heed the warning sign: Watch out for holes. Deep holes are in the sandy bottom, and you may suddenly find yourself in over your head. The best pool for swimming is the one on the Diamond Head end, but the water circulation is questionable—there sometimes appears to be a layer of suntan lotion floating on the surface. If the waves are up, watch the boogie boarders surf by the seawall. They ride toward the wall and at the last minute veer away with a swoosh.

After watching the surfers, walk down Kalakaua Avenue (toward Diamond Head) to the entrance of Kapiolani Park, where you'll see the:

❺ Kapiolani Park Kiosk

On the corner of Kalakaua and Kapahulu avenues, this small display stand contains brochures and actual photos of the park's history. It also carries information on upcoming events at the various sites within the park (Aquarium, Zoo, Waikiki Shell, and Kapiolani Bandstand). An informative map will orient you to the park grounds.

Continue up Kapahulu Avenue to the entrance of the:

❻ Honolulu Zoo

The city's 42-acre zoo is open every day from 9am to 4:30pm, but the best time to go is as soon as the gates open—the animals seem to be more active and we agree—it is a lot cooler than in the hot midday sun. See p. 197.

Trace your steps back to Kapahulu and Kalakaua avenues and head mauka down Monsarrat Avenue to the:

❼ Kapiolani Park Bandstand

Once upon a time, from 1937 to 2002, the **Kodak Hula Show** presented the art of hula to visitors, with some 3,000 people squeezed into the bleachers around a grassy stage area every day. The Kodak Hula Show is gone now, but the bandstand is still used for concerts and special events.

Back on Monsarrat Avenue, on the fence facing the zoo, you'll find the:

❽ Art Mart

The Artists of Oahu Exhibit is the new official name of this display. Here, local artisans hang their artwork on a fence for the public to view and buy. Not only do you get to meet the artists, but you also have an opportunity to purchase their work at a considerable discount from the prices you'll see in galleries. Exhibits are Saturday, Sunday, and Wednesday, 10am to 4pm.

Cross Monsarrat Avenue, and you'll see the:

❾ Waikiki Shell

This open-air amphitheater hosts numerous musical shows, from the Honolulu Symphony to traditional Hawaiian music.

Continue walking down till the end of the block (corner of Monsarrat and Paki aves.) to the:

❿ Queen Kapiolani Garden

You'll see a range of hibiscus plants and dozens of varieties of roses, including the somewhat rare Hawaiian rose. The tranquil gardens are always open and are a great place to wander and relax.

Across the street, on a Wednesday morning, you'll find the:

⓫ People's Open Market

Open from 10 to 11am on Wednesdays, the farmers' market with its open stalls is an excellent spot to buy fresh produce and flowers.

After you make your purchases, continue in the Diamond Head direction down Paki Avenue to the:

⓬ Diamond Head Tennis Courts

Located on the mauka side of Paki Avenue, the free City and County tennis courts are open for play during daylight hours 7 days a week. Tennis etiquette suggests that if someone is waiting for a court, limit your play to 45 minutes.

After watching or playing, turn onto Kalakaua Avenue and begin walking back toward Waikiki to:

⓭ Sans Souci Beach

Located next to the New Otani Kaimana Beach Hotel, this is one of the best swimming beaches in Waikiki. The shallow reef, which is close to shore, keeps the waters calm. Farther out is good snorkeling in the coral reef by the Kapua Channel. Facilities include outdoor showers and a lifeguard.

After a brief swim, keep walking toward Waikiki until you come to the:

⓮ Natatorium

This huge concrete structure next to the beach is both a memorial to the soldiers of World War I and a 100-meter saltwater swimming pool. Opened in 1927, when Honolulu had hopes of hosting the Olympics, the ornate swimming pool fell into disuse and disrepair after World War II, and was finally closed in 1979. The last mayor of The City and County of Honolulu wanted to reopen the saltwater pool and poured $4.4 million into restoring the outside arches to the building, construction of modern restrooms and showers, and refurbishment of the bleacher seating. The new mayor is balking at spending the estimated $11.5 million more needed to make the saltwater swimming pool usable again. The controversy rages on. Stop by and take a peek at this once-magnificent site.

After a brief stop here, continue on to the:

⓯ Waikiki Aquarium

The Aquarium is located at 2777 Kalakaua Ave. Try not to miss this stop—the tropical aquarium is worth a look if only

The President Lived Here, and Here, and Here....

President Barack Obama was born and raised on the island of Oahu. Several visitors have expressed interest in tracing the roots of our 44th president. His family moved several times during his childhood, but generally stayed within the **Makiki-Manoa neighborhoods,** a lush residential area, nestled between the blue waves of Waikiki Beach and the verdant green vegetation of Mt. Tantalus.

The story really starts at the **University of Hawaii at Manoa** in 1960, where the president's father, Barack Obama Sr., a student from Kenya and the school's first African student, meet his mother, Stanley Ann Dunham, during a Russian language class. The couple got married on the island of Maui on February 2, 1961. On August 4, 1961, Ann gave birth to Barack Jr. at the **Kapiolani Hospital for Women and Children.**

The future president's first home was about five miles from the Makiki neighborhood in the very swank address of **Hawaii Kai** (6085 Kalaniana'ole Highway) in a small bungalow behind the main house.

In 1962, Obama's parents separated when his father went to Harvard on a scholarship. The next year, his mother, still a college student at the University of Hawaii, moved to **2277 Kamehamaha Ave.,** a few blocks from the university (unfortunately the building has been torn down and replaced with a new structure). During this time, Barack and his mother frequently visited her parents, Stanley and Madelyn Dunham, who lived in the **Makiki area** in a two-bedroom apartment (#110) at **1427 Alexander Street.**

In 1964, the Dunhams, along with their daughter and now-famous grandson, moved to a prestigious address in **Manoa Valley,** at **2234 University Ave.,** into a four-bedroom, single-story house (built in 1947) with wide lanais and a spacious lawn. A desired address of university professors, Manoa Valley offered an older, mature neighborhood of swaying eucalyptus trees and fragrant flowers. The home also was walking distance to the future president's first school, **Noelani** (which translates as "heavenly mist"), **Elementary School,** which still today is considered one of the best elementary schools on Oahu.

In 1967, Ann Dunham married another UH student, Lolo Soetoro. The 6-year-old Barack, his mother and new stepfather moved to Jakarta, Indonesia.

to see the only living **chambered nautilus** born in captivity. For more details, see p. 200.

Your final stop is:

⓰ Kapiolani Beach Park

Relax on the stretch of grassy lawn alongside the sandy beach, one of the best-kept secrets of Waikiki. This beach park is much less crowded than the beaches of Waikiki, plus it has adjacent grassy lawns, barbecue areas, picnic tables, restrooms, and showers. The swimming is good here year-round, a surfing spot known as "Public's" is offshore, and there's always a game going at the volleyball courts. The middle section of the beach park, in front of the pavilion, is known as Queen's Beach or Queen's Surf and is popular with the gay community.

When he was 10 years old, Barack returned to Hawaii and lived with his grandparents, the Dunhams, who had moved back to **Makiki** to an apartment building, called **Punahou Circle,** located at **1617 S. Bertania St.** They lived in apartment #1206, and in 1973, moved into unit #1008. Barack's grandmother, Madelyn Dunham (whom he called "Toot," short for tutu, the Hawaiian word for grandmother) lived here until her death on November 3, 2008. The 96-unit building is still standing today.

A couple of years later, the president's mother, now known as Ann Dunham Sutoro (a modern spelling of her former husband's last name), returned to Hawaii with Barack's new 3-year-old sister, Maya. His mother had separated from her second husband and came back to Hawaii to study anthropology at the University of Hawaii. The family moved about 6 blocks from her parents into a small apartment building at **1839 Poki St.**

The future 44th president attended Hawaii's most prestigious private school, **Punahou,** from the fifth grade until his graduation in 1979. Founded in 1841, Punahou (which translates as "new spring") is where the movers and shakers in Hawaii send their children. The 76-acre complex resembles a college campus, where some 3,750 students in grades kindergarten to 12 wander the mani- cured grounds between the historic and architecturally-designed buildings. In fact, *Sports Illustrated* recently ranked the Punahou sports program the best out of some 38,000 high schools in the United States.

Obama, who was called "Barry" in high school, was nicknamed "Obomber" for his antics on the high school basketball team. The future president also worked during high school, scooping ice cream at the local **Baskin Robbins** (1618 S. King St., near Punahou St.), within walking distance of his school and home.

Since becoming the 44th president, Barack Obama has returned to the 50th state a few times: playing at Olomana Golf Links, Luana Hills Country Club, and Mid-Pacific Country Club; visiting the **Valley of the Temples Memorial Park** (p. 226); visiting the **Punchbowl Cemetery** (p. 193); stopping at the **Pali Look- out** (p. 202); spending time at the **USS** *Arizona* **Memorial at Pearl Harbor** (p. 194); having a picnic lunch at **Ala Moana Beach Park** (p. 153); and taking the kids to the **Honolulu Zoo** (p. 197).

6 BEYOND HONOLULU: EXPLORING THE ISLAND

The moment always arrives—usually after a couple of days at the beach, snorkeling in the warm, blue-green waters of Hanauma Bay, enjoying sundown mai tais—when a certain curiosity kicks in about the rest of Oahu, largely unknown to most visitors. It's time to find the rental car in the hotel garage and set out around the island. You can also explore Oahu using **TheBus** (p. 34 for details on the transit system).

For great places to stop for a bite to eat while you're exploring, see chapter 5, "Where to Dine." You also might want to check out chapter 8, "Shopping." Beaches, nature hikes, camping, and other outdoor activities outside of Honolulu are covered in chapter 6.

OAHU'S SOUTHEAST COAST

From the high-rises of Waikiki, venture down Kalakaua Avenue through tree-lined Kapiolani Park to take a look at a different side of Oahu, the arid south shore. The landscape here is more moonscape, with prickly cacti onshore and, in winter, spouting whales cavorting in the water. Some call it the South Shore, others refer to it as Sandy's (after the mile-long beach here), but Hawaiians call it **Ka Iwi,** which means "the bone"—no doubt because of all the bone-cracking shore breaks along this popular bodyboarding coastline. The beaches here are long, wide, and popular with local daredevils.

This open, scenic coast is the best place on Oahu to watch sea, shore, and even land birds. It's also a good whale-watching spot in season, and the night sky is ideal for amateur astronomers on the lookout for meteors, comets, and stars.

To get to this coast, follow Kalakaua Avenue past the multitiered Dillingham Fountain and around the bend in the road, which now becomes Poni Moi Road. Make a right on Diamond Head Road and begin the climb up the side of the old crater. At the top are several lookout points, so if the official Diamond Head Lookout is jammed with cars, try one of the other lookouts just down the road. The view of the rolling waves is spectacular; take the time to pull over.

Diamond Head Road rolls downhill now into the ritzy community of **Kahala.** At the V in the road at triangular Fort Ruger Park, veer to your right and continue on palm-tree-lined Kahala Avenue. Make a left on Hunakai Street, then a right on Kilauea Avenue, and look for the sign: H-1 WEST—WAIMANALO. Turn right at the sign, although you won't get on the H-1 Freeway; get on the Kalanianaole Highway, a four-lane highway interrupted every few blocks by a stoplight. This suburban bedroom community to Honolulu is marked by malls on the left and beach parks on the right.

About a half-hour outside of Waikiki, you'll see the turnoff to **Hanauma Bay ★★** (p. 156) on the right. This marine preserve is a great place to stop for a swim; you'll find the friendliest fish on the island here. *A reminder:* The beach park is closed on Tuesdays.

Around mile marker 11, the jagged lava coast itself spouts sea foam at the **Halona Blowhole.** Look out to sea from Halona over Sandy Beach and across the 26-mile gulf to neighboring Molokai and the faint triangular shadow of Lanai on the far horizon. **Sandy Beach** (p. 157) is Oahu's most dangerous beach; it's the only one with an ambulance always standing by to whisk injured wave catchers to the hospital. Bodyboarders just love it.

The coast looks raw and empty along this stretch, but the road weaves past old Hawaiian fishponds and the famous formation known as **Pele's Chair,** just off Kalanianaole Highway (Hwy. 72) above Queen's Beach. From a distance, the lava-rock outcropping looks like a mighty throne; it's believed to be the fire goddess's last resting place on Oahu before she flew off to continue her work on other islands.

Ahead lies 647-foot-high **Makapuu Point,** with a lighthouse that once signaled safe passage for steamship passengers arriving from San Francisco. The automated light now brightens Oahu's south coast for passing tankers, fishing boats, and sailors. You can take a short hike up here for a spectacular vista (p. 157).

If you're with the kids, you may want to spend the day at **Sea Life Park ★** , a marine amusement park described earlier in this chapter (p. 201).

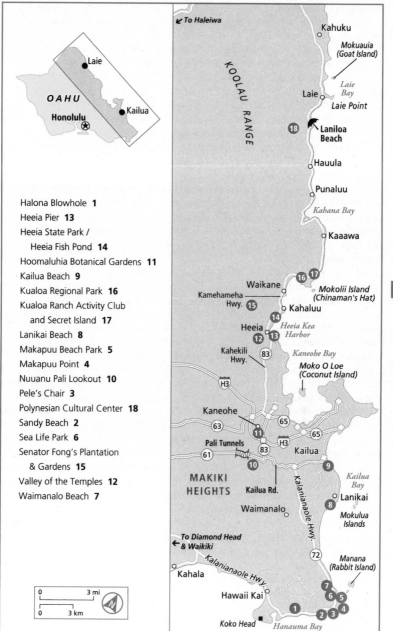

Halona Blowhole **1**
Heeia Pier **13**
Heeia State Park /
 Heeia Fish Pond **14**
Hoomaluhia Botanical Gardens **11**
Kailua Beach **9**
Kualoa Regional Park **16**
Kualoa Ranch Activity Club
 and Secret Island **17**
Lanikai Beach **8**
Makapuu Beach Park **5**
Makapuu Point **4**
Nuuanu Pali Lookout **10**
Pele's Chair **3**
Polynesian Cultural Center **18**
Sandy Beach **2**
Sea Life Park **6**
Senator Fong's Plantation
 & Gardens **15**
Valley of the Temples **12**
Waimanalo Beach **7**

To Haleiwa

Kahuku

Mokuauia
(Goat Island)

KOOLAU RANGE

Laie

Laie
Bay

Laie Point

Laniloa
Beach

Hauula

Punaluu

Kahana Bay

Kaaawa

Waikane

Mokolii Island
(Chinaman's Hat)

Kamehameha
Hwy.

Kahaluu

Heeia Kea
Harbor

Heeia

Kahekili
Hwy.

Kaneohe Bay

Moko O Loe
(Coconut Island)

Kaneohe

Pali Tunnels

Kailua

MAKIKI
HEIGHTS

Kailua Rd.

Kailua
Bay

Lanikai

Mokulua
Islands

Waimanalo

Kalanianaole Hwy.

To Diamond Head
& Waikiki

Manana
(Rabbit Island)

Kahala

Kalanianaole Hwy.

Hawaii Kai

Koko Head

Hanauma Bay

OAHU

Honolulu

Laie

Kailua

0   3 mi
0   3 km

Turn the corner at Makapuu, and you're on Oahu's windward side, where cooling trade winds propel windsurfers across turquoise bays; the waves at **Makapuu Beach Park** are perfect for bodysurfing (p. 157).

Ahead, the coastal vista is a profusion of fluted green mountains and strange peaks, edged by golden beaches and the blue, blue Pacific. The 3,000-foot-high sheer green Koolau Mountains plunge almost straight down, presenting an irresistible jumping-off spot for hang-glider pilots, who catch the thermals on hours-long rides.

Winding up the coast, Kalanianaole Highway (Hwy. 72) leads through rural **Waimanalo,** a country beach town of nurseries and stables, fresh-fruit stands, and some of the island's best conch and triton shell specimens at roadside stands. Nearly 4 miles long, **Waimanalo Beach** is Oahu's longest beach and the most popular for bodysurfing. Take a swim here or head on to **Kailua Beach ★★**, one of Hawaii's best (p. 160).

If it's still early in the day, you can head up the lush, green Windward Coast by turning right at the Castle Junction, Highway 72, and Highway 61 (which is also Kailua Rd. on the makai, or seaward, side of the junction, and Kalanianaole Hwy. on the mauka, or inland, side of the junction), and continuing down Kailua Road (Hwy. 61). After Kailua Road crosses the Kaelepulu Stream, the name of the road changes to Kuulei Road. When Kuulei Road ends, turn left onto Kalaheo Avenue, which becomes Kaneohe Bay Drive after it crosses the Kawainui Channel. Follow this scenic drive around the peninsula until it crosses Kamehameha Highway (Hwy. 83); turn right and continue on Kamehameha Highway for a scenic drive along the ocean.

If you're in a hurry to get back to Waikiki, turn left at Castle Junction and head over the Pali Highway (Hwy. 61), which becomes Bishop Street in Honolulu and ends at Ala Moana. Turn left for Waikiki; it's the second beach on the right.

THE WINDWARD COAST

From the **Nuuanu Pali Lookout ★**, near the summit of the Pali Highway (Hwy. 61), you get the first hint of the other side of Oahu, a region so green and lovely that it could be an island sibling of Tahiti. With its many beaches and bays, the scenic 30-mile Windward Coast parallels the corduroy-ridged, nearly perpendicular cliffs of the Koolau Range, which separates the windward side of the island from Honolulu and the rest of Oahu. As you descend on the serpentine Pali Highway beneath often gushing waterfalls, you'll see the nearly-1,000-foot spike of **Olomana,** the bold pinnacle that always reminds us of Devil's Tower National Monument in Wyoming, and beyond, the Hawaiian village of **Waimanalo.**

From the Pali Highway, to the right is **Kailua,** Hawaii's biggest beach town, with more than 50,000 residents and two special beaches, Kailua and Lanikai, begging for visitors. Funky little Kailua is lined with million-dollar houses next to tarpaper shacks, antiques shops, and bed-and-breakfasts. Although the Pali Highway (Hwy. 61) proceeds directly to the coast, it undergoes two name changes, becoming first Kalanianaole Highway—from the intersection of Kamehameha Highway (Hwy. 83)—and then Kailua Road as it heads into Kailua town; but the road remains Highway 61 the whole way. Kailua Road ends at the T-intersection at Kalaheo Drive, which follows the coast in a northerly and southerly direction. Turn right on South Kalaheo Drive to get to Kailua Beach Park and Lanikai Beach. No signs point the way, but you can't miss the beaches.

If you spend a day at the beach here, stick around for sunset, when the sun sinks behind the Koolau Range and tints the clouds pink and orange. After a hard day at the beach, you'll work up an appetite, and Kailua has several great, inexpensive restaurants (see chapter 5, "Where to Dine").

If you want to skip the beaches this time, turn left on North Kalaheo Drive, which becomes Kaneohe Bay Drive as it skirts Kaneohe Bay and leads back to Kamehameha Highway (Hwy. 83), which then passes through Kaneohe. The suburban maze of Kaneohe is one giant strip mall of retail excess that mars one of the Pacific's most picturesque bays. After clearing this obstacle, the place begins to look like Hawaii again.

Incredibly scenic Kaneohe Bay is spiked with islets and lined with gold-sand beach parks like **Kualoa,** a favorite picnic spot (p. 160). The bay has a barrier reef and four tiny islets, one of which is known as Moku o loe, or Coconut Island. Don't be surprised if it looks familiar—it appeared in *Gilligan's Island.*

At Heeia State Park is **Heeia Fish Pond,** which ancient Hawaiians built by enclosing natural bays with rocks to trap fish on the incoming tide. The 88-acre fishpond, which is made of lava rock and had four watchtowers to observe fish movement and several sluice gates along the 5,000-foot-long wall, is now being restored.

Stop by **Heeia Pier,** which juts onto Kaneohe Bay. You can take a snorkel cruise here, or sail out to a sandbar in the middle of the bay for an incredible view of Oahu that most people, even those who live here, never see. If it's Tuesday through Sunday between 7am and 6pm, stop in at the **Deli on Heeia Kea Pier** (© **808/235-2192**). They have served fishermen, sailors, and kayakers the beach town's best omelets and plate lunches at reasonable prices since 1979.

Everyone calls it **Chinaman's Hat,** but the tiny island off the eastern shore of Kualoa Regional Park is really named **Mokolii.** It's a sacred *puu honua,* or place of refuge, like the restored Puu Honua Honaunau on the Big Island of Hawaii. Excavations have unearthed evidence that this area was the home of ancient alii. Early Hawaiians believed that Mokolii ("fin of the lizard") is all that remains of a *mo'o,* or lizard, slain by Pele's sister, Hi'iaka, and hurled into the sea. At low tide, you can swim out to the island, but keep an eye on the changing tide, which can sweep you out to sea. The islet has a small, sandy beach and is a bird preserve, so don't spook the red-footed boobies.

Little poly-voweled beach towns, such as **Kaaawa, Hauula, Punaluu,** and **Kahaluu,** pop up along the coast, offering passersby shell shops and art galleries to explore. Famed hula photographer **Kim Taylor Reece** lives on this coast; his gallery at 53-866 Kamehameha Hwy., near Sacred Falls (© **808/293-2000**), is open Thursday to Saturday, noon to 6pm. You'll also see working cattle ranches, fishermen's wharves, and roadside fruit and flower stands vending ice-cold coconuts (to drink) and tree-ripened mangoes, papayas, and apple bananas.

Sugar, once the sole industry of this region, is gone. But **Kahuku,** the former sugar-plantation town, has found new life as a small aquaculture community with prawn farms that supply island restaurants.

From here, continue along Kamehameha Highway (Hwy. 83) to the North Shore.

Attractions Along the Windward Coast

The attractions below are arranged geographically as you drive up the coast from south to north.

Hoomaluhia Botanical Gardens ★   At the foot of the steepled Koolau Mountains, this 400-acre botanical garden is the perfect place for a picnic. Its name means "a peaceful refuge," and that's exactly what the Army Corps of Engineers created when they installed a flood-control project here, which resulted in a 32-acre freshwater lake and garden. Just unfold a beach mat, lie back, and watch the clouds race across the rippled cliffs of the majestic Koolau Range. This is one of Oahu's few public places that provides a close-up view of the steepled cliffs. The park has hiking trails and—best of all—the island's only free inland campground (p. 116). If you like hiking and nature, plan to spend at least a half-day here.

45-680 Luluku Rd., Kaneohe. © **808/233-7323.** www.co.honolulu.hi.us/parks/hbg/hmbg.htm. Free admission. Daily 9am–4pm. Guided nature hikes Sat 10am and Sun 1pm. Take H-1 to the Pali Hwy. (Hwy. 61); turn left on Kamehameha Hwy. (Hwy. 83); at the 4th light, turn left onto Luluku Rd. Bus: 55 or 56 will stop on Kamehameha Hwy.; it's a 2-mile walk to the visitor center.

Kualoa Ranch and Activity Club   This once-working ranch now has various adventure packages covering numerous activities on its 4,000 acres. Activities include horseback riding, ATV rides, ranch tours, and more.

49-560 Kamehameha Hwy., Kaaawa. © **800/231-7321** or 808/237-7321. www.kualoa.com. Reservations required. Various activity packages: single activities $21–$93. Daily 8am–5pm. Take H-1 to the Likelike Hwy. (Hwy. 63), turn left at Kahekili Hwy. (Hwy. 83), and continue to Kaaawa. Bus: 52.

Polynesian Cultural Center ★ Kids   Experience the natural beauty and culture of the entire vast Pacific in a single day at the Polynesian Cultural Center, a kind of living museum of Polynesia. Here you can see firsthand the lifestyles, songs, dance, costumes, and architecture of seven Pacific islands or archipelagos—Fiji, New Zealand, the Marquesas, Samoa, Tahiti, Tonga, and Hawaii—in the re-created villages scattered throughout the 42-acre lagoon park. A recent $1.1-million renovation project remodeled the front entrance and added an exhibit on the story of the Polynesian immigration.

You travel through this museum by foot or in a canoe on a man-made freshwater lagoon. Each village is "inhabited" by native students from Polynesia who attend Hawaii's Brigham Young University. The park, which is operated by the Mormon Church, also features a variety of stage shows celebrating the music, dance, history, and culture of Polynesia. A luau takes place every evening. Because a visit can take up to 8 hours, it's a good idea to arrive before 2pm. Just beyond the center is the **Hawaii Temple** of the Church of Jesus Christ of Latter-Day Saints, which is built of volcanic rock and concrete in the form of a Greek cross and includes reflecting pools, formal gardens, and royal palms. Completed in 1919, it was the first Mormon temple built outside the continental United States. An optional tour of the Temple Visitors Center, as well as neighboring Brigham Young University Hawaii, is included in the package admission prices.

55-370 Kamehameha Hwy., Laie. © **800/367-7060,** 808/293-3333, or 808/923-2911. www.polynesia. com. Various packages available for $60–$225 adults, $45–$175 children 3–11. Mon–Sat 12:30–9:30pm. Take H-1 to Pali Hwy. (Hwy. 61) and turn left on Kamehameha Hwy. (Hwy. 83). Bus: 55. Polynesian Cultural Center coaches $19 round-trip; call numbers above to book.

Senator Fong's Plantation & Gardens   Senator Hiram Fong, the first Chinese American elected to the U.S. Senate, served 17 years before retiring to this 725-acre tropical garden years ago. This land originally belonged to King Lunalilo. In 1950, Senator Fong purchased it. The landscape you see today is relatively the same as what early Polynesians saw hundreds of years ago, with forests of kukui, hala, koa, and *ohia-'ai* (mountain apple). Ti and pili grass still cover the slopes. It's definitely worth an hour—if you haven't already seen enough flora to last a lifetime.

47-285 Pulama Rd., Kaneohe. © **808/239-6775.** www.fonggarden.net. Admission $15 adults, $13 seniors, $9 children 5–12. Daily 10am–2pm; guided walking tours daily 10:30am and 1pm. Take the H-1 to the Likelike Hwy. (Hwy. 63); turn left at Kahekili Hwy. (Hwy. 83); continue to Kaneohe and turn left on Pulama Rd. Bus: 20 then transfer to Bus: 55; it's a 1-mile walk uphill from the stop.

Valley of the Temples   This famous cemetery in a cleft of the pali is stalked by wild peacocks and about 700 curious people a day, who pay to see the 9-foot meditation Buddha,

2 acres of ponds full of more than 10,000 Japanese koi carp, and a replica of Japan's 900-year-old Byodo in the Temple of Equality. The original, made of wood, stands in Uji, on the outskirts of Kyoto; the Hawaiian version, made of concrete, was erected in 1968 to commemorate the 100th anniversary of the arrival of the first Japanese immigrants to Hawaii. It's not the same as seeing the original, but it's worth a detour. A 3-ton brass temple bell brings good luck to those who can ring it—although the gongs do jar the Zen-like serenity of this little bit of Japan. If you're in a rush, you can sail through here in an hour, but you'll probably want to stay longer.

47-200 Kahekili Hwy. (across the street from Temple Valley Shopping Center), Kaneohe. (C) **808/239-8811.** Admission $2 adults, $1 children under 12 and seniors 65 and over. Daily 8:30am–4:30pm. Take the H-1 to the Likelike Hwy. (Hwy. 63); after the Wilson Tunnel, get in the right lane and take the Kahekili Hwy. (Hwy. 63); at the 6th traffic light is the entrance to the cemetery (on the left). Bus: B, then transfer to Bus: 65.

CENTRAL OAHU & THE NORTH SHORE

If you can afford the splurge, rent a bright, shiny convertible—the perfect car for Oahu, since you can tan as you go—and head for the North Shore and Hawaii's surf city: **Haleiwa** ★, a quaint turn-of-the-20th-century sugar-plantation town designated a historic site. A collection of faded clapboard stores with a picturesque harbor, Haleiwa has evolved into a surfer outpost and major roadside attraction with art galleries, restaurants, and shops that sell hand-decorated clothing, jewelry, and sports gear (see chapter 8, "Shopping").

Getting here is half the fun. You have two choices: The first is to meander north along the lush Windward Coast, through country hamlets with roadside stands selling mangoes, bright tropical pareus, fresh corn, and pond-raised prawns. For attractions along that route, see above, p. 224.

The second choice is to cruise up the H-2 through Oahu's broad and fertile central valley, past Pearl Harbor and the Schofield Barracks of *From Here to Eternity* fame, and on through the red-earthed heart of the island, where pineapple and sugar cane fields stretch from the Koolau to the Waianae mountains, until the sea reappears on the horizon. If you take this route, the tough part is getting on and off the H-1 freeway from Waikiki, which is done by way of convoluted routing on neighborhood streets. Try McCully Street off Ala Wai Boulevard, which is always crowded but usually the most direct route.

Once you're on H-1, stay to the right side; the freeway tends to divide abruptly. Keep following the signs for the H-1 (it separates off to Hwy. 78 at the airport and reunites later on; either way will get you there), then the H-1/H-2. Leave the H-1 where the two "interstates" divide; take the H-2 up the middle of the island, heading north and following signs directing you toward the town of Wahiawa.

The H-2 runs out and becomes a two-lane country road about 18 miles outside downtown Honolulu, near Schofield Barracks (see below). The highway becomes Kamehameha Highway (Hwy. 99 and later Hwy. 83) at Wahiawa. Just past Wahiawa, about a half-hour out of Honolulu, the **Dole Pineapple Plantation,** 64-1550 Kamehameha Hwy. ((C) **808/621-8408;** www.dole-plantation.com; bus no. 52), offers a rest stop with pineapples, pineapple history, pineapple trinkets, and pineapple juice, open daily from 9am to 6pm. This agricultural exhibit/retail area also features a maze kids will love to wander through, open daily from 9am to 5pm; admission is $6 for adults and $4 for children 4 to 12 (free for ages 3 and under). The Pineapple Express is a single-engine diesel locomotive with four cars that takes a 22-minute tour around 2¼ miles of the plantation's grounds, with an educational spiel on the legacy of the pineapple and agriculture in Hawaii. The first tour departs at 9:30am, and the last tour gets back to the station at 5:20pm. Cost is $8 for adults, $6 for children 4 to 12 (free for ages 3 and under). The Plantation Garden tour is a self-guided tour through the various crops that have been grown on Oahu's North Shore. The tour costs $4 for adults and $3.50 for children. "Kam" Highway, as everyone calls it, will be your road for most of the rest of the trip to Haleiwa.

Central Oahu Attractions

On the central plains of Oahu, tract homes and malls with factory-outlet stores are now spreading across abandoned sugar cane fields, where sandalwood forests used to stand at the foot of Mount Kaala, the mighty summit of Oahu. Hawaiian chiefs once sent commoners into thick sandalwood forests to cut down trees, which were then sold to China traders for small fortunes. The scantily clad natives caught cold in the cool uplands, and many died.

On these plains in 1908, the U.S. Army pitched a tent that later become a fort. And on December 7, 1941, Japanese pilots came screaming through Kolekole Pass to shoot up the Art Deco barracks at Schofield, sending soldiers running for cover, and then flew on to sink ships at Pearl Harbor.

Kukaniloko Birthing Stones   This is the most sacred site in central Oahu. Two rows of 18 lava rocks once flanked a central birthing stone, where women of ancient Hawaii gave birth to potential alii. The rocks, according to Hawaiian belief, held the power to ease the labor pains of childbirth. Birth rituals involved 48 chiefs who pounded drums to announce the arrival of newborns likely to become chiefs. Children born here were taken to the now-destroyed Holonopahu Heiau in the pineapple field, where chiefs ceremoniously cut the umbilical cord.

Used by Oahu's *alii* for generations of births, the *pohaku* (rocks), many in bowl-like shapes, now lie strewn in a grove of trees that stands in a pineapple field. Some think the site also may have served ancient astronomers—like a Hawaiian Stonehenge. Petroglyphs of human forms and circles appear on some of the stones. The Wahiawa Hawaiian Civic Club recently erected two interpretive signs, one explaining why this was chosen as a birth site and the other telling how the stones were used to aid in the birthing process.

Off Kamehameha Hwy., btw. Wahiawa and Haleiwa, on Plantation Rd., opposite the road to Whitmore Village.

U.S. Army Schofield Barracks   James Jones, author of *From Here to Eternity,* called Schofield Barracks "the most beautiful army post the U.S. has or ever had." The *Honolulu Star Bulletin* called it a country club. More than a million soldiers called Schofield Barracks home. With its broad, palm-lined boulevards and Art Deco buildings, this old army cavalry post is still the largest operated by the U.S. Army outside the continental United States. And it's still one of the best places to be a soldier.

You can no longer visit the barracks themselves, but the history of Schofield Barracks and the 25th Infantry Division is told in the small **Tropic Lightning Museum.** Displays range from a 1917 bunker exhibit to a replica of Vietnam's infamous Cu Chi tunnels.

Schofield Barracks, Building 361, Waianae Ave. (C) **808/655-0497.** www.25idl.army.mil/tropic%20lightning%20museum/history.htm. Free admission. Tues–Sun 1–4pm. Bus: 52 to Wahiawa; transfer at California Ave. to no. 72, Schofield Barracks Shuttle.

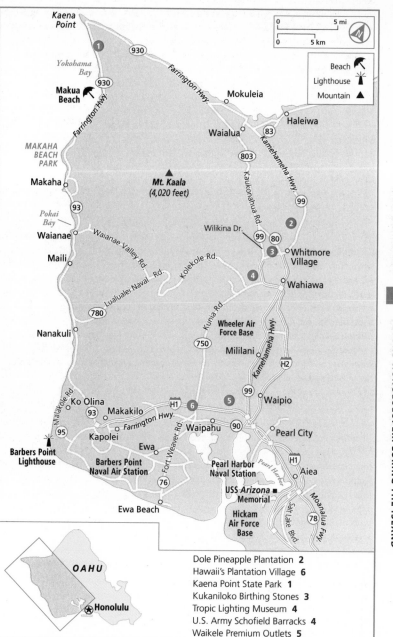

Kaena
Point

930

Yokohama
Bay

930

*Makua
Beach*

Farrington Hwy.

Farrington Hwy.

Mokuleia

MAKAHA
BEACH
PARK

Waialua

Haleiwa

83

803

Kamehameha Hwy.

Makaha

▲
Mt. Kaala
(4,020 feet)

Kaukonahua Rd.

99

Pokai
Bay

93

Wilikina Dr.

2

Waianae

Waianae Valley Rd.

99 80

Maili

Kolekole Rd.

3 Whitmore
Village

Lualualei Naval Rd.

4 Wahiawa

Nanakuli

780

Kunia Rd.

Wheeler Air
Force Base

750 Mililani

Kamehameha Hwy.

H2

Malakole Rd.

99

Ko Olina

93 Makakilo

H1 6 5 Waipio

95

Kapolei

Farrington Hwy.

Waipahu

90 Pearl City

**Barbers Point
Lighthouse**

Ewa

Fort Weaver Rd.

H1 Aiea

**Barbers Point
Naval Air Station**

76

**Pearl Harbor
Naval Station**

Pearl Harbor

Ewa Beach

USS *Arizona* ■
Memorial

Salt Lake Blvd.

78

Moanalua Hwy.

**Hickam
Air Force
Base**

Beach ☂
Lighthouse 🗼
Mountain ▲

0   5 mi
0   5 km

OAHU

★Honolulu

Dole Pineapple Plantation **2**
Hawaii's Plantation Village **6**
Kaena Point State Park **1**
Kukaniloko Birthing Stones **3**
Tropic Lighting Museum **4**
U.S. Army Schofield Barracks **4**
Waikele Premium Outlets **5**

EXPLORING OAHU

7

BEYOND HONOLULU: EXPLORING THE ISLAND

Only 28 miles from Waikiki is Haleiwa, the funky ex-sugar-plantation town that's the world capital of big-wave surfing. This beach town really comes alive in winter, when waves rise up, light rain falls, temperatures dip into the 70s, and practically every surfer in the world is here to see and be seen.

Officially designated a historic cultural and scenic district, Haleiwa thrives in a time warp recalling the turn of the 20th century, when it was founded by sugar baron Benjamin Dillingham, who built a 30-mile railroad to link his Honolulu and North Shore plantations in 1899. He opened a Victorian hotel overlooking Kaiaka Bay and named it Haleiwa, or "house of the Iwa," the tropical seabird often seen here. The hotel and railroad are gone, but Haleiwa, which was rediscovered in the late 1960s by hippies, resonates with rare rustic charm. Tofu, not taro, is a staple in the local diet. Arts and crafts, boutiques, and burger stands line both sides of the town. Haleiwa's busy fishing harbor is full of charter boats and captains who hunt the Kauai Channel daily for tuna, mahimahi, and marlin. The bartenders at **Jameson's** ★, 62-540 Kamehameha Hwy. (✆ **808/637-6272**), make the best mai tais on the North Shore; they use the original recipe by Trader Vic Bergeron.

Once in Haleiwa, the hot and thirsty traveler should report directly to the nearest shave-ice stand, usually **Matsumoto Shave Ice** ★★, 66-087 Kamehameha Hwy. (✆ **808/637-4827**). For 40 years, this small, humble shop operated by the Matsumoto family has served a popular rendition of the Hawaii-style snow cone flavored with tropical tastes. The cooling treat is also available at neighboring stores, some of which still shave the ice with a hand-crank device.

Just down the road are some of the fabled shrines of surfing—**Waimea Beach, Banzai Pipeline, Sunset Beach**—where some of the world's largest waves, reaching 20 feet and more, rise between November and January. They draw professional surfers as well as reckless daredevils and hordes of onlookers, who jump in their cars and head north when word goes out that "surf's up." Don't forget your binoculars. (For more details on North Shore beaches, see chapter 6.)

North Shore Surf and Cultural Museum   Even if you've never set foot on a surfboard, you'll want to visit Oahu's only surf museum to learn the history of this Hawaiian sport of kings. This collection of memorabilia traces the evolution of surfboards from an enormous, weathered redwood board made in the 1930s for Turkey Love, one of Waikiki's legendary beach boys, to the modern-day equivalent—a light, sleek, racy, foam-and-fiberglass board made for big-wave surfer Mark Foo, who drowned while surfing in California in 1994. Other items include classic 1950s surf-meet posters, 1960s surf-music album covers, old beach-movie posters with Frankie Avalon and Sandra Dee, the early black-and-white photos by legendary surf photographer LeRoy Grannis, and trophies won by surfing's greatest. Curator Steve Gould is working on a new exhibit of surfing in the ancient Hawaiian culture, complete with Hawaiian artifacts.

North Shore Marketplace, 66-250 Kamehameha Hwy. (behind KFC), Haleiwa. ✆ **808/637-8888.** www.captainrick.com/surf_museum.htm. Free admission. Wed–Mon 11am–6pm (unless the surf is up).

More North Shore Attractions

If you're on the North Shore, don't miss **Puu o Mahuka Heiau,** the largest sacrificial temple on Oahu (p. 202) and the **Waimea Valley Audubon Center,** which has a huge park and kid-pleasing activity center (p. 176).

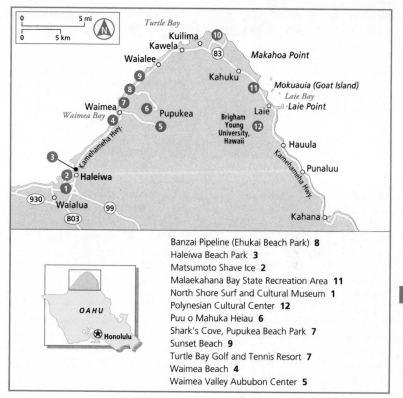

Banzai Pipeline (Ehukai Beach Park) **8**
Haleiwa Beach Park **3**
Matsumoto Shave Ice **2**
Malaekahana Bay State Recreation Area **11**
North Shore Surf and Cultural Museum **1**
Polynesian Cultural Center **12**
Puu o Mahuka Heiau **6**
Shark's Cove, Pupukea Beach Park **7**
Sunset Beach **9**
Turtle Bay Golf and Tennis Resort **7**
Waimea Beach **4**
Waimea Valley Aububon Center **5**

8

Shopping

It's a no-brainer: Honolulu is a shopping destination. Shopping competes with golf, surfing, and sightseeing as a bona fide Honolulu attraction. The proliferation of top-notch made-in-Hawaii products, the vitality of the local crafts scene, and the unquenchable thirst for mementos of the islands lend respectability to shopping here. More than 1,000 stores occupy the 11 major shopping centers on this island, with a tsunami of new retail stores to come.

By 2009, retail shops will increase an unprecedented 25% over current space, mostly in leeward Oahu, the fastest-growing population on the island. Planned are two regional malls, five big-box discount stores, a handful of community shopping centers, and major additions to Ala Moana Shopping Center and the two Ward centers.

From T-shirts to Versace, posh European to down-home local, avant-garde to unspeakably tacky, Oahu's offerings are wide-ranging indeed. Nestled amid the Louis Vuitton, Chanel, and Tiffany boutiques on Waikiki's Kalakaua Avenue are plenty of tacky booths hawking airbrushed T-shirts, gold by the inch, and tasteless aloha shirts.

But this chapter won't help you discover cheap souvenirs or tony items from designer fashion chains; you can find these things on your own. Rather, we offer a guide to finding the special treasures that lie somewhere in between. Be aware that small shops and boutiques have their own hours. Some don't open until 10am, some close for lunch, and some close their doors at 5pm, while others are open until 9pm. To make sure, call the store before you go.

1 IN & AROUND HONOLULU & WAIKIKI

ALOHA WEAR

One of Hawaii's lasting afflictions is the penchant tourists have for wearing loud, matching aloha shirts and muumuus. I applaud such visitors' good intentions (to act local), but no local resident would be caught dead in such a get-up. Muumuus and aloha shirts are wonderful, but the real thing is what island folks wear on Aloha Friday (every Fri), to the Brothers Cazimero Lei Day Concert (every May 1), or to work (where allowed). It's what they wear at home and to special parties where the invitation reads "Aloha Attire."

Aside from the vintage Hawaiian wear (1930s–1950s) found in collectibles shops and at swap meets, my favorite contemporary aloha-wear designer is Hawaii's **Tori Richards.** **Tommy Bahama,** which never calls its shirts "aloha shirts" but claims, instead, a Caribbean influence, is another Hawaii shirt icon, and so is the up-and-coming **Tiki** brand, quirky and distinctive, with elements that hark back to the 1950s.

The best aloha shirts are pricey these days, going for $80 to $125. For the vintage look, **Avanti** has a corner on the market with its line of silk shirts and dresses in authentic retro patterns. **Kahala Sportswear,** a well-known local company established in 1936, is also popular. Kahala has faithfully reproduced, with astounding success, the linoleum-block prints of noted Maui artist Avi Kiriaty and the designs of other contemporary artists. Kahala is sold in department stores, surf shops, and stylish boutiques throughout Hawaii and the mainland.

For the most culturally correct aloha wear, and for a graphic identity that is rare in the aloha shirt realm, check out the shirts, dresses, and pareus of **Sig Zane Designs** (www. sigzane.com), found in many department stores (and on the Big Island, in Hilo, they have their only outlet. Zane, an accomplished hula dancer married to one of Hawaii's most revered hula masters, has an unmistakable visual style and a profound knowledge of Hawaiian culture that brings depth and meaning to his boldly styled renditions. Each Sig Zane pareu and aloha shirt, in pure cotton, tells a story. No wonder it's the garb of cultural connoisseurs, who also buy fabrics by the yard for interior accents.

Reyn Spooner is another source of attractive aloha shirts and muumuus in traditional and contemporary styles, with stores in Ala Moana Center, Kahala Mall, and the Sheraton Waikiki. Reyn has popularized the reverse-print aloha shirt—the uniform of downtown boardrooms—and has also jumped aboard the vintage-look bandwagon with Old Hawaii cotton prints, some of them in attractive two-color pareu patterns.

Well-known muumuu labels in Hawaii include **Mamo Howell,** with a boutique in Ward Warehouse, and **Princess Kaiulani** and **Bete** for the dressier muumuus, sold along with many other lines at Macy's and other department stores. **Hilo Hattie's** Ala Moana store (© **808/973-3266**) is a goldmine for affordable aloha wear. Hilo Hattie also offers free daily shuttle service from Waikiki to its retail outlet, 700 N. Nimitz Highway (© **808/535-6500**). You'll also find macadamia nuts, Hawaiian coffees, and other souvenirs at these Hilo Hattie's stores, as well as live Hawaiian entertainment. Quality and selection have improved noticeably in recent years.

See also "Fashion Boutiques," later in this chapter.

Avanti Fashion   This leading retro aloha shirt label turns out stunning silk shirts and dresses in authentic 1930s to 1950s fabric patterns. The shirts, though made of thin silk, are hip and nostalgic, without the web-thin fragility of authentic antique shirts. The line is distributed in better boutiques and department stores throughout Hawaii, but the best selections are at its Waikiki retail stores. 2229 Kuhio Ave. (© **808/924-1668**); 2250 Kalakaua Ave., Waikiki Shopping Plaza (© **808/922-2828**); 307 Lewers St. (© **808/926-6886**); and 2160 Kalakaua Ave. (© **808/924-3232**). www.avantishirts.com.

Bailey's Antiques & Aloha Shirts (**Finds**   A large selection (thousands) of vintage, secondhand, and nearly new aloha shirts and other collectibles fills this eclectic emporium. It looks as though the owners regularly scour Hollywood movie costume departments for odd ball gowns, feather boas, fur stoles, leather jackets, 1930s dresses, and scads of other garments from periods past. Bailey's has one of the largest vintage aloha-shirt collections in Honolulu, with prices ranging from inexpensive to sky-high. Old Levi's jeans, mandarin jackets, vintage vases, household items, shawls, purses, and an eye-popping assortment of bark-cloth fabrics (the real thing, not repros) are among the mementos in this monumental collection. 517 Kapahulu Ave. © **808/734-7628.**

Hilo Hattie (**Value**   Hilo Hattie, the largest manufacturer of Hawaiian fashions, attracts more than a million visitors to its ever-expanding empire throughout the state. Its Ala Moana store is a leap in image, quality, range of merchandise, and overall shopping options. You can find great gifts here, from coconut utensils to food products and aloha shirts in all price ranges and motifs. There are some inexpensive silk aloha shirts as well as brand-name aloha shirts such as Tommy Bahama and the store's own Hilo Hattie label. Ala Moana Center, 1450 Ala Moana Blvd. © **808/973-3266.** Also at 700 N. Nimitz Hwy. © **808/535-6500.**

Oahu's Vibrant Gallery Scene

Like restaurants, galleries come and go in Chinatown, where efforts to revitalize the area have moved in fits and spurts. Two exceptions are the **Ramsay Galleries,** Tan Sing Building, 1128 Smith St. ((✆ **808/537-2787**), and the **Pegge Hopper Gallery,** 1164 Nuuanu Ave. ((✆ **808/524-1160**). Both are housed in historic Chinatown buildings that have been renovated and transformed into stunning showplaces. Nationally known quill-and-ink artist Ramsay, who has drawn everything from the Plaza in New York to most of Honolulu's historic buildings, maintains a vital monthly show schedule featuring her own work, as well as shows of her fellow Hawaiian artists. A consummate preservationist, Ramsay has added a courtyard garden with an oval pond and exotic varieties of bamboo.

Pegge Hopper, one of Hawaii's most popular artists, displays her widely collected paintings (usually of Hawaiian women with broad, strong features) in her attractive gallery, which has become quite the gathering place for exhibits ranging from Tibetan sand-painting by saffron-robed monks to the most avant-garde printmaking in the islands.

The **Gallery at Ward Centre,** in Ward Centre, 1200 Ala Moana Blvd. ((✆ **808/ 597-8034**), a cooperative gallery of Oahu artists, features fine works in all media, including paper, clay, scratchboard, oils, watercolors, collages, woodblocks, lithographs, glass, jewelry, and more.

Art lovers now have a wonderful new resource: a 34-page full-color brochure offering an overview of the music, theater, history, and visual arts of Oahu. The free brochure, which includes a map, phone numbers, websites, and more information, is put out by Arts with Aloha, representing 11 major Honolulu cultural organizations. For current info or for a free copy of the brochure, send a 4¹/₄x9-inch letter-sized envelope with $1.11 postage on it to **Arts with Aloha,** c/o Honolulu Academy of Arts, 900 S. Beretania St., Honolulu, HI 96814 ((✆ **808/532-8713**), or download it from their website (www.artswithaloha.com).

Macy's If it's aloha wear, Macy's has it. The extensive aloha shirt and muumuu departments here feature every label you can conjure, with a selection—in all price ranges—that changes with the times. 1450 Ala Moana Blvd., Ala Moana Center. ✆ 808/941-2345.

Reyn's Reyn's used to be a prosaic line but has stepped up its selection of women's and men's aloha wear with contemporary fabric prints and styles that appeal to a hipper clientele. Ala Moana Center, 1450 Ala Moana Blvd. ✆ 808/949-5929. Also at Kalala Mall, 4211 Waialae Ave., ✆ 808/737-8313; Sheraton Moana Surfrider, 2377 Kalakaua Ave., ✆808/923-7640; and the Downtown Rack, 125 Merchant St., ✆ 808/524-1885.

ANTIQUES & COLLECTIBLES

For the best in collectible aloha wear, see "Aloha Wear," above (especially the listing for **Bailey's Antiques & Aloha Shirts**).

Anchor House Antiques This highly eclectic collection of Hawaiian, Asian, and European pieces sprawls over thousands of square feet. You'll find wooden calabashes, camphor chests, paintings, Hawaiian artifacts, and trinkets, priced from $10 to $2,000. 471 Kapahulu Ave. (C) 808/732-3884.

Antique Alley This narrow shop is chockablock with the passionate collections of several vendors under one roof. With its expanded collection of Old Hawaii artifacts and surfing and hula nostalgia, it's a sure winner for eclectic tastes. The showcases include estate jewelry, antique silver, Hawaiian bottles, collectible toys, pottery, cameras, Depression glass, linens, plantation photos and ephemera, and a wide selection of nostalgic items from Hawaii and across America. At the rear is a small, attractive selection of Soiree clothing, made by Julie Lauster out of antique kimonos and obis. 1347 Kapiolani Blvd. (C) 808/941-8551.

Antique House Small but tasteful, the low-profile Antique House is hidden below the lobby level of the illustrious Royal Hawaiian Hotel. Come here for small items, such as Asian antiques, Chinese and Japanese porcelains, and a stunning selection of snuff bottles, bronzes, vases, and china. In the Royal Hawaiian Hotel, 2259 Kalakaua Ave. (C) 808/923-5101.

Garakuta-Do This huge warehouse/store has a sublime collection of Japanese antiques. It's worth finding for its late-Edo period (1800s–early 1900s) antiques, collected and sold by cheerful owner Wataru Harada. The selection of gorgeous tansus, mingei folk art, Japanese screens, and more makes shopping here feel like a treasure hunt. 433 Koula Ave., Ste. 100. (C) 808/955-2099.

Robyn Buntin Robyn Buntin's 5,000-square-foot gallery and picture-framing department—called Robyn Buntin's Picture Framing and Oceania Gallery—along with his gallery for Hawaiian art, at 820 S. Beretania St., are among the features of this burgeoning art resource, located three doors from the Honolulu Academy of Art. This is Honolulu's stellar source of museum-quality Asian art and contemporary and traditional Hawaiian art. 848 S. Beretania St. (C) 808/523-5913.

T. Fujii Japanese Antiques This long-standing icon in Hawaii's antiques world is an impeccable source for *ukiyo-e* prints, scrolls, obis, Imari porcelain, tansus, tea-ceremony bowls, and screens, as well as contemporary ceramics from Mashiko and Kasama. Prices range from $25 to $18,000. 1016 Kapahulu Ave. (C) 808/732-7860.

BOOKSTORES

Barnes & Noble With more than 150,000 titles, a respectable music department, and strong Hawaiiana, fiction, and new-release departments, as well as a popular coffee bar, Barnes & Noble has become the second home of Honolulu's casual readers and bibliophiles. Kahala Mall, 4211 Waialae Ave. (C) 808/737-3323.

Bestsellers Books & Music Hawaii's largest independent bookstore, located in downtown Honolulu, has a complete selection of nonfiction and fiction titles with an emphasis on Hawaiian books and music. There's another Bestsellers in the Hilton Hawaiian Village (2005 Kalia Rd.). 1001 Bishop St. (C) 808/528-2378.

The Bookmobile Think back to your childhood when the library's bookmobile would come around the neighborhood. That is exactly what Bryde Cestare, executive director of the Friends of the Library Hawaii, wanted to create with this 12×27-foot RV, refitted to be an air-conditioned, well-lit bookstore on wheels. All profits support the state's 51 public libraries. 690 Pohukaina St. (next to Mother Waldron Park). (C) 808/536-4174.

Borders   Borders is a beehive of literary activity, with weekly signings, prominent local and mainland musicians at least monthly, and special events almost daily that make this store a major Honolulu attraction. Borders has six branches on Oahu, including those listed here. Victoria Ward Centre (© **808/591-8995**); Windward Mall, 46-056 Kamehameha Hwy., Kailua (© **808/235-8044**); and Waikiki Shopping Plaza, 2250 Kalakaua Ave. (© **808/922-4154**).

Friends of Kailua Library Bookstore   Located in the community meeting rooms of the Kailua Library, this bargain bookstore has a range of books from that perfect beach read to college textbooks and bestselling nonfiction. Every used book is either 50¢ or $1. Call for hours, as staffing is done by volunteers. Kailua Library, 239 Kuulei Rd., Kailua. © **808/266-9911**.

Rainbow Books and Records   A little weird but totally lovable, especially among students and eccentrics (and insatiable readers), Rainbow Books is notable for its selection of popular fiction, records, and Hawaii-themed books, secondhand and reduced. Because it's located in the university area, it's always bulging with textbooks, Hawaiiana, and popular music. It's about the size of a large closet, but you'll be surprised by what you'll find. 1010 University Ave. © **808/955-7994**.

EDIBLES

In addition to the stores listed below, we recommend **Executive Chef** (© **808/596-2433**), in the Ward Warehouse, and **Islands' Best** (© **808/949-5345**), in the Ala Moana Center. Both shops contain wide-ranging selections that include Hawaii's specialty food items.

Asian Grocery   Asian Grocery supplies many of Honolulu's Thai, Vietnamese, Chinese, Indonesian, and Filipino restaurants with authentic spices, rice, noodles, produce, sauces, herbs, and adventurous ingredients. Browse among the kaffir lime leaves, tamarind and fish pastes, red and green chilies, curries, chutneys, lotus leaves, gingko nuts, jasmine and basmati rice, and shelf upon shelf of medium to hot chili sauces. The chefs for most of Honolulu's Asian and ethnic restaurants shop here. 1319 S. Beretania St. © **808/593-8440**. www.asianfood.com.

Don Quijote   Stands offering takeout sushi, Korean *kal bi*, pizza, Chinese food, flowers, Mrs. Fields cookies, and other items for self and home surround this huge emporium. Inside, you'll find household products, a pharmacy, and inexpensive clothing, but it's the prepared foods and produce that excel. The fresh-seafood section is one of Honolulu's best, not far from where regulars line up for the bento lunches and individually wrapped sushi. When Kau navel oranges, macadamia nuts, Kona coffee, Chinese taro, and other Hawaii products are on sale, savvy locals arrive in droves to take advantage of the high quality and good value. Additional branches are at 345 Hahani St., Kailua (© **808/266-4400**); 850 Kam Hwy., Pearl City (© **808/453-5509**); and 94-144 Farrington Hwy., Waipahu (© **808/678-6800**). 801 Kaheka St. © **808/973-4800**.

Fujioka's Wine Merchants   Oenophiles flock here for a mouthwatering selection of excellent wines, single-malt Scotches, and affordable, farm-raised caviar—food and libations for all occasions. Everyday wines, special-occasion wines, and esoteric wines are priced lower here than at most places. The wine-tasting bar at the rear of the store is a new attraction. Market City Shopping Center, 2919 Kapiolani Blvd., lower level. © **808/739-9463**.

Honolulu Chocolate Co.   Life's greatest pleasures are dispensed here with abandon: expensive gourmet chocolates made in Honolulu, Italian and Hawaiian biscotti, boulder-size turtles (caramel and pecans covered with chocolate), truffles, chocolate-covered coffee beans, and jumbo apricots in white and dark chocolate, to name a few. You pay dearly for them, but the dark-chocolate-dipped macadamia-nut clusters are beyond compare. Ward Centre, 1200 Ala Moana Blvd. © **808/591-2997.**

It's Chili in Hawaii This is *the* oasis for chili-heads, a house of heat with endorphins aplenty and good food to accompany the hot sauces from around the world, including a fabulous selection of made-in-Hawaii products. Scoville units (measurements of heat in food) are the topic of the day in this shop, lined with thousands of bottles of hot sauces, salsas, and other chili-based food products. Not everything is scorching, however; some products, such as Dave's Soyabi and the lime-habanero sauce called Makai, are everyday flavor enhancers that can be used on rice, salads, meats, and pasta. If you're eating in, the fresh-frozen tamales, in several varieties (including meatless), are now in regular supply. Every Saturday, free samples of green-chili stew are dished up to go with the generous hot-sauce tastings. 3133 Waialae St. (corner 3rd Ave.) © **808/945-7070.**

Mauna Kea Marketplace Food Court Hungry patrons line up for everything from pizza and plate lunches to quick, authentic, and inexpensive Vietnamese, Thai, Italian, Chinese, Japanese, and Filipino dishes. The best seafood fried rice comes from the woks of **Malee Thai/Vietnamese Cuisine**—it's perfectly flavored, with morsels of fish, squid, and shrimp. Tandoori Chicken Cafe serves Indian culinary pleasures, from curries and jasmine-chicken rice balls to spiced rounds of curried potatoes and a wonderful lentil dal. **Masa's** serves bento and Japanese dishes, such as miso eggplant, which are famous. You'll find the best dessert at **Pho Lau,** which serves *haupia* (coconut pudding), tapioca, and taro in individual baskets made of pandanus. Join in the spirit of discovery at the produce stalls (pungent odors, fish heads, and chicken feet on counters—not for the squeamish). Vendors sell everything from fresh ahi and whole snapper to yams and taro, seaweed, and fresh fruits and vegetables. 1120 Maunakea St., Chinatown. © **808/524-3409.**

People's Open Markets Truck farmers from all over the island bring their produce to Oahu's neighborhoods in regularly scheduled, city-sponsored open markets, held Monday through Saturday at various locations. Among the tables of ong choy, choi sum, Okinawan spinach, opal basil, papayas, mangoes, seaweed, and fresh fish, you'll find homemade banana bread, Chinese pomelo (like large grapefruit), fresh fiddleheads (fern shoots) when available, and colorful, bountiful harvests from land and sea. Various sites around town. Call to find the open market nearest you. © **808/527-5167.** www.honolulu. gov/parks/programs/pom/sked.htm.

Pampered Pedicure: A Must-Have in Hawaii

In Hawaii, where going barefoot is as common as breathing, and open-toed sandals and slippers are the shoes of necessity, a pedicure is a must. Most resort spas will offer pedicures among their list of services, but my favorite pedicure is from **Honolulu Nails Salon,** 2570 S. Beretania St (© **808/949-1600**). I recommend the Special Spa Pedicure, a five-step procedure with soaking, scrubs, rubs, masks, and a wonderful refreshing gel before you get down to the polish (OPI and Essie). Allow an hour. The entire relaxing experience is $25—worth every penny.

R. Field Wine Co. Foodland has won countless new converts since Richard Field— oenophile, gourmet, and cigar aficionado—moved his wine shop here. The thriving gourmet store offers gemlike vine-ripened tomatoes and juicy clementines, sparkling bags of Nalo gourmet greens, designer cheeses, caviar, Langenstein Farms macadamia nuts, vegetarian and salmon mousses, vinegars, and all manner of epicurean delights, including wines and single-malt Scotches. The warm, just-baked breads (rosemary–olive oil, whole-wheat, organic wheat, and others) baked on the premises with dough flown in from Los Angeles' famous La Brea Bakery, are a huge hit. Foodland Super Market, 1460 S. Beretania St. (C) 808/596-9463.

Sushi Company   It's not easy to find premium-grade *hamachi* (yellowtail), ahi, *ikura* (salmon roe), *ika* (cuttlefish), and other top-grade fresh ingredients in anything but a bona-fide sit-down sushi bar. But here it is, a small, sparkling gem of a sushi maker that sells fast-food sushi of non-fast-food quality, at great prices. Order ahead or wait while they make it. The combinations range from minisets (27 pieces) to large-variety sets (43–51 pieces), ideal for picnics and potlucks. Sushi Company has one small two-person table; most of the business is takeout. 1111 McCully St. (at Young St.). (C) 808/947-5411.

Bakeries

If you're looking for a bakery, **Saint-Germain,** in Shirokiya, at Ala Moana Shopping Center ((C) 808/955-1711), and near Times Supermarket, 1296 S. Beretania St. ((C) 808/593-8711), sells baguettes, country loaves, and oddball delicacies such as mini mushroom-and-spinach pizzas. The reigning queen of bakers, though, is **Cafe Laufer,** 3565 Waialae Ave. ((C) 808/735-7717); see p. 146. Nearby, old-timers still line up at **Sconees,** 1117 12th Ave. ((C) 808/734-4024), formerly Bea's Pies. Sconees has fantastic scones, pumpkin-custard pies, and danishes. For warm bread, nothing can beat **Foodland,** 1460 S. Beretania St. ((C) 808/949-4365 for the bakery department), where R. Field is located. The Foodland bakery flies in dough from Los Angeles' famous La Brea bakery and bakes it fresh at this location, so you can pick up fresh-from-the-oven organic wheat, rosemary–olive oil, roasted garlic, potato-dill, and other spectacular breads.

Cake Works   If creating cakes is an art form, former Hilo native, Chef Abigail "Abi" Langlas, the chef/owner of Cake Works, is a genius. This wonderful bakery, which specializes in custom wedding cakes, can also produce a specialty cake for any occasion. 2820 S. King St., across from the Hawaiian Humane Society. (C) 808/946-4333. www.cakeworks.org.

Fish Markets

Safeway on Beretania Street has a seafood counter with fresh choices and a staff that takes pride in its deftness with prepared foods. (Don't be shy about asking for a taste.) The prepared foods (fresh ahi poke, seaweed salad, marinated crab) are popular among busy working folks heading home. **Foodland,** on Beretania Street, occasionally offers good buys on live lobster and Dungeness crab, fresh ahi and aku poke, ahi sashimi and steaks, and a wide variety of fresh fish and shellfish, including whole snappers and oysters when available.

Honolulu Fish Auction   If you want to experience the high drama of fish buying, head to this auction at the United Fishing Agency. The fishermen bring their fresh catch in at 5:30am (sharp) Monday through Saturday, and buyers bid on a variety of fish, from fat tunas to weird-looking hapupu. Don't be surprised if you don't recognize much of the language the bidders are using; it is an internal dialect developed over decades, which

only the buyers and the auctioneer understand. You'll be happy you woke up so early!
Pier 38, 1131 N. Nimitz Highway. ✆ **808/536-2148.**

Tamashiro Market   This is the granddaddy of fish markets and the ace in the hole for home chefs with bouillabaisse or paella in mind. A separate counter sells seaweed salad, prepared poke, Filipino and Puerto Rican ti-wrapped steamed rice, and dozens of other ethnic foods. You'll think you're in a Fellini movie amid the tanks of live lobsters and crabs, and the dizzying array of counters glistening with fresh slabs of ahi, opakapaka whole, and, in filets, *onaga,* and *ehu.* Point and ask if you don't know what you're looking at, and one of the fish cutters will explain and then clean and fillet your selection. Good service and the most extensive selection in Honolulu make Tamashiro a Honolulu treasure. 802 N. King St., Kalihi. ✆ **808/841-8047.**

Yama's Fish Market   Neighbor islanders have been known to drive directly from the airport to Yama's for one of the best plate lunches in Honolulu. Robust Hawaiian plates with pork or chicken *lau lau* (20 combinations!), baked ahi, chili, beef stew, shoyu chicken, and dozens of other varieties stream out to those who line up at the counter. Many Honolulu businesses order by the dozen for their offices. But Yama's is also known for its inexpensive fresh fish (mahimahi is always less expensive here than in the supermarkets), tasty poke (ahi, aku, Hawaiian-style, Oriental-style, with seaweed), lomi salmon, and many varieties of prepared seafood. Chilled beer, boiled peanuts, and fresh ahi they'll slice into sashimi are popular for local-style gatherings, sunset beach parties, and festive *pau hana* (end of work) celebrations. At its new, larger location just a few hundred feet away, Yama's is offering more prepared foods and bakery items than ever before; and let me tell you, their chocolate-chip/mac-nut cookies are peerless. 2332 Young St., Moiliili. ✆ **808/941-9994.**

Health Food
Down to Earth   This university district shop sells organic vegetables and bulk foods, with a strong selection of supplements, herbs, and cosmetic products. Everything here is vegetarian, down to the last drop of tincture. Cereals, bulk grains and nuts, breads, many varieties of honey, nonalcoholic beer, teas, snacks, environment-friendly paper and household products, and a vegetarian juice and sandwich bar are among the reasons shoppers of all ages come here. 2525 S. King St., Moiliili. ✆ **808/947-7678.**

House of Health   Tiny, with a loyal clientele that has stuck by it through management and name changes and a hefty dose of parking problems, Hou Ola has competitive prices and a wide and user-friendly selection of health-food supplements. The supplements are good enough reason to shop here. No produce, but there are frozen vegetarian foods, cosmetics, bulk grains, and healthy snacks. 1541 S. Beretania St. ✆ **808/955-6168.**

Huckleberry Farms   Located in Nuuanu across town from the university area, Huckleberry Farms has two locations in the same shopping plaza. One houses a wide selection of vitamins, nutritional supplements, beauty creams and cosmetics, books, and nonperishable health products. A few feet away, the other store offers prepared health foods, fresh produce, and food products for the health-conscious. The selection at both stores is good. 1613 Nuuanu Ave., Nuuanu. ✆ **808/524-7960.**

Kokua Market   Kokua is Honolulu's best source for healthy provisions in all categories but vitamin supplements. The market is trying, however, and the vitamin selection is expanding noticeably. Voluminous, leafy organic vegetables; an excellent variety of cheeses; pastas and bulk grains; sandwiches, salads, and prepared foods; poi as fresh as can be; organic coffee beans; breads and pastries; and a solid selection of organic wines give Kokua a special place in the hearts of health-minded shoppers. There's ample parking behind the store. 2643 S. King St., Moiliili. ℭ **808/941-1922.**

Whole Foods Market   This national chain (the "queen" of organic and health food stores) finally has come to Hawaii, and not in a small way. At 28,670 square feet, it is one of the largest grocery stores on Oahu. Even bigger stores are planned for the Ward complex and Kailua in 2010. Kahala Mall, 4211 Waialae Ave. ℭ **808/738-0820.**

FASHION BOUTIQUES

For those looking for unique, personal style, these hot new boutiques offer exclusive (and somewhat unexpected) fashions you won't find anywhere else.

Hot Mama   Owner Paige McGuire has filled her store with fashionable (and comfortable) clothes for those who are expecting, such as designer tops (with hidden spandex), trendy skirts (that will fit through several months), and diaper bags that resemble the latest handbags. 3435 Waialae Ave. (entrance on 9th Ave.). ℭ **808/737-2737.**

House of Flys   This is the place of extremes, both the retail and the retail outlet. Selling clothes isn't the only draw; events such as DJ nights or a skateboard-a-thon in the nearby parking lot periodically take place here, too. Owned by local surfers and sports enthusiasts Saree Chirayunion and Sci Fly, this boutique features their own line, Black Flys, which includes sunglasses, cargo pants, T-shirts, skateboards, caps, and high-tech backpacks. International Market Place, 2330 Kalakaua Ave. upstairs across from the Food Court. ℭ **808/923-3597.**

In4mation   This is a boutique for guys who are tired of seeing the same old stuff in every men's store. This hip, hot boutique has the latest clothes, unusual baseball caps, limited-release Nike and DC shoes, collectible toys, and a great collection of T-shirts. Waikiki Shopping Plaza, 2250 Kalakaua Ave., ℭ **808/923-0888;** Ward Warehouse, 1050 Ala Moana Blvd., ℭ **808/597-1447.**

Kicks   Attention sneaker aficionados, collectors, and those looking for shoes as a fashion statement—this is your store. Limited editions and classic footwear by Nike and Adidas can be found here. Owners Edward Haus and Ian Ginoza carry clothing lines produced by their friends, as well as Anx, Freshjive, Creative, Subase, and Poetree. The store looks like a gallery, with the clothes and shoes as art. 1530 Makaloa St., Ste. 211 (upstairs, across from Walgreens). ℭ **808/941-9191.**

Modern Amusement   The limited-edition clothing sold here (perfect for the artsy type or nonconformist surfers, skateboarders, or clubbers) is both sophisticated surf wear and classic club outfits. Only quality fabrics and top-quality items are found, but each one is unique and creates a picture of individuality. This is one of only four Modern Amusement stores in the world. 449 Kapahulu Ave., Ste. 102. ℭ **808/738-2769.**

Valerie Joseph   Word is getting out about this newcomer on the fashion scene. Off the beaten tourist track, the small store has some unique clothing lines (BCBG Girls, French Connection, and its own private label), featuring everything from ultra-casual to very, very dressy. Be sure to check the table in the back for earrings, necklaces, and other well-priced bling. McCully Shopping Center, 1960 Kapiolani Blvd. ℭ **808/942-5258.**

At most lei shops, simple leis sell for $10 and up, deluxe leis for $25 and up. For a special-occasion designer bouquet or lei, you can't do better than Michael Miyashiro of **Rainforest Plantes et Fleurs** (℃ **808/738-0999**). He's an ecologically aware, highly gifted lei maker—his leis are pricey, but worth it. He custom-designs the lei for the person and occasion. Order by phone or stop by the Kilohana Square, 1016 Kapahulu Ave., where his shop is an oasis of green and beauty. Upon request, Miyashiro's leis will come in ti-leaf bundles called *pu'olo,* custom gift baskets (in woven green coconut baskets), and special arrangements. You can even request the card sentiments in Hawaiian, with English translations.

The other primary sources for flowers and leis are the shops lining the streets of Moi-liili and Chinatown. Moiliili favorites include **Rudy's Flowers,** Isenburg at Beretania (℃ **808/944-8844**), a local institution with the best prices on roses, Micronesian ginger lei, and a variety of cut blooms. Across the street, **Flowers for a Friend,** 2739 S. King St. (℃ **808/955-4227**), has good prices on leis, floral arrangements, and cut flowers. Nearby, **Flowers by Jr. and Lou,** 2652 S. King St. (℃ **808/941-2022**), offers calla lilies, Gerbera daisies, a riot of potted orchids, and the full range of cut flowers along with its lei selection.

In Chinatown, lei vendors line Beretania and Maunakea streets, and the fragrances of their wares mix with the earthy scents of incense and ethnic foods. My top picks are **Lita's Leis,** 59 N. Beretania St. (℃ **808/521-9065**), which has fresh puakenikeni, gardenias that last, and a supply of fresh and reasonable leis; **Poohala Lei and Flowers,** 69 N. Beretania St. (℃ **808/537-3011**), with a worthy selection of the classics at fair prices; **Lin's Lei Shop,** 1017-A Maunakea St. (℃ **808/537-4112**), with creatively fashioned, unusual leis; and **Cindy's Lei Shoppe,** 1034 Maunakea St. (℃ **808/536-6538**), with terrific sources for unusual leis, such as feather dendrobiums and firecracker combinations, and such everyday favorites as ginger, tuberose, orchid, and pikake. "Curb service" is available with phone orders. Just give them your car's color and model, and you can pick up your lei curbside—a great convenience on this busy street.

HAWAIIANA & GIFT ITEMS

Our top recommendations are the fabulous, newly expanded **Academy Shop,** at the Honolulu Academy of Arts, 900 S. Beretania St. (℃ **808/523-8703**), and the **Contemporary Museum Gift Shop,** 2411 Makiki Heights Rd. (℃ **808/523-3447**), two of the finest shopping stops on Oahu—worth a special trip whether or not you want to see the museums themselves. (And you will want to see the museums, especially the recently expanded Honolulu Academy of Arts.) The Academy Shop offers a brilliant selection of art books, jewelry, basketry, ethnic fabrics and native crafts from all over the world, posters and books, and fiber vessels and accessories. The Contemporary Museum shop focuses on arts and crafts such as avant-garde jewelry, cards and stationery, books, home accessories, and gift items made by artists from Hawaii and across the country. We love the glammy selection of jewelry and novelties, such as the twisted-wire wall hangings. (For details on the collections at both museums, see p. 203.)

Other good sources for quality gift items are the **Little Hawaiian Craft Shop,** in the Royal Hawaiian Shopping Center, and **Martin and MacArthur,** in the Aloha Tower Marketplace.

Hula Supply Center   Hawaiiana meets kitsch in this shop's marvelous selection of Day-Glo cellophane skirts, bamboo nose flutes, T-shirts, hula drums, shell leis, feathered rattle gourds, lauhala accessories, fiber mats, and a wide assortment of pareu fabrics. Although hula dancers shop here for their dance accoutrements, it's not all serious shopping. This is fertile ground for souvenirs and memorabilia of Hawaii, rooted somewhere between irreverent humor and cultural integrity. 2346 S. King St. (at Isenberg), Moiliili. ⒸＣ 808/941-5379.

Mana Hawaii Get some authentic Hawaiian culture in the heart of Waikiki at this unusual store, where the owners are five successful Native Hawaiians who have combined their talents. The partners include Native Books (see below), which sells books, CDs, and educational material about Hawaii; Na Mea Hawaii, featuring Hawaiian-made gifts, clothing, jewelry, and art; Hula Supply Center (see above) with everything for hula from fabric to implements; Ukulele House, offering ukuleles; and the Lomi Shop Va'a, specializing in health and wellness through massage. They also offer free cultural activities; call for schedule. Waikiki Beach Walk, 226 Lewers St., 2nd level. Ⓒ 808/923-2220.

Native Books & Beautiful Things Ⓕ**Finds** This *hui* (association) of artists and craftspeople is a browser's paradise featuring a variety of Hawaiian items from musical instruments to calabashes, jewelry, leis, and books. You'll find contemporary Hawaiian clothing; handmade koa journals; Hawaii-themed home accessories; lauhala handbags and accessories; jams, jellies, and food products; etched glass; hand-painted fabrics and clothing; stone poi pounders; and other high-quality gift items. Some of Hawaii's finest artists in all craft media have their works available here on a regular basis, and the Hawaiian-book selection is tops. Ward Warehouse, 1050 Ala Moana Blvd. Ⓒ 808/596-8885.

Nohea Gallery A fine showcase for contemporary Hawaii art, Nohea celebrates the islands with such thoughtful, attractive selections as pit-fired raku, finely turned wood vessels, jewelry, handblown glass, paintings, prints, fabrics (including Hawaiian-quilt cushions), and furniture. Nohea's selection is always evolving and growing, with 90% of the works by Hawaii artists. Ward Warehouse, 1050 Ala Moana Blvd., Ⓒ 808/596-0074; and Sheraton Moana Surfrider, A Westin Resort, 2365 Kalakaua Ave., Ⓒ 808/923-6644; www.nohea gallery.com.

Shop Pacifica Local crafts, lauhala and Cook Island woven coconut, Hawaiian music tapes and CDs, pareu, and a vast selection of Hawaii-themed books anchor this gift shop. Hawaiian quilt cushion kits, jewelry, glassware, seed and Niihau shell leis, cookbooks, and many other gift possibilities will keep you occupied between stargazing in the planetarium and pondering the shells and antiquities of the esteemed historical museum. In the Bishop Museum, 1525 Bernice St. Ⓒ 808/848-4158.

KIDS

Baby Emporium Parents will be grateful that Tom Kim opened this one-stop shopping mecca for everything you could possibly need, from breast pumps and a range of strollers in a variety of styles and sizes, to clothes, blankets and even tiny T-shirts with a selection of sayings that will leave you laughing. 614 Cooke St. Ⓒ 808/596-4868.

Zuke's Magic & Jokes You don't have to be Harry Potter to enter here, but you may feel like him as you enter the store with the soda sign proclaiming C. ZUKEMURA STORE GENERAL MERCHANDISE. Amateur and professional magicians from around the island stream into this magic store that opens another world. Kids love this place, filled with shelves packed with tricks: candles that magically become flowers, a sponge ball that morphs into two balls, then three balls. . . . Go early, when it opens (call for hours), for a chance to "talk story" with 73-year-old owner Jimmy Zukemura, who doesn't just tell

his young patrons how to do a trick, but how to make the trick into real magic. Open
Saturdays only. 1516 Auld Lane (off Halona St.). ℂ **808/847-7788.**

SHOPPING CENTERS

Ala Moana Center   Many of the shops here are the familiar names of mainland
chains, such as **DKNY, Macy's, Neiman Marcus, Nordstrom, Sears,** and **Old Navy.**
The three-story, superluxe **Neiman Marcus,** opened in 1998, was a bold move in
Hawaii's troubled economy and has retained its position as the shrine of the fashionistas.
But there are practical touches in the center, too, such as banks, a U.S. Post Office, several optical companies (including 1-hr. service by **LensCrafters**), **Longs Drugs,** and a
handful of photo-processing services. The smaller locally owned stores are scattered
among the behemoths, mostly on the ground floor. Nearly 400 shops and restaurants
sprawl over several blocks (and 1.8 million sq. ft. of store space), catering to every imaginable need, from over-the-top upscale (**Tiffany, Chanel, Versace**) to mainland chains
such as **Gap** and **Banana Republic.** Department stores, such as **Macy's,** sell fashion,
food, cosmetics, shoes, and household needs. Need shoes? They're a kick at **Nordstrom,**
and **Walking Co.** has first-rate comfort styles by Mephisto, Ecco, and Naot.

A good stop for gifts is **Islands' Best,** which spills over with Hawaiian-made foodstuffs, ceramics, fragrances, and more. **Splash! Hawaii** is a good source for women's
swimwear. For aloha shirts and men's swimwear, try **Macy's, Town & Country Surf,**
Reyn's, or the terminally hip **Hawaiian Island Creations.** The **food court** is abuzz with
dozens of stalls purveying Cajun food, ramen, pizza, plate lunches, vegetarian fare, green
tea and fruit freezes (such as frozen yogurt), panini, and countless other treats. Hours are
Monday through Saturday 9:30am to 9pm, Sunday 10am to 7pm. 1450 Ala Moana
Blvd. ℂ **808/955-9517.** www.alamoanacenter.com. Bus: 8, 19, or 20. For Ala Moana
Shuttle Bus runs and Waikiki Trolley information, see "Getting There & Getting
Around," in chapter 2.

Aloha Tower Marketplace   There is a perpetual parking shortage here, and if you
do manage to find a parking spot, the rates are sky-high. Take the trolley if you can. The
refurbished Aloha Tower, once the tallest structure in Honolulu, still stands high over the
complex.

Dining and shopping prospects abound: **Hawaiian Ukulele Company, Don Ho's**
Island Grill, Chai's Island Bistro, and **Gordon Biersch Brewery Restaurant** (see chap-
ter 5 for details on the restaurants). Retail shops are open Monday through Saturday 9am
to 9pm, Sunday 9am to 6pm; dining and entertainment, daily 8am to midnight. Various
Honolulu trolleys stop here; if you want a direct ride from Waikiki, take the free Hilo
Hattie trolley or the Waikiki Red Line trolley, which continues on to Hilo Hattie in
Iwilei. 1 Aloha Tower Dr., on the waterfront btw. piers 8 and 11, Honolulu Harbor.
ℂ **808/528-5700.** www.alohatower.com. Aloha Tower Entertainment Hotline ℂ **808/**
566-2333.

DFS Galleria   "Boat days" is the theme at this newly renovated (to the tune of $65
million) Waikiki emporium, a three-floor extravaganza of shops ranging from the superluxe (such as **Givenchy** and **Coach**) to the very touristy. Great Hawaii food products
range from the incomparable **Big Island Candies'** shortbread cookies to a spate of coffees
and preserves. **The Tube,** a walk-through aquarium, is a big attraction. There are multi-
tudes of aloha shirts and T-shirts, a virtual golf course, surf and skate equipment, a terrific
Hawaiian music department, and a labyrinth of fashionable stores once you get past the
Waikiki Walk. Fragrances and cosmetics make a big splash at **DFS. Starbucks** and **Jamba**

Juice serve up coffee and smoothies, and **Kalia Grill** features rotisserie and deli items for casual dining. *Caveat:* Some sections are duty-free and therefore restricted to international travelers only. Free live Hawaiian entertainment, featuring hula styles from the 1920s through the 1940s, takes place nightly at 7pm. Daily 9am to 11pm. 330 Royal Hawaiian Ave. (corner of Kalakaua and Royal Hawaiian aves.). ℂ 808/931-2655. www.dfsgalleria. com.

Kahala Mall Chic, manageable, and unfrenzied, Kahala Mall is home to some of Honolulu's best shops. Located east of Waikiki in the posh neighborhood of Kahala, the mall has everything from a small **Macy's** to chain stores such as **Banana Republic** and **Barnes & Noble**—nearly 100 specialty shops (including dozens of eateries and eight movie theaters) in an enclosed, air-conditioned area. Java-magnet **Starbucks** sits a stone's throw from **Godiva Chocolatier,** with its sinfully wonderful treats. Smoothie lovers form long lines at **Jamba Juice.** For gift, fashion, and specialty stores, my picks of the mall's best and brightest are **Riches Kahala,** a tiny kiosk with a big, bold selection of jewelry; the **Compleat Kitchen;** and the **Body Shop,** with its lotions and potions. Monday through Saturday 10am to 9pm, Sunday 10am to 5pm. 4211 Waialae Ave., Kahala. ℂ 808/ 732-7736. www.kahalamallcenter.com.

Royal Hawaiian Shopping Center After 2 years and $115 million in renovations, a new, larger, upscale shopping center recently opened with 110 shops, restaurants, a nightclub and theater, and a garden grove of 70 coconut trees with an entertainment area. The result is a 310,000-square-foot open-air mall (17,000 sq. ft. larger than before), with shopping, dining, and activities on four levels, stretched along three blocks in the heart of Waikiki. The most exciting addition is the $15-million, 760-seat theater, with moving stages and acrobatic rigging. After the show, half of the theater's seating will retract to create a nightclub which holds up to 1,000 people. Upscale is the operative word here. Although there are drugstores, lei stands, restaurants, and food kiosks, the most conspicuous stores are the European designer boutiques (**Cartier, Hermès, L'Occitane, Fendi, Kate Spade, Bvlgari, Salvatore Ferragamo,** and more) that cater largely to visitors from Japan. Daily 10am to 10pm. 2201 Kalakaua Ave., Honolulu. ℂ 808/922-0588. www. shopwaikiki.com.

Waikele Premium Outlets Just say the word *Waikele* and my eyes glaze over. So many shops, so little time! There are two sections to this sprawling discount shopping mecca: the **Waikele Premium Outlets,** some 51 retailers offering designer and name-brand merchandise; and the **Waikele Value Center** across the street, with another 25 stores that are more practical than fashion-oriented (**Eagle Hardware, Sports Authority).** The 64-acre complex has made discount shopping a travel pursuit in itself, with tours for visitor groups and carloads of neighbor islanders and Oahu residents making pilgrimages from all corners of the state. They come to hunt down bargains on everything from perfumes, luggage, and hardware to sporting goods, fashions, vitamins, and china. Examples: **Armani Exchange, Saks Fifth Avenue, Anne Klein, Brooks Brothers, Calvin Klein, Izod, Polo Ralph Lauren, Banana Republic,** and the ultra-chic **Barneys.** Monday through Friday 9am to 9pm, Sunday 10am to 6pm. To find out which companies offer shopping tours with Waikiki pickups, call the **Information Center** at ℂ 808/ 678-0786. 94-790 Lumiaina St., Waikele (about 20 miles from Waikiki). ℂ 808/676-5656. www. premiumoutlets.com/waikele. Take H-1 west toward Waianae and turn off at exit 7. Bus: 42 from Waikiki to Waipahu Transit Center, then 433 from Transit Center to Waikele.

Ward Centre   Although it has a high turnover and a changeable profile, Ward Centre is a standout for its concentration of restaurants and shops. **Ryan's** and **Kakaako Kitchen** are as popular as ever, the former looking out over Ala Moana Park and the latter with lanai views of the sprawling **Pier 1 Imports** across the street. **Nordstrom Rack** and **Office Depot** have sprouted in a new development area that includes a 16-theater movie megaplex now being built. All these establishments are part of developer Victoria Ward's Kakaako projects, which take up several blocks in this area: Ward Centre, Ward Farmers' Market, Ward Village Shops, Ward Gateway Center, and Ward Warehouse.

Ward Centre's gift shops and galleries include **Crazy Shirts Factory Outlet** for T-shirts, **Honolulu Chocolate Co.** (see "Edibles," earlier in this chapter). **Borders** is action central, bustling with browsers. Monday through Saturday 10am to 9pm, Sunday 10am to 5pm. 1200 Ala Moana Blvd. ℂ 808/591-8411. www.victoriaward.com.

Ward Entertainment Center   This large, multiblock complex includes Ward Centre, mentioned above, and Ward Warehouse, mentioned below, at the corner of Auahi and Kamakee streets. The complex has undergone enormous expansion, beginning with a new 16-movie megaplex, and a new retail-and-restaurant complex, with such eateries as **Dave & Buster's** (with virtual golf, games, interactive entertainment, bars, and a restaurant), **Buca di Beppo,** and **Cold Stone Creamery.** Monday through Saturday 10am to 10pm, Sunday 10am to 9pm. Auahi and Kamakee sts. ℂ **808/591-8411.** www.victoriaward.com.

Ward Warehouse   Older than its sister property, Ward Centre, and endowed with an endearing patina, Ward Warehouse remains a popular stop for dining and shopping. **Native Books & Beautiful Things** and the **Nohea Gallery** (see "Hawaiiana & Gift Items," above, for both) are excellent sources for quality Hawaii-made arts and crafts.

Other recommended stops include **C. June Shoes** for designer footwear; **Mamo Howell** for distinctive aloha wear; and **Quiksilver Youth,** brimming with tasteful gifts for kids and babies. For T-shirts and swimwear, check out the **T& C Surf Shop,** and for an excellent selection of sunglasses, knapsacks, and footwear. Monday through Saturday 10am to 9pm, Sunday 10am to 5pm. 1050 Ala Moana Blvd. ℂ **808/591-8411.** www.victoria ward.com.

The New Royal Hawaiian Shopping Center

The Royal Hawaiian Shopping Center has just finished a massive 2-year renovation, to the tune of $115 million, and is updated with a new look: Instead of clusters of stores, one right next to another, the renovated mall is filled with open space, lots of light, big windows, and breezeways between shops. The 310,000-square-foot, open-air mall is 17,000 square feet larger and has four stories of 110 restaurants, stores, and entertainment attractions, and stretched over three blocks in the heart of Waikiki. The central performance area features a landscaped courtyard with a pond, artesian fountain, stream, performance area with seating, and a statue of Princess Bernice Pauahi Bishop. The second level has a nine-restaurant food court. The biggest change is the exterior finish, with a Polynesian-kapa look, and an open-air bridge that connects the central area to the wings of the mall (with a panoramic view of the Royal Hawaiian Hotel).

The surf-and-sports shops scattered throughout Honolulu are a highly competitive lot, with each trying to capture your interest (and dollars). But we can't live without them.

The Bike Shop Excellent for cycling and backpacking equipment for all levels, with major camping lines such as North Face, MSR, and Kelty. 1149 S. King St., near Piikoi St. ⓒ 808/596-0588.

Hawaiian Island Creations HIC is a super-cool surf shop offering sunglasses, sun lotions, surf wear, surfboards, skateboards, and accessories galore. In the Ala Moana Center, 1450 Ala Moana Blvd. ⓒ 808/973-6780. Other locations are in Pearlridge (ⓒ 808/483-6700) and Haleiwa (ⓒ 808/637-0991).

McCully Bicycle & Sporting Goods Find everything from bicycles and fishing gear to athletic shoes and accessories and a stunning selection of sunglasses. 2124 S. King St. ⓒ 808/955-6329.

The Sports Authority This discount mega-outlet offers a huge variety of sporting equipment—including clothing and shoes—cycles, all sorts of fishing gear, camping gear, beach chairs, and everything else you can imagine for life outside the office. 333 Ward Ave. ⓒ 808/596-0166. Also at Waikele Center (ⓒ 808/677-9933).

2 WINDWARD OAHU

KAILUA

Longs Drugs and **Macy's** department store, located side-by-side on Kailua Road in the heart of this windward Oahu community, form the shopping nexus of the neighborhood.

Agnes Portuguese Bake Shop (**Finds**) This Kailua treasure is the longtime favorite of Hawaii's *malassada* mavens. *Malassadas*—sugary Portuguese dumplings that look and taste like doughnuts without holes—fly out of the bakery, infusing the entire neighborhood with an irresistible aroma. The Bake Shop also offers a variety of pastries, cookies, scones, Portuguese bean and other soups, and local- and European-style breads. 46 Hoolai St. ⓒ 808/262-5367.

Alii Antiques of Kailua II Abandon all restraint, particularly if you have a weakness for vintage Hawaiiana. Koa lamps and rattan furniture from the 1930s and 1940s, hula bobbleheads, rare 1940s koa tables, Roseville vases, Don Blanding dinnerware, and a breathtaking array of vintage etched-glass vases and trays are some of the items in this unforgettable shop. Across the street, the owner's wife runs **Alii Antiques of Kailua,** which is chockablock with jewelry, clothing, Bauer and Fiesta Ware, linens, Bakelite bracelets, and floor-to-ceiling collectibles. 9-A Maluniu Ave., Kailua. ⓒ 808/261-1705.

BookEnds BookEnds is the quintessential neighborhood bookstore, run by a pro who buys good books and knows how to find the ones she doesn't have. There are more than 60,000 titles here, new and used, from *Celtic Mandalas* to C. S. Lewis's *Chronicles of Narnia* and the full roster of current bestsellers. Volumes on child care, cooking, and self-improvement; a hefty periodicals section; and mainstream and offbeat titles are among the treasures to be found. 600 Kailua Rd., Kailua. ⓒ 808/261-1996.

Heritage Antiques & Gifts This Kailua landmark is known for its selection of Tiffany-style lamps (ranging $200–$2,000). The mind-boggling inventory also includes

European, Asian, American, local, and Pacific Island collectibles. The shop is fun, the people friendly, and the selection diverse enough to appeal to the casual as well as serious collector. Glassware; china; and estate, costume, and fine jewelry are among the items of note. Heritage has its own jeweler who does custom designs and repairs, plus a stable of woodworkers who turn out custom-made koa rockers and hutches to complement the antique furniture selection. 767 Kailua Rd. ✆ **808/261-8700.**

KANEOHE

Windward Oahu's largest shopping complex is the **Windward Mall,** 46-056 Kamehameha Hwy., in Kaneohe (✆ **808/235-1143**), open Monday through Saturday from 10am to 9pm and Sunday from 10am to 5pm. The big draw here is the 10-screen theater complex. The 100 stores and services at this standard suburban mall include **Macy's** and **Sears,** health stores, airline counters, and surf shops. A small food court serves pizza, Chinese fare, tacos, and other morsels, and the new theaters are a big draw for Windwardites.

---

3 THE NORTH SHORE: HALEIWA

Haleiwa means serious shopping for those who know that the unhurried pace of rural life can conceal vast material treasures. Ask the legions of townies who drive an hour each way just to stock up on wine and clothes at Haleiwa stores. Below are our Haleiwa highlights.

ART, GIFTS & CRAFTS

Haleiwa's shops and galleries display a combination of marine art, watercolors, and sculptures, as well as a plethora of crafts trying to masquerade as fine art. This is the town for gifts, fashions, and surf stuff—mostly casual, despite some very high price tags. **Haleiwa Gallery** in the North Shore Marketplace displays a lot of local art of the non-marine variety, and some of it is appealing.

Global Creations Interiors   Global Creations offers casual clothing as well as international imports for the home, including Balinese bamboo furniture and colorful hammocks for the carefree life. There are gifts and crafts by 115 local potters, painters, and artists of other media. 66-079 Kamehameha Hwy. ✆ **808/637-1505.**

Oceans in Glass   You can watch as local artists create beautiful sea-life sculptures of dolphins, sea turtles, humpback whales, sharks, and colorful reef fish all blown from glass in their studios within the gallery. North Shore Marketplace, 66-250 Kamehameha Hwy. ✆ **808/637-3366.**

EDIBLES

Haleiwa is best known for its roadside shave-ice stands: the famous **Matsumoto Shave Ice** ★, with the perennial queue snaking along Kamehameha Highway, and nearby **Aoki's.** Shave ice is the popular island version of a snow cone, topped with your choice of syrups, such as strawberry, rainbow, root beer, vanilla, or passion fruit. Aficionados order it with a scoop of ice cream and sweetened black adzuki beans nestled in the middle.

Tiny, funky **Celestial Natural Foods,** 66-443 Kamehameha Hwy. (✆ **808/637-6729**), is the health foodie's one-stop shop for everything from wooden spine-massagers to health supplements, produce, cosmetics, and bulk foods.

Although Haleiwa used to be an incense-infused surfer outpost, where zoris and tank tops were the regional uniform and the Beach Boys and Ravi Shankar the music of the day, today it's one of the top shopping destinations for those with unconventional tastes. Specialty shops abound.

Top-drawer **Silver Moon Emporium,** North Shore Marketplace, 66-250 Kamehameha Hwy. (© **808/637-7710**), features the terrific finds of owner Lucie Talbot-Holu. Exquisite clothing and handbags, reasonably priced footwear, hats straight out of *Vogue,* jewelry, scarves, and a full gamut of other treasures pepper the attractive boutique. The entire line of chic Brighton accessories—shoes, handbags, fragrance, belts, and jewelry—are a prized addition.

Other highlights of the prominent North Shore Marketplace include **Patagonia** (© **808/637-1245**) for high-quality surf, swim, hiking, kayaking, and all-around adventure wear; **North Shore Swimwear** (© **808/637-6859**) for excellent mix-and-match bikinis and one-piece suits, custom-ordered or off the rack; and **Jungle Gems** (© **808/ 637-6609**), the mother lode of gemstones, crystals, silver, and beadwork.

Nearby **Oogenesis Boutique,** 66-249 Kamehameha Hwy. (© **808/637-4422**), in the southern part of Haleiwa, features a storefront lined with vintage-looking dresses that flutter prettily in the North Shore breeze.

SURF SHOPS

Haleiwa's ubiquitous surf shops are the best on earth, surfers say.

Barnfield's Raging Isle Sports & Cycle Shop Barnfield's is the surf-and-cycle center of the area, with everything from wet suits and surfboards to surf gear and clothing for men, women, and children. The adjoining surfboard factory puts out custom-built boards of high renown. There's also a large inventory of mountain bikes for rent and sale. In the North Shore Marketplace, 66-250 Kamehameha Hwy. © **808/637-7707.**

Northshore Boardriders Club Cream of the crop, this is the mecca of the board-riding elite, with sleek, fast, elegant, and top-of-the-line boards designed by North Shore legends such as long board shaper Barry Kanaiaupuni, John Carper, Jeff Bushman, and Pat Rawson. This is a Quicksilver "concept store," which means that it's the testing ground for the newest and hottest trends in surf wear put out by the retail giant. In the North Shore Marketplace, 66-250 Kamehameha Hwy. © **808/637-5026.**

Surf & Sea Surf Sail & Dive Shop A longtime favorite among old-timers is this newly expanded, flamboyant roadside structure just over the bridge, with old wood floors and blowing fans. It sports a tangle of surf and swimwear, T-shirts, surfboards, boogie boards, fins, watches, sunglasses, and miscellaneous goods; you can also rent surf and snorkel equipment here. 62-595 Kamehameha Hwy. © **808/637-9887.**

Tropical Rush Tropical Rush has a huge inventory of surf and swim gear: surfboards, long boards, bodyboards, Sector 9 skateboards, and all the accessories to go with an ocean-minded life, such as slippers and swimwear for men and women. T-shirts, hats, sunglasses, and visors are among the scads of cool gear, and you can rent equipment and arrange surf lessons, too. An added feature is the shop's surf report line, for the up-to-the-minute lowdown on wave action (© **808/638-7874**); it covers the day's surf and weather details for all of Oahu. 62-620-A Kamehameha Hwy. © **808/637-8886.**

9

Oahu After Dark

A must-do on your Hawaii vacation—take the time every day to stop and enjoy the sunset. You can watch the big yellow ball descend slowly into the blue water of the Pacific from anywhere on the Waikiki-Honolulu-Leeward side of the island. Some insist on viewing the sunset with a locally made tropical mai tai. When the sun is low, make the tropical mix with fresh lime juice, fresh lemon juice, fresh orange juice, passion-orange-guava juice, and fresh grapefruit juice, if possible. Pour this concoction on ice in tall, frosty glasses, and then add Meyer's rum, in which Tahitian vanilla beans have been soaking for days. (Add cinnamon, if desired, or soak a

cinnamon stick with the rum and vanilla beans.) A dash of Angostura bitters, a few drops of Southern Comfort as a float, a sprig of mint, a garnish of fresh lime, and voilà!—you have a tropical, homemade mai tai, a cross between planter's punch and the classic Trader Vic's mai tai. As the sun sets, lift your glass and savor the moment, the setting, and the first sip—not a bad way to end the day.

In Hawaii, the mai tai is more than a libation. It's a festive, happy ritual that signals holiday, vacation, or a time of play, not work. Computers and mai tais don't mix. Mai tais and hammocks do. Mai tais and sunsets go hand in hand.

IT BEGINS WITH SUNSET . . .

Nightlife in Hawaii begins at sunset, when all eyes turn westward to see how the day will end. Like seeing the same pod of whales or school of spinner dolphins, sunset viewers seem to bond in the mutual enjoyment of a natural spectacle.

On Fridays and Saturdays at 6:30pm, as the sun casts its golden glow on the beach, and surfers and beach boys paddle in for the day, **Kuhio Beach,** where Kalakaua Avenue intersects with Kaiulani, eases into evening with hula dancing and a torch-lighting ceremony. It's a thoroughly delightful, free weekend offering. Start off earlier with a picnic basket and your favorite libations and walk along the oceanside path fronting Queen's Surf, near the Waikiki Aquarium. (You can park along Kapiolani Park or near the Honolulu Zoo.) There are few more pleasing spots in Waikiki than the benches at the water's edge at the Diamond Head end of Kalakaua Avenue, where lovers and families of all ages stop to peruse the sinking sun. A short walk across the intersection of Kalakaua and Kapahulu avenues takes you to the Duke Kahanamoku statue on Kuhio Beach and the nearby Wizard Stones.

1 THE BAR & CLUB SCENE

ON THE BEACH

Waikiki's beachfront bars offer many possibilities, from the Royal Hawaiian Hotel's **Mai Tai Bar** (© 808/923-7311), a few feet from the sand, to the unfailingly enchanting **House Without a Key,** at the Halekulani (© **808/923-2311**), where the breathtaking former Miss Hawaii, Kanoelehua Miller, dances hula to the riffs of Hawaiian steel–pedal guitar under a century-old kiawe tree. With the sunset and ocean glowing behind her and Diamond Head visible in the distance, the scene is straight out of Somerset Maugham—romantic, evocative, nostalgic. It doesn't hurt, either, that the Halekulani happens to make the best mai tais in the world. Halekulani has the after-dinner hours covered, too, with light jazz by local artists from 10:15pm to midnight nightly.

Another great bar for watching the sun sink into the Pacific is **Duke's Waikiki** (© 808/922-2268; www.dukeswaikiki.com), in the Outrigger Waikiki on the Beach (p. 126). The outside Barefoot Bar is perfect for sipping a tropical drink, watching the waves and sunset, and listening to music. It can get crowded, so get here early. Hawaii sunset music is usually from 4 to 6pm on weekends, and there's live entertainment nightly from 10pm to midnight.

IN THE ALOHA TOWER MARKETPLACE

Unlike Waikiki, palm trees don't sway at **Aloha Tower Marketplace,** which is on the waterfront, between piers 8 and 11, Honolulu Harbor (© 808/528-5700). But the landmark Aloha Tower at Honolulu Harbor, once Oahu's tallest building, does occupy Honolulu's prime downtown location—on the water, at a naturally sheltered bay, near the business and civic center of Honolulu. Since its construction, the Aloha Tower Marketplace, 1 Aloha Tower Dr., has gained popularity as an entertainment and nightlife spot, with more than 100 shops and restaurants, including several venues for Honolulu's leading musical groups.

In the **Gordon Biersch Brewery Restaurant** (p. 137; © 808/599-4877; www. gordonbiersch.com), diners swing to jazz, blues, and island riffs with a changing slate of entertainers from sunset through the evening Wednesday through Saturday. The food and beer are great, too. The roster of performers includes the cream of the local contemporary music crop, and the **Atrium Center Court** features ongoing programs of foot-stomping good times. Hours at the Marketplace are daily 8am to midnight.

Most notable, however, is **Don Ho's Island Grill** (© 808/528-0807), a local hotspot, with Willie K. and other musical icons taking the stage throughout the year. It's worth calling to see who's playing. Also check out **Chai's Island Bistro** (© 808/585-0011), one of Honolulu's hottest nightspots (see "Hawaiian Music," below, for more on Chai's).

See chapter 5 for reviews of the Gordon Biersch Brewery Restaurant, Don Ho's Island Grill, and Chai's Island Bistro mentioned above.

DOWNTOWN

The downtown scene is awakening from a long slumber, thanks to the performances at the **Hawaii Theatre** and the popular Nuuanu Avenue block parties, courtesy of some tenacious entrepreneurs who want everyone to love Nuuanu as much as they do. **Hank's Café** on Nuuanu between Hotel and King streets (© 808/526-1410; www.hankscafe honolulu.com) is a tiny, kitschy, friendly pub with nightly live music, open-mic nights, and special events that attract great talent and a supportive crowd. On some nights, the music spills out into the streets and it's so packed you have to press your nose against the window to see what you're missing. At the *makai* end of Nuuanu, toward the pier, **Murphy's Bar & Grill** (© 808/531-0422; www.gomurphys.com) and **O'Toole's Irish Pub** (© 808/536-6360), which recently built an entertainment stage, are the downtown ale houses and media haunts that have kept Irish eyes smiling for years.

Bar 35, 35 N. Hotel St. (*©* **808/537-3535;** www.bar35hawaii.com), is a great watering hole/grill with full bar (110 beers), eats (from pizza to oysters on the half shell), and rock-n-roll music in the background. Happy hour (Mon–Fri 4–8pm) features excellent prices, with beers discounted.

At the edge of Chinatown is something straight out of 1940s film noir: **Indigo's,** 1121 Nuuanu Ave. (*©* **808/521-2900;** www.indigo-hawaii.com), which serves sizzling food during the day, turns to cool jazz in the early evening, and progresses to late-night DJs spinning Top 40, disco, rock, funk, and more.

Another Chinatown "in" spot is **thirtyninehotel,** 29 N. Hotel St., between Smith Street and Nuuanu Avenue (*©* **808/599-2552;** www.thirtyninehotel.com), where live jazz and visiting and resident DJs rock all night (but during the day, it morphs into an art gallery, featuring contemporary local artists; Tues–Sat noon–6pm). The door is unmarked, with only the address to tell you where you are. Enter and walk up the stairs to the second floor. The cover is $8 to $10.

WAIKIKI & SURROUNDIING AREA

The nightclub scene in Waikiki and Honolulu is just as hot as the sun-kissed beaches during the day. It's more laid-back than in such big cities as New York; dress is casual (though usually slippers, tank tops, or athletic wear are a no-no), and there's no point in even showing up until midnight. The **Wave Waikiki,** 1877 Kalakaua Ave. (btw. Ala Wai Blvd. and Ena Rd.; *©* **808/941-0424;** www.wavewaikiki.com), is one of Hawaii's top dance clubs, with two levels (and two bars), featuring a huge variety of live music and every type of DJ you can think of. Open nightly from 9pm to 4am; cover is $5 to $7 on weekdays and $7 to $10 on weekends (more for special events). Dress code is so laid-back—all they care about is if you have something on your back and on your feet.

Twice the size of the Wave and filled with dancing, darts, pool, and a sports bar with huge TVs is the **Pipeline,** 805 Pohukaina St., in Kakaako (*©* **808/589-1999;** www.pipelinecafe.net). Patrons here tend to be younger than at the Wave (you can get in at 18 years old, but some events specify 21 and over) and dressed to go clubbing. The cover is generally $5 to $10; concerts are around $20 to $25.

The 20-something crowd, visitors, and military personnel head to **Moose McGillycuddy's,** 310 Lewers St., in Waikiki (*©* **808/923-0751;** www.mooserestaurantgroup.com/waikiki-hawaii.html). Downstairs is a cafe serving breakfast, lunch, and dinner; upstairs is a happening entertainment and dance club. Tuesday is $2 drink night, but with a $5 to $7 cover (it's the busiest night of the week).

Rumours Nightclub, in the lobby of the Ala Moana Hotel, 410 Atkinson Dr. (*©* **808/955-4811**), is the disco of choice for those who remember Paul McCartney as something other than Stella's father. The theme changes by the month, but generally, it's the "Big Chill" '60s, '70s, and '80s music on Friday; the "Little Chill" on Saturday; ballroom dancing from 5 to 9pm on Sunday; Top 40 on Tuesday; karaoke on Wednesday; and an "after-work office party" until midnight on Thursday. A spacious dance floor, a good sound system, and Top 40 music draw a mix of generations.

GAY BARS & CLUBS

The reigning queen of gay bars and clubs in Waikiki is **Hula's Bar & Lei Stand,** Waikiki Grand, 134 Kapahulu Ave., second floor (*©* **808/923-0669**), still going strong after 3½ decades. Overlooking Kapiolani Park, Queen's Surf Beach, and the Honolulu Zoo,

Waikiki's most popular and best known gay bar is packed from the 10am opening until last call at 2am the next day. **Angles Waikiki,** 2256 Kuhio (corner of Seaside Ave.), second floor, (📞 **808/926-9766;** www.angleswaikiki.com), is a more relaxed place with people lounging outside on the lanai under a tropical moon. Patrons can also shoot pool, dance, or check out the eye candy posing at the bar. Gay catamaran cruises set sail Sundays (3–7pm). Drag queens gather at **Fusion Waikiki,** 2260 Kuhio Ave. (near Seaside Ave.), second floor (📞 **808/924-2422**), for the Gender Bender Lip Gloss Revue on Fridays and the Paper Doll Revue on Saturdays, plus a male strip show both nights ($5 cover). The clientele tends toward local Hawaii residents at this only after-hours (till 4am) gay bar. **The In-Between,** 2155 Lauula St. (near Lewers St.; 📞 **808/926-7060;** www.inbetweenonline.com), is a neighborhood gay bar with a great karaoke sound system (you can belt out everything from contemporary hits and Broadway to Hawaiian and country and western).

2 HAWAIIAN MUSIC

"Aloha shirt to Armani" is what we call the night scene in Honolulu—mostly casual, but with ample opportunity to dress up if you can bear to part with your flip-flops.

Oahu has several key spots for Hawaiian music. A delightful (and powerful) addition to the Waikiki music scene is Hawaii's queen of falsetto, **Genoa Keawe,** who fills the Lobby Bar of the **Hawaiian Regent Hotel** (📞 **808/922-6611**) with her larger-than-life voice. You'll find her here from 5:30 to 8:30pm every Thursday; the rest of the week, except Monday, other contemporary Hawaiian musicians fill in.

Brothers Cazimero remains one of Hawaii's most gifted duos (Robert on bass, Roland on 12-string guitar), appearing every Wednesday at 7pm at **Chai's Island Bistro** (📞 **808/585-0011**), in the Aloha Tower Marketplace. Also at Chai's: Robert Cazimero plays by himself on the piano on Fridays at 7pm; and **Jerry Santos and Olomana** performs on Sundays and Mondays at 7pm. If you're here on May 1, Lei Day, the Brothers Caz give

Get Down with ARTafterDark

The last Friday of every month (except Nov and Dec), the place to be after the sun goes down is the **Honolulu Academy of Arts' ARTafterDark** ★★★, a *pau-hana* (after-work) mixer in the art museum that brings residents and visitors together around a theme combining art with food, music, and dancing. In addition to the exhibits in the gallery, ARTafterDark also features visual and live performances. Last year the themes ranged from "Plant Rice"—with rice and sake tastings, Asian beers, live Asian fusion music, and a tour of the "Art of Rice" exhibit—to "'80s Night," "Turkish Delights," "Cool Nights," "Hot Jazz and Blues," and "Havana Heat."

The party gets going about 6pm and lasts until 9pm. The crowd—ranging in age from their 20s to 50s—dresses in everything from jeans and T-shirts to designer cocktail party attire. Entry fee is $10. For more information, call 📞 **808/532-6091** or visit www.artafterdark.org.

a special concert at the Waikiki Shell, as they do every year—one of the loveliest events in Hawaii. Locals dress up in their leis and best aloha shirts, the air smells like pikake and pakalana, and the moon sometimes rises over Diamond Head.

Impromptu hula and spirited music from the family and friends of the performers are an island tradition at places such as the Hilton Hawaiian Village's **Paradise Lounge** (*© 808/949-4321*), which, despite its pillars, serves as a large living room for the full-bodied music of **Olomana.** The group plays Friday and Saturday from 8pm to midnight (no cover, one-drink minimum). At **Duke's Canoe Club** at the Outrigger Waikiki (*© 808/923-0711*), it's always three deep at the beachside bar as the sun sets; extra-special entertainment is a given here—usually from 4 to 6pm on Friday, Saturday, and Sunday, and nightly from 10pm to midnight.

Nearby, the Moana Surfrider offers a regular nightly program of live Hawaiian music and piano in its **Banyan Veranda** (*© 808/922-3111*), which surrounds an islet-size canopy of banyan tree and roots where Robert Louis Stevenson loved to linger. The Veranda serves afternoon tea, a sunset buffet, and cocktails.

My best advice for Hawaiian music lovers is to scan the local dailies (especially Friday's pull-out TGIF section in the *Honolulu Advertiser*, www.honoluluadvertiser.com) or the *Honolulu Weekly* (www.honoluluweekly.com) to see if and where the following Hawaiian entertainers are appearing: **Kekuhi Kanahele,** an accomplished, award-winning chanter and *kahiko* (ancient hula) dancer; **Hookena,** a symphonically rich quintet featuring **Manu Boyd,** one of the most prolific songwriters and chanters in Hawaii; **Kealii Reichel,** premier chanter, dancer, and award-winning recording artist; **Robbie Kahaka-lau,** another award-winning musician; **Kapena,** for contemporary Hawaiian music; **Na Leo Pilimehana,** a trio of angelic Hawaiian singers; the **Makaha Sons of Niihau,** pioneers in the Hawaiian cultural renaissance; **Fiji,** a performer whose music is classified as Hawaiian Soul; and slack-key guitar master **Raymond Kane.**

Consider the gods beneficent if you happen to be here when the hula *halau* of **Frank Kawaikapuokalani Hewett** is holding its annual fundraiser. It's a rousing, inspired, fam-ily effort that always features the best in ancient and contemporary Hawaiian music. For the best in hula, check the dailies for halau fundraisers, which are always authentic, enriching, and local to the core.

---

3 THE BLUES

The blues are alive and well in Hawaii, with quality acts both local and from the main-land drawing enthusiastic crowds. **Junior Wells, Willie & Lobo, War,** and surprise appearances by the likes of **Bonnie Raitt** are among the past successes of this genre of big-time licks. The best-loved Oahu venue is **Anna Bannanas,** 2440 S. Beretania St., between University Avenue/Isenberg Street. (*© 808/946-5190*), still rocking after 30 years in the business, with reggae, blues, and rock—plus video games and darts.

---

4 JAZZ

Jazz lovers should watch for the **Great Hawaiian Jazz Blow-Out** every March, at Mid-Pacific Institute's Bakken Hall, which is at the south end of Honolulu, near Diamond Head (*© 808/734-0397*).

To find out what's happening in the jazz scene while you're in town, check out www. honolulujazzscene.net. **Diamond Head Grill** (© 808/922-3734; p. 121) features live music nightly; and **Duc's Bistro** (© 808/531-6325; p. 137), downtown, presents live jazz nightly except Thursday, when vocalist Mihana Souza brings her style of Hawaiian music to the cozy venue. Also in Chinatown, **thirtyninehotel,** 29 N. Hotel St. (© 808/ 599-2552; www.thirtyninehotel.com) has live jazz at night; during the day, the same space morphs into an art gallery.

In Waikiki, tops in taste and ambience is the perennially alluring **Lewers Lounge,** in the Halekulani, 2199 Kalia Rd. (© 808/923-2311; www.halekulani.com). Recently renovated (higher ceiling, contemporary color scheme, and comfy intimate seating around the pillars), this a great spot for contemporary jazz nightly from 8:30pm to midnight. And with expert mixologist Dale DeGroff (the "king of cocktails") now the hotel's director of beverages, the drinks are better than ever. Be sure to try the Hpnotiq Liqueur (Dale's own creation), a blend of premium vodka, cognac, and fruit juices from France, served over ice or in various concoctions.

Also in Waikiki, **Nick's Fishmarket,** Waikiki Gateway Hotel, 2070 Kalakaua Ave. (© 808/955-6333), offers live entertainment nightly in its lounge—mild jazz or contemporary Top 40 hits.

Outside of Waikiki, the **Veranda,** at the Kahala Resort, 5000 Kahala Ave. (© 808/ 739-8888; www.kahalaresort.com), is a popular spot for the over-40 crowd, with nightly jazz music and a dance floor.

In Honolulu, jazz fans will love **Jazz Wednesdays** at the **Honolulu Club,** 932 Ward Ave. (© 808/543-3900), where the seventh-floor lounge of this ultra-upscale fitness center turns into a jazz nightclub with a wall of windows overlooking the Honolulu skyline. Music begins at 6pm (and lasts until 9pm), but the tables start filling up at 5:30pm. Cover is $5 and the crowd, often from the surrounding offices, generally ranges from people in their mid-20s to 50s. Skip the high-priced *pupu* (appetizers), but the local jazz musicians are well worth the price of drinks (martinis, ranging from $6.75 to $7.75, are your best bet).

Around town, watch for **Sandy Tsukiyama,** a gifted singer (Brazilian, Latin, jazz) and one of Honolulu's great assets, as well as for jazz singers **Rachel Gonzales** and **Loretta Ables.** Other noteworthy groups in jazz, blues, and r&b include **Blue Budda, Bongo Tribe, Secondhand Smoke, Bluzilla, Piranha Brothers,** and the **Greg Pai Trio.**

5 THE PERFORMING ARTS

Audiences have stomped to the big Off-Broadway percussion hit *Stomp* and have enjoyed the talent of *Tap Dogs,* Momix, the Hawaii International Jazz Festival, the American Repertory Dance Company, and John Kaimikaua's *halau*—all at the **Hawaii Theatre,** 1130 Bethel St., downtown (© 808/528-0506; www.hawaiitheatre.com), Hawaii's Carnegie Hall of the Pacific, still basking in its renaissance following a 4-year, $22-million renovation (it was built in 1922). The neoclassical Beaux Arts landmark features an original 1922 dome, 1,400 plush seats, and a hydraulically elevated organ. Breathtaking murals create an atmosphere that's making the theater a leading multipurpose center.

Other smaller theaters on Oahu are: the **Manoa Valley Theatre,** 2833 E. Manoa Rd. (© 808/988-6131; www.manoavalleytheatre.com), Honolulu's equivalent of Off Broadway, with well-known shows performing; **Diamond Head Theatre,** 520 Makapuu Ave.

If you are on island the first Thursday of the month, head for the **Poetry Slam** at the Hawaiian Hut, Ala Moana Hotel, 410 Atkinson Dr. ((C) **808/387-9664;** www. hawaiiislam.com), where standing-room-only crowds (500 is not uncommon) come to listen to Hawaii's best performance poets and live music, while painters and DJs keep the energy high. Show starts at 8:30pm, $3 before and $5 after showtime.

((C) **808/733-0274;** www.diamondheadtheatre.com), hosting a variety of performances from musicals to comedies to classical dramas; **Kumu Kahua Theatre,** 46 Merchant St. ((C) **808/536-4222;** www.kumukahua.org), producing plays dealing with the island experience, often written by residents; **Army Community Theatre,** Richardson Theatre, Fort Shafter ((C) **808/438-5230**), offering revivals of Broadway musicals; and **Leeward Community College Theatre,** 96-045 Ala Ike St. ((C) **808/455-0385**), featuring an eclectic slate of productions, from visiting performing companies to local students' work.

The **Honolulu Symphony Orchestra** performs at the Waikiki Shell and the **Neal Blaisdell Center** ((C) **808/591-2211;** www.honolulusymphony.com), Hawaii's premier performance center for the best in entertaining. This arena/concert hall/exhibition building can be divided into an intimate 2,175-seat concert hall or an 8,805-seat arena, serving everyone from symphony goers to punk rockers. The Symphony is in house from September to May and then the highly successful **Hawaii Opera Theatre** ((C) **808/596-7858;** www.hawaiiopera.org) takes to the stage from January to March. Started in 1960 (past hits have included *La Bohème, Carmen, Turandot, Romeo and Juliet, Rigoletto,* and *Aida*), the Opera still draws fans to the Neal Blaisdell Concert Hall. In the summer during July, the Hawaii Opera Theatre (HOT) puts on a lighter performance such as *South Pacific.* Dance also makes the list at the center with **Ballet Hawaii** ((C) **808/521-6514;** www.ballethawaii.org) performing twice a year in August—in 2007, Tchaikovsky's *Sleeping Beauty* was presented—and the annual *Nutcracker* ballet (generally sold out) in December.

SHOWROOM ACTS & REVUES

Showroom acts that have maintained a following start with the **Society of Seven's** nightclub act (a blend of skits, Broadway hits, popular music, and costumed musical acts), in the **Outrigger Waikiki on the Beach** ((C) **808/923-0711;** www.outriggeractivities.com). Shows are Tuesday through Sunday at 8pm; dinner costs $75; show-only is $37 adults and $24 children 2 to 20. Across the street at the **Waikiki Beachcomber** is the performance of *The Magic of Polynesia* ((C) **808/971-4321;** www.magicofpolynesia.com), a show with illusionist **John Hirokana,** nightly at 8pm (dinner $85 adults, children $57 ages 4–11; show-only $53 adults, $35 children ages 4–11, *note:* book on their website for 20% discount).

Also on Kalakaua Avenue is the still-sizzling Polynesian revue, **"Creation—A Polynesian Odyssey"** ((C) **808/931-4660;** www.princess-kaiulani.com/de_creation.htm) in the **Sheraton Princess Kaiulani**'s second-floor Ainahau Showroom. Produced by **Tihati** (pronounced tea-*hot*-tea), the state's largest entertainment company, the show is a theatrical journey of fire dancing, special effects, illusions, hula, and Polynesian dances from

Hawaii and the South Pacific. Dinner shows are Tuesday, Thursday, Friday, Saturday, and Sunday and cost $85 to $135 adults and $64 to $100 for children 5 to 12 years.

The best in comedy is **Andy Bumatai,** who performs local stand-up sketches that will have you not only understanding local residents, but also screaming with laughter. Another excellent comic is **Frank Delima.** If he's playing anywhere on Oahu, it's worth the drive to see this comic genius, who sings, dances, and performs comic routines that will have you laughing until your sides hurt.

LUAU!

The sun is setting, the tiki torches are lit, the pig is taken from the *imu* (an oven in the earth), the drums begin pounding—it's luau time. Recently, three new luau have started: in Waikiki, on the North Shore, and in windward Oahu at Sea Life Park. Regrettably, there's no commercial luau on Oahu that comes close to Maui's Old Lahaina Luau, or Hawaii Island's legendary Kona Village Luau. In Waikiki, the **Royal Hawaiian Hotel,** 2259 Kalakaua Ave. (at Seaside Ave.; ℭ **888/808-4668;** www.royal-hawaiian.com), is Waikiki's only oceanfront luau. Upon arrival, you'll be greeted with a Hawaiian flower lei and a refreshing drink, followed by a feast: a variety of traditional Hawaiian as well as continental American dishes. The buffet menu features delicacies such as roasted kalua pig, mahimahi, teriyaki steak, poi, sweet potatoes, rice, vegetables, *haupia* (coconut pudding), and a selection of delicious cakes. It all ends with the Royal Polynesian Extravaganza, which features songs and dances from Hawaii and other Polynesian island nations. Luau is Monday and Thursday at 5:30pm; cost is $175 adults and $75 for children (ages 5–12).

The largest luau venues are **Germaine's** (ℭ 808/941-3338; www.germainesluau.com) and **Paradise Cove Luau** (ℭ 808/842-5911; www.paradisecovehawaii.com), both about a 40-minute drive away from Waikiki on the Leeward Coast. Bus pickups and drop-offs in Waikiki are part of the deal.

Germaine's tries awfully hard and is a much more intimate affair than those legendary shows, but the experience is not as complete. Cost for Germaine's is $72 per adult, $62 for 14- to 20-year-olds, and $52 for 6- to 13-year-olds (5-year-olds and younger are free)—the prices include tax and transportation. The shows are held nightly from 5:30 to 9:30pm.

Paradise Cove, too, is a mixed bag, with 600 to 800 guests a night. The small thatched village feels more like a Hawaiian theme park, with Hawaiian games, *hukilau* net throwing and gathering, craft demonstrations, and a beautiful shoreline looking out over what is usually a storybook sunset. Tahitian dance and ancient and modern hula make this a fun-filled evening for those spirited enough to join in. The food is safe, though not breathtaking: Hawaiian *kalua* pig, lomi salmon, poi, and coconut pudding and cake, as well as more traditional fare. Paradise Cove is extremely popular because of its idyllic setting and good entertainment quality. Tickets, including transportation and taxes, are $80 for adults, $70 for ages 13 to 18, $60 for ages 4 to 12, and free for those 3 and under. Shows are nightly from 5 to 8:30pm.

On the North Shore, the **Turtle Bay Resort** presents **"Voyages of Luau,"** on the lawn overlooking the ocean with a "Taste of the Islands" luau buffet and a Polynesian revue featuring the songs and dances of the Tuamotu Islands, Samoa, Tahiti, Fiji, and Hawaii. Tickets for the dinner and show are $95 adults and $55 children ages 4 to 11. To book, call ℭ **808/293-6000** or go to www.turtlebayresort.com/activities/luau.asp.

6 MORE ENTERTAINMENT

FILM

A new 16-theater megaplex has opened in the **Victoria Ward** entertainment center, at the corner of Auahi and Kamakee streets, and the **Windward Mall's** 10-screen megaplex is also bringing movies to the masses more conveniently. Honolulu's film scene continues to sprawl with more screens, more seats, and more multiplexes.

A quick check in both dailies and the *Honolulu Weekly* will tell you what's playing where in the world of feature films. For film buffs and esoteric movie lovers, **The Movie Museum,** 3566 Harding Ave. (© **808/735-8771;** www.kaimukihawaii.com/businesses/current/956.html), has special screenings of vintage films and rents a collection of hard-to-find, esoteric, and classic films. The **Honolulu Academy of Arts Theatre,** 900 S. Beretania St. (© **808/532-8768;** www.honoluluacademy.org/cmshaa/academy/index. aspx?id=2402), is the film-as-art center of Honolulu, offering special screenings, guest appearances, and cultural performances, as well as noteworthy programs in the visual arts.

The Kahala Mall's **Kahala 8-Plex** (© **808/593-3000**) and **Kapolei Megaplex,** a 16-theater complex (© **808/593-3000**), are now eclipsed by the 18-screen **Dole Cannery** (© **808/526-FILM** [3456]), at Nimitz Highway and Pacific.

At the nine **Wallace Theatres** (© **808/263-4171**), on Restaurant Row, 500 Ala Moana Blvd., near downtown Honolulu, free parking in the evenings, discount matinees, and special discounted midnight shows make the movies here more affordable.

10

Oahu Fast Facts & Websites

1 FAST FACTS: HONOLULU, WAIKIKI & OAHU

AAA Hawaii's only American Automobile Association (AAA) office is located at 1130 N. Nimitz, Ste. A-170, in Honolulu (© **808/593-2221**). Some car-rental agencies now provide auto club–type services, so you should inquire about their availability when you rent your car.

AMERICAN EXPRESS The Honolulu office is at 677 Ala Moana Blvd. (© **808/585-3200**) and is open Monday through Friday from 9am to 5pm. There is also an office at **Hilton Hawaiian Village,** 2005 Kalia Rd. (© **808/947-2607** [7am–9pm] or 808/951-0644 [7am–6pm]), offering financial services daily.

AREA CODE All the Hawaiian Islands are in the **808** area code. Note that if you're calling one island from another, you'll have to dial 1-808 first.

BUSINESS HOURS Most offices are open Monday through Friday from 8am to 5pm. Bank hours are Monday through Thursday from 8:30am to 3pm and Friday from 8:30am to 6pm; some banks are open on Saturday as well. Shopping centers are open Monday through Friday 10am to 9pm, Saturday 10am to 5:30pm, and Sunday noon to 5 or 6pm.

DRINKING LAWS The legal drinking age in Hawaii is 21. Bars are allowed to stay open daily until 2am; places with cabaret licenses are able to keep the booze flowing until 4am. Grocery and convenience stores are allowed to sell beer, wine, and liquor 7 days a week. Proof of age is required and often requested at bars, nightclubs, and restaurants, so bring ID when you go out.

Do not carry open containers of alcohol in your car or any public area that isn't zoned for alcohol consumption. The police can fine you on the spot. And nothing will ruin your trip faster than getting a citation for DUI ("driving under the influence"), so don't even think about driving while intoxicated.

DRIVING RULES See "Getting Around," p. 30.

ELECTRICITY Like Canada, the United States uses 110 to 120 volts AC (60 cycles), compared with 220 to 240 volts AC (50 cycles) in most of Europe, Australia, and New Zealand. Downward converters that change 220 to 240 volts to 110 to 120 volts are difficult to find in the United States, so bring one with you.

EMBASSIES & CONSULATES All embassies are located in the nation's capital, Washington, D.C. Some consulates are located in major U.S. cities, and most nations have a mission to the United Nations in New York City. If your country isn't listed below, call for directory information in Washington, D.C. (© **202/555-1212**) or log on to **www.embassy.org/embassies**.

The embassy of **Australia** is at 1601 Massachusetts Ave. NW, Washington, DC

20036 (© **202/797-3000;** www.austemb. org). There are consulates in New York, Honolulu, Houston, Los Angeles, and San Francisco.

The embassy of **Canada** is at 501 Pennsylvania Ave. NW, Washington, DC 20001 (© **202/682-1740;** www.canadianembassy.org). Other Canadian consulates are in Buffalo (New York), Detroit, Los Angeles, New York, and Seattle.

The embassy of **Ireland** is at 2234 Massachusetts Ave. NW, Washington, DC 20008 (© **202/462-3939;** www.irelandemb.org). Irish consulates are in Boston, Chicago, New York, San Francisco, and other cities. See website for complete listing.

The embassy of **New Zealand** is at 37 Observatory Circle NW, Washington, DC 20008 (© **202/328-4800;** www.nzembassy.com). New Zealand consulates are in Los Angeles, Salt Lake City, San Francisco, and Seattle.

The **United Kingdom**'s embassy is at 3100 Massachusetts Ave. NW, Washington, DC 20008 (© **202/588-7800;** www.britainusa.com). Other British consulates are in Atlanta, Boston, Chicago, Cleveland, Houston, Los Angeles, New York, San Francisco, and Seattle.

EMERGENCIES Dial © **911** for police, fire, or ambulance. The **Poison Control Center** is located at 1319 Punahou St. (© **808/941-4411**).

GASOLINE (PETROL) At press time, the cost of gasoline in Hawaii is abnormally high. Taxes are already included in the printed price. One U.S. gallon equals 3.8 liters or .85 imperial gallons. Fill-up locations are known as gas stations or service stations. As we went to press, gas was averaging $3.59 a gallon.

HOLIDAYS Banks, government offices, post offices, and many stores, restaurants, and museums are closed on the following legal national holidays: January 1 (New Year's Day), the third Monday in January

(Martin Luther King, Jr., Day), the third Monday in February (Presidents' Day), the last Monday in May (Memorial Day), July 4 (Independence Day), the first Monday in September (Labor Day), the second Monday in October (Columbus Day), November 11 (Veterans Day/Armistice Day), the fourth Thursday in November (Thanksgiving Day), and December 25 (Christmas). The Tuesday after the first Monday in November is Election Day, a federal government holiday in presidential-election years (held every 4 years, and next in 2012).

For more information on holidays see "Oahu Calendar of Events," in chapter 2.

HOSPITALS Hospitals offering 24-hour emergency care include **Queens Medical Center,** 1301 Punchbowl St. (© 808/538-9011); **Kuakini Medical Center,** 347 Kuakini St. (© 808/536-2236); **Straub Clinic and Hospital,** 888 S. King St. (© 808/522-4000); **Moanalua Medical Center,** 3288 Moanalua Rd. (© 808/834-5333); **Kapiolani Medical Center for Women and Children,** 1319 Punahou St. (© 808/973-8511); and **Kapiolani Medical Center,** at Pali Momi, 98-1079 Moanalua Rd. (© 808/486-6000). Central Oahu has **Wahiawa General Hospital,** 128 Lehua St. (© 808/621-8411). On the windward side is **Castle Medical Center,** 640 Ulukahiki St., Kailua (© 808/263-5500).

INSURANCE If you think your travel plans may change, you might want to look into travel insurance. For information on traveler's insurance, trip cancellation insurance, and medical insurance while traveling, please visit www.frommers.com/planning.

INTERNET ACCESS See "Staying Connected," in chapter 2.

LEGAL AID If you are "pulled over" for a minor infraction (such as speeding), never attempt to pay the fine directly to a police officer; this could be construed as attempted bribery, a much more serious crime. Pay fines by mail, or directly into the hands of the clerk of the court. If accused of a more serious offense, say and do nothing before consulting a lawyer. Here the burden is on the state to prove a person's guilt beyond a reasonable doubt, and everyone has the right to remain silent, whether he or she is suspected of a crime or actually arrested. Once arrested, a person can make one telephone call to a party of his or her choice. International visitors should call your embassy or consulate. Call the **Legal Aid Society of Hawaii,** 924 Bethel St., Honolulu, HI 96813 (© **808/536-4302**).

LOST & FOUND Be sure to tell all of your credit card companies the minute you discover your wallet has been lost or stolen, and file a report at the nearest police precinct. Your credit card company or insurer may require a police report number or record of the loss. Most credit card companies have an emergency toll-free number to call if your card is lost or stolen; they may be able to wire you a cash advance immediately or deliver an emergency credit card in a day or two. Visa's U.S. emergency number is © **800/847-2911** or 410/581-9994. American Express cardholders and traveler's-check holders should call © **800/221-7282.** Master-Card holders should call © **800/307-7309** or 636/722-7111. For other credit cards, call the toll-free number directory at © **800/555-1212.**

If you need emergency cash over the weekend, when all banks and American Express offices are closed, you can have money wired to you via **Western Union** (© **800/325-6000;** www.westernunion. com).

MAIL At press time, domestic postage rates were 28¢ for a postcard and 44¢ for a letter. For international mail, a first-class letter of up to 1 ounce costs 75¢ to 98¢ (depending on the destination); a first-class postcard costs 75¢ (69¢ to Canada

and 79¢ to Mexico). For more information, go to **www.usps.com** and click on "Calculate Postage."

NEWSPAPERS *The Honolulu Advertiser* is Oahu's daily newspaper. *Midweek, Pacific Business News,* and *Honolulu Weekly* are weekly papers. *Honolulu Weekly,* available free at restaurants, clubs, shops, bookstores, and newspaper racks around Oahu, is the best source for what's going on around town. It features discriminating restaurant reviews and an informed critique of the nightclub scene, plus a weekly Calendar of Events.

PASSPORTS **Residents of Australia** can pick up an application from your local post office or any branch of Passports Australia, but you must schedule an interview at the passport office to present your application materials. Call the **Australian Passport Information Service** at © **131-232,** or visit the government website at www.passports.gov.au.

Passport applications for **residents of Canada** are available at travel agencies throughout Canada or from the central **Passport Office,** Department of Foreign Affairs and International Trade, Ottawa, ON K1A 0G3 (© **800/567-6868;** www. ppt.gc.ca). *Note:* Canadian children who travel must have their own passports. However, if you hold a valid Canadian passport issued before December 11, 2001, that bears the name of your child, the passport remains valid for you and your child until it expires.

Residents of Ireland can apply for a 10-year passport at the **Passport Office,** Setanta Centre, Molesworth St., Dublin 2 (© **01/671-1633;** www.irlgov.ie/iveagh). Those under age 18 and over 65 must apply for a 3-year passport. You can also apply at 1A South Mall, Cork (© **021/272-525**) or at most main post offices.

Residents of New Zealand can pick up a passport application at any New Zealand Passports Office or download it from their website. Contact the **Passports Office** at ℭ **0800/225-050** in New Zealand, or 04/474-8100; or log on to www.passports. govt.nz.

Residents of the United Kingdom can pick up an application for a standard 10-year passport (5-year passport for children under 16) at your nearest passport office, major post office, or travel agency; or contact the **United Kingdom Passport Service** (ℭ **0870/521-0410;** www.ukpa. gov.uk).

POLICE Call **911** for police, fire, or ambulance.

SMOKING See the box "Hey, No Smoking in Hawaii," in Chapter 5.

TAXES The United States has no value-added tax (VAT) or other indirect tax at the national level. Every state, county, and city may levy its own local tax on all purchases, including hotel and restaurant checks and airline tickets. These taxes will not appear on price tags. Hawaii's sales tax on Oahu is 5.5%. The hotel-occupancy tax is 7.25%, and hoteliers are allowed by the state to tack on an additional .1666% excise tax. Thus, expect taxes of about 12.92% to be added to your hotel bill.

TIME The continental United States is divided into four **time zones:** Eastern Standard Time (EST), Central Standard Time (CST), Mountain Standard Time (MST), and Pacific Standard Time (PST). Alaska and Hawaii have their own zones. Hawaii is 2 hours behind Pacific Standard Time and 5 hours behind Eastern Standard Time. In other words, when it's noon in Hawaii, it's 2pm in California and 5pm in New York during Standard Time on the mainland.

Daylight saving time takes effect at 2am the second Sunday in March until 2am the first Sunday in November, except in Arizona, Hawaii, the U.S. Virgin Islands, and Puerto Rico. Daylight saving moves the clock 1 hour ahead of standard time. When daylight saving time is in effect on the mainland, Hawaii is 3 hours behind the West Coast and 6 hours behind the East Coast; when it's noon in Hawaii, it's 3pm in California and 6pm in New York.

Hawaii is east of the International Date Line, putting it on the same day as the U.S. mainland and Canada, and a day behind Australia, New Zealand, and Asia.

TIPPING Tips are a very important part of certain workers' income, and gratuities are the standard way of showing appreciation for services provided. (Tipping is certainly not compulsory if the service is poor!) In hotels, tip **bellhops** at least $1 per bag ($2–$3 if you have a lot of luggage) and tip the **chamber staff** $1 to $2 per day (more if you've left a disaster area for him or her to clean up). Tip the **doorman** or **concierge** only if he or she has provided you with some specific service (for example, calling a cab for you or obtaining difficult-to-get theater tickets). Tip the **valet-parking attendant** $1 every time you get your car.

In restaurants, bars, and nightclubs, tip **service staff** 15% to 20% of the check, tip **bartenders** 10% to 15%, tip **checkroom attendants** $1 per garment, and tip **valet-parking attendants** $1 per vehicle.

As for other service personnel, tip **cab drivers** 15% of the fare; tip **skycaps** at airports at least $1 per bag ($2–$3 if you have a lot of luggage); and tip **hairdressers** and **barbers** 15% to 20%.

TOILETS You won't find public toilets or "restrooms" on the streets in most U.S. cities but they can be found in hotel lobbies, bars, restaurants, museums, department stores, railway and bus stations, and service stations. Large hotels and fast-food restaurants are often the best bets for clean facilities. If possible, avoid the toilets at parks and beaches, which tend to be dirty; some may be unsafe. Restaurants and bars in resorts or heavily visited areas may reserve their restrooms for patrons.

VISAS For information about U.S. visas go to **http://travel.state.gov** and click on "Visas." Or go to one of the following websites:

Australian citizens can obtain up-to-date visa information from the **U.S. Embassy Canberra,** Moonah Place, Yarralumla, ACT 2600 (℅ **02/6214-5600**); or by checking the U.S. Diplomatic Mission's website at **http://usembassy-australia.state.gov/consular.**

British subjects can obtain up-to-date visa information by calling the **U.S. Embassy Visa Information Line** (℅ **0891/200-290**) or by visiting the "Visas to the U.S."

section of the American Embassy London's website at **www.usembassy.org.uk.**

Irish citizens can obtain up-to-date visa information through the **Embassy of the USA Dublin,** 42 Elgin Rd., Dublin 4, Ireland (℅ **353/1-668-8777**) or by checking the "Consular Services" section of the website at **http://dublin.usembassy.gov.**

Citizens of **New Zealand** can obtain up-to-date visa information by contacting the **U.S. Embassy New Zealand,** 29 Fitzherbert Terrace, Thorndon, Wellington (℅ **644/472-2068**; http://wellington. usembassy.gov).

---

2 AIRLINE, HOTEL & CAR RENTAL WEBSITES

MAJOR U.S. AIRLINES

(*flies internationally as well)

Alaska Airlines
www.alaskaair.com

American Airlines*
www.aa.com

Continental Airlines*
www.continental.com

Delta Air Lines*
www.delta.com

go!
www.iflygo.com
(interisland Hawaii only)

Hawaiian Airlines*
www.hawaiianair.com

Island Air
www.islandair.com

Mokulele Airlines
www.mokuleleairlines.com

Northwest Airlines
www.nwa.com

United Airlines*
www.united.com

US Airways*
www.usairways.com

MAJOR INTERNATIONAL AIRLINES

Air Canada
www.aircanada.com

Air France
www.airfrance.com

Air New Zealand
www.airnewzealand.com

Air Pacific
www.airpacific.com

Air Tahiti Nui
www.airtahitinui-usa.com

Alitalia
www.alitalia.com

All Nippon Airways (ANA)
www.fly-ana.com

American Airlines
www.aa.com

British Airways
www.british-airways.com

China Airlines
www.china-airlines.com

Continental Airlines
www.continental.com

Delta Air Lines
www.delta.com

Hawaiian Airlines
www.hawaiianair.com

Japan Airlines
www.jal.co.jp

Korean Air
www.koreanair.com

Philippine Airlines
www.philippineairlines.com

Qantas Airways
www.qantas.com

United Airlines
www.united.com

US Airways
www.usairways.com

CAR-RENTAL AGENCIES

Alamo
www.alamo.com

Avis
www.avis.com

Budget
www.budget.com

Dollar
www.dollar.com

Enterprise
www.enterprise.com

Hertz
www.hertz.com

National
www.nationalcar.com

Rent-A-Wreck
www.rentawreck.com

Thrifty
www.thrifty.com

MAJOR HOTEL & MOTEL CHAINS

Best Western International
www.bestwestern.com

Doubletree Hotels
www.doubletree.com

Embassy Suites
www.embassysuites.com

Four Seasons
www.fourseasons.com

Hilton Hotels
www.hilton.com

Holiday Inn
www.holidayinn.com

Hyatt
www.hyatt.com

Marriott
www.marriott.com

Radisson Hotels & Resorts
www.radisson.com

Renaissance
www.renaissance.com

Sheraton Hotels & Resorts
www.starwoodhotels.com/sheraton

Westin Hotels & Resorts
www.starwoodhotels.com/westin

Wyndham Hotels & Resorts
www.wyndham.com

INDEX

See also Accommodations and Restaurant indexes, below.

RESTAURANTS